Jörg Rüpke
Urban Religion

Jörg Rüpke
Urban Religion

A Historical Approach to Urban Growth
and Religious Change

DE GRUYTER

ISBN 978-3-11-062868-5
e-ISBN (PDF) 978-3-11-063442-6
e-ISBN (EPUB) 978-3-11-063136-4

Library of Congress Control Number: 2019952763

Bibliographic information published by the Deutsche Nationalbibliothek
The Deutsche Nationalbibliothek lists this publication in the Deutsche Nationalbibliografie;
detailed bibliographic data are available on the Internet at http://dnb.dnb.de.

© 2020 Walter de Gruyter GmbH, Berlin/Boston
Printing and binding: CPI books GmbH, Leck

www.degruyter.com

Acknowledgements

My growing interest in and reflection on urban religion from a historical perspective was one of the rather surprising results of the research pursued and supported under the umbrella of three different programmes: the Kolleg-Forschungsgruppe 'Religious individualisation in historical perspective' (financed by the German Science Foundation, DFG, FOR 1080 from 2008 to 2018); 'Lived ancient religion: Questioning cults and polis religion' (an Advanced Grant financed by the European Research Council from 2012–17); and an International Graduate School on 'Resonant Self-world-relationships in ancient and modern socio-religious practices' (financed by the DFG from 2017 onwards, GRK 2283). Traces of the enduring insights I acquired while working on these projects can be detected more or less plainly throughout the book. Many colleagues have furthered the development of questions and concepts that I draw on herein, including Jan Bremmer, Harry O. Maier, Rubina Raja, Emiliano Rubens Urciuoli, and Markus Vinzent in particular. Martin Fuchs, Paul Lichterman, and Anna Sun ensured that the historical and sociological breadth of the topic was kept at the front of my mind. Finally, Susanne Rau enabled me to professionalise the historical, as much as the urban studies, side of this work, and also shared in the effort involved in enlisting the support of the DFG, again lavishly provided in the wonderful form of a Kolleg-Forschungsgruppe 'Religion and urbanity: Reciprocal formations' (FOR 2779, from 2018 onwards). It was the time provided by this latter project and conferences organised by it that allowed me to systematise and complete an initial stage of research in the form of this book. Colleagues and fellows within the group have offered both critical and encouraging comments on the text (each equally valuable). In addition to those mentioned above, I would also like to thank Rana Behal, Supriya Chaudhuri, Pralay Kanungo, Asuman Lätzer-Lasar, Antje Linkenbach, and Martina Stercken. The unstinting and ongoing support of the Max Weber Centre for Advanced Cultural and Social Studies at the University of Erfurt has been vital here and has taken on material form in the shape of Elisabeth Begemann, Bettina Hollstein, and Diana Püschel.

For some of the chapters I owe thanks to further individuals and institutions for their support in a variety of forms. Chapter 2 is based on the August-Boeck-Lecture at the Humboldt University, Berlin, and I am grateful to Markus Asper for the invitation, as well as to Georgia Petridou and Federico Santangelo, and the additional audiences they invited for talks at Liverpool and Newcastle. Chapter 4 was instigated by a conference on Cicero's *De natura deorum*, organised by Christoph Schubert and Christopher Diez at Erlangen University. A research stay at the Norwegian Centre for Advanced Study, Oslo, in the framework of the research group 'The Demise of Religion' (Michael Stausberg/James T. Lewis), provided the leisure time required for wide reading and the writing of the first draft of Chapter 3, while discussions at the Max Weber Centre improved the text. I am grateful to Maren Niehoff and her colleagues for the invitation to her research group at the Israel Institute of Advanced Study, Jerusalem and also am grateful for the feedback at the Centre and from other readers of Chapter 8. Work on an earlier version of parts of Chapter 9 was supported by a grant from the Federal Ministry of Education and Research (BMBF) "Dynamics of Jewish rituals in multireligious contexts from Antiquity to the Present" at the Max Weber Centre for Advanced Cultural and Social Studies at the University of Erfurt (directed by Benedikt Kranemann). I am grateful to the audience and, in particular, to Guenther Stemberger and Charlotte Fonrobert for their detailed critique. Other parts were presented as a Keynote at the 2018 annual conference of the European Association for the Study of Religion at Berne and I am grateful to Jens Schröter for the invitation. Further debts are noted in footnotes.

My gratitude also goes to Manuela Seifert, who fought with my endless handwritten corrections to the first draft of the book. Frederic Arning, Maximilian Gutberlet and Claudia Heise helped with the bibliography, Carmina Volkers and Johannes Benjamin Vonderschmidt with the index. Sophie Wagenhöfer encouraged me to develop my argument for a broader audience and found an adequate material form, while Katrin Mittmann and Anett Rehner helpfully guided me through the process of production.

Paul Scade has not only corrected my English. His careful readings of the text and the many discussions that have built upon them have not only improved the textual surface but have also challenged time and again the flow and wording of my arguments and, ultimately, have made for a different book. The responsibility for any remaining mistakes rests nevertheless with me.

Contents

Introduction: Urban religion in a historical perspective —— 1
1 Religion in the metropolis —— 1
2 From lived to urban religion —— 6
3 The plan of the book —— 8

1 Looking at religion in the city —— 16
1.1 Introduction —— 16
1.2 Religious agency and sacralisation —— 18
1.3 Selectivity and canonicity as intensification of sacralisation —— 23
1.4 Reflecting on the urban —— 25
1.5 Urbanism and the formation of religious groups —— 27

2 Before urban religion: Fustel de Coulanges and narratives of civic religion —— 30
2.1 The problem —— 30
2.2 Polis religion —— 31
2.3 Critique —— 37
2.4 Comparative perspectives on cities in other regions and periods —— 40
2.5 Urbanised religion —— 43

3 Urbanising and urbanised religion —— 47
3.0 Introduction —— 47
3.1 Religion as spatial practice —— 47
3.2 Religion and urbanisation —— 51
3.3 Religions as urbanising factors —— 53
3.4 Urbanised religion —— 58
3.5 Conclusion —— 60

4 Presupposing the city: Philosophical piety as urbanised religion —— 62
4.1 Urban literature —— 62
4.2 The city as the ideal place for a good life —— 64
4.3 Religious phenomena as phenomena in a city —— 67
4.4 Philosophical debate as an indicator of urbanity —— 73
4.5 Conclusion: Urbanised religion —— 75

5	**Crafting complex place: Religion and urban development** — 77
5.1	Introduction — 77
5.2	'On places' — 79
5.3	Time and place — 81
5.4	The idea of a city? — 83
5.5	Multiple appropriations — 85
5.6	Trajectories — 86

6	**Materiality of religion in urban space: Neighbourhoods of a metropolis** — 88
6.1	Visible and material religion — 88
6.2	Religion and material objects — 90
6.3	Urban space — 95
6.4	Religious practices and the city — 98
6.5	Religion at the crossroads — 102
6.6	Conclusion: Religion and public space — 112

7	**Urban resilience and religion: Attaching time to place** — 114
7.1	Resilience and religion — 114
7.2	A wealth of practices — 118
7.3	Historical background: The first written Roman calendar — 120
7.4	Adding urban history — 124
7.5	Negative history — 127
7.6	Urban practices in the face of empire building — 132
7.7	Attachment to urban places — 135
7.8	Spatial interest and attachment to place in contemporary literary texts — 139
7.9	Conclusion — 142

8	**Urban Selves: Individualisation in urban space** — 145
8.1	The problem — 145
8.2	The concept of the self — 145
8.3	An urban market for the shaping of the self — 150
8.4	Urban identities — 153
8.5	Citizenship and imagined cities — 161
8.6	Conclusion — 165

9	**Urbanity and multiple religious identities** — 166
9.1	Introduction — 166
9.2	Religious identities as seen by urban observers — 167

9.3	Semantics —— 176
9.4	Construing identity boundaries in hindsight —— 177
9.5	Mapping differences —— 179
9.6	Prescribing differences in the Mishnah —— 182
9.7	Urbanity in the Mishnah —— 184
9.8	A particular and a general conclusion —— 187

Conclusion: Religion and urbanity —— 190

References —— 195

Index —— 233

Introduction: Urban religion in a historical perspective

1 Religion in the metropolis

Urban studies are flourishing. That this should be so is no surprise. For the first time in human history, we are now at a point at which more than half of the global population lives in cities. In 2016, thirty-five cities had populations above the threshold of ten million inhabitants.[1] Megacities and large metropolitan areas are the economic backbones of global production and exchange. The 'Northeast Megalopolis' in the United States, for instance, stretches from Boston to Washington DC and comprises one sixth of the US population and one fifth of its gross domestic product.[2] These vast cities are regarded as the motors of innovation and the epicentres of globalisation, even if much of the economic activity they contain is still performed by low-paid local clerical and manual labour.[3] At the same time, many of them have grown up outside of the economically leading regions of the world.[4] Urban experiences are vastly different in different places and it is this diversity within and across metropolises, as much as the problems posed by their size and development, that has driven research into the specifics of urban sociology, urban planning, and urban history since the 1920s and, in particular, from the 1950s onwards. This research began in Europe and North America but has now become a global concern.[5]

Religion has been marginal to this research. In a recent handbook on urban planning, religion figures only in a chapter on cultural diversity, and not even prominently in this limited context.[6] It is, at least, one among the 'themes' of a recently published handbook on urban history[7] and the more specific topic of 'ritual' appears in a few further chapters of the volume. In a recent handbook of urban sociology, religion figures in chapters on 'affect' and the visibility of religious space.[8] This comparative neglect stands in stark contrast to the self-images of many inhabitants of cities and their narratives about the origins of

---

1 Robinson, Scott and Taylor 2016, 18.
2 Short 2013, 26.
3 Sassen 2013, 212.
4 Robinson, Scott and Taylor 2016, 18.
5 See for instance the handbooks of Bridge and Watson 2013; R. Weber and Crane 2015;
6 Umemoto and Zambonelli 2015.
7 Baird 2013.
8 Bridge and Watson 2013; Hill 2013.

their cities, and also, likewise, to early comparative studies of the city, admittedly written with prominence given to the ancient Mediterranean Greek *polis*.⁹ Scholarship has bridged this gap by exploiting the master narrative of rationalisation. Max Weber's more parochial vision of the occidental city as the locus of rationality, of '*systematische Erwerbsarbeit*' or systematic paid and professional labour,¹⁰ that created places in which humans can ascend from serfdom to freedom,¹¹ has implicitly been universalised. It is clear that even Weber considered that certain types of religious practice, organisation, and belief played important roles in making possible the rise of the medieval European city, offering means by which free and individual bearers of political and economic rights (and military means) could form bonds against regal, feudal, or clerical powers. According to Weber, some religious tenets, in particular that of double destination, the belief that an individual is predestined for heaven or hell, even played a vital role in the accumulation of capital that was necessary for, and gave its name to, capitalist production and industrialisation.¹² Yet, despite the religious roots of the phenomenon, in the mainstream narrative it was secularisation and *Entzauberung* or 'disenchantment' that were central to the whole process of rationalisation. This image of secularised industrial cities was produced and propagated from the early industrial period onwards by many observers, including religious people, town planners, and academics, and still remains influential in contemporary scholarship today.¹³ A great deal of religious innovation in Western cities – from the building of parish churches and organised spiritual welfare, through awakening movements, the Salvation Army, and the YMCA, to specifically urban forms of assembly rooms and rituals – developed in reaction to this view. Nevertheless, it is only as academic research has examined cities through the lenses of immigration and immigrant religions that it has rediscovered anew the importance of religion in these urban contexts.

In the face of the presence of religious phenomena in urban space, the high visibility and the massive scale of the religious practices of immigrants, and the global presence of organised religious actors and 'religions', things are beginning to change. A new wave of interest in religion in contemporary cities has sprung up in the fields of Religious Studies and Anthropology. This development has been triggered by scholarly reflection on modernisation and globalisation –

---

9 Mumford 1961; Müller 1961; recently Russo 2016 (I am grateful to Susanne Rau for the reference *and* the book).
10 M. Weber 1972 [1922], 774.
11 Ibid., 742.
12 M. Weber 2014.
13 Thus Orsi 1999, 41.

above all, in the form of migration motivated by the 'urban aspirations' that are themselves produced by images and imaginaries of cities and the lives lived within them[14] –, and by the concomitant development of new forms of religious practices and the appropriation of urban space by non-elites.[15] These disciplines are now fully aware of spatiality and the social character of space as articulated by Michel Foucault, Henri Lefebvre, and Edward Soja (exploring the counter-cultural space in particular)[16] and as then taken up by the sociology of space and the study of class-based differences in the appropriation of space and 'place making'.[17]

In Religious Studies, the 'spatial turn' advanced by Kim Knott has rapidly been taken up by other scholars who have given her 'spatial analysis' of 'the location of religion' a programmatic role.[18] More recently, anthropologist Stephan Lanz has proposed a comprehensive definition of 'urban religion' as 'a specific element of urbanisation and urban everyday life ... intertwined with ... urban lifestyles and imaginaries, infrastructure and materialities, cultures, politics and economies, forms of living and working, community formation, festivals and celebrations'.[19] 'Urban religion' is further specified as 'a continual process in which the urban and the religious reciprocally interact, mutually interlace, producing, transforming and defining each other'.[20] Lanz enlarges the class of agents that are of interest by invoking 'subaltern urbanism' and characterising religious practices as a '"prescriptive regime" (...), where technologies of power and technologies of the self intermesh in its practice of governmentality'.[21] The interest here is in practices involving the mediation of the urban and the religious, thus opposing the idea that the character of the city is principally secular.

Lanz's definition is deictic rather than delineative. It draws attention to the thoroughness of the interaction between the urban and what people think of as religious actions. The object defined by 'urban religion' is a process in which these religious practices and the urban are both involved, a context in which re-

---

14 van der Veer 2015b, 2–12.
15 E.g. Goh and van der Veer 2016; Knott, Krech and Meyer 2016.
16 Foucault 1984; Lefebvre 1974; and the sequence of E. W. Soja 1989; E. Soja 1996; E. W. Soja 2000; E. Soja 2013.
17 Massey 1984; Löw 2001/Löw 2016; Löw 2008, 2012; Berking et al. 2006; Berking and Löw 2008. For cities, these reflections go back to the Chicago School of Urban Studies of the 1930s and their successors.
18 Knott 2005, 2008; exemplary: Knott 2015.
19 Lanz 2014, 25.
20 Ibid., 26.
21 Ibid., 24 and 28 (quotation); he adds the characterisation as 'sensational form' (quoting B. Meyer 2009, 201). The reference is to Marshall 2009, 11.

ligious actions take place, rather than an identifiable subset of 'religion' (or the 'urban'). The boundaries of the object under scrutiny are only implicit in the framework of the 'Global Prayers' project in which Lanz is a leading participant. They are spelled out more clearly in a review of the field by David Garbin and Anna Strhan.[22] Apart from older issues concerning, for example, the role of religion in welfare and justice, two further related, but not necessarily convergent, processes define urban religion. The first is the rise of the post-secular. Despite the range of scholarly perspectives on the recent developments in the variety of secular-religious divides and their associated regimes,[23] all are in agreement that there has been 'a pluralisation of options',[24] to the extent that religion is now regarded as a central element for the phenomenon of 'super-' or 'hyper-diversity'. This diversity is the result of the crossing of many different dividing lines and of the complex processes of situational salience of one category or the other (these categories can even become hegemonic, as demonstrated by the development of 'Muslim' as a religious category in recent European discourses).[25] On the other hand, globalisation is not only a major force for urbanisation and pluralisation by way of the many types of migration,[26] but also in the presence of flows that involve and trans-localise cities. With regard to religion, trans-local contacts and the trans-local presence of an ever-growing number of 'universal' religions shape local religion – as much as cities – without denying the importance of locality. Here, we need to both accommodate and account for a multi-layered 'glocalisation' that shows very different and, at times, quite contrary effects, sometimes questioning and sometimes reinforcing local religious or urban power.[27] Further, it is important that we not lose sight of the broad range of 'deviant' forms of religious practices and beliefs that are frequently set aside as mere 'folk religion'.

The concept of 'urban religion' thus opens up a wide field of urgently needed research and this volume sets out to explore these new vistas. Some qualifications are, however, necessary. We can summarise and enlarge upon the observations of Garbin and Strhan by identifying three important implications and consequences of the dominant use of 'urban religion'. First, the real object of study is not religion at all but globalisation, with 'religion' serving as a 'lens'

---

[22] Garbin and Strhan 2017, in particular 6–11.
[23] On the latter see Burchardt and Wohlrab-Sahr 2013.
[24] Beyer 2013, 676.
[25] Aspinall and Song 2013.
[26] The large differences are only occasionally stressed, already for antiquity see Tacoma 2016 and G. Woolf 2015.
[27] Garbin and Strhan 2017, 15–18; see e.g. Moser 2013 on 'new Islamic cities' or van der Veer 2015b on 'worlding'.

through which to examine globalisation. This interlacing of globalisation, cities, and religion does not open up a space for historical research, even if historians of religion have been willing to employ this concept in examining specific pre-modern instances of translocality, universalisation, regionalisation, and localisation, as well as the interactions among them.[28] The underlying theories of Modernity, even if non-Eurocentric, put a stop sign here as they condition the concept of 'urban religion' in such a way as to make it of only limited use for studying the pre-modern world. This contemporary use of religion has a second implication. Religion is never closely defined in this context by reference to its spatial properties. Rather, it just happens to be confronted with, and has to employ tools to deal with, space. It is only in the discourse on 'iconic religion' that scholars have come closer to addressing this problem.[29] The variability of post-secular religious pluralism seems to exclude the possibility of a more specific relationship between religious practices and the spaces within which they occur. Finally, and rather surprisingly, 'the city' or 'the urban' is treated as a given by these scholars, unquestionable in the face of global megalopolises with their populations in excess of eight or ten million inhabitants.[30] Cities are not regarded as culturally produced orders that construct differences – urban and non-urban, religious and secular – which 'make a difference'.[31]

By contrast, the primary interest of this book is in religion and the history of religion. It is the historical dimension of religious, rather than urban, transformations that has been overlooked in considerations of their mutual entanglement. This book will situate urban religion in a historical perspective and pursue it beyond the modern metropolis.

'Religion' is not a given but is, rather, construed as both the theoretical object that underlies the empirical historical research I envisage and pursue here, and also the theoretical object on which I have reflected as I carried out this work.[32] The research briefly reviewed above, with its interest in the relationship between religion and the urban, suggests that the concept of 'urban religion' should provide a useful starting point for my project, even if it is in need of con-

---

28 Cancik and Rüpke 1997, 2003; Rüpke 2007a, 2011b, 2011d. Translocality: Freitag and Oppen 2010.
29 Knott, Krech and Meyer 2016, but again above all pointing to space as a contingent parameter.
30 See Robinson, Scott, Taylor 2016, 18.
31 Adopting a phrase of Hirschauer 2014, 183.
32 I use the distinction of J. Z Smith 2001, 142, understanding 'religion' as follows: 'The generic category supplies the field with a theoretical object of study, different from, but complimentary to their particular subject matters.'

siderable modification. As is the case with 'visible religion', 'material religion', or 'iconic religion',[33] the language of 'urban religion' preconditions an approach to religion from a particular angle. As we have seen, urban religion does not focus on the aesthetic or, in terms of practice, on the media properties of religion but, rather, on a specific spatial setting, namely religion in the city and, in particular, post-secular religion in the contemporary globalised city.

'Urban religion' offers a loose umbrella term that may be helpful in connecting an almost exclusively presentist line of research with much longer-term processes. However, in order to be used as an analytical instrument of a contingent constellation (religion that happens to be urban religion) rather than as a theorised concept of religion (religion if seen as urban religion), this approach needs to be supplemented by a more fundamental reflection on religion as a spatial practice. Only on such a basis can it be put to use in a search for the most fruitful perspective from which to approach religion and 'the city'.

When viewed from a historical perspective, religion can be seen to have been responsible for dramatic developments in the history of cities, playing important roles in waves of immigration, transformation, and ghettoisation, as well as in the founding and destruction of cities. We can say with certainty that religion has been a decisive factor in the development of the concept of citizenship, as well as in justifying the expulsion of large groups. It has also contributed to the monumentalisation of city centres and has given importance to places outside the centre. And yet, even when pursuing this type of historical research, little attention has been paid to the urban character of religious ideas, practices, and institutions, or to the role of urban space in shaping this very 'religion'.

2 From lived to urban religion

From the point of view of the historian, the study of the relationship between religion and the city has been framed by two very different lines of research. On the one hand, religion has been viewed as an important factor in stabilising cities and rendering them governable. In studies of the ancient Mediterranean world, for instance, the terms 'polis religion' and 'civic religion' have been coined to capture this role, and in doing so have produced the image of a coherent and long-term traditional religion that is both local and focused on the city. On the

---

33 For these concepts see e.g. Uehlinger 2006 and the earlier journal 'Visible Religion' (1982–1990, Brill); the journal 'Material Religion' (2005–, Berg) and Knott, Krech and Meyer 2016 for 'iconic religion'.

other hand, the fresh approach to contemporary cities sketched out above has discovered new forms of religion and interpreted the wide variety of religious phenomena by drawing on modernisation theory and identifying a non-traditional 'urban religion'. In this second section, I will briefly review the older of these two strands in order to bring them together. In doing so, I attempt to lay the groundwork for the replacement of these comparatively simple explanatory models, with their foci on diversity and the legitimisation of power, with a more complex view. This new view seeks to acknowledge the divergent, even contradictory, processes across different historical periods and geographical spaces that I address under the broader notion of 'urban religion'. 'Urban religion', as I use the term here, focuses primarily on processes of this sort rather than simply on phenomena.

The observation that religion has been the cause of major developments in the history of cities is not new. Even a recent introductory encyclopaedia entry on 'Religion and space in the United States' goes so far as to state that, 'historically religion has been largely an urban phenomenon: religion and cities have been inextricably related throughout human history, mutually dependent in their development'.[34] However, drawing on a rare example of a historically-oriented sociological account given by Robert N. Bellah, the author of the entry quickly makes clear that the claim is to be understood in a much narrower sense than a reader might initially expect. 'Religion, power, and the places of power were intricately interconnected in symbiotic relationships—in cities. This pattern of the co-production of religion and urban life has continued throughout much of history'. Even if such statements are frequently illustrated with images of Mesopotamian temple-mounts (ziggurats), the European tradition of research has given greater prominence to a later period which, due to the extensive survival of sources, has allowed for much more detailed investigation or urban and religious phenomena. This is a period characterised by renewed and extended waves of urbanisation, stretching from the Greek Archaic age to the late Roman Empire in the Mediterranean basin (with de-urbanisation beginning in its Western part at the end of the 2nd century CE).

Evidently, 'urban religion' cannot simply be added to traditional historical accounts of religion as the latest phase. 'Urban religion', as this book will show, offers an integrative long-term perspective if embedded into further conceptual tools. 'Lived religion' is one such tool. While Orsi's 'lived religion' approach led him to detect 'Gods of the city',[35] my own research into ancient 'met-

---

34 Day 2017.
35 In the sequence of Orsi 1985, 1997, 1999; briefly: Garbin and Strhan 2017, 5.

ropolitan religion' has led me to adapt and enlarge the 'lived religion' concept into the 'Lived Ancient Religion' approach.[36] This approach has shown that funerary ritual and domestic religion, the social and ritual practices of voluntary associations ('cults' and 'religions'), and the political use of religion by administrators and political elites, are neither independent strands of religious practice nor replications of, or counter-models to, 'polis religion'.

The Lived Ancient Religion approach has developed tools for analysing the religious practices of political elites, writers, practitioners, and the general populace in all its diversity.[37] By focusing on practices and religious action as forms of communication,[38] this approach has questioned the simplistic dichotomy between public and private,[39] and has developed concepts for exploring religious agency, the instantiation of religion in practices and media, the effects of such instantiated religion upon action and experience, the (re-)narration of religion, and, finally, the roles of narrated religion. Religion is seen from this perspective as 'religion in the making'.[40] This study of premodern South and West European, West Asian, and North African religion made it clear that it is necessary to address the city as the focal point of movements and relations, as a particular social and spatial arrangement crucial to religious practices, and, ultimately, as *the driving force of religious change*. This book will explore how this research can be conceptualised and pursued, starting from, but also modifying, the notion of 'urban religion'.

3 The plan of the book

The objective of this monograph is to demonstrate how important changes in religion can be understood more fully when they are seen cross-culturally as being a result of the reciprocal formation of urban space and urban ways of living, on the one hand, and religion, on the other. Such an approach can shed light on paths of urbanisation, such as those found in China, in the ancient Mediterranean, in India, Mesoamerica, late ancient West Asia, medieval and early modern Europe. This general claim is developed, conceptualised, and supported in the first group of three chapters. In the subsequent chapters, I go on to apply this framework specifically to the ancient Mediterranean world from the Hellenistic

---

36 Rüpke 2012c, 2016b, 2019a.
37 Raja and Rüpke 2015a, 2015b.
38 Rüpke 2015c.
39 See Clifford Ando and Rüpke 2015.
40 Albrecht et al. 2018.

period to the late Imperial period, and to the city of Rome in particular. Many features of ancient religion can be more plausibly viewed as the outcome of specific effects and uses of space and the social and cognitive bases of such uses, rather than as inherent features of a specific 'religion'. These features include the development of certain mass-rituals connected to theatre and circus structures, the widespread staging of theatrical processions, the declining role of animal sacrifice, the 'intellectualisation' of religion, and the establishment of specifically religious networks and (initially small) group religions. They include also the forms in which gods were tied to specific places and the very structure of a polytheism informed by a plurality of local temples. It is, however, not these well-known changes, which I (and certainly others!) have discussed in earlier books, that needs to be addressed. Rather, what is at issue is the reflection of this situation in the lives of intellectuals and simple people, that is the lived religion of these individuals and collectives. It was their appropriation and claiming of urban space that changed them from objects to subjects of these processes and that mutually altered and shaped religion, on the one hand, *and* city-space as well as urban ways of life, on the other.

The recurring focus on Rome and the ancient Mediterranean here offers some advantages from a methodological and historiographical perspective. The period from the Hellenistic age through to Late Antiquity was crucial for the establishment of concepts and institutions of 'religion' and was also a period of renewed and extended waves of urbanisation. As such, the Mediterranean basin and the Roman Empire in this era offer a rich and comparatively well-documented area within which to investigate the nature of urban religion. By examining this region throughout this period, the present volume also aims to fill significant gaps in the scholarship on urban religion and ancient Mediterranean history. If we take seriously the proposition that space is a condition, medium, and outcome of social relations, then the development of 'urban religion' in lived urban spaces offers a lens onto processes of religious change that have been neglected in the study of both the history of religion and ancient urbanism. My key thesis is, thus, first, that city-space – understood as the array of urban spatial and structural forms, forces, processes, and agents – engineered the major changes that revolutionised Mediterranean religions, and, second, that this process is a paradigmatic model against which is it fruitful to compare other processes of urbanisation and their histories of religious practices, ideas, and institutions.

My argument in this volume will be developed over four sections of two or three chapters each. The first section, *Religion in urban space: Methodological reflections*, will address major conceptual and historiographical questions. Here, basic notions of religion, religious agency, and the materiality of religious communication will be developed and applied to the problems of the entangled development of urban settlements and religion. Urban religion will be developed as a two-sided process in which religious practices shape urban space and urban space shapes religion. The second section, *Thinking religion in urban space*, addresses changes in religious reflection that follow from an engagement with contemporary urban growth. In the first instance, I show how textual analysis can detect the implicit presupposition of an urban frame of reference for the development of religious notions while the analysis in the second starts from an indigenous taxonomy of places; both case studies are taken from ancient Rome. The third section, *Shaping urban space*, turns from the intellectual to the material dimension. Starting from the notions of material religion and urban resilience, I show how practices of writing and implementing material objects allowed the short- and long-term appropriation of urban space. Again, both instances focus on the invention and change of religious practices in urban environments. Both are taken from the city of Rome in longer chronological perspectives. The fourth and final section, *Grouping and subjectivisation in urban religion*, addresses, in a wider chronological and geographical framework, changes in individual and collective religious identities as consequences of urban settings.

In the first section, *Religion and the city: Methodological reflections*, three chapters deepen and develop the initial sketch of the theoretical foundation and conceptual apparatus underpinning my research question. 'Looking at religion in the city' (Chapter 1) will add the notion of sacralisation to the concept of the fluidity of religion, which latter is captured, even in historical contexts, by the concepts of 'lived religion' and 'religion in the making'. This chapter focuses on the inherently dynamic quality of those cultural products that I identify as 'religion' in cities. At the same time, the continuing materiality of religion and the undeniable presence of traditions and even *canones* needs to be conceptualised as something more than a world of individually fragmented religious practices and beliefs, and incipient, ever-changing, and also sometimes dissolving, institutions. However, one should not simply cluster together these phenomena in the form of narrative shorthand terms, such as the 'Greek Religion' or 'Islam' used by historians or the 'urban religion' of social anthropologists. The chapter offers a theoretical reflection on a concept of religion that is useful for asking questions about such fixations and intensifications of 'sacredness'.

'Before urban religion: Fustel de Coulanges and narratives of civic religion' (Chapter 2) takes a fresh look at religion in the cities of the ancient Mediterranean in the light of present-day urbanisation. The models of 'polis religion' and 'civic religion', a potential legacy of the study of Mediterranean antiquity that might be of use in the study of urban religion in other periods and regions, are considered in the context of their origins in Numa Fustel de Coulange's 1864 work *La cité antique*. A re-reading of this text draws attention to a number of deficiencies in the popular model of the coextension of political dominion and identity with religious practices and identity. This critical review will then be extended to interpretations of the relationship between city and religion in other periods and areas. It is only once this background is in place that it will be possible to propose a new concept of 'urbanised religion'.

The third chapter, 'Beyond Urban Religion: Urbanising and urbanised religion', takes as its starting point the brief comparative review of narratives concerning the role of religion in cities throughout history with which Chapter 2 ends. It discusses both sides of the reciprocal formation of religion and urban ways of life using a dual terminology in which religion is an active factor, promoting and acting upon urban settlements ('urbanising'), and a passive factor, being acted upon by urban factors ('urbanised religion'). However, my argument starts from an even more fundamental reflection. If what can loosely be termed 'urban religion' is able to serve as a lens onto the historical entanglement of cities, or 'urban settlements', then it is the specifically spatial character of religion that needs to be understood and theoretically modelled. Is religion more, or better differently, spatial than are other cultural practices? 'Sacred places' have played a prominent role in the history of research as loci of epiphanic character, above all in phenomenological approaches to religion but also in studies of sacred centres or pilgrimage. The temporal aspects of religion (routine, crisis rituals and rites of passage, conversion, calendar) have been foregrounded in many other approaches to the subject, with place being reduced to a mere setting. This chapter thus attempts to reconstruct religious action as a spatial practice that is sensitive to and creative of the character of settlements. On this basis, it attempts to develop a grid of analytical perspectives for studying the mutual interactions of religious practices and beliefs with urban space that were introduced in the previous chapter.

The second section of the book, *Thinking religion in urban space*, begins to analyse certain historical material with regard to specific forms of religious practices or discourses and the concomitant results for religious change and religion being 'urbanised'. The fourth chapter, 'Presupposing the city: Philosophical piety as urbanised religion', focuses on literary discourses in mid-1st century BCE Rome. Cicero's political and philosophical reflections react not only to the social and political conditions of the late Roman Republic and the Imperial expansion, but also specifically to changes in the social and spatial fabric of the city of Rome. I focus on this latter aspect, considering his *On the nature of the gods* both on the level of its content – arguments, choice of examples – and on the meta-level of the intellectual and communicative enterprise of the dialogue as such. It is astonishing to see that this universalist theological discussion presupposes the city as the best place to live. However, my analysis deals not with Cicero's participation in a widespread ancient urban ideology but, rather, with his implicit rendering of the specifics of urbanised religion. Thus, the chapter develops perspectives for close reading that might be employed in the study of texts produced in different processes of urbanisation.

Recent evolutionary theorising has drawn on cognitive studies to suggest that the formation of large societies and the social coherence necessary for their upkeep depends on the development of omniscient and moral gods that are able to observe and punish individuals in a way that extends beyond the ordinary mechanisms of social control. In contrast, Chapter 5, 'Crafting complex place: Religion and urban development', advances the hypothesis that large urban societies need practices that craft urban places by relating people and space, by disrupting continuous space, and by selectively appropriating space. These three processes are stabilised and furthered when they become reflexive, that is when they are accompanied by mental representations and discourses that are able to interpret urban experiences and to motivate urban development by providing further services. My argument draws on the example of the late Republican city of Rome and, in particular, on the rise of what is usually treated as 'aetiological myth' and 'antiquarian literature'. The textual basis is given by Vitruvius and by book 5 of Marcus Terentius Varro's *On the Latin language*, which is dedicated to the treatment of 'Place'. At Rome, it was ritual and textual religious practices that provided important tools for the creation of the highly complex, shared *and* divided, space called 'city' that was brought to a new level of complexity *and* coherence in the subsequent period.

While the focus of the second section of this volume is on the cognitive appropriation of space, the third section, *Shaping urban space*, turns to the materiality of this process and considers the long term consequences of this appropriation. Chapter 6, 'Materiality of religion in urban space: Neighbourhoods of a metropolis', leads the way. Materiality, which is to say the touchability and visibility of religion, is of particular importance in urban contexts. As systematically developed in Chapter 1, in the multi-layered and over- or under-determined urban space, religious practices use material forms in order to imprint a lasting religious character on spaces and thus appropriate them for temporary or permanent use. How does this work on the spatial level of neighbourhoods and neighbourhood religion? This chapter will explore fundamental mechanisms, focusing on practices in the *vici*, the small official sub-divisions of the city of Rome. The concept of 'public' spaces in Rome as areas for such religious practices is of particular interest, as the category of 'public' constitutes a fundamental trait of the contemporary concept of what characterised cities. From this perspective, religion is employed in such a way as to constitute the public character of places.

Starting from a brief analysis of 'quarters' and the cult of the Lares, I will offer a new view of the institution and institutionalisation of the *vicomagistri* and of what has been seen as the popularisation of Imperial cult in the city of Rome. The chapter thus argues for a heterarchical view of urbanised, as well as urbanising, religion, from which perspective questions naturally arise concerning the validity of the dichotomy of public and private as an analytical concept.

The seventh chapter, 'Urban resilience and religion: Attaching time to place', focuses on the relationship between urban resilience and religion, with resilience providing a lens through which to analyse religion and religion serving the same role with respect to resilience. By focusing on those religious practices that might reasonably be seen as fostering resilience (and hence urbanising religion), I assume that change in ancient Roman religion is related to a constellation of material and social action that can be described as 'urban resilience'. An important question to ask is how forms of attachment to one's city and urban space actually changed over time. A rare and important source of historical data that allows us to relate specific religious practices to the ups and downs of urban history (and hence to urbanised religion) is preserved in the material, frequently monumental, form of Roman calendars. This chapter argues that the development of certain features of the calendar offers a glimpse into different forms of practices that might have reflected, and helped foster, urban resilience. In the material form of the *fasti* and related media, individual and group memories of disasters (defeats, especially those including a massive loss of individual life; pestilences; floods) and memories of resilience, or the overcoming of disasters, are fixed and communicated through annual dates. This is not an inherent feature of just any calendar but, rather, a specific characteristic of the Republican Roman development of the calendar and its medial representation. The structural and historical continuity of the city are emphasised in these forms, acknowledging that disasters occur but stressing their temporary nature. The actual copies of the Roman calendar from the early Imperial period (the only period for which we can trace the material distribution, due to the fashion of inscribing calendars on stone) indicate a bottom-up interest in the places that made up the city of Rome. Whether this interest and the related practices actually contributed to resilience cannot be proven. However, by examining these religious practices we can shed some light on the peculiar ways in which Romans dealt with the fear of disaster and with its actual manifestation. As far as the study of urbanised religion is concerned, looking for resilience can help historicise religious practices that can be understood better within the framework of such memories and fears and in the context of changing urban and Imperial constellations.

The last section of this volume, *Grouping and subjectivisation in urban religion*, further highlights questions surrounding the religious changes that take place under urban conditions by shifting the focus onto the agents involved. In looking for a social and experiential framework for intellectual reflection on 'selves', the eighth chapter, 'Urban Selves: Individualisation in urban space', scrutinises not only concepts of the self but, above all, socio-religious practices and experiences related to such self-concepts. The argument here builds on recent research into the processes of religious individualisation in Mediterranean antiquity. In particular, I suggest that specifically urban developments during the Hellenistic and (early) Imperial phases of urbanisation contributed, to a certain extent at least, to the development of notions of 'selves'. I attempt to show how cities not only conditioned religious actions and reflections in this context but also served as motifs of such reasoning.

The final chapter, 'Urbanity and multiple religious identities', builds on this argument. The view of religious identities as collective and publicly affirmed came late to the ancient Mediterranean world, slowly developing in the Hellenistic and Roman empires. Prior to this, people were comfortable engaging with a range of different cults and easily shifted their piety from one local god to the next when they moved from one locale to another. Only in rare situations were self-definitions invoked with regard to religious beliefs or belongings. Family or political belonging might be expressed by reference to religious symbols but only very specific religious roles produced anything like religious identities. This last chapter explores changes in the use of specifically religious identities and the driving forces behind such changes. Building on the concepts developed in the preceding chapters, I pay particular attention to processes related to urbanisation and urban growth as the most important dynamic factors for changes in the degree of institutionalisation of religious identities. Such factors include the kind of urban aspirations that triggered migration, including identification and ethnogenesis, but also the density and diversity of living quarters, and the political interests involved in the administration and domination of urban space. A closer inspection of these combined factors highlights their role in the development of intermittent and multiple religious identities as forms of urbanity that combined, rather than mutually excluded, the enlargement of options and control. Collective religious identities, and hence religious plurality in the sense of a plurality of such imagined or interacting groups, were a phenomenon triggered by migration to and between cities and were furthered by urban conditions of density. The necessary boundary work, performed by urban intellectuals in the role of religious specialists, can, as the second part of the chapter shows, be identified even in the case of ancient Judaism as we find it in the world of Imperial cities.

The volume closes with a short summary of the individual chapters and their integrated results at the end of the book, under the heading of 'Religion and the City'. Here I critically evaluate the possibility of generalising my broader findings concerning religious change and other related changes in urban fabrics.

1 Looking at religion in the city

1.1 Introduction

How exactly should we define the 'religion' that has been so frequently invoked in the Introduction to this volume? Is it the wholly traditional, and as such legitimised, cultural system that has served to stabilise cities for millennia but that is now unable to adapt to the rapidly changing environment of the globalised city? Is it the traditional religion that is being driven out of its previous strongholds by new forms of 'urban religion' or by the inhumanity that is fossilised in 'fundamentalist cities', where protagonists of one religion subject everybody to the same oppressive requirements and marginalise or suppress any other religion?[1] Taking its start from polemics against the notion of a unified 'public religion', an important focus of research during the past decade has been 'religious individualisation' and the related fluidity of religion. These have been brought together in the notion of 'lived religion', that is the idea of individual religious practices that exist beyond the boundaries of established traditions and institutionalised forms of religion.[2] This notion is no longer restricted to contemporary forms of religiosity but has, more recently, been applied to the religiosity of the ancient world as well, with the introduction of the notion of 'lived ancient religion'. However, 'lived ancient religion' encompasses much more than just ancient 'popular religion', extending so far as to include the very making of 'public religion', understood in terms of the strategies pursued by members of the elite using their dramatically superior resources.[3] These resources typically dominate the archaeological, and frequently also the textual, records of earlier periods and their cities, obliterating our view of the dynamic character and situational meaning-making of even these practices, to say nothing of the practices of those who were less rich in resources.

I have tried to capture this dynamic dimension of religion in the phrase 'religion in the making'. This phrase is also the title of an early work by Alfred North Whitehead, published in 1926 and containing four of his lectures. This coincidence did not present itself to me when I first started to use the phrase, as my own reading of the book occurred many years ago and in a German translation

---

[1] AlSayyad 2011; Furseth 2011. I am grateful to audiences at Leiden and Erfurt to discuss the arguments presented here.
[2] Such as proffered by Ammerman 1997; Hall 1997; Orsi 1997; McGuire 2008.
[3] Rüpke 2016b; Albrecht et al. 2018.

entitled *Wie entsteht Religion?*⁴ Whitehead's title is not repeated as a phrase at any point throughout the book but it nevertheless helps to define my own wording *ex negative*. Whitehead writes at the very beginning of his preface: 'The aim of the lectures was to give a concise analysis of the various factors in human nature which go to form a religion, to exhibit the inevitable transformation of religion with the transformation of knowledge, and more especially to direct attention to the foundation of religion on our apprehension of those permanent elements by reason of which there is a stable order in the world, permanent elements apart from which there could be no changing world'. Whitehead's account is of a universal history of religion, its necessary change in the course of the development of a rational world view, and its permanent individual reproduction on the basis of aesthetic experiences that bring together the material and the noetic worlds. In historical terms, the religion of the Roman Empire is viewed as the most advanced rational form of 'communal religion' before a rational religious world view was formulated by humans in reaction to their perception of the universe as a whole, the all-encompassing unit within which everyone is located. Such an encompassing view, even if necessarily built on earlier forms of religion, by definition distances the individual from concrete localised social formations, helping the individual to arrange her- or himself in their solitariness and bringing a sort of transcendence into their limited and mortal immanence.⁵ Whilst, in Whitehead's preface, it is philosophical critique that calls into question the stability of religion and dogmas, my own 'making' focuses rather on the *inherent* dynamic quality of those cultural products that I identify as religion in the course of historical analyses.

The question remains as to how the undeniable presence of 'traditions' and their distillation into 'canons' can be conceptualised. Such forms of religious practices and knowledge evidently surpass individually fragmented religious practices and beliefs, and the incipient, ever-changing, and sometimes also dissolving institutions. It is not sufficient to group all of these traditions and practices together under the narrative shorthand terms – such as 'Buddhism', 'Christianity', 'Islam', or 'Judaism' – used by historians, or to place them within the category of 'urban religion' that has been used by recent social anthropologists. The approach I take in seeking to answer this question is, rather, to examine the concept of religion by means of a theoretical reflection upon it. This reflection will be framed by a historical assumption, namely that the processes that are

---

4 Whitehead 1926, 1990.
5 Indeed, subchapter 6, 'The Ascendance of Man' of his first lecture, dates the decisive shift to the first millennium BCE, thus approaching the notion of an 'axial age' *ante litteram* (1990, 31–33).

of interest here are furthered and accelerated in urban environments. Whether this relationship amounts to being 'originated in' needs to be discussed ultimately on the basis of specific historical evidence.

1.2 Religious agency and sacralisation

Drawing on my research into the ancient Mediterranean world, I have suggested that religion can be theorised as a form of communication with special agents (sometimes including objects) that are frequently conceptualised as god or gods, ancestors or demons. By the very existence of such communicative actions and the particular contents of this communication, these special agents are accorded agency in a way that is not unquestionably plausible: to employ religious communication at all in a specific situation, or to employ *this type* of religious communication, or to address this special addressee – all these decisions might be criticised by a given observer as being based on implausible suppositions, even if religious communication is deemed plausible in that particular society, which is to say that people would not question the existence of god or gods *per se*. Communication with or concerning such 'divine' agents might reinforce or reduce human agency, create or modify social relationships, and change power relationships.[6] 'Religious agency' is, thus, actually a constellation of two forms of agency: A) the agency attributed to such non-human or supra-human agents, and B) the agency of the human instigators of such communication. I am well aware that there is a great deal of phenomenologically comparable ritual action that does not assume the inclusion of such non-human agents. However, I deliberately restrict my definition of religion to the consequences of the invention of this specific type of agency, which I will call 'divine agency' (type A) in order to differentiate it from human religious agency (type B). In the eyes of contemporaries, the latter type of agency would be understood as deriving from the former, which is to say that the god grants agency to his or her human venerator (whether male or female, spontaneous or habitual, and whether conceptualised as 'mediators', 'saints', or just 'pious' and exemplary). Agency could also be attributed and arrogated by further participants or the peers, family, followers, or contacts of the primary group. It might also be used in a reversed manner, by negating the power, legitimacy, honesty, or piety of those excluded from the temporary or lasting relationship established in the initial or repeated act of communication:

---

6 Rüpke 2015c.

those not present, not listening, heathens or unbelievers, or simply 'the others', are all powerless or will ultimately be rendered powerless.

Expanding the dyadic model of speaker and addressee to a triadic model that also accounts for an audience to the communication leads us back to the problem of plausibility, briefly touched on above. Plausibility is a notion that ties the success of an act of communication to the approval of an audience, as I have discussed elsewhere.[7] However, if we turn our attention to the discipline of Semiotics we can provide a more detailed description of what is going on in such communication. So far, I have deliberately avoided talking about the medium of communication or the use of signs. This approach allows us to start with a simple model in which the speakers' own body and speech constitute the most basic form of symbolic communication. However, it is certainly true that, historically, ritual behaviour often precedes language.[8]

While I will continue to put off further discussion regarding signs for the moment, I do, of course, admit that my initial dyad of speaker and addressee already has an implicit triadic structure if we consider, to use Charles S. Peirce's terms, the sign proper (*representamen*), the interpretant, and the object represented.[9] The interpretant is not simply the religious agent speaking, but her or his conception of the sign. This conception includes, from the perspective of Peirce's pragmatist turn, all the possible practical effects of the sign, and thus ties in with the concept of the individual's religious agency and range of possible action. The semiotic perspective and the semiosis, that is the creation of a chain of meaningful signs, do not stop here. The process of interpretation continues, as the interpretation is an interpretation for an audience now itself engaging in its own interpretation of the semiotic complex set before its eyes and ears.

Neither the attribution of meaning nor the imagining of effects come from nothing. Rather, they draw on previous experiences, shared meanings and imaginings, and shared strategies, that is, traditions of interpretation.[10] Even if limitless in principle, the probable range of interpretations is thus restricted, even if such a restriction does not exclude the capacity for creative acts.[11] There is no zero point in an encounter between a user and a sign. Any articulation of this encounter – or, more precisely, of the experience in which such a sign is involved – is already framed by language and the shared meaning inherent within it.[12]

---

[7] Rüpke 2015c in more detail.
[8] See Bellah 2011, 134–5.
[9] See Peirce 1986; Peirce 1991; Klostergaard Petersen 2012, 156–7.
[10] For the latter see Fish 1995.
[11] Joas 1996.
[12] See Jung 2005.

This is not to advocate a culturalist approach. Linguistic research has demonstrated the rapidly changing character of language, as well as interpersonal and inter-group differences in its use.[13] The variety of meaning, often implicit or communicated through narratives or images, goes far beyond the clear-cut dichotomies favoured by structuralist interpreters or the systematisations attempted by indigenous or academic 'intellectuals' that generate in turn the 'religious traditions' of our handbooks.[14]

My own approach involves conflating the perspectives of articulation (focusing on the initiator) and interpretation (focusing on the audience) against the backdrop of the specific character of religious communication. Religious communication is communication with special agents that are not undeniably relevant. As it is, the very communication that brings the divine agents into situational relevance, and thus situational existence, and the pragmatic efficiency of this communication, as well as its plausibility, which latter needs to be assented to by the audience, are stressed for the agent as well as for the audience by the intensive use of media. In fact, the very act of communication and the vast range of media involved advance the existence of the otherwise invisible addressees.[15] The media-intensity of religious communication is far from the least significant reason for its presence in the archaeological records of different cities and periods.

We can now turn to the notions of sacralisation and the sacred. I propose to use 'sacralising' to refer to actions and processes that include elements of the situation – objects, space, time – within the act of communication and which thus ascribe meaning to them. Sunrise or the day of the full moon are thus marked as specifically conducive; a hot spring or the top of a hill or a tomb are places associated with more successful communication; a torch, a sacrificed animal, a valuable dress, or a block of stone might support the formulation and conveyance of one's message. Thus, the instigators make their communicational intent more relevant to their addressees and their communication as a whole more relevant and plausible to any audience. The speakers are heard by the gods and seen by their fellow humans thanks to intensive sacralisation.[16]

The notion developed so far allows us to speak of 'temporary sacralisation'. A place is used for religious communication and subjected to specific interpretations, perhaps even rules of behaviour, for the duration of the communication (usually this would take the form of a ritual but, for the moment, I will try to

---

13 Keller 1994; Bowern and Evans 2015, 225–553; Brinton 2017; Filppula et al. 2017.
14 B.-C. Otto, Rau and Rüpke 2015; Rüpke 2018b.
15 See Rüpke 2007c.
16 Sacralisation is here developed on the model of Catherine Bell's 'ritualization' (Bell 1992).

avoid introducing additional concepts). A marketplace might be used for a prayer or a street for a procession. Usually, such a temporary sacralisation would not leave any traces in the city, unless, perhaps, a bronze plaque is placed to commemorate the visit of a particularly important religious actor, such as a guru, saint, pope, or the like. Nor would such a place strengthen the 'religious' character of an action in a future instance, unless great efforts are made to re-activate the former ascription of a special character by way of remembrance or full re-enactment. Sacralisation also need not encompass the whole of a large site. It might focus instead on single, even small, objects that happen to be available or are consciously introduced into or produced within the situation. 'Gifts' or 'tokens' that refer in some way to the communicants involved or the message to be transferred are widespread.[17] Particular forms of dress or objects attached to the body – festive garments, crowns, ornaments, or body painting – are also used.

It is now easier to imagine the processes of interpretation in their temporal development. Sacralised objects (and places or times marked out using these objects) would create presuppositions that would serve to guide the processes of interpretation connected with the communicative action (scheduled for such a place or time). Re-use of objects or sites, or the addition of new objects into the process of framing, can strengthen and intensify the religious character of the event. Sacralisation is a matter of both quantity and scale.[18] Perhaps only under certain conditions and in specific cultural contexts can such processes produce debates about the dichotomy between that which is 'sacred' and that which is 'profane' (from the Latin *profanus*, literally 'in front of the sanctuary').[19] Space in a crowded city is scarce and the presence of observers, commentators, and systematisers in a given urban space would certainly be supportive of such distinctions. As is well known, these distinctions, reformulated as religion, on the one hand, and society, one the other, have remained important in Europe and other regions up to the present day.[20]

The argument has come full circle back to the notion of agency. By invoking in specific situations agents or authorities held to be divine, human agents extend their possibilities for imagining and acting. In this way, religious agency, the attribution of agency to 'divine agents' or the like, allows the human agent

---

17 See e.g. van Straten 1981; Linders and Nordquist 1987; also Auffarth 1995; Rüpke 2018c.
18 Thus, concepts like 'sacral topography' or 'sacred landscape' (e. g. Cancik 1985; MacCormack 1990; Caseau 1999; Clifford Ando 2001; Steinsapir 2005; Ceccarelli 2008; J. Hahn 2008) need also to be discussed with regard to the degree of sacralisation – as much as to visibility, readability and intentionality,
19 On *profanus* see Rüpke 2006a.
20 See e.g. M. Burchardt and Wohlrab-Sahr 2013.

to develop ideas that transcend the situation in question. This may lead to creative strategies that suit the situation, such as are deployed by principals in ritual performances or individuals who claim to be in a state of possession attributed to a divine being. Performing ritual actions or claiming religious knowledge creates powerful allies, spaces, audiences, and, in the long run, even networks. But the converse is also possible. The same mechanism can also trigger an abjuration of personal agency that results in impotence and passivity for the individual human, when acting with agency is seen to be the preserve of divine agents. Quietism, or even voluntary death, provide illustrations of the effect such perceptions can have.

Evidently, such agency or patiency could find expression and temporal extension in processes of sacralisation and in the spaces, times, or objects thus sacralised. Conversely, such agency could be supported by means of employing previously sacralised objects or situating itself in previously sacralised contexts. Praying in a temple, sacrificing on a holiday, preaching in a priestly garment, all could serve to enhance religious agency so long as the position of power held by the actor allows her or him to enlist such resources.[21] The use of such resources is a process of negotiating and appropriating such institutional resources within the overlapping networks of urban space. This is the case whether such actions are the outcome simply of previous, comparable actions of prestigious individuals or the outcome (and further development) of a powerful organisation, such as a priesthood running a temple, or a ruler who had dedicated a place, building, altar, etc. before and might use it again. The performance and novelty of religious agency interfere with institutionalised sacrality in many different ways, some of which may potentially conflict with one another. A new actor might be regarded as an impostor or heretic, as illegitimate or simply unworthy. All this depends on the audience present at the time or on later indirect observers, and on the relationships holding between the observers and the human religious actor. These relationships might range from hostility or disinterested neutrality, through contemporaries who could possibly be mobilised in support, through to people with obligations to existing institutional powers or who might simply be the family or followers of the initiator. As audiences widen and the public position of the actor grows, so are both potential and risk increased.

Such an understanding of sacralisation and the resulting degrees of sacredness clearly differs markedly from the notions of 'the sacred' that have been used

---

[21] For a detailed discussion see e. g. Patzelt 2018 (for praying) or Rüpke 2013e and Rüpke 2018d (for sanctuaries).

in sociological or theological reflections from Rudolf Otto through Mircea Eliade to Hans Joas.[22] In contrast to my approach, these notions of the sacred are inspired first and foremost by the Latin concept of *sacer*, the property of the gods, but also by the Hebrew concept of *qadosh*, which describes God and the manifestation of his radiance into the world in its varying degrees of intensity. My own version of sacralisation stresses rather the *transformation* of ownership in relation to the concept of *sacer* and inverts the agency involved in *qadosh*: it is the human, not the god, who sacralises.

1.3 Selectivity and canonicity as intensification of sacralisation

The concepts laid out in the preceding sections provide the basis for my attempt to adapt the term 'canonicity' for use within the framework of 'religion in the making'. Here, a canon is produced by the selectivity and intensity of sacralisation.[23] Power is translated into decisions about the restriction of access to and production of high degrees of sacredness. This interpretation can be supported by reference to a few examples, again taken from ancient Rome.

Only certain calendar dates, chosen by the decision of the Roman senate, are qualified by the letters *NP*, which means that something is forbidden by sanction of an expiating ritual (*nefas piaculo*). On these days a number of political and juridical activities are forbidden or made precarious, while other days with religious significance lack the same restrictions.[24] Similarly, only certain places are accorded the quality of being *sacer*. This characterisation depends, in part, on the decisions and participation of officials, but is limited in geographic extent to Roman soil only and within those boundaries to public properties, which preclude private occupation and the possibility of the sale of the property, in principle at least.[25] Again, only certain rituals (of course addressed to certain gods) were paid for from the public funds, in the form of *sacra publica*. This neither excludes other gods nor other forms of worship but, rather, awards the necessary means to those officially sanctioned while also providing the protection of tradition and respectability. This status is demonstrated by the involvement of the *magistratus* or *sacerdotes publici*, state officials and religious practitioners

---

22 R. Otto 1917, 2014 (on whom Deuser 2014); Eliade 1961; Urban 2003b; 2003a; Joas 2017.
23 For concepts of 'canon' see e.g. A. Assmann and Assmann 1987; A. Hahn 1987; Cancik 1997; E.-M. Becker 2012b; Wallraff 2013, Folkert 1989; Citroni 2006; Thomassen 2010.
24 See Rüpke 2011c.
25 Gai. *inst.* 2.3–5; on the problem Clifford Ando 2011, 2015.

from the upper echelons of society legitimised by formal elections or co-optations.[26] Finally, knowledge that might be termed 'canonical' is defined by texts only in exceptional cases. The notable exception that springs to mind is the Sibylline books, oracular texts that were collected, reviewed, and endorsed (after the loss of the original collection through fire in the first third of the 1st century BCE) by the authority of Augustus at the end of the 1st century BCE, an authority that included the decision to burn some of those collected books as not genuine.[27] Apart from this exception, knowledge is conceptualised as traditional and hence bound to persons rather than texts. In the version of a regulated religion laid out by Cicero in his *On laws*, it is the public priests who authoritatively 'know' about religious matters and prescribe rituals and gods to people or accept the latter's choice of rituals and gods.[28] In the period of Tiberius' rule, before the middle of the 1st century CE, Valerius Maximus fully endorsed this idea and built his collection of contemporary and earlier religious *exempla* around this notion.[29]

If canonisation is a medium of control found, not exclusively but also, *within* the realm of religion, it presupposes that there is competition within this very domain. That is to say, there must be a form of conflict that cannot be solved by subduing, driving out, or destroying the competitor, as in the case of external enemies. Obviously, canonisation does not in this context have an 'international' scope beyond the boundaries of one's own city, since religion is a domain a defining rule of which is 'every state has its religion and we have ours'.[30] Universality comes in as a local argument only.[31]

The thesis that I will try to make plausible is that the formation of social groups in the form of religious traditions that are organised and controlled by processes of canonisation is a phenomenon related to urbanity, to urban styles of life, and to the conditions of the city. I will dedicate the rest of this chapter to this issue by reconstructing certain characteristics of life in cities that made such developments seem adaptive to urban developments.[32]

---

26 See Scheid 2003; Rüpke 2007d.
27 Suet. *Aug.* 31.1.
28 Cic. *leg.* 2.20. See Rüpke 2016e, 21–31. The authoritative character of Cicero's priests reflects both Roman attitudes and those of Plato in his *Laws*, on which Cicero's work is modelled.
29 Rüpke 2016a.
30 Thus formulated in Cic. *Flacc.* 69.
31 Rüpke 2009a.
32 See Klostergaard Petersen 2012.

1.4 Reflecting on the urban

As I have shown above, the city, understood as a focal point of movements and relations and as a particular social and spatial arrangement, has never been treated as a condition crucial to the religious practices of the past or as the driving force behind religious change. It is clear that a vague notion of 'the city' cannot do justice to the full range of forms of larger or denser settlements, central places, and functional centres offering multiple services[33] that have either been described as 'cities' or consciously denied the label. For the present argument, with its focus on Mediterranean antiquity, this problem can be set aside by falling back on a polythetic definition formulated in a tradition that both originated in and was concerned with modern American cities,[34] although it will be necessary to modify the definition somewhat to fit the ancient subject matter.[35] The core of this definition is an understanding of urban space as a 'lived space', a built environment that is appropriated, used, and reshaped by agents who entertain their individual (and collective) notions of these spaces and what it means to live within them.[36] It is not the city *tout court*, but life in the city, the way of life developed in and shaped by cities, that provides the focus here.[37]

We can begin by noting that a 'city' is a spatial form that organises and regulates the phenomena of the density of population on a larger scale. In social terms, the 'high density' of a 'city' is marked above all by an increase in the contact zones and contacts of inhabitants and visitors.[38] As urban growth relies primarily on immigration, either permanent or temporary, the attractiveness of cities was and is a critical factor for their development. A city is, thus, a place that offers specific opportunities and evokes certain hopes. This dimension of the city is encapsulated in the concept of 'urban aspirations'.[39]

The heterogeneity of the city is an important dividing line marking such places (and I include smaller towns) off from larger villages. The city is a place that

---

33 E.g. M. E. Smith et al. 2015.
34 Wirth 1938, 1964.
35 Thanks go to Emiliano Urciuoli, Asuman Lätzer-Lasar, Maik Patzelt and Harry O. Maier as collaborators in the drawing of this list.
36 See Lefebvre 1974; Löw 2016.
37 E.g. Manderscheid 2004; for antiquity e.g. Kolb 1984; Cunliffe and Keay 1995.
38 Löw 2008.
39 The term has been developed in recent urban studies that have taken up the language of 'aspirations' from studies of social mobility (Appadurai 2004a) in order to describe the driving motifs and attitudes of immigrants as well as inhabitants, that is, the hopes and ideas connected with urban life and the employment of religion for such ends, which latter addition gives us 'urban religious aspirations' (van der Veer 2015a, 2–12; Goh and van der Veer 2016).

engenders diversity, not only as a result of the heterogeneous origins of its inhabitants but as its permanent production. Conflict is, thus, endemic. As a consequence, homogenisation and standardisation are crucial for the government. To make the city 'legible', systems of documentation, principally in written forms, were invented and developed in the dense settlements of alluvial plains from the Nile to the Yangtze.[40] The city is a place subject to administrative attempts at comprehensive organisation. Ancient religion has tended to be framed by scholars in the context of the pursuit of this latter goal, an approach that has resulted in a very narrow view of both religion and religious change.[41]

A division of labour is another central characteristic of the city, even if the occupations or livelihoods of many ancient (and later) city-dwellers were related in some way to agriculture, whether in terms of actual practice or indirectly through investment and financing. A city is a place inhabited by a substantial population of non-food-producing individuals who pursue a variety of trades (including intellectual occupations) sustained by an agricultural surplus. Intellectualisation, with its basis in urban writing systems, was a major consequence of growing specialisation below the ruling elites.[42] Urban intellectuals are also important for the elaboration, albeit not the instigation, of the final characteristic of the city: a city is a place that is recognised as such and is defined by contrast with (culturally variable forms of) the 'non-city'. Such general notions were made more specific with regard to actual places. In the long run, imaginaries of cities, one's own and others', were developed.

These characteristics fit well with a definition that has recently been proposed:

> Cities are distinguished from other human settlements by two key features: they constitute dense and large clusters of people living and working together, and they are the focus of myriad internal and external flows. This is what makes cities uniquely active and vibrant places that are always more cosmopolitan than culturally uniform.[43]

A city is not an isolated place and nor is its context restricted to its relationship with its hinterland. Rather, it is necessarily connected to and part of the migratory, economic, and/or intellectual flows that transcend the local.

Given the ability of religious communication to produce a specific agency, religious practices might be intimately bound up with the dichotomous striving

---

40 Mann 1986; Law et al. 2015.
41 See Rüpke 2018d.
42 M. L. Smith 2019, 185–201.
43 Robinson, Scott and Taylor 2016, 5.

for both homogeneity, that is power and administration, and diversity, that is the securing of spaces for the preservation or development of specific identities and ways of living. This potential need not be exploited in every path of urbanisation nor in every phase of a city's lifetime, but it was certainly important and much mobilised in the classical Greek, Hellenistic, and Imperial phases of Mediterranears urbanisation.[44] It is with a view to these periods and forms of urban life that I develop my argument here.

1.5 Urbanism and the formation of religious groups

As stated above, cities are typified by frequent encounters and dense networks, but also by fluid and exchangeable relationships.[45] Religious communication that brings the 'beyond' temporarily or permanently into a communicative space is a practice induced and shaped by, while also recreating, space.[46] In the ancient Mediterranean world, religious communication was reinforced by sacralising objects or spaces and was manifest in material form even in non-religious uses of space.[47] Creating religious space was part of an ongoing process of claiming and appropriating urban space as a whole. Within the many overlapping spaces, religion thus could also create, overdetermine, and negate other spaces. This change might be temporary, as in the case of dances or processions,[48] or it might be permanent, as in the case of images and architecture. In both cases, the presence of signs or traces of religious practices shapes urban 'lived space' and stimulates particularly tenacious memories.[49]

The same holds true if we turn to the appropriation of time and its relationship with spatial processes. Synchronisation and de-synchronisation are simultaneously interests and activities. Large spaces were laid out for religious action in a way that brought together multitudes of people at the very same moment. 'Games', races, and plays performed on *scaenae* were religious techniques directed towards centralisation and synchronisation that spread rapidly in the ancient Mediterranean world.[50] Nevertheless, for centuries ancient Rome shunned the building of permanent theatres in order not to provide spaces for counterpub-

---

[44] A short overview: Zuiderhoek 2017.
[45] Simmel 1917; Blum 2003.
[46] Becci and Burchardt 2013; Rüpke 2017a.
[47] Insoll 2009; Droogan 2013; Raja, Rüpke 2015b.
[48] See e.g. Connor 1987; Fless and Moede 2007; Chaniotis 2013; Stavrianopoulou 2015.
[49] Rau, Schwerhoff 2008; Hurlet 2014; Dey 2015; Galinsky 2016; Latham 2016.
[50] Bernstein 2007.

lics.[51] The use of religion to produce such counterpublics is generally very hard to detect in Rome during the Republic, but appears in an exemplary manner and in an exceptionally conflictual form when the cult places of Dionysos, the so-called *Bacchanalia*, were closed down, destroyed, or restricted by legal and military means following the *Senatus consultum de Bacchanalibus* in 186 BCE.[52] Otherwise, it is the many small sanctuaries that appear in the Imperial period alongside the circuses and amphitheatres, rarely as archaeologically identifiable as the Mithraic caves, which best demonstrate the parallel strands of unity and diversity.[53]

In Athens and other Greek poleis, Orphic groups might have developed early on[54] as part of an urbanity that found its expression of unity (of the male and freeborn citizen body above all) in rituals and monumentalised central places and architectures. For a long period, the development of different textualised bodies of knowledge was a means of developing and supporting diversity rather than unity. Or it seems that this is the case when we confine ourselves to taking a bird's eye view of the matter. If we zoom in instead to the level of competing intellectuals and their attempts to forge stable networks of followers, we find that the opposite is true. It is new texts that claim authority, investing in a self-canonisation by means of authorial personae and narrative voices.[55] This approach aimed at exclusion and internal stabilisation by polarising groups on the basis of even minimal differences.

For all this competition, urban space was not a merely spatial setting. To capture its wider scope, an additional term will be useful. Recent urban studies have borrowed the language of 'aspirations' from studies of social mobility[56] in order to describe the driving motivations and attitudes of immigrants as well as inhabitants. 'Urban aspirations' describe the hopes and ideas connected with urban life and, when we add in the employment of religion in pursuit of such ends, we can speak also of 'urban religious aspirations'.[57] It is part of the way of life that I have described as urbanity to develop an image of the chosen or given city that might motivate temporary or permanent migration and provide a driving force for adaptation and integration with regard to survival, economic

---

[51] Dupont 1986; Sear 2006; Goldberg 2007; Manuwald 2011.
[52] See Pailler 1988; de Cazanove 2000; H. I. Flower 2002.
[53] Arnhold 2015; Van Andringa 2015.
[54] See Guthrie 1966; Obbink 1997; Bernabé Pajares 2008; Burkert 2011; Edmonds 2011; J. N. Bremmer 2016; Jackson 2016 and Edmonds III 2013.
[55] E.-M. Becker 2012b, 2012a; E.-M. Becker and Rüpke 2019.
[56] Appadurai 2004.
[57] Goh and van der Veer 2016.

1.5 Urbanism and the formation of religious groups — 29

success, and possibly even the development of cultural capital. It is here that religion and religious agency again comes in, with urban identities being couched in religious terms even as late as the fourth to sixth centuries CE.[58] The high-density network of urban activities has plausibly been claimed to foster human reflexivity and to lead to cultural innovations by addressing problems in novel ways.[59]

The creative stimulus is two-fold. On the one hand, religious innovations enlarge agency by attempting to deal with the specific problems raised and opportunities provided by cities. On the other hand, new cultural productions may generate new urban issues, challenge socio-political and religious leaderships, and, eventually, complicate the lives of city dwellers rather than simply facilitating them. Prophecy and the struggle to contain it offer an example of this tension.[60] As outlined above, religious communication is part and parcel of this, a reflection of the tensions and strife as much as a resource and driving force. Non-urban space might invite religious communication in a plurality of distant places around a village. Such rural sanctuaries do not enter inter direct competition with each other as they lack a diversity of stakeholders. Villages enforce social unity even in domestic space by way of social pressure in the overlapping of primary and secondary groups, that is of kinship groups and economic or cultural groupings. In contrast, city-space demands explicit forms of shared meanings or identities or networks. High visibility and a large range of aesthetic forms are characteristics of the iconic religion prominent in city-space,[61] phenomena that are captured by the concept of sacralisation developed above. In a way unknown to smaller settlements and their social groups, religious communication produces and depends on sacralising space, time, and the material environment, and participates in shaping the built environment as well. It is cities and the urbanity developed therein that afford and necessitate the formation of recognisable traditions and perhaps even the form of intensiveness and selectivity called 'canonisation' to offer points of reference and orientation in the complex networks of their inhabitants.

---

58 Caseau 1999; Dey 2014; Jacobs 2014.
59 Soja 2000, 14–15; see also Storper 1997.
60 E.g. the Roman *carmina Marciana*, late Republican and early Imperial *vates* or Judaeo-Christian apocalyptics, see Potter 1990; Momigliano 1992a; Wiseman 1992; Bendlin 2002, 2011b.
61 See Knott, Krech and Meyer 2016.

2 Before urban religion: Fustel de Coulanges and narratives of civic religion

2.1 The problem

It was the new focus on lived religion, rather than organised and intellectually elaborated religion, practiced in people's houses and flats, rather than restricted to traditional ritual spaces, that led to the discovery by contemporary scholarship of both non-traditional and very active and vivid forms of religion in contemporary city-space.[1] The growing academic interest in the cities of Asia and the 'global South' in recent years has started to pay proper attention to these newly discovered, even if not always recent, practices and material forms. This attention has opened up a wealth of new material concerning the religious practices that continue to take place in, and to define spaces within, industrial and post-industrial metropoleis.[2] Ancient places of worship are memorialised in contemporary cities through small devotional practices, as, for example, when shrines are set up in the middle of shopping malls or in the backyards of houses, workshops, and factories.[3] These practices not only represent a continuation of the ancient into the contemporary world but can also help us better imagine that ancient world, reflecting as they do the practices of, for instance, ancient Mediterranean cities. When we read in one late ancient urban catalogue that Alexandria housed nearly 2,500 temples, we should envision not several thousand grand buildings on the Capitoline scale, but a multitude of smaller, more personal and local shrines.[4]

The city had and has a central place in thinking about ancient religion, at least in terms of those religious practices and beliefs that were characteristic of the Mediterranean basin in the period stretching from the spread of Hellenic urbanism through to Late Antiquity. Of course, we must not be fooled by mere similarities in phenomena, as such similarities do nothing to defuse or deny the many important differences between the urban conditions of antiquity and the present day. However, the similarities *do* invite us to confront the past with the present in order to better understand the development of cities *and* religion. The concepts of 'polis religion' and 'civic religion', as developed by Classics scholars, placed the city centre stage for explaining religious change long

---

[1] See Introduction. An earlier Germany version of this chapter: Rüpke 2019.
[2] E.g. Sun 2013; J. Becker et al. 2014; Veer 2015.
[3] Sinha 2016.
[4] Haas 1997, 141.

before the rise of the concept of 'urban religion'. However, looking back at these concepts, it is evident that their development in the twentieth century fell short of exploring the full intellectual breadth of these ideas as envisioned by their founding father Numa Fustel de Coulanges (1830–1889). Instead of focusing on religion as a tool of the political and social elites, his analysis offers wider insights that can be developed into an analytic framework that is just as able to comprehend perspectives on social and religious agency as it is findings from the history of urbanism. The development of such a framework promises to produce questions and answers that will make important contributions to contemporary urban and religious studies.

If the concepts of 'Lived Ancient Religion' and religious agency, as developed at the Max Weber Centre and outlined above,[5] can help to broaden and shift the focus of 'polis religion', they nevertheless fall short of adequately dealing with the specifics of the urban. For this reason, I will begin with a re-reading of Fustel de Coulanges' *La cité antique*.[6] I then turn to questions concerning comparative evidence, in the light of which I attempt to develop a new analytical framework that integrates recent findings in Urban Studies and the History of Ancient Religion and that also helps to develop and enrich the notion of an 'urbanised religion' that is an object *of* change as much as an instrument *for* change.

2.2 Polis religion

While common in the works of scholars who focus on Urban Studies,[7] the name of Numa Denis Fustel de Coulanges is surprisingly absent from most studies of ancient polis religion. Nevertheless, his ideas are never far from the surface. This holds true, for example, in Zaidman and Pantel's *Religion in the Ancient Greek City*,[8] the authors of which limit their study to the period between the foundation of the polis (for which Athens stands as the primary example) and the turn towards a personalised notion of individual contact with the divine, which rendered meaningless the collective dimension of such contact and thus the gods' safeguarding of the community. This also holds true for John Scheid's masterly *Introduction to Roman Religion*, which stresses the 'fundamen-

---

5 Rüpke 2012c, 2016b; Rüpke 2015c; see Ch. 1.
6 Fustel de Coulanges 1864, 1956.
7 See Yoffee and Terrenato 2015, 7.
8 Bruit Zaidman and Schmitt Pantel 1992, French title: *La religion grecque*.

tal importance of *city ideology*' and the co-originating of the city of Rome and the historical Roman religion.[9] Fustel de Coulanges' underlying presence is no less implicit in Kurt Latte's handbook of Roman religion, published in 1960 but conceived already by the end of the 1920s,[10] in which he regards the unity of the community to be represented ('sinnfällig') through the unity of cult. This urban cult was, according to him, the result of the transferal of domestic rites onto the city. However, Latte did not claim a historical priority for isolated households, focusing instead on Vesta and thus distancing himself from Fustel.[11]

It was, in fact, the study of Vesta and of ritual fire that led Fustel to write his more expansive treatise on the ancient city, with its 'books' on, first, religion ('Antiques croyances'), the family, and the city, before turning to the contingent history of social revolutions within Greek and Roman cities. The sequence of the first three books reflects the conceptual link between these three elements, the inquiry into which is driven by the question of how the ancients thought ('que pensaient les hommes', Introduction), or, to put it in terms familiar to twentieth-century sociology, of what the shared imaginaries were that gave meaning to their actions.

On this analysis, Greco-Roman religion in its earliest, original form (Fustel de Coulanges does not make any broader evolutionary claims) was exclusively domestic,[12] with a double focus on the hearth in the house and the family tomb close by.[13] The cult was not public but, rather, performed in the *foyer* (literally 'the place of the fire') of the house, at an altar invisible to those outside. As a consequence, there were no rules governing the practice of religion and every family could do what it liked.[14] Just as the family created its own practices, so too was the family constituted by this cult and, hence, by religion, as the second book argues in great detail.

Families were not just small nuclear units. In the form of the *gens*, the clan, they might comprise many thousands of people. In order to understand Fustel (and similarly his pupil Émile Durkheim),[15] it is vital to grasp that he sees fam-

---

9 Scheid 2003, 16–7.
10 See Rüpke 1994a, 131.
11 Latte 1960, 108.
12 'La religion était purement domestique', book 1, ch. 4 = 1984, 34.
13 Here Fustel de Coulanges had mitigated his earlier 'ordinairement voisin de la maison' (still in the 5th edition of 1874) to 'Aux temps très-antiques, le tombeau était dans la propriété même de la famille, au milieu de l'habitation, non loin de la porte', book 1, ch. 4, 1984, 34.
14 Fustel de Coulanges refers to Varro, *ling.* 7.88: *suo quisque ritu sacrificia faciat*, 'everybody performed sacrifices according to his own rite' (book 1, ch. 4 = 1984, 36).
15 See R. A. Jones 1993 and Pettenkofer 2014, 100.

ilies (and clans), like cities, as being fully-fledged forms of 'society'. On that basis, the general rule is that the size of a society grows in parallel with the expansion of the reach of religious concepts, in the sense of the degree to which these concepts can include more people and settlements within their conceptual horizon.[16] It is religion – that is, cult on a higher level – that enables new types of societies, phratries, and *curiae*. Cult at the level of religion is built on the same fundamental principle as the lower-level family cult: a shared meal is prepared at an altar and is, hence, 'sacred'.[17]

What, then, are the mechanisms that allow religion to transcend the limits of the family? In the second chapter of his third book, entitled '*Novelles croyances religieuses*', Fustel develops a more complex model of religion as he addresses this question. Right from the start (and again he limits this observation to his historical subjects: 'those peoples'), there were two different religions.[18] The first was built on the experience of one's own life and self, and located the divine forces in one's own soul and in the ancestors, the heroes, and the *lares*. The other was related to the wider world, to the external physical forces that enabled life. This religion thus located the divine forces in external objects but imbued them with the same kind of personality and will found in the divinities that were located in human agents.

This second religion is still domestic, family religion, since its concepts and understanding of the divine forces are developed independently by each individual (or at least by many individuals). It was not a common doctrinal origin but, rather, the uniformity of the conditions of life, that led to the similarity of the divinities thus generated and to the shared everyday religious language, drawing as it did on a restricted reservoir of names for natural phenomena (here Fustel de Coulanges is close to the thinking of his contemporary, Friedrich Max Müller, concerning the origins of divine names). There were, thus, many 'glorious ones' (Heracles) or 'luminous ones' (Phoebos), but these 'thousands of Jupiters' (and the like) were all gods of individual families; they were gods who shared a name, rather than the same shared god with minor familial variations.[19] Yet, in the long run,[20] these gods of the second religion had enough in common that they could become generalised in a way that the ancestors could not. I might, for instance, be interested in getting the help of *your* Jupiter, with all

---

[16] 'L'idée religieuse et la société humaine allaient donc grandir en même temps', book 3, ch. 1 = 1984, 132, a paragraph of just this sentence.
[17] The reference is to Dionys of Halikarnassos, *Antiquities* 2.23.
[18] 'Deux religions', 1984, 136.
[19] 1984, 139.
[20] 'Il fallut beaucoup de temps', 140.

the might and power that it appears to possess, but I would never be able to make use of your family hero. You might wish to maintain the sacerdotal position with regard to your Jupiter (as the clan of the Potitii is said to have been responsible for the cult of Hercules before the Middle Republic),[21] but in the end you would not object to me venerating him.

The formation of such shareable religious concepts, and the idea that the Jupiters of different families might be the same divine force, preceded the creation of larger social units. This was the case not least because this second type of deity also implied another type of morality, as they were referred to or associated with phenomena of the shared social and natural world, thus favouring hospitality even to strangers and asking for concord even if occasionally they were party to one side of a conflict. Society could enlarge in parallel with the rise of these gods and their associated morality.[22] The domestic 'foyer' is thus transformed into an extra-domestic small *naos* or *cella*, and finally into a full-size temple, a clear indicator of the larger society in which it is now embedded. These mechanisms shape the very form of the city, as Fustel de Coulanges theorises in his third chapter, '*La cité se forme*'. The fundamental units do not merge with one another but, rather, associate on a higher level: families grow into *curiae*, *curiae* into 'tribes', and tribes into a city, all while remaining individual and independent units that are held together by their own form of cult, their *religion comune*.[23] It follows that 'the city is not an assembly of individuals, but a confederation of several groups'.[24] Material forces are insufficient for keeping it together; a shared belief (*croyance*), the strongest bond imaginable, is also necessary.

> A belief is the product of our thinking, but we are not free to modify it at whim. It is our creation, but we do not know it. It is human, but we believe it to be the god.[25]

What Fustel imagines here is an individual intellectual construct. This is not yet Durkheim's idea of an 'effervescent' bond, a spontaneous production of solidar-

---

21 Ibid.
22 'A mesure que cette seconde religion alla se développant, la société dut grandir', 1984, 142.
23 Book 3, ch. 3 = 1984, 143. See 1984, 144: 'En religion il subsista une multitude de petits cultes au-dessus desquels s'établit un culte commun; en politique, une foule de petits gouvernements continuèrent à fonctionner, et au-dessus d'eux un gouvernement commun s'éleva'.
24 'Ainsi la cité n'est pas un assemblage d'individus: c'est une confédération de plusieurs groups que étaient constitués avant elle et qu'elle laisse subsister', 1984, 145.
25 1984, 149: 'Une croyance est l'oeuvre de notre esprit, mais nous ne sommes pas libres de la modifier à notre gré. Elle est notre création, mais nous ne le savons pas. Elle est humaine, et nous la croyons dieu'.

ity, generated by emotions in social rituals.²⁶ Rather, it is still some form of human mass production, the character of which is veiled from the producers.

Fustel de Coulanges writes as a good historian when he admits that the path described above need not be the history of each city, as the final structure might also be instituted in a top-down way. However, he is also a good sociologist when he claims that the successful result of such a top-down implementation would need to reproduce the same pattern as would come from the bottom-up mechanism. In either case, a city is the coming together of people who have the same tutelary deities and who perform cult practices at the same altar – at the temple of Vesta in the case of Rome.²⁷ And it is this *de facto* political and religious association (*cité*), which initially comes together in an informal and un-organised way, that then decides collectively to constitute a proper town (*ville*) (book 3, Chapter 4), the people of which will later venerate the leading figure of this foundation as a 'holy man' (*homme sacré*) (book 3, Chapter 5). In the end, the city's religion will consist of a number of meals and festivals, which together will form the city's calendar (book 3, Chapter 7).²⁸

In the chapters that follow, Fustel describes the political institutions of the city in great detail. These need not, on the whole, concern us here, but it is important to recall his conclusions with regard to religion in the final chapter of the book (18, originally 17), conveniently entitled '*De l'omnipotence de l'état; les anciens n'ont pas connu la liberté individuelle*' ('The state's omnipotence; the ancients did not know individual liberty'). Both conclusions are attributed not to the density of political institutions but to the religious character of the ancient city. This dimension of the city's character appears time and again throughout the work, as, for instance, with regard to the religious impossibility of having two citizenships (Chapter 12 '*Le citoyen et l'étranger*') due to the embedding of citizenship within a hierarchy of religious commitments rising from the level of family to that of the city. The religious character of the city is now generalised:

> The city had been grounded on a religion and constituted like a Church. Hence its power, hence, too, its omnipotence and unrestricted command over its members.²⁹

---

26 Durkheim 1947 [1912].
27 'La cité était la réunion de ceux qui avaient les mêmes dieux protecteurs et qui accomplissaient l'acte religieux au même autel', book 3, ch. 6 = 1984, 166.
28 'Le calendrier n'était pas autre chose que la succession des fêtes religieuses ... établi par les prêtres', 1984, 185.
29 'La cité avait été fondée sur une religion et constituée comme une Église. De là sa force; de là aussi son omnipotence et l'empire absolu qu'elle exerçait sur ses membres', 1984, 265.

Given the status of a city as a confederation, Fustel de Coulanges needs to explain the city's ability not only to draft individuals for military service but also to force those who held certain roles into a persistent celibacy or to forbid them to mutilate themselves. It is this doubling of political and religious authority, that is to say of magistrates and priests, with the first always built on the blueprint of the second,[30] that is critical for achieving this end.

Likewise, religious liberty is not granted at the level of the domestic, the phratries/curiae, or the city as described so far. This sort of liberty is conceptually related only to religion at an even higher level: the belief in universal gods and a universal god, a possibility grounded in the expansion of the 'second religion' and one that will, ultimately, bring about the end of the ancient Greco-Roman city. This ending of the ancient city is helped along on the political side by the growing number of people who fall outside the ultra-dense structure of the ancient city and the ancient state (which is unable to expand beyond the city, since it can develop only *within* the spatial and organisational context of the city), and who fight (without knowing it) for a wider and more universal structure than the city can offer (book 4, Introduction). Thus, the beginning of the end of the ancient city is dated to the seventh century BCE by Fustel de Coulanges, that is, to the time immediately following the first steps in Greco-Roman urbanisation. In the end, however, it was not the historically contingent, even if fairly uniform, series of social and political revolutions undertaken by, for instance, patricians and plebeians (studied at length in book 4), but the transformation of Rome into an empire (again led by a change in thinking), that led to the demise of the 'municipal regime' (book 5).[31] The growing distance between practices addressed to the dead and concepts of the divine and divine intelligence, that is the growing distance between habitualised cultic practices that lacked an adequate explanatory framework and the new philosophical discourse that opened up new existential perspectives, served to undermine the principles of polis religion (book 5, Ch. 1).[32]

---

30 Here the influence of Cicero's *De legibus* is decisive, see for this text Rüpke 2012f, 188–191; in short form Rüpke 2016e, 28.
31 See e.g. Fustel de Coulanges 1984, 415f.
32 1984, 418.

2.3 Critique

It should be plain that we cannot simply agree with Fustel de Coulanges' claim that the city has been replaced by something more important, even if we suggest that it is a modern phenomenon such as globalisation that provides the replacement. Max Weber solved the problem of the inherent limitations to the structure of the Greco-Roman cities by postulating a radical break with the ancient city, an idea that has become almost impossible to sustain.[33] Without explicitly criticising Fustel de Coulanges' view of the ancient city, Weber posited a radically different character for the occidental medieval city. The legitimate rule (*legitime Herrschaft*) in the ancient city, which grew quasi-organically out of the process of delegating the self-evident and religiously sanctioned power of heads of families and clans to ever higher levels, is replaced by the *illegitime Herrschaft* of the medieval city, founded by people who wished to defend themselves against the oppression of the legitimised power of external bishops or kings by voluntarily associating in the form of a town.

With my own focus on the similarities between ancient and modern cities, I clearly cannot follow the Weberian solution in any sort of straightforward manner. Rather, I need to provide a theoretical underpinning for the permanent influx of migrants that drives urbanisation and that contributed to the number and, above all, the growth of ancient cities,[34] and that was itself driven by the urban aspirations, the imaginaries, and the hopes associated with the urban life held by those in the areas surroundings these cities.[35] Central administration and the dominant position of cities as an instrument of power for wider regions[36] was challenged by the everyday fluidity and diversity of an immigration the motifs of which were not under control.

Similarly, I am unable to follow those (implicit) critics of Fustel de Coulanges who point to the fact that a millennium of flourishing ancient cities can hardly be reconciled with a coextensive decline and dysfunctionality. Such critics are certainly correct that the actual social practices of later and historically accessible stages cannot be reduced to traces of practices in earlier periods.[37] However, it is not a legitimate move to abbreviate the logic of the argument and focus only on the top layer of this model, retaining the idea of the strength and obligatory

---

[33] See Zuiderhoek 2017.
[34] Scheidel 2001a; Scheidel 2003; De Ligt 2012; Hin 2013; Rizos 2017.
[35] Goh and van der Veer 2016 for contemporary Asian cities; for antiquity see Schalles and Hesberg 1992, 394; Revell 2009, 78.
[36] Revell 2014, 91.
[37] Scheid 2001, 24.

force of 'public' religion, i.e. religion on the level of the city, without acknowledging the even more fundamental character of the social levels underneath, upon which the higher-level conclusions rely. The basic question Fustel de Coulanges tries to answer is how could a city function without a power structure kept in place by force? The answer is not just found in the rich evidence for religious practices. Instead, this broad presence of religious practices is in itself a curious fact that needs to be explained. It is by bringing both problems together that Fustel de Coulanges develops a narrative that makes both developments plausible at the same time. However, he did not, himself, follow through on the explanation that he started to develop. Rather, his own solution to the problems turned the city into a transitional phase in a longer-term religious development. This transitional view quickly shifted his own interest from the question of the stability of the city to that of its decline, and from the question of the ongoing relevance of the basic units to that of the universalistic transcending of the city. Fustel de Coulanges' primarily intellectualist framing of his argument made it easy to disregard his analysis. This framing put belief centre stage rather than the practices, and the tacit conceptions implied by these practices, that were foregrounded by his pupils.[38] Nevertheless, if we go beyond these problems and reformulate his questions (and findings) in the light of later theory, the approach Fustel de Coulanges takes in *The ancient city* remains highly interesting. At the heart of his theory were the religious creativity of individuals, the centrality of religious practices and beliefs as socially inclusive and exclusivist strategies, the continuation of practices and related conceptions across different levels of social aggregation, the co-presence of the institutions and actions of these levels within the city, and, finally, the heterogeneity of the imaginaries entertained by co-present inhabitants.

Clifford Ando has demonstrated how vital the notion of urban religion is for the cognitive apparatus necessary for dealing with religion in the Roman empire.[39] The same holds true for 'sub-urban' religious concepts (in a Fustelian sense), usually implied in practices rather than being fully explicit and coherent. In my recent longitudinal study of religious transformations at Rome within its Mediterranean context, I discuss the centrality of ancestor cult and tomb-related practices and their transferal onto, or their being substitutes for, other religious practices.[40] This holds true from the early Iron Age practices of addressing dead humans and deities in the same manner through the doubling of Lares and Di

---

38 See Pettenkofer 2014, 106–7.
39 Ando 2015.
40 Rüpke 2016d, see now also MacMullen 2017.

Manes, through sacrificial meals, the creating of epiphanic space in domestic contexts, and the focusing of religious creativity on extra-urban tomb sites, all the way up to the emperor-related and Christological issue of deification. Priestly colleges, which were at the very heart of polis religion in ancient thinking, were modelled on domestic symposiastic groups.[41] These groups provided a blueprint for many voluntary associations as well, which made shared professions, and frequently also neighbourhoods, a basis for religiously conceptualised grouping and served as a major instrument for entangling newcomers into urban networks.[42]

Against this backdrop, a closer look at the central empirical data for Fustel de Coulanges' idea of a unifying religion for the city lays open its feebleness: the cult of Vesta, one of the primary examples for his theory, is centrally located but it is invisible; the distribution of a salt-grain mix from this cult is of unknown age and unknown impact; the distribution should thus be seen as an attempt at centralisation, probably limited to rituals belonging to the same circle of 'public' (i.e. elite) agents, by introducing a ritual detail into the preparation of a major sacrificial victim.[43] Triumphs, another important example for the theory, were as much a ritual for a public appropriation of victory as for the self-extolling of the victorious general and could be celebrated outside the city as well as within.[44] For the metropolis of Rome, we can find the perceived threat produced by religious innovation, above all by imports and immigrants, in Cicero's 'laws' concerning religion;[45] the almost unlimited openness to re-interpretation of publicly displayed religious artefacts in Propertius' poem on dedications to Vertumnus;[46] people without a proper place in traditional grids in Ovid's account of the Fornacalia (*fast.* 2,531–2); and the production of shared knowledge in clandestine 'magical' practices in the interaction of client and magician.[47] Even Fustel de Coulanges' implied complex model of the religion of the city requires additional complexity if we are to take it seriously.

---

41 Rüpke 1998a.
42 See Noy 2000; Rüpke 2007d, Ch. 10 'Religion in the Metropolis'; Orlin 2010.
43 See Rüpke 2007d, 115; cf. Harders 2014.
44 Rüpke 2006f; Östenberg 2009a; Lange and Vervaet 2014.
45 Rüpke 2016e, 29.
46 Rüpke 2016b, 58–63.
47 Gordon 2013a, 2013b; already elaborated in M. Mauss: Pettenkofer 2014.

2.4 Comparative perspectives on cities in other regions and periods

Are these findings and perspectives concerning ancient cities isolated or do they tie in with cities in other regions and/or periods? The recently published third volume of the *The Cambridge World History* is dedicated to *Early Cities in Comparative Perspective, 4000 BCE-1200 CE* and offers a large sample of comparative data that we can use to answer this question.[48] In addition to ecological, economic, and political factors, it is the question of the atmosphere of early cities and the imaginaries of the inhabitants that is foregrounded in this volume, leading to a focus on ideology and religion.[49] The very first group of chapters on Pharaonic Egypt, the Classical Mayan period, and Southeast Asian cities analyses cities as performance arenas. To this end, the volume focuses on visibility and ritual spaces. Agency is ascribed to rulers and elites, and religion is typically seen as being involved in this ascription of agency to the rulers, with gods and the dead being relevant co-citizens.[50] This sort of performance is presented in its many dimensions of sound, smell, taste, atmosphere, duration, and embodiment, in addition to its visual dimension. However, the interpretation of these rituals is confined to the production of solidarity, which leaves unanswered a number of important questions. Would this solidarity extend beyond the small percentage of actual observers and performers, estimated at one to two per cent of the population in Maya cities?[51] How does the production of fear by ostensive destruction and violence[52] relate to any binding effects the performances might have? It is important to note that, already in ancient cities, rituals were staged by very different agents and could mark competing claims to (e.g. religious) authority. The rituals of the elites were frequently invisible, could be copied, or might be subject to ridicule by non-elite actors. Literary and epigraphic texts from ancient Mediterranean cities demonstrate that very different groups could take to the street and that actors from different genders or social strata had very different experiences, as well as making use of very different spaces for individual participation.[53]

---

48 Yoffee 2015.
49 Yoffee and Terrenato 2015, 17–8.
50 Baines et al. 2015, 95.
51 Ibid., 106.
52 Ibid., 107.
53 E.g. Hüsken and Brosius 2010; Michaels 2010; Chaniotis 2011; Grimes 2011; van Nuffelen 2012; G. Woolf 2013; Raja and Rüpke 2015a.

It is worth briefly considering the next section of the volume as well, even if religion is not the focus here. Studies here of fourth-millennium Uruk, second-millennium Chinese Zhungzhou and Yinxu, lowland Mayan cities of the first millennium CE, and second millennium CE Andean Cuzco focus on information technologies. They argue in each case that the vastly different techniques for storing information (phonological writing, iconographies, knots) and the materials used for this storage were above all urban inventions. These inventions enabled the administration of systems of growing social and economic complexity, enabled accountability for those in charge, and, by means of standardisation, enabled the 'legibility' of the flows and structures of the incipient states. Taken together these features allowed for control.[54]

These discussions are entirely lacking in any reference to the subversive or counterfactual usage of writing. This usage is widely attested for the Mediterranean: experts collected omens, prophets diffused political and social critique,[55] historians or mythographers fixed *their* version of events, and philosophers reflected on better ways of life and utopian cities. At the same time, the many political opponents produced graffiti,[56] the suppressed hid curse tablets, and magicians impressed clients and themselves with meaningless pictograms.[57] Writing was not confined to cities but the chance of finding actual readers there was much higher. Cities were not only controlled by information technologies but also offered a space for these new types of communication. Beyond being a neutral space that could be used by the owners or instigators of the built environment for display or hiding, this space could also be appropriated by others, for instance in the form of further types of graffiti on the walls of private buildings or in temple interiors.[58] Even more, urban space could be shaped in order to create space for written forms of communication (libraries) or for the ostensive storing or hiding of information (archives). Urban spaces could even be developed in such a way as to conform to the imaginaries stored in and communicated by such technologies. At Rome, the former line of the wall that had fallen into disuse was marked out at some places and extended according to theories of Empire, while a place at the temple of Bellona was marked out as 'foreign ground' to perform a ritual developed in literature.[59]

---

54 Law et al. 2015, 225.
55 For ancient Israel, Potter 1990; R. R. Wilson 1980; Nissinen and Carter 2009.
56 Morstein-Marx 2012; Hillard 2013.
57 Gordon 2014, 2016.
58 Rüpke 2018d, 258.
59 Rüpke 2019b.

The complex and frequently antagonistic character of cities comes to the fore in the volume when the actual arrangement of living quarters and the topography of city come under scrutiny, as they do in the cases of Mesopotamia and Central and South America. While providing for the safety of their inhabitants, cities also created new social divisions at the same time as sustaining the continuation of earlier ones.[60] Rulers and temples 'had a variety of relationships', with rulers serving and maintaining the temples but also employing them to manage agricultural production, for manufacturing purposes, or to draw legitimacy from them.[61] Yet talking of 'rulers' oversimplifies matters. The cities of the Indus civilisation (2600–1900 BCE) and the 'Early Historic cities' of the alluvial plain between the Ganges and Yamuna were places without clearly differentiated palaces and, thus, places the structure of which reflected a very complex economic and social composition and a high degree of resilience against the many changes in power holding.[62] Actors in Greek cities undertook monumentalisation without strong rulers while Jenne-jeno on the middle Niger and East African cities such as Nubian Kerma (from c. 3000 BCE onwards) also provide arguments against the equation of urbanism and centralised power, as the often claimed nexus of kingship, religious institutions, and centralised administration is not to be found in these places.[63] Rather, religious concepts and practices could serve to hinder the processes by which divisions of labour and social differentiations could turn into hierarchies of power, for instance by way of forging castes or guilds or through political and religious ideologies that sanction the display of wealth.[64]

Further studies on early Islamic Baghdad, Jerusalem, and 11th- to 14th-century Cahokia on the Mississippi demonstrate the entanglement of the histories of memories and the built environments.[65] The authors of these studies join in the chorus of a major line of recent archaeological theory which claims that ancient built cities were above all an expression of cosmic order.[66] This is far from self-evident and fully neglects the role of religious experience.[67] First of all, such cosmologies were far from stable and were subject to change, sometimes even within a single generation of rulers. Secondly, cosmologies of this sort were sys-

---

60 Emberling, Clayton and Janusek 2015, 305.
61 Ibid., 307.
62 Sinopoli 2015.
63 Sinopoli et al. 2015, 383.
64 Ibid., 388 and 391.
65 Pauketat, Killebrew and Micheau 2015.
66 For instance Rykwert 1976; more recently Timothy Insoll 2001, 2011.
67 Raja and Rüpke 2015c.

tematised and over-determined by their producers, who tried to bring into line the ecological conditions of a specific city's existence, the technical possibilities available, and the economic constraints on specific building projects, but also possible constraints of time, visibility, and acoustics that applied to the users of such built environments. These users, however, brought along their own 'aesthetics of reception' and were rarely able or willing to decode the cosmologies implied according to the original intentions of the producers. Thirdly, diverse instigators, financers, architects, and actual builders might bring very different interests and even patches of ideologies into their uncoordinated and competitive building or their reworking of existing and previously differently experienced spaces.[68] The Imperial cities treated in the last section of the handbook offer ample material for such diversity and discrepancies, even if the authors again regard religion and rulership as indivisible.[69] These cities are characterised by their highly diverse populations – in terms of identities, ethnicities, and languages – and show strong social differences and degrees of specialisation, even in the religious realm.

2.5 Urbanised religion

What is the result of the above review of comparative data and their interpretations? Recent work in the field of urban studies has focused on the very complexity of cities, and not only in terms of the functions and services offered or the diversity of their populations. This complexity has been described from a variety of perspectives as the overlapping of different networks, as the variations of differing groups in the ways in which they make urban space, and as the varying forms of appropriation of spaces as 'espace vécu' by diverse agents.[70] Diversity is also reflected in classical sociological theory, which focuses on the *individual*[71] who is located in spaces and networks that differ from those of the other city-dwellers he or she encounters. From a similar starting point, those approaches that focus on economic factors stress the diversity, the division of labour, and the hindrances of exchange that need to be overcome even in ancient cities. By contrast, narratives focusing on the political dimension in 'early cities' presume hierarchy rather than heterarchy as the default situation.

---

[68] E.g. Arnhold 2015; Rieger 2016; Rüpke 2017d.
[69] Gutiérrez, Terrenato and Otto 2015, 536, 541–2; 539–540 for the following.
[70] Lefebvre 1974; Soja 1989; see also Löw 2001.
[71] Simmel 1917.

Religion, then, finds two very different places in such narratives. In the former, dominant in recent studies of today's cities and focusing on diversity and heterarchy, religion is a tool for the urban aspirations of the inhabitants of or migrants to the city, often in contrast to the established religion. By taking the risk of enlarging the given situational constellation of powerful human agents by further introducing god or gods into social interactions, religious practices open up or recall horizons and resources beyond present power structures. This happens on a scale that ranges from the demanding of redress for wrong-doings that one has experienced, through the distortion of competition among equals by the introduction of higher powers, on up to globalising or universalist projects that can be envisaged only with the support of supernatural helpers.[72]

Is the approach implied in this first way of situating religion in narratives about cities also applicable to cities from the past alongside those of the contemporary world for which it is typically employed? The concept of 'lived ancient religion', that is a focus on everyday religious practices and the individual appropriation of religion, has made a case for not starting from a preconceived divide between the past and the present, but instead carefully exploring differences, similarities, and continuities.[73] However, religious practices not only appropriate but also create urban space and are reciprocally also shaped by it. 'Lived religion' alone cannot account for this. For contemporary cities, the term 'urban religion' has been coined 'as a specific element of urbanization and urban everyday life ... intertwined with ... urban lifestyles and imaginaries, infrastructure and materialities, cultures, politics and economies, forms of living and working, community formation, festivals and celebrations'.[74] The concept will come under closer scrutiny in the next chapter but, for the moment, it will suffice to repeat that any easy generalisation of the term is hindered by the fact that it is exclusively used for focusing on contemporary phenomena and innovation.[75] For the approach implied in the second way of situating religion within narratives about cities, the simple extension of 'urban religion' to cities of the past does not yet offer a great deal of assistance.

In the narratives belonging to this second group, which focus on politics and hierarchy, the city takes centre stage and serves as the primary area of application for religion. In a way, the polis is presupposed and the pre-urban beyond reach. Urban space is created in a top-down manner, aided by religion. Religion is, from this perspective, a resource administered by elites and rulers, who en-

---

[72] Rüpke 2015c.
[73] Rüpke 2018d.
[74] Lanz 2014, 25.
[75] See Introduction, above, 2–5.

large their power by monopolising alliances with even more powerful agents. Strangely enough, in the approach that underlies this view of the role played by religion, it is taken for granted that the acceptance of this partial alliance was fully interiorised by the powerless so that they felt compelled into obedience. Thus, the whole struggle brought to light by the analysis of 'fundamentalist cities'[76] is ignored. It was precisely this contradiction that Fustel de Coulanges' *The ancient city* sought to explain, yet as much as his overstated conclusion has been accepted, his complex explanation has been rejected. Religious agency is thus left to a few or regarded as insignificant; 'urban religion' as defined above has no place.

The historical evidence, as much as a closer look at the history of theory, suggests that we need analytical and descriptive models that bring to bear the agency of religious actors and religious imaginaries in creating urban space *and* the agency of urban space and urbanity in shaping religious practices and rooting them in the specific local context. I propose the term 'urbanised religion', not as a theory and explanation, but as a programme of research and a definition of the object of this research: the co-evolution and reciprocal formation of religion and urbanity, or even potentially many urbanities.[77] Or to put the object of research in a more precise form: religious practices, ideas, and institutions, on the one hand, and urbanities in their historical and geographical diversity, on the other. Urbanised religion is thus just as much a religion changed by urbanity as an urbanity in which religion is sedimented. It is not the random spatial constellation of religious signs and institutions that is foregrounded. Rather, it is the fundamental spatial character of religious practices[78] and its long-term consequences under the conditions of local or global urbanisation processes that come into view.

At this point we need to return to Fustel de Coulanges as a historian. The relationship between urbanity and religion is a contingent one. It is only in certain instances of urbanisation (and for Fustel de Coulanges, in a specific, not easily generalisable, form of urbanisation that is witnessed in Greco-Roman antiquity) that this relationship becomes a conceptual one, determining the shape of both religion and urbanisation in the long term. When these are applied to other processes of urbanisation, too – and these should be defined more closely from the perspective of 'urbanised religion' – a surprising reversal of perspective occurs. If we live in a moment in which the assertion that more than half of the world's

---

76 AlSayyad and Massoumi 2011.
77 For the term, Rau 2014.
78 Knott 2005, 41–2.

population are living in 'cities' is part of our own urbanity, our own concept of what it is to live in a city, then it is not the sudden appearance of phenomena of urban religion on a vast scale that is relevant. What becomes urgent is the question of a new historical perspective on religion: how strongly, and in what way, has what we consider to be 'religion' already become 'urbanised religion'? Does it present itself as practices, conceptions, and even institutionalisations that are shaped by interaction with urban spaces, living conditions, and urban cultural techniques such as writing to an extent that owes more to the cultural dominance and attractiveness of urban life (or its deliberate rejection) than to the pre-modern low share of urban populations in the total population? To answer this question, we need to cast our net even wider.

3 Urbanising and urbanised religion

3.0 Introduction

The aim of this chapter is to further develop the concept of urban religion, differentiated already in Chapter 2 above, with a view to its employment in historical research. To begin with, it will be useful to consider the way in which religion is entangled with urbanisation, rather than with 'the city' or even with 'urban space'. To analytically disentangle the two requires a two-pronged approach. First, I will briefly discuss the role of religious practices and ideas in processes of urbanisation. I will then go on to consider the effects on religion of urbanisation and the city dwellers' urbanity as they turn settlements into 'cities'. My intention with these reviews is not to attempt to summarise the multitude of paths involved in this mutual formation. Rather, I aim to show that it is plausible to treat the historical turn in research on urban religion as important. Both sections thus end by offering up more nuanced terminology for use in our further inquiries, namely the language of 'urbanising religion' and (just introduced) 'urbanised religion'. The chapter concludes by reflecting on the limitations of both terms. However, before pursuing these two lines of argument, it will be necessary to first explore the very character of religious practices with regard to space. In doing so, we can come to understand the *specific* role played by religion in its relationship to urban space and urban life.

3.1 Religion as spatial practice

The generic objects in which I am interested are those forms of human action and experience that are set apart from other cultural forms in that they consist of or build on communication with special[1] agents (sometimes including objects). These agents have properties that differ from those of everyday humans: they might be dead (ancestors) or unborn (angels) entities, slightly (demon) or fully superhuman (gods). However, it is not the properties of these addressees that differentiates this type of communication but, rather, the way in which the addressees are addressed. To accord agency to them in the course of communication is not unquestionably plausible. The potential implausibility involved relates as much to the ascribed quality of the addressees as it does to the situational context of this ascription. In the second case, it is also the relevance given

---

1 For the concept of 'special', see Taves 2009, 2010.

to these special agents in the situation, their role in the solution of the problem at hand, that is at issue, as I have pointed out in Chapter 1. Religious communication is, thus, a risky form of communication. What I try to capture from the perspective of agents can also be aggregated into a systemic view in which 'religion has to do with the problem of how one can describe the transcendence that *cannot be represented in everyday experience with immanent means,* or how one can transform the unavailable into the available'.[2]

From the point of view of the agents, religious communication is a consequential form of communication. Communication with or concerning such 'divine' agents might reinforce or reduce human agency, create or modify social relationships, and change power relationships.[3] Religious agency is a coin with two sides: the agency attributed to the non-human or even super-human agents, and the agency thus arrogated by or attributed to the speaker that enters into such communication. Such a speaker can, thus, not only attribute agency to the 'divine' (however the divine is construed in a particular situation and in the underlying traditions). Often she or he also claims to be attributed agency of her or his own by those very addressees, an agency either arrogated by the speaker or further attributed to other members of her or his group, whether present or absent. Religion, as stated before, thus serves as much as a technique for negotiating power relationships as a technique for shaping the self.

As is the case with any other cultural practice, religious communication is a spatio-temporal practice. It is both located *in* space and time and it *engages with* space and time. 'Appropriation' is one way of describing this engagement. It is not a simple copying of patterns of action established by tradition, as Michel de Certeau has insisted.[4] The use of religious communication is preceded by a selection. It recognises and accepts the character of spaces as defined by previous, common, or prescribed usage, but it also modifies the space through performance and, in doing so, changes the *future* memory of the place. I have introduced the term 'sacralisation' to describe this modification of space. Even religious 'traditions' are not simply given. On the contrary, they require constant reproduction and are modified by the micro- (and sometimes revolutionary) modifications of their users.

This sort of appropriation relates to space as much as it does to time, as the usage of both can be flexible or, to use a temporal metaphor, ephemeral. Usage of space can also be rhythmical or permanent. Given the problem that religious

---

[2] Krech 2012, 24.
[3] Rüpke 2015c.
[4] de Certeau 2007/1984.

communication faces in addressing the not unquestionably given, that is, the problem of transforming the unavailable transcendent into something available, religious communication tends to employ on a vast scale media that go beyond sounds and gestures. These include gifts, architecture, inscriptions, and tools such as knives and books. In other words, religious communication tends to be 'material religion'. The media of this religious communication, i.e. the tools used for or in the communication, might be more or less, and temporarily or permanently, associated with it and, thus, 'sacralised' by virtue of association with the special addressees. As such, spaces might be contested by different religious or non-religious agents, occupied visibly or invisibly, legally or illegally. Open, accessible space (not always centrally administered or in 'public' ownership) might be fought over or, occasionally, ceded.

'Place-making' offers a different perspective on such processes, and we might also think metaphorically of something like 'calendar-making' as similarly organising and differently qualifying time as well. This perspective stresses the mental maps, the feeling-at-home and the patterns of actual usage that correlate with the experience of a certain atmosphere, as well as the emotional relationships formed with places, conceived, above all, as an *attachment* to places. Identifiable relationships, clear marks, or even ownership are central for such an analysis. Religious practices and signs can serve as tools for such 'place-making' but just as relevant are processes of grouping, such as the formation of networks or the creation of even closer organisations. The closing of a thoroughfare by neighbours in order to create a space for a sanctuary or the setting up of small shrines at street corners, the former an act of significance for the neighbourhood alone while the latter has the potential to be more widely visible, are examples of such place-making. The results that follow are sometimes permanent and sometimes not. Here, we are more and more dealing with the specifics of practices that were seen explicitly as 'religion' by contemporary or later observers, and, as a consequence, with 'sacralised' places. Yet these places, too, might be appropriated by others or might be 'disappropriated' by some authority, which might, perhaps, declare the place to belong to the 'heritage' of some other or larger group (such as the nation). This latter trend has been hugely influential on the national level since the 1980s[5] but can also be triggered by something as simple as an influx of tourists overturning the localised appropriation of a place.[6]

---

5 Narayanan 2015.
6 See Stausberg 2010.

The initial definition suggests that there is a specific spatial character to religious communication, a conceptual relationship that is not comparatively valid for other cultural practices. If place-making can be equated with 'dwelling', that is, with identifying oneself with a place, and is frequently achieved through religious practices, then religious communication is inherently also a practice of 'crossing', of going beyond that place – to borrow the terminology used by Thomas Tweed in pointing out this tension.[7] 'Religion' as used here is *defined* as action that transcends (in a very simple sense) the immediate and unquestionably given situation. There is no sharp dividing line between 'immanent' and 'transcendent' religion.[8] Even the sacralisation of present objects and institutions, whether domestic or public (Jonathan Zittel Smith's *here* and *there* in the 'locative' type of his classification of religion),[9] is not entirely concerned with the spatially present but also contains a reference to a beyond; even sacral kingship contains elements of risks, whether empirical, such as droughts, or staged in ritual contests.[10] This is the basis for usefully employing the conceptualisation as 'religion'. The trans-local references inherent to religious communication by way of its claims to agency need not wait for a radicalised axial-age-style transcendence that opposes a celestial order to the norms and power relationships of the contemporary society within which these religious activities are located. Such trans-local references, and the feebleness of their claims, have been the basis for debates about icons, representation, and presence, about anthropomorphic or non-anthropomorphic forms, and about images or no image.[11]

If urbanisation is about the densification and differentiation of space, about inclusion (or even trapping) and exclusion on a larger scale, then religion is uniquely conducive to and uniquely clashes with urbanisation – or, at least, it held such a unique status until the rise of efficient telecommunication. According to this perspective, religious places would also, at the same time, be places in an eminent, super-empirical sense. They would be heterotopias, in the words of Michel Foucault, rather than non-places or transit zones without identities, as Marc Augé would put it.[12] They would be places that signal, focus, and intensify specifically urban identities.[13] Ritual can be miniaturised or virtualised; the pray-

---

[7] Tweed 2006; cf. Tweed 2011.
[8] See Strathern 2019, despite his interest in the differentiation of both.
[9] J. Z. Smith 2003.
[10] See e.g. Hooke 1958; Weinfurter 1992; King 1999; Alexander, Giesen and Mast 2006; J. Assmann 2006; Wengrow 2013; Nygaard 2016.
[11] Bibliography is endless within and across religious traditions.
[12] Augé 1992.
[13] For the concept of cultural intensification, see Davies 2008.

er in the heart can take place *anywhere*. Urban techniques of control via representation in the form of maps, numbers, or texts have been used to escape place by shifting religious practices into intellectual debate and engagement with scripture, into commenting on ritual rather than practicing ritual. If we are to grasp the complexities of the entanglement of religion and urbanisation, then this aspect must also be taken into account.

3.2 Religion and urbanisation

It has become a frequently stressed truism among scholars of religion that religion is not simply a given. The fact that it is a scholarly construct needs to be made explicit in order to allow for open discussion of the limits and usefulness of the notion. As I have argued elsewhere,[14] an agent-centred version of religion, such as that briefly sketched above, avoids many of the pitfalls that are identified by the standard criticism of the notion of 'religion' as being a Christian-biased or inherently Western concept, because the agent-centred approach allows us to model religion cross-culturally as a spatial practice. The conceptual status of the 'urban', and even of 'cities', is no different. To give just one example, despite the pre-reflective overwhelming evidence for the proliferation of cities and urban growth, these terms need to be delineated more closely. Even if such details seem unnecessary in the face of the present reality of urban growth, we have to be aware that an unknown, but certainly substantial, portion of recent 'urban growth' is the result of a reclassification of settlements to class them as parts of urban settlements,[15] thus reflecting administrative approaches and ideas about cities rather than changed patterns of settlement. Cities such as (Greater) London demonstrate how such conceptualisations can change within just a few decades, and sometimes in even shorter periods.

As a consequence of such variances over time and certainly across places, I take 'city' as an object language term, a term used by the people I am studying. This term implies a self-differentiation from the non-city, whether the counterpart is described as 'rural', 'wilderness', 'uncivilised', or, in a less derogatory way (sometimes, at least), as villages and countryside. Thus, 'city' is just an invitation to look for the classificatory operations used by people to differentiate and often rank forms of settlements (including nomadic ways of life or transhumance).

---

14 Rüpke 2015c.
15 See Robinson, Scott and Taylor 2016, 18.

In the following, I will use 'urban' as a meta-language term, implying, on the one hand, dense settlement patterns of a large number of people (far beyond the number of inhabitants that would be the upper limit of a community in which it would be possible for all members to maintain face-to-face contacts with all others) that are characterised by a corresponding density of interaction, and, on the other hand, external links with other settlements that are likewise seen as 'cities' in the aforementioned culturally and historically variable sense.[16] The second element has two important consequences: urban settlements do not appear individually but in networks – even if these might have only very distant corresponding nodes. And urban diversity transcends the mere effect of numbers but is, rather, reinforced by inter-cultural contacts and migration – even if this is restricted to more regional variants and distances.

On this basis, I follow Susanne Rau in differentiating between 'urbanisation' and 'urbanity'. 'Urbanisation', or more precisely urbanisations, are different and reversible paths of the growth and spread of settlements as 'urban settlements' ('the history of the constitution, perception and appropriation of urban spaces'). 'Urbanity', on the other hand, is the specific way of life in such cities, defined by the fact that the inhabitants realise that they are living *in a city* (again, however they define 'city').[17] It is urbanisation as a larger historical process that offers us a 'lens' through which to view religious change here. This is not a matter of stopping up one's ears against claims of an encompassing 'planetary urbanisation', as diagnosed by, for instance, Christian Schmid.[18] It is part of the unequal, hegemonic character of urbanity that elements of urban ways of life have been acknowledged and partly copied in far-distant areas. After all, it is just such a widespread notion of the superiority of city life that has produced, and continues to produce, immigration into cities. And yet the urban has also caused violent or whole-hearted rejections of its way of life, seen in emigration from the city to places where alternative models of living and settlement can be pursued, whether these be extra-urban monasteries, garden cities with a 'back to nature' focus, or remote islands. Whether the agents are urban agents opting out or non-urban agents rejecting absorption is an important question, not least for the history of religion. That the 'global city' today is the solution to all problems regarding climate change, demographics, and sustainability is a claim made by urban scientists that might well be correct but that still must be tested against the possibility that it is merely an ideologically-maintained position that belongs to the

---

16 Cf. the definition by Robinson, Scott and Taylor 2016, 5 as given above, 26.
17 Rau 2014, 405–6.
18 E.g. Brenner and Schmid 2014.

hegemonic urban ideology. My own enterprise here must thus remain self-reflective with regard to claims about the urban as much as it is about religion.

3.3 Religions as urbanising factors

It is only very recently that the potentially disruptive effects of religion have been addressed in discussions on religion and urbanisation, by pointing out that the close proximity of groups that are exclusionary to one another can produce tension and cause division, and that religion might well reinforce other dimensions of difference.[19] The focus in this discourse has typically been on religion as a way of legitimising power or increasing the sociability of people, an approach that is far more simplistic than the starting point offered by Fustel de Coulanges' reconstruction, discussed in Chapter 2 above.[20] Religious communication is to be found on both sides of the characteristic urban divide between trapping, ruling, and homogenising, on the one hand, and stabilising diversity and carving out individual space, on the other. It serves both as a tool for enlarging the agency of holders of power, and for opposing or mitigating the current power structure when used by marginalised agents. Analyses of the relationship between religion and urbanisation thus need to follow complex and conflicting lines, even when looking back into pre- and early urban settlement periods.

We need not start from the notion of religion as social glue. Neolithic cave paintings, preserved in south-east Spain and south-west France, in areas that became accessible from the Mediterranean in the final phase of the last Ice Age, have been adduced as early manifestations of religion.[21] The debate over whether they represent forms of hunting magic or binding rituals has remained indecisive and has provided grounds for a widespread suspense of judgement and an attempt to decolonialise views of the neolithic period by drawing attention to the excessive use of the terms 'art' and 'artists'. Classifying these practices as religion makes them much more easily understandable. These practices evidently represented, in a fairly consistent manner, beings that were more powerful than humans: horses, aurochs (*bos primigenius*), mammoths, and rhinoceroses seem to have been depicted at a considerably earlier date than the first representations of human creations such as arrows. These depictions were placed in a

---

19 Thus Furseth 2011, 46. On the role of religion in warfare, see Rüpke 1993, 2006c, 2006 g.
20 For the latter, see e.g. Norenzayan 2013, criticised by Rüpke 2014b. More generally, see Stausberg 2014.
21 See the discussion and further bibliography in Wunn 2005. The following is also based on site visits in summer 2018.

controlled environment in which they could not be seen by the actual animals. The many repetitions and overlapping features demonstrate that the practice of painting itself was more important than its results. Instead of being finalised products of permanent character they invited further painting at the same spot. In several instances, the very places at which the paintings were made, and their enormous distances from the entrances to the caves – Rouffignac is paradigmatic, even if perhaps an extreme case – exclude the presence of any large group gathering in those locations.

With regard to the social developments that led towards urbanisation, it is, thus, the division of labour visible here that is of paramount importance. The simple quality of the lines, the labour invested in the production of different colours, the degree of realism, or the abstraction and referential power achieved by the producers, all these features demonstrate an investment of time and a degree of specialisation that amounts to a division of labour. Certainly, many members of the same group were never witnesses to these practices. Indeed, many might have never even seen the images while a few joined the more accomplished painters by contributing simpler additions, miniaturising the practice in the form of painting dots or perhaps printing their hands. It is, thus, not possible to build up an interpretation exclusively on the basis of find spots that were easily accessible and probably used by all members of the local group. With regard to those who never went deep enough inside, these activities and the energy and time spent on them was justified by claims, not by unquestionably relevant achievements (not even as a decoration of a space used for living). This is comparable with later practices that have been classified as religion. Similarly, copying by visitors from other groups, whether contemporary or much later, is the most likely explanation for the regional spread of the practice.

The practices referred to so far were one result of the development of technologies and the division of labour. But religion takes on a new relevance during the early stages of social development that led towards urbanisation. The religious practices that are relevant here are those which refer to that which is beyond the spatial bounds of the situation in which the practices take place and typically outside the city. Of particular significance are those practices which represent what lies outside the city *within* the highly controlled city environment. The monumentalisation of space is important in the contexts of both religion and urbanisation. The artificial creation of monumental structures required a vast pool of labour, and, as such, their construction was a highly controlled process that created highly controlled space. At Göbekli Tepe in the 10th and 9th millennia BCE, references to non-human beings were articulated by the use of images of animals, and perhaps also by the use of stylised pillars that referred to dead humans. Similar references to the beyond are found in the circular arrangements of wooden structures or stones in central Europe. Structures of this type, such as 'henges', integrated references to solstices and other solar phenomena into the architectural design of the places by means of doors or lines of sight which allowed the beyond to play a role in well-arranged performances. In both cases, these places were probably used by groups of nearby settlements without being parts of the permanent settlements. They all fell into disuse after longer or shorter periods of usage, and were never subject to processes of urbanisation themselves. Both presuppose specialised planning and labour,[22] and in both cases the religious practices carried out in these places were about network activities, rather than serving to reflect the urban trappings of a central administration.

It will be worth briefly considering one last example of the rise of 'religious' monumentalisation outside of towns. In the case of the massive, stone-built Etruscan necropolises, the initial phases of construction preceded, in at least some places, the monumentalisation of the adjacent settlements, which is to say that massive stone-built tumuli were, in some cases, contemporary with settlements composed of wattle and daub huts. The funerary, and clearly religiously articulated, practices of not only remembering but also communicating with ancestors were polyfocal, in that they were performed (and monumentalised) by different, and competing, families and groups of families.[23]

In many narratives, religion is used as a tool in the actual foundation of cities. Motifs that can be found elsewhere also show up in some of the narratives concerning the foundation of Rome, as, for example, when we read about the transfer of sacralised 'stuff', such as images of gods. The *penates*, a group of deities related to the household, were transferred from Troy to Rome according to the complex succession myths of the Aeneades, referred to already in early central Italian pottery finds but made explicit perhaps only in the late 4th or 3rd century BCE.[24] Another motif used in the same way is that of a divinatory decision concerning places, as we find narrated in a Roman context by Ennius in the early 2nd century BCE.[25] Only slightly later are attestations of a supposed foundation ritual that defined the lines of the wall and the location of the gates, the places of the boundary's interruption.[26] The commonality of motifs became increasingly present as Rome itself became more and more frequently responsible for instigat-

---

22 Schmidt 2006, 2013; for the 'calendar structures', briefly Rüpke 2006 h, 37–38.
23 See my brief discussion in Rüpke 2018d, 41, with further references.
24 See Barchiesi 2006; Cancik 2006 for the motifs and its late Republican or early Augustan settings. On the wider issue, see Erskine 2001; Rüpke 2009b.
25 Ennius, *Annales* fr. 72–91 Skutsch. See Rüpke 2004, 27–28.
26 Cato, *Origines* fr. 20 Peter = 1.20 Beck/Walter. See Bremmer 1987 and cf. Detienne 2002.

ing the foundation of cities, in particular in the Western part of the emerging empire. Yet such narratives and the (mostly but not always) fictitious rituals with which they are concerned are products of an urbanised religion rather than an urbanising one. In functional terms, the most important religious practices appropriated from, rather than actively distributed by, the centre were those relating to the cult of the emperors. The spread of such practices furthered the establishment of central regional sanctuaries (as at Lugdunum/Lyon) and urban growth in subsequent periods, and also contributed to the monumentalisation of the cult as part of local political elites attempted to upgrade their own status.

From the perspective of agents more generally, the character of religious practices that allows them to be used in the appropriation, and sometimes the marking or even the sacralising, of space, seems much more important. In the diversity and density of urban settlements, religious communication and its association with space and people supports making 'places' out of underdefined space.[27] At Rome, the separation of settlement space and tombs, enforced from a very early time, drove the ancestors, and all the place-claiming strategies that were frequently related with funerary practices and ancestor cult, out of the space within the walls. Here, perhaps, provides the context for the conceptual separation of the Lares, as a type of divine addressee found at the hearth and in the home, from one's ancestors, who came to be located outside the home. The new divinities enabled an appropriation of the domestic space belonging to the living that was not possible in the earlier and now forbidden practice of closely relating the space of the living and the dead through carrying out burials close to the accommodation of the living.[28]

It should be pointed out in passing at least that the history of Latin Christianity, situated in the Western part of the Imperium Romanum from the end of Antiquity onwards, took place in a space that witnessed significant de-urbanisation over a period of centuries and then only very slow re-urbanisation prior to the early modern period – far below development in the circum-Mediterranean Muslim-dominated regions, India, or China.[29] That is to say that the very religious tradition on which Western historiography was focused[30] was a tradition embedded within a complex and changing relationship with urbanisation.

---

[27] For the differentiation, see Tuan 1977; see also Berking 2006. For Rome, see Dumont 2000; Galvao-Sobrinho 2008; Maier 2015 and Ch. 5 below.
[28] For the debate, see Chapter 6 below.
[29] See Erdkamp 2013, 245–6 for the different paths of urbanisation in late Antiquity and Robinson, Scott, Taylor 2016, 8–19 in general.
[30] Thus Weltecke 2016.

This fact certainly bears closer examination, although it cannot, unfortunately, be pursued in more detail here.

To sum up the argument so far, I do not claim that religious practice was the primary factor in all, or even most, urbanisation processes. It was, however, an important factor from early on. As such, it contributed towards enabling, if not outright co-creating, heterarchy in urban settlements.[31] This is not to deny that religious practices might, in the course of the history of an urban settlement, shape the urban topography, architecture, and even the atmosphere and the 'branding' of such settlements, in terms of their collective memories and 'heritage'.[32] However, what is much more fundamental is that these practices catered for urban aspirations and place-making as much as they did for ruling and administration. The temples on the Roman *forum* that were close to a small number of aristocratic houses needed shops in their basements or spectacular rituals to draw significant public attention in the form of large numbers of visitors. This interplay of politics, economics, and religious practices can be observed in different, not spatially bound, forms, as well. Religious groups profited from senatorial or Imperial recognition and thus gained from financial support as much as they did from the visibility granted to them in the permanent form of architecture or the ephemeral form of rituals such as public processions.[33] Religious and urban diversity and heterarchy was not restricted to space, but can be detected as well in their temporal dimensions. Again, religious communication, with its use and marking, if not sacralising, of time 'spots', led to complex and far from unified urban calendars. Their dates invited religious communication that was initialised at the top ranks of society as much as it was by the ordinary citizens or even slaves within the city. Calendrical dates also offered or secured many references to or even two-way relationships with places, people, or powers outside of the city, whether in the suburbs, Latium, Asia minor, or North Africa (Carthage).[34]

---

31 For the concept of a diversity of conflicting or at least changing systems of ranking power or prestige, see Rautman 1998, 327 with Crumley's definition: 'heterarchies are systems in which the component elements have (1) "the potential of being unranked (...)" and/or (2) ... of being "ranked in a number of ways, depending on systemic requirements"'.
32 Cf. Moser 2013. For Antiquity, see Sulzbach 2013.
33 For the importance of urban infrastructure for religion, see Burchardt, Stefan; Simone, AbdouMaliq 2015; Burchardt 2016, and Becci, Burchardt and Casanova 2013.
34 For an in-depth case-study, see Rüpke 1995b/Rüpke 2011c (partial translation).

3.4 Urbanised religion

If religion is a factor in urbanising processes that stretch far beyond the occasional growth of a pilgrimage destination into an urban settlement or the application of foundation rituals for new urban settlements, either actually performed or part of a later narrative embellishment – note that I do not suggest that such constellations were unimportant –, then religious practices, ideas, and social forms of institutionalisation were also changed or, better, formed by urban conditions, that is by urban space and the further characteristics of urban settlements. Whilst later chapters will deal with some of the specific constellations and developments involved, at this point it will be more useful to make some general remarks and suggest some potentially fruitful questions rather than arguing for causal relationships.

We can start by considering the use by religious agents and organisations of cultural techniques. Above all, we can consider the use of writing systems, which some have suggested were developed in, and for the administration of, urban settlements. Religious writing and the 'religions of the book', with all their correlates of learning and commenting, are features of urbanised religion, not least because they depend on the high levels of division of labour associated with (even if not exclusive to) urban production. 'Intellectualisation', as Max Weber proposed in his analyses a century ago, offers a heuristic term that we might look for in particular text-related processes of rationalisation and in the specific agents of these processes.[35] Such 'intellectuals' might act as clerks to the central administration or as providers of religious services in a competitive and potentially socially disruptive manner, as was the case with prophets and diviners. The cultural techniques employed were, however, not restricted to systems of writing and counting. The fight for visibility within such settlements, as well as competition *between* settlements, must have been an important driving force for religious architecture. The counterpart to this impetus was camouflage and secrecy, the holding back of strong group identities from public visibility, which was an important strategy for minimising as well as for living differences under the conditions of urban density and diversity.[36]

For any sort of fine-grained analysis, it is essential to focus on single urban settlements within an urban network. I will, thus, restrict my list of suggestions to the city of Rome in its network of, initially, Etruscan and Greek cities (such as

---

[35] M. Weber 1922, passim. For the Roman Republican period, Rüpke 2012f; for the Imperial period, Rüpke 2018e.
[36] See the studies in J. Assmann and Stroumsa 1999.

Veii, Cumae, Corinth, and Athens), then later (mostly coastal) circum-Mediterranean cities (such as Alexandria, Pergamon, Antioch, and Jerusalem), and, finally, Roman Imperial cities (such as Carthage, Trier, Palmyra, and Constantinople). One of the things that becomes clearly visible when we take such a perspective is the long rise and resilient status of the mass rituals that the Romans called 'games'. During the games, processions of gods and actors drew the attention of crowds throughout the city and sporting competitions (above all races, *ludi circenses*, but also boxing in the *ludi Capitolini*) or dramatic performances (*ludi scaenici*) offered entertainment for hours, if not days.[37] As we can see in the works of ancient authors, some of whom commended such events as occasions on which one could meet people of the opposite sex (Romans advocated homosexuality much less than the Greeks),[38] such festivals generated 'shared microspaces of intimacy and inclusion', to borrow Kim Knott's description of the function of 21st-century festivals.[39]

The development of religious signs, that is to say 'divine addressees', in the self-conceptualisation of the agents was deeply influenced by the economic investments of different groups in urban conditions. Varro, an ancient philosopher and historian of religion, accounted for the demise of the sky god Summanus (related to nocturnal lightning) in terms of architectural developments, that is by reference to the growth in the popularity of and common knowledge about his counterpart Jupiter (related to day-time lightning) that was due to the construction of his important temple. This, we learn, enabled Jupiter to outgrow the temple-less Summanus.[40] The very size and diversity of the urban settlement is reflected in a growing number and an (un-coordinated) diversity of 'gods', a diversity stabilised in ritual praxis as well as in memory (the basis for further systematisation) by architecture.[41]

I suggest that we can usefully employ as a further heuristic device the concept of urban 'services' developed by Michael E. Smith and others.[42] On their account, religion is rather marginal and the services it offered to the inhabitants of cities are reduced to the role played by sanctuaries and temples, and their central importance for social identity. In fact, religious providers developed in the course of time a much broader range of services. During the Hellenistic and Im-

---

37 On the process, see Rüpke 2012d, for the chronology, see Cancik 1978; Manuwald 2011.
38 Such advice is given in Ovid's *Art of loving*.
39 Knott 2015, 17.
40 Varro, *Antiquities of divine things* fr. 42 Cardauns.
41 Unfortunately, the many accounts of the production of Roman gods have never delved into this type of spatial diversity and its effects (see e.g. Wissowa 1912; Ziolkowski 1992).
42 M. E. Smith et al. 2015.

perial periods, health care, finally professionalised by medical staff in Asclepian temples, was provided for in the form of god-patient relationships.[43] At Rome, rituals, religious concepts, and places were developed to cater for legal transactions on the basis of a (vaguely) codified civil law, as, for instance, when a *sacramentum*, a material pledge by a party in a legal suit about ownership, was stored in a temple. Oaths, conditional self-inflictions of retribution by selected gods, substituted for material evidence in certain cases.[44] I restrict myself to the city of Rome for further examples. Augustus built an all-compassing fire fire-fighting organisation based at the neighbourhood level by relying on neighbourhood-based religious specialists.[45] The idea of a central Christian ritual, the Eucharistic 'breaking of the bread', might have been developed in the city of Rome in the 2nd century CE in order to allow the distribution of parts of the consecrated bread to fellow Christians who were absent,[46] but whose location in the neighbourhood must, I presume, have been known. Roman sanctuary areas developed into artificial parks, featuring water surfaces, fountains, or dense rows of trees[47] that provided space for leisure and recreation. The inclusion of shops in temple structures, I have already referred to above. None of these elements were inherent and timeless components of 'ancient religion' or 'Mediterranean polytheism' but, rather, were developments at a certain urban settlement, Rome, that often profited from innovations and inventions in other urban settlements of the same network. These developments at Rome did not just add certain unimportant features to a stable tradition. Rather, the exchange was a process that rendered the sum and details of local religious practices into a thoroughly 'urbanised religion'. This urbanised religion then provided models and established norms far beyond the spatial limits of the agglomeration and became an inseparable part of urbanity, of the way of life, in circum-Mediterranean and Imperial cities.

3.5 Conclusion

In an attempt to overcome a presentist bias in many, even if not all, instances in which the concept of 'urban religion' is employed, I have argued that we need to understand the spatial character of religious practices more intimately and that

---

43 In general Steger 2016; Petridou and Thumiger 2016.
44 Overview: Tellegen-Couperus 2012; see also on the problematic historiography Rüpke 2015a.
45 See Ch. 6.
46 Cf. Leonhard 2017.
47 See e.g. de Cazanove 2015; Neudecker 2015.

we should replace the timeless pair of 'religion in the city' or 'religion and the city' with a focus on the entanglement of religious change and urbanisation. Finally, I have argued that in pursuing such a historical enterprise it would be useful to analyse religion as an (active) agent, preparing and pushing forward processes of urbanisation, as well as a (passive) patient, reacting and adapting to urban conditions and thus becoming part and parcel of urbanity. I have suggested the terminological pair of 'urbanising' and 'urbanised' religion to describe these two different but interlinked perspectives on the same complex of phenomena.

One of the main arguments of the preceding chapter was that the specific spatial character of religious communication refers in a very different manner and with multi-layered meanings to that which is spatially beyond the situation, to physically distant places and heterotopias, but that religious communication was also, at the same time, a primary tool for the situational appropriation of specific places. As such, religious practices are compatible with globalisation as well as localisation. But they are also compatible with a *tertium*, something that is beyond distance and closeness. Religious practices can also serve not only to employ, but also to actively create, 'no-place', negating the importance of the spatial character, and hence the spatial limits, of a place.[48] This might be translated as the 'anywhere' of Jonathan Z. Smith or be equated with the transcendence and the *sui generis* character attributed to religion in a lot of classic works on the subject in the History of Religion. However, I would urge readers to resist this temptation. It is only from a spatial perspective that the place of no-place can be seen.

---

48 Cf. the concept of no places by Waghorne 2017.

4 Presupposing the city: Philosophical piety as urbanised religion

Urbanity and religion are as much the products of discourse as they are of other types of social interaction and of built environments. The wide use of the cultural technique of writing in ancient Mediterranean cities produced texts that allow us to study religion and urbanity, not only individually, but also in their interaction with each other. Focusing on very different type of treatises written at Rome in the 1st century BCE, this chapter and the following are invitations to analyse theological and technical treatises more generally as – always historically contingent – results and indicators of such interaction.

4.1 Urban literature

In her book *Tarpeia: Workings of a Roman Myth*, Tara Welch characterises the rise of Latin literature as 'a phenomenon' that 'emerged to give voice to the evolving Roman elite class'.[1] Although late in terms of the history of Latin literature, Cicero's project of making Greek philosophy accessible to Latin-speaking Romans can be regarded as part of this process. The latter also had a spatial dimension, that is, to write the city into existence, as Catherine Edwards suggested two decades earlier.[2] It was Cicero who praised Varro's *Antiquitates rerum divinarum*, his 'Antiquities of divine matters', published in 47 BCE, as a work that helped Romans to feel at home in their city.[3] It should not be forgotten that Varro's work was far more than just a local antiquarian or historical account. Varro's focus on the city of Rome and its institutions went together with a universalistic philosophical framework and a wide comparative horizon that aimed at building bridges towards other religious practices in Italy, Greece, and beyond.[4]

Those of his works that Cicero considers to be philosophical certainly lack the clear focus on the city of Rome that is on display in Varro's *Antiquitates rerum humanarum et divinarum*. However, his *De legibus* (*On laws*), which *does* have such a local focus even if it also argues within a broader universalistic framework, is not included by Cicero as one of his philosophical works in his review of these texts at the beginning of the second book of *De divinatione* (*On div-*

---

1 Welch 2015, 285.
2 Edwards 1996, 7.
3 Cicero, *Academica posteriora* 1.9.
4 Rüpke 2012f, 172–185, and 185 in particular; bridging: Rüpke 2014a.

ination) (44 BCE).⁵ Clearly, Greek philosophy (in the same manner as Greek rhetoric) was, in principle, treated as a universalistic enterprise, something that was even more the case for religious topics.⁶ The very attraction of such universalistic reasoning derives from the fact that, from this point of view, Greek reflexions were also a resource for Rome and its citizens. Cicero's audience is captured by his use of the term *res publica*, to which Cicero tries to offer his services even when not acting in a political role, and by his addressing his readers as 'my citizens' (*meis civibus*)⁷ or 'Romans' (*Romanisque hominibus*).⁸ Such a 'Roman' audience need not, indeed cannot, be restricted to the cityscape of Rome. The locations of some of the dialogues – *in Puteolano* and *in Tusculano*, set in villas in the suburban area around Rome or further afield – demonstrate that the social and political elite Cicero has in mind when thinking of educating the 'youth' (*iuventus*)⁹ conceives of Rome and these properties as a unified communicative space, dominated by urban political functionaries and their offspring.

Nevertheless, these treatises are not firmly grounded in a communicative space centred around the city. The firm and institutional belief in divination at Rome is the starting point for *De divinatione*.¹⁰ This belief is less evident in the three books of *De natura deorum* (*On the nature of the gods*), published in 45 BCE, some two years after Varro's massive work. In this chapter, I argue that Cicero's way of dealing with religion in this text is, like Varro's, informed by an urban framework. More precisely, I will argue first that there is an urban horizon to his argument: the city is presupposed as the ideal place for a good life and the discussion is, thus, necessarily developed within the context of urban perspectives. Secondly, my claim is that the individual religious practices named in the course of the interlocutors' arguments are overwhelmingly practices that have been shaped by the cityscape or, more loosely, by urban contexts. As such, they are examples of urbanised religion, not time honoured expressions of an ethnic 'Roman' religion. Finally, this chapter seeks to demonstrate that the very manner in which religion is discussed in *On the nature of the gods* is a performance of urbanity. In considering this point, we touch upon a meta-level, reaching from the style of the discussion as a discussion

---

5 Cicero, *On divination* 2.1–7.
6 For that reason, I have argued, Cicero has opened his discussion of laws in *De legibus* with religious issues (book 2) rather than the magistrates treated in book 3: Rüpke 2016e, 24. Cf. Rexine 1968.
7 Cicero, *On divination* 2.1 and *De fato* 1.6–7.
8 Cicero, *On divination* 2.5; also *De fato* 1.4.
9 Cicero, *De fato* 1.4.
10 Cicero, *On divination* 1.1, 3.

among people who perform their elite status to the fact that the publication of such discussions about religious beliefs, practices, and the resulting norms in the form of a book was part of a specifically urban religion in Antiquity.

4.2 The city as the ideal place for a good life

At a number of places in *On the nature of the gods,* the city is invoked or presupposed by Cicero's speakers as the *Lebenswelt,* the world as lived, which serves as the measuring rod. In order to make the argument as clear as possible, I provide the relevant Latin texts whenever necessary.

> Also, why should god take a fancy to decorating the firmament with figures and illuminations, like an aedile? (1.2)[11]

Here, constellations and stars are compared to the statues and illuminations erected by the Roman magistrate who was responsible for the city of Rome itself, an office Cicero himself held in 69 BCE.[12]

> In an inquiry as to the nature of the gods, the first question that we ask is, do the gods exist or do they not? 'It is difficult to deny their existence.' No doubt it would be if the question were to be asked in an assembly, but in this type of conversation and in sitting together it is perfectly easy. (1,61)

The discussion is opened in these striking terms by the most public figure among the characters present, the pontiff Cotta, who is ironically given the task of arguing for scepticism about the gods. Cotta insists that the question of whether gods exists must be dealt with seriously in the context of a philosophical inquiry and that it cannot simply be pushed aside with reference to widespread consent or any similarly loose evidential standard. The transmission of the text at the end of the sentence is distorted, with the transmitted *consensu* being hard to retain since it is this very consent that is questioned by Cotta. He clearly distinguishes between public and private discussion here, but instead of simply repeating the widespread *topos* of the contrast between the uneducated public and the talk of experts,[13] he adds a spatial (and perhaps even temporal) component. This is the contrast he draws between the standing assembly in an open space and the spa-

---

[11] I basically, but not always follow the latin text of Wolfgang Gerlach and Karl Baier, Tusculum. The translation is by Harris Rackham: Rackham 1933.
[12] See Pease 1955, 193 *ad loc.*
[13] Fully documented ibid., 351.

tially confined and seated assembly exemplified by audiences in theatres, by the assembly of jurors in a legal context, or, indeed, by the interlocutors now sitting down together in an *exedra* (1.15). *Contio* and *consessus* both evoke urban institutions and locations. It is worth spelling out that the city thus imagined is a city of diverse and different publics and opinions. The space of open political assemblies, which gives a limited, but important voice to the crowd,[14] is rivalled by lesser, but even more valuable publics.

At the same time, the city's manifold institutions, which are simply presupposed by the speakers as their shared world of phenomena, are each characterised by their instantiation of a premeditated order:

> When a man goes into a house, a wrestling-school, or a public assembly and observes in all that goes on arrangement, regularity, and system, he cannot possibly suppose that these things come about without a cause: he realises that there is someone who presides and controls. Far more ...
>
> *Ut, si quis in domum aliquam aut in gymnasium aut in forum venerit, cum videat omnium rerum rationem, modum, disciplinam, non possit ea sine causa fieri iudicare, sed esse aliquem intellegat, qui praesit et cui pareatur, multo magis ...* (2.15)

The argument here is an argument *a minore ad maiorem*, from the type of order in the city to the type of order found in the universe, with its orderly movements of sun, moon, and fixed stars. The reasoning is presented from the perspective of a hypothetical visitor who is imagined as being unfamiliar with the phenomena of cities, presumably arriving from somewhere beyond this ordered world. Rural life does not inspire the same sense of order. Speaking in a Stoicising mode, Cotta notes that meadows, fields, and herds are loved for their utility and the gain they generate (1.122). In terms of civilisation, dealing with the necessities of life, from the protection of the body to agriculture, is an affordance of the form of human hands. It is upon these fundamentals that the refinements of urban life are built:

> Hence we realise that it was by applying the hand of the artificer to the discoveries of thought and observations of the senses that all our conveniences were attained, and we were enabled to have shelter, clothing and protection, and possessed cities, fortifications, houses and temples.

---

14 See Millar 1998; Jehne 2006.

> *Ex quo intellegitur ad inventa animo percepta sensibus adhibitis opificum manibus omnia nos consecutos, ut tecti, ut vestiti, ut salvi esse possemus, urbes, muros, domicilia, delubra haberemus* (2.150).

This does not imply that rural life is backward. In the strongly developmental and teleological perspective offered by the Stoic speaker here,[15] the natural world of flat land and mountains, lakes and rivers, is ultimately radically transformed into 'another nature' (*altera natura*, 2.152).[16] Cities must be seen as a prominent part of this transformed nature. Single houses and whole cities give islands and beaches their distinct, cultivated appearance according to the Stoic Balbus (2.99). But the importance given to cities is not a doctrine restricted to a single school. Cotta, the 'academic' sceptic, argues on the same basis even in a passage directed against Balbus. The passage deals with the quality of the 'world':

> 'There is nothing in the universe superior to the world.' No more is there anything on earth superior to our city (3.21).

Other, less important but nevertheless telling, features of the text corroborate the image of a work that simply presupposes an urban *Lebenswelt*. Cotta and Balbus share the idea that houses are necessarily built on the plans of architects (1.72; 2.141). In order to encounter examples of vice and crime, Balbus invites his small audience to move from the theatre and the comedies performed therein to the *forum* and the criminal courts at work there (2.72, 74). The city praised by the speakers elsewhere is seen here in its complex and ambivalent reality, a place of vice and crime and a place that is self-reflexive about this fact.

By and large, Cicero has his speakers explicitly proffer a broadly positive view of cities in Antiquity, without denying the presence of problems and strife. Shared across speakers, this view reflects the author's own perception and evaluation. Economically, the city is dependent on the exploitation of the countryside, which is above all the property of the city-dwellers – here Cicero shares the perspective of what later came to be seen as the consumer-city. However,

---

[15] See more generally Cancik 1979, repr. in Cancik 1998, 55–80. The notion of 'progress' is lacking here, see Altini 2015; *in rerum natura* suggests an evolutionary perspective leading towards a final stage *(denique)*.

[16] The reference is not fully clear. *Denique* at the beginning of the sentence suggests a further step, not just a summing up. Cicero might think of artificial landscapes as exemplified by contemporary gardens in cities, see Giesecke 2007; Stackelberg 2009; Neudecker 2015.

his emphasis on the inventiveness and productivity of artisans working in professions outside agriculture is notable.[17]

4.3 Religious phenomena as phenomena in a city

What is the place of religion in the world that appears on and between the lines of Cicero's dialogue? The dialogue features protagonists who held the most important positions in the major contemporary philosophical schools, including a notable Epicurean. Given the broad lack of interest in religious activity on the behalf of many Epicureans , it is the exchange between the Stoic, Balbus, and the Academic sceptic, Cotta, that produces most of the material that is relevant for our discussion here. The Stoic representative cites the evidence of tangible religious practice in order to bolster his overarching theoretical claims about the gods. The sceptic returns to these concrete 'proofs' in order to point out the limited value of the insights that could potentially be drawn from such arguments, as well as their lack of validity. For the most part, the evidence is presented and discussed without reference to any spatial markers: it is about what *the* Greeks or *the* Romans do in general, or about what can be read in their literature. An urban character is never designated specifically as such. Cicero is, thus, clearly not thinking along the lines of a division between urban and non-urban religion. It is all the more telling, then, that he has his characters build up crucial arguments on the foundations of urban practices and institutions. The urban character of the religion used for this purpose is taken for granted in a way that never applies to the non-urban space. I am not claiming that the author (or his characters) argues that certain religious phenomena are specifically urban. Rather, I make the observation that, in a number of places, Cicero associates religious phenomena with urban space or practices in a way that points towards deep-rooted assumptions about a close entanglement that need not be spelled out in theories of origin or other causal relationships. The short list of such phenomena consists of temples, calendars, and individual gods.

Let us consider temples first. The Stoic Balbus ridicules Velleius' atomistic Epicurean physics by posing a rhetorical question:

> Yet if the clash of atoms can create a world, why can it not produce a portico, a temple, a house, a city, which are less and indeed much less difficult things to make?

---

[17] For the discussion about Max Weber's consumer city and Moses Finley's analysis of the lack of capitalist developments see summarily Zuiderhoek 2017, 43–49.

> *Quod si mundum efficere potest concursus atomorum, cur porticum, cur templum, cur domum, cur urbem non potest, quae sunt minus operosa et multo quidem faciliora?* (2.94)

As the leading 'portico' indicates, the sequence does not simply provide a list of architectural features that ends with cities. Rather, urban architecture is depicted here in a sequence of growing complexity. The architects of houses, we are told in a later passage, have to consider such complex issues as how to keep the smell of wastewater and sewerage away from the owners (2.141, although not from his slaves, obviously). Thus houses figure even after the mentioning of porticos and temples that frequently include porticos. I will, however, focus on temples here.

Temples or architecturally articulated sanctuaries (*delubra*)[18] are associated with cities throughout the text. Such temples are fundamental in providing opportunities for the recognition of gods. Balbus draws up a list of powers that are regarded as being gods and that have, consequently, had dedicated temples to them at Rome (2.61). These, he argues, are each so potent that it is necessary to assume they are under the guidance of some divine force:

> In other cases some exceptionally potent force is itself designated by a title of divinity, for example Faith and Mind; we see the shrines on the Capitol lately dedicated to them both by Marcus Aemilius Scaurus, and Faith had previously been deified by Aulus Atilius Calatinus. You see the temple of Virtue, restored as the temple of Honour by Marcus Marcellus, but founded many years before by Quintus Maximus in the time of the Ligurian war. Again, there are the temples of Wealth, Safety, Concord, Liberty, and Victory, all of which things, being so powerful as necessarily to imply divine governance, were themselves designated as gods. In the same class the names of Desire, Pleasure, and Venus Lubentina have been deified ... (2.61)

In Balbus' argument, such deities supplement astral deities and are further supplemented by deified human benefactors and natural forces in great numbers. Balbus admits the problem involved with this multiplication of gods (2.70f.) without questioning the validity of the principles. Cotta not only points to the problem of multiplication (3.40) but engages with the argument directly. Nobody among the audience would choose to address the bright bare sky itself rather than the concrete Capitoline Jupiter (3.11). Balbus interrupts his host Cotta's critique of the power of unbelievable narratives by pointing to the physical evidence of the temple of Castor and Pollux on the forum (3.13). In doing so, he accidentally strengthens Cotta's point: it is the existence of approachable, urban temples that renders all these gods plausible to the public (also 3.59) without

---

18 See e.g. 1.14; 2.150; 3.49f., 52, 59, 84, 88, 94.

producing any philosophical argument for the existence of gods. This part of the argument is summarised somewhat later in a *reductio ad absurdum:*

> If gods exist, are the nymphs also goddesses? If the nymphs are, the Pans and Satyrs also are gods; but they are not gods; therefore the nymphs also are not. Yet they possess temples vowed and dedicated to them by the nation; are the other gods also therefore who have had temples dedicated to them not gods either?
>
> *Si di sunt, suntne etiam Nymphae deae? si Nymphae, Panisci etiam et Satyri; hi autem non sunt; ne Nymphae [deae] quidem igitur. at earum templa sunt publice vota et dedicata. ne ceteri quidem ergo di, quorum templa sunt dedicata?* (3.43)

I will not sketch the lengthy argument in detail, but point instead to its culmination in the critique of the institution of sanctuaries (*fanum, ara*) even for pernicious powers such as Fever and Bad Luck:

> So far did this sort of error go, that even harmful things were not only given the names of gods but actually had forms of worship instituted in their honour: witness the temple to Fever on the Palatine, that of Orbona the goddess of bereavement close to the shrine of the Lares, and the altar consecrated to Misfortune on the Esquiline (3.63).

The excessively large number and the many implausibilities of the traditional gods are stabilised by religious practices and, above all, by architecturally articulated spaces that can be *seen* in the city.

I must admit from the outset that my second point, concerning the calendar, is weaker with regard to its explicit embeddedness in cities. The passage I have in mind is part of the Stoic praise of the teleological nature of humans as indicative of divine providence and follows directly on from the introduction of the notion of *altera natura*.

> Then moreover has not man's reason penetrated even to the sky? We alone of living creatures know the risings and settings and the courses of the stars, the human race has set limits to the day, the month and the year, and has learnt the eclipses of the sun and moon and foretold for all future time their occurrence, their extent, and their dates. And contemplating the heavenly bodies the mind receives knowledge of the gods, from which arises piety, with its comrades justice and the rest of the virtues, the sources of a life of happiness that vies with and resembles the divine existence and leaves us inferior to the celestial beings in nothing else save immortality, which is immaterial for happiness.
>
> *Quid vero hominum ratio non in caelum usque penetravit? soli enim ex animantibus nos astrorum ortus obitus cursusque cognovimus, ab hominum genere finitus est dies mensis annus, defectiones solis et lunae cognitae praedictaeque in omne posterum tempus, quae quantae quando futurae sint. Quae contuens animus accipit [ad] cognitionem deorum, e qua oritur pietas, cui coniuncta iustitia est reliquaeque virtutes, e quibus vita beata existit par et similis*

deorum, nulla alia re nisi immortalitate, quae nihil ad bene vivendum pertinet, cedens caelestibus (2.153).

The previous passage draws for its evidence on the form of the hands and the manual ingenuity of the human race. The focus here now turns to the reasoning power of the mind (*ratio*). It is the mind alone that is capable of coming to know the mechanisms of the celestial bodies. *Cognoscere* here stresses the perception, the mastery of a given fact. This resonates with the lengthy description of the celestial order (*ordo, ratio*) given by Balbus earlier in book 2 (2.49–56), in which he argued for the existence of a divine agency lying behind, or implicit in, these ordered movements. However, the focus here is rather different. 'Rising' and 'setting', as well as the 'courses' of the bodies, anchor the current description in the perspective of the human observers, not the perfect 'orbits' and 'circles' as seen from the celestial pole. This perspective is immediately made explicit by giving agency to humans to 'define' the day, month, and year. This – I presume consciously and in close reception of Plato's description of human faculties[19] – clashes with Varro's probably slightly earlier dealing with the language of time in *De lingua latina*, where these three terms are associated with 'natural discrimination' as opposed to the *civilia vocabula dierum*.[20]

However, Varro's train of thought can help us to understand the further progress of Balbus' argument, which is characterised by a perspective that departs in important ways from that of Plato. When Varro moves from natural units of time to human institutions, he starts off with days that are instituted *deorum causa*.[21] In Cicero's dialogue, Balbus develops a somewhat different sequence of argumentative steps. Like Plato, he moves from astronomic observation to recognising gods. In Plato, the divinely granted gift of sight allows humankind to

---

19 See in particular Plato, *Timaios* 47a–d: 'For I reckon that the supreme benefit for which sight is responsible is that not a word of all we have said about the universe could have been said if we had not seen stars and sun and heaven. *As it is, the sight of day and night, the months and returning years, the equinoxes and solstices, has caused the invention of number, given us the notion of time, and made us inquire into the nature of the universe*; thence we have derived philosophy, the greatest gift the gods have ever given or will give to mortals ... the cause and purpose of god's invention and gift to us of sight was that we should see the revolutions of intelligence in the heavens and use their untroubled course to guide the troubled revolutions of our own understanding, which are akin to them, and so, by learning what they are and how to calculate them accurately according to their nature, correct the disorder of our own revolutions by the standard of the invariability of those of god' (transl. Lee). Cf. Cicero, *On the nature of gods* 2.153. I am grateful to Paul Scade for the observation.
20 Varro, *On Latin language* 6.12.
21 Ibid.

correct their imperfect calendars, and thus eventually their imperfect souls, through empirical observation and, ultimately, mathematical calculation. Cicero further sharpens this argument. It is human *ratio* that leads to astronomical knowledge, cognition of the gods, and, consequently, the piety that flows from this understanding. Early in this argument, he replaces Plato's equinoxes and solstices with eclipses of the sun and moon, classic examples used in explaining the rise of religious fear and the taking of ritual action in order to support benevolent (sun, moon) divine forces and to avert their threatening counterparts (shadow understood as having a demonic aspect).[22] This is a forced transition, as can be seen from the fact that the human ability to calculate such eclipses, an ability that is often celebrated as an antidote to religious interpretation, is not followed up. The next sentence does not build on these calculations but, rather, takes up the observations of the eclipses as motivating the recognition of gods. Such recognition, the reader learns, necessarily leads to *pietas* and religious cult, as is made clear in the introduction to the dialogue as a whole.[23]

Balbus' argument now moves on from piety to other virtues, but mine stops here. Cicero's modification of Plato's argument points towards an external, contemporary referent: the Roman calendar and Caesar's reform of it. This reform was brought into effect on the 1st of January, 45 BCE, preceded by an exceptional year of 445 days and sharp public discussions. It brought the civic and religious calendar in the form of the *fasti* (it should be pointed out that there was no concept of 'calendar' in contemporary Latin, only its graphic form, the *fasti*, or the abstract *annus Romanus*) into line with the solar (and stellar) year. Only against this background does Cicero's phrase *ab hominum genere finitus est dies* ('the day has been defined by humans') make sense, with its stress on direct human agency in contrast to Plato's stress on the discovery of limits with a divine origin, as Pease points out in his commentary on *De natura deorum*.[24] Thus again, a very urban, if not *the* urban, religious instrument is declared central for metaphysical recognition and practical piety.

The last element in my list is as explicit as it is surprising.

> Nor is the care and providence of the immortal gods bestowed only upon the human race in its entirety, but it is also wont to be extended to individuals. We may narrow down the entirety of the human race and bring it gradually down to smaller and smaller groups, and finally to single individuals. For if we believe, for the reasons that we have spoken of before, that the gods care for all human beings everywhere in every coast and region of the

---

22 Briefly with evidence from pre-Ciceronian traditions Rüpke 1995b, 219.
23 Cicero, *On the nature of gods* 1.3, see Rüpke 2007b.
24 Pease 1955, 946 *ad loc.*

lands remote from this continent in which we dwell, then they care also for the men who inhabit with us these lands between the sunrise and the sunset. But if they care for these who inhabit that sort of vast island which we call the round earth, they also care for those who occupy the divisions of that island, Europe, Asia and Africa. Therefore they also cherish the divisions of those divisions, for instance Rome, Athens, Sparta and Rhodes; and they cherish the individual citizens of those cities regarded separately from the whole body collectively, for example, Curius, Fabricius and Coruncanius in the war with Pyrrhus, Calatinus, Duellius, Metellus, and Lutatius in the First Punic War, and Maximus, Marcellus, and Africanus in the Second, and at a later date Paulus, Gracchus, and Cato, or in our fathers' time Scipio and Laelius; and many remarkable men besides that both our own country and Greece have given birth to, none of whom could conceivably have been what he was save by god's aid. It was this reason which drove the poets, and especially Homer, to attach to their chief heroes, Ulysses, Diomede, Agamemnon, or Achilles, certain gods as the companions of their perils and adventures; moreover the gods have often appeared to men in person, as in the cases which I have mentioned above, so testifying that they care both for communities and for individuals (2.164–6).

Despite its length, the contents of this passage are quite straightforward. It is the final argument of Balbus' speech, claiming that the gods care even for individuals, or at least for important people or those with important business. Theodicy is supported here by the claim that the gods care for the big issues and neglect the small (2.167). The gods, hence, care for everybody, not only humankind as such but also smaller portions of humanity and even (some) individuals. These levels are defined as 'world', 'continents', 'cities' (*urbes*), and *singuli*, big men such as Curius, Fabricius, and so on. Balbus' examples form a chronological sequence, moving from the early 3rd century BCE to the second half of the second, without excluding unnamed later cases. Great men claiming the support of specific deities were a contemporary phenomenon, exemplified by Sulla, as well as by Pompey and Caesar in Cicero's lifetime. These figures would present themselves to the minds of Cicero's readers, even if we should not forget that the dialogue is set in the mid-80s. Far from being just religious figures of speech, these close relationships were amply communicated not only in anecdotes, legends, and nicknames, but in material form, in coins, dedications, temples, or complex urban architectural forms such as Pompey's temple-theatre or Caesar's forum.

To sum up, the main characteristics of the contemporary religious reality that serves as the basis for argumentation in the dialogue are considered, mostly implicitly but at certain times explicitly, as features that are peculiar to cities. This image of a complex urban religious reality is characterised by an incoherent and even contradictory plurality of religious agents and of gods made plausible by temples, images (3.61), or narratives (3.62). Cotta – anachronistically considering the fictitious date of the dialogue – shares Marcus' position in the earlier dialogue *On laws*, in which Cicero has the latter (his own persona) argue against the proliferation of gods by individual invention or import. Whereas Marcus focuses on the threat of *confusio religionum* which might derive from such behaviour,[25] Cotta highlights the problems that follow from Balbus' uncritical support of the proliferation of gods in cult, stories, and Stoic philosophical argumentation in order to avoid such a state: *ne perturbentur religiones* (3.60). The solution offered by both is adherence to tradition under the surveillance of 'public priests' (see 1.5–10).

4.4 Philosophical debate as an indicator of urbanity

The realities of contemporary religion as encountered in the city of Rome (and certainly in other cities as well) have a threatening aspect. This is the starting point of *On the nature of the gods*, as the very first sentence makes clear:

> There are a number of branches of philosophy that have not as yet been by any means adequately explored; but the inquiry into the nature of the gods, which is both highly interesting in relation to the theory of the soul, and fundamentally important for the regulation of religion, is one of special difficulty and obscurity, as you, Brutus, are well aware (1.1).

As is evident from the dialogue as a whole, such control (not to speak of sanctions, hardly ever mentioned, even in *On laws*) is only one among a number of possible options, and an option proposed by only one speaker in the dialogue: *habes, Balbe, quid (sc. ego) Cotta, quid pontifex sentiat* (3.5). The solution, or rather, the way to deal with the problem, is different. It is an intellectual approach, a philosophical enquiry, with religious practices made the object of intellectual reflection and discussion. If religious diversity – fundamental contradictions and incoherences rather than some colourful plurality – is part of the urban condition, then the urban way of dealing with this problematic diversity is philosophical debate. For this debate, *urbanitas* is a meta-norm, which is mutually accorded to by the participants in the debate (2.74). It is the city that is the highest form of artisanship and rationality, as can be seen from the development of painting and architecture (see 2.35). It is the city that provides the best comparison for the rationality of the cosmos (2.78). And it is the power of speech that, at the end of the process of civilisational development from savage nature, has enabled this societal form:

---

25 Cicero, *On laws* 2.25.

> It is this that has united us in the bonds of justice, law and civil order, this that has separated us from savagery and barbarism.
>
> *Haec nos iuris, legum, urbium societate devinxit, haec a vita inmani et fera segregavit* (2.148).

Such urbanity is performed in *On the nature of gods*. This performance is self-reflexive. It is not by chance that the quotations in this and the previous section are all are taken from the speech of the Stoic Balbus, for it is he who does not accord the necessary qualities of rationality to his opponents:

> Therefore the existence of the gods is so manifest that I can scarcely deem one who denies it to be of sound mind (2.44).

It is also Balbus who is reprimanded in the sharpest way by his opponent Cotta:

> Now oblige me by letting me know yours. You are a philosopher, and I ought to receive from you a proof of your religion, whereas I must believe the word of our ancestors even without proof (3.6).

It is Balbus who, himself, needs to adhere to the norms of a *philosophical* debate by offering cogent arguments rather than invoking common sense. After all, intellectuals are part and parcel of the urban perturbation of religion. The so-called 'theologians' already start from three Jupiters instead of one (3.53). Philosophical inquiry, as undertaken by the few Romans communicating via books, involves, as Cicero, the author, demonstrates, the following of certain norms of discourse.[26]

The social position of the participants is not without importance for the performance of such a debate.[27] If we neglect (as Cicero himself invites us to do by the shortness of the exposition) the Epicurean arguments voiced in *On the nature of gods*, the positions most critical of current practice in the two related dialogues *On the nature of gods* and *On divination* are given to those with the highest standing and greatest religious engagement: the pontiff Cotta in the earlier work and the augur Marcus Tullius Cicero in the later. The authority thus given to their statements ensures that their critical arguments are taken seriously and that their stance is judged to be sincere. This does not mean that one has to endorse their position, as the authorial voice demonstrates when it supports Balbus over Cotta, the host and senior, at the end of *On the nature of gods*:

---

26 For the concept of ‚norms of discourse' see Baumhauer 1997.
27 The following is taken from Rüpke 2012f, 202.

> Here the conversation ended, and we parted, Velleius thinking Cotta's discourse to be the truer, while I felt that that of Balbus approximated more nearly to a semblance of the truth.
>
> *Haec cum essent dicta, ita discessimus, ut Velleio Cottae disputatio verior, mihi Balbi ad veritatis similitudinem esse propensior.* (3.95)

This passage demonstrates for a final time that the characters have, throughout the text, been enacting norms of philosophical discussion at Rome.[28] The performative aspects are highly important: the use of *otium* offered by festivals as the impetus to pursue such discussions; the decorum exercised in addressing each other and in finding consensus about further proceedings; *dignitas, gravitas, constantia*.[29] Philosophising is as honourable as acting in the Forum, and it follows similar norms. This respectability was, of course, particularly important for Cicero, who was out of political office in the 40s, just as he had been earlier in the 50s,[30] but it was also a norm that applied universally. We have to remember that the whole Ciceronian project of presenting Greek philosophy in the Latin language starts with a *protreptikos*. Cicero's *Hortensius* was an invitation to do philosophy for 'the Roman man' who is 'only timidly tackling this type of discussion'.[31] If philosophy leads to a good life, a *vita beata*, as all schools claimed, the practice of philosophising itself must adhere to the norms of such a life.[32] If philosophy is able to deal with the complexities of urban religion, it must itself display the qualities of urbanity.

4.5 Conclusion: Urbanised religion

The positive and critical remarks of the main character and pontiff Cotta, as well as the author's introductory remarks, underline the fact that rational reflection on religion is not an activity separate from and above religion but one that is intimately intertwined with it. Mary Beard and John Scheid have taught us to see the literary form of such discourse as part and parcel of late Republican Roman religion.[33] The analysis of Cicero's dialogue *On the nature of gods* in this chapter adds a further dimension. This literary discourse about religion is a reflection of

---

28 Henderson 2006.
29 See ibid., 177; Krostenko 2000, 357.
30 See Cicero, *On laws* 1.9–10.
31 Cicero, *De fato* 1.4.
32 Henderson 2006.
33 Beard 1985, 1991; Scheid 1990a; Feeney 1998, 2007b; Rüpke 1994b, 1997, 1998b, 2001b, 2003a.

the complexities of a specifically urbanised religion and is, moreover, part and parcel of that specifically urbanised religion. Again, I employ 'urbanised religion' as a term here to catch the interaction of urban space and urban conditions of life with the shape of religious practices, beliefs, and institutions. In contrast to the idea of 'urbanising religion', it focuses on how religious practices, imaginaries (ideas, discourses, 'beliefs'), and institutions (taken broadly) are impacted by their urban environments. The thesis underlying this term is the intuition, developed in the introductory chapter to this volume, that city-space engineered the major changes that revolutionised Mediterranean religions, where this space is understood as the array of urban spatial and structural forms, forces, processes, and agents. Cicero's dialogue offers a first confirmation of this view. At the same time, the work of this religious thinker exemplifies an impact of urbanity on religious discourse that is not restricted to Antiquity and thus invites further comparative studies. However, the compass of the current discussion is necessarily more restricted, and the next chapter will remain in the company of the very same period discussed here. It takes a closer look at texts that are much more explicit concerning spatial concepts and are even more indicative of the contemporary process of massive urbanisation and its relation to urban discourses.

5 Crafting complex place: Religion and urban development

5.1 Introduction

The development of large-scale cities is a comparatively recent feature in human history. For a long time, the viability of this new development was also extremely precarious. The permanent cohabitation of a large number of people, surpassing the scale of face-to-face societies by orders of magnitude, had its ups and downs for several millennia. Large cities grew and shrank, and, at certain times and in certain regions, even appeared to be under threat of disappearing completely. What role, if any, did religion play in this precarious developmental process?

Historically, the periods of urbanisation beginning in the third millennium BCE ran in parallel with a rise in visible, and partly institutionalised, activities characterised by their specifically religious form of communication, which sought to bring not unquestionably plausible agents 'down' from a place beyond the immediate situational context and into present interaction 'here and now'.[1] The psychologist Ara Norenzayan has recently argued, from a cultural evolutionary perspective, that the development of societies beyond the size boundaries of pre-neolithic hunter-gatherer groups (not explicitly quantified but an example suggests a threshold of around thirty members) was fundamentally enabled by the evolution of a specific type of religion. The pivotal trait of this type of religion was the appearance of Big Gods, that is gods that are all-observing from the position 'above' yet still human enough to be 'intuitively graspable and emotionally potent', and, above all, characterised by a concern with morality, reading to punish amoral behaviour, even if such behaviour was not witnessed by other group members. With this range of properties, such gods were thus able to ensure prosocial behaviour and, ultimately, to inculcate standards of morality.[2] Norenzayan's thesis that the formation of large societies and the social coherence necessary for their upkeep depends on the development of omniscient and moral gods, able to observe and punish individuals even beyond ordinary social control, has been sharply criticised from a historical perspective.[3] But this does not invalidate his identification of the problem. By shifting from the numerical quantity of the human group to the complexity of the group's spatial framework,

---

1 On this concept of religion, see above Ch. 1.2 and Rüpke 2015c.
2 Norenzayan 2013, quotation 27.
3 See e.g. Rüpke 2014b.

I will develop the hypothesis that large urban societies require practices that craft place in the city by relating people and space, disrupting continuous space, and selectively appropriating space. Religion, I suggest, provided precisely such services.

My argument for this claim will be developed again using the example of the late Republican metropolis of Rome. Rome was an exceptionally large city already by the early 1st century BCE and, by the end of the century, accommodated a population of somewhere between five hundred thousand and one million free and servile people.[4] My aim in this chapter is limited to the claim that religion is a possible provider of the kind of practices that can craft space, and that, historically and contingently, it played this role as a provider of an important range of practices to craft space in the classical Mediterranean world. Whether this role can be extended further, to urbanisation in the early cultures of the Indus, Mesopotamian, and Nile valleys, and/or to the civilisations of Central America for instance, must be the subject of a further inquiry. For Rome, as we have seen in the preceding chapter, ritual and textual religious practices provided important tools for the creation of a highly complex, shared *and* divided, space called 'city'. Similar to its development in the late-Republican period, Rome was brought to a new level of complexity *and* coherence on the same basis in the subsequent period, the Augustan age.

Sensu stricto the value of the available evidence is even more limited than the term 'hypothesis' suggests. Given the lack of statistical data that might suggest causal relationships, the lack of explicit testimony from agents, and even the lack of testimonies from observers or evidence for reception in general, my hypotheses can only provide a model for interpreting the parallelism in the rise of a certain type of literature and the growth and attempted reorganisation of the city. This suggests that a process of urban growth is stabilised and furthered if the process becomes reflexive, that is, if it is accompanied by mental representations and discourses that are able to interpret urban experiences and to motivate urban development by providing further services. The rise of what is usually treated as 'aetiological myth' and 'antiquarian literature' is central in this context.

What I will not deal with at all here is the line of research in Religious Studies that collects and studies those religious ideas that give special prominence to certain cities or places. I am thinking here of the idea that a given place is the centre of the earth, or the location for some vertical connection between heaven

---

[4] For the order of magnitude and the methodological problems, see Brunt 1987; Scheidel 2001a; Hin 2013.

and earth, a mythical *axis mundi* such as a tree rooted in the underworld and reaching up to heaven, or some spring or chasm that makes a connection downwards to the underworld instead.[5] I will briefly touch on this idea as it relates to Rome but my purpose in doing so will be to point out its lack of significance, since ideas of this sort were limited to a special type of intellectual discourse. My primary interest in what follows will be the complexity that is created and stabilised by religious practices and ideas.

5.2 'On places'

Marcus Terentius Varro (114–27 BCE), a polymath who had reached the rank of praetor and was entrusted with a military command even in his old age, had, by the early 40s BCE, written twenty-five books *On the Latin language* (*De lingua Latina*). The work opens with an introductory book, followed by three books on the method of etymology. Books 5–7, the second triad, were dedicated to the famous lawyer, politician, and philosopher Marcus Tullius Cicero (116–43 BCE), whom we have just met, and are among the few books of the work to have survived. Here Varro discusses the treatment of 'places' (*de locis*, 5.14), 'times' (*temporum*, 6.1), and words characteristic for poetic usage (7).

Varro was no parochialist. He had been born in Sabine Reatinum but pursued his career at Rome. He was aware of both the divisions and the close relationships, alliances, and exchanges between polities and peoples in older and more recent Italian history. Heaven and earth are his starting points, the former inhabited by the gods and the latter by humans (5.16). He then goes on to systematically divide the earth into *Asia* and *Europa* (5.31). *Europa* he explains, is inhabited by many *nationes*, the Romans among them, and its parts are each named after those groups who live there. Varro then inserts a lengthy treatment of generic terms for places that he understands as being named so as to represent the activities that take place there (5.34–40). Immediately following this, Varro dedicates sixteen paragraphs to places in the city of Rome (5.41–56). His attention then turns to the terrestrial places inhabited, first, by the immortals and, second, by mortals. Animals take pride of place with regard to air and water (5.75–79) while humans are given priority over domestic and wild animals with regard to the land (he discusses Roman magistrates, priests, military personnel, people with differing levels of wealth, and artisans, 5.80–94, before reaching cattle). Natural products and manufactured objects follow, including

---

5 E.g. Rykwert 1976.

a lengthy discussion of the built environment (5.141–159) and the parts of the house (5.160–168). Finally, the book closes with Varro's discussion of the terminology of money (5.169–183).

Rome is not treated in this work as if it is the only city or even the only city that matters. '[M]any founded *oppida* in Latium using the "Etruscan rite"', Varro freely admits (5.143), and these were all, according to his definition (5.141), places that were suitable for securing and defending wealth. Rome is not assigned any special place in Varro's systematic division. Rather, it is the contingent features of Rome, the many gods, the many localities, the types of functional spaces and streets, that are treated in unbalanced length and detail. Book 6 of the work follows the same trend. After a very systematic introduction to the cosmos and astronomical movements, the treatment of the 'civil names of days' (*ciuilia vocabula dierum*, 6.12) then follows. This relates the days to gods as well as to humans and is restricted to the Roman calendar (6.12–34). Varro's interest then shifts to terms that are used to describe activities in time.

In many of the passages just mentioned, religion is used to define places and times and places via times. This is done not just by attesting to the ubiquity of religion. On the contrary, Varro attributes religious practices and qualities to specific places. In his *Antiquities of things divine* (*Antiquitates rerum divinarum*), the same author assumes that communities wanted to have sacralised spots in order to have places within the continuous area of buildings to which they could flee in the case of a fire.[6]

The emphasis placed on the religious function and history of spaces in the city of Rome in both works is interesting precisely because *On the Latin language* is a treatment with different foci. The same holds true for other texts that focus on the relationship between religion and urban space. The 'widely' read (given ancient rates of literacy) poet Propertius dedicated his fourth book of poems around the year 16 BCE, that is, about a decade before Augustus' reform of the administrative organisation of the city, to the topic of rites and places. 'I will sing of gods and the old names of places' (*sacra deosque canam et cognomina prisca locorum*)[7] is the programmatic formulation of the first elegy, with this programme being confirmed by all the following poems of the book, each of which takes its point of departure from a certain place or has a clear reference to areas of the city.[8] This programme was explicitly taken up shortly afterwards

---

[6] Varro, *Ant. rer. diu.* fr. 69 Cardanus. Cf. fr. 68, which formulates the norm that every ritual activity needs a place for a fire *(focus)*.
[7] Propertius 4.69.
[8] Fantham 1997; Rüpke 2009c.

by the poet Ovid, who transformed it into a commentary on the graphic representation of the Roman calendar, the so-called *fasti*, thus producing his *Libri fastorum*.[9] Here, the topographical itinerary imagined by the anonymous speaker in Propertius' first elegy is replaced by the rigorous temporal sequencing of the calendar. However, Ovid continued to share with his forerunner the interest in associating with a specific place the activities and stories that were related to a date.

5.3 Time and place

Why are both the Varronian and the incipient Propertian systematics of space set aside in favour of a systematic of time? Varro's starting point for the first detailed ancient treatment of the topography of Rome is the most complex topographical rite we know of, the rite of the *Argei*. This rite was based on 27 small sanctuaries distributed across the city[10] and was, in Augustan times, thought to have been founded by Numa, the second of Rome's legendary 'kings' and the city's mythical lawgiver.[11] We have no information about the actual performance of the ritual, which involved the participants moving from location to location across the city but we do know that it lasted for two days.[12] Varro offers a list of the 27 locations, which cover the old urban nucleus of Rome spread over several hills. The ritual also included the throwing of 27 straw puppets from a bridge into the Tiber. The interpretation of this ritual was hotly debated probably as early as the second half of the 2nd century BCE.[13] Most ancient observers – and their position is important for our topic – interpreted this as a rite enacting the expulsion of inhabitants of Argive, that is, Greek, origin. Many commentators compared it to the saying 'sixty-years-old off the bridge', thus relating the expulsion of some sort of 'foreigners' to the denying of voting rites to elderly people, the latter being a story that reflected ancient attitudes more than any contemporary legal reality. Involved into the ritual was the, conceptually and topographically

---

9 Rüpke 1994b, 1996, 2006i.
10 For the problematic evidence and widely diverging interpretations, see Clemen 1930; Nagy 1985; Radke 1990b; Versnel 1996; Ziolkowski 1998; Wifstrand Schiebe 1999. For the ritual of throwing images from a wooden bridge (by the late Republic and early Empire into the Tiber), Varro, *On Latin language* 7.44; Ovid, *Fasti* 5.621–2; Festus p. 450.22–452.22 L; Plutarch, *Roman questions* 32; Paulus ex Festo p. 14,22–23 Lindsay.
11 Livy 1.21.5.
12 Ovid, *Fasti* 3.791–2.
13 Festus p. 452.21–2 L mentions Afranius (on whom Stärk 1996).

most central, priesthood of the Vestals, who, being female, were rather distant from any formal political agency. That these priestesses were given a leading role in the ritual of the Argei would have underlined the hypothetical character of the exclusion. The straw puppets likewise indicated a clear distance from any real exclusion. In any case, these were religious practices that addressed the topographical complexity of the city as much as its ethnic composition. The concrete shape of the ritual was probably a reflection of a widespread historical narrative which gave Greek migrants a role in the prehistory of the city of Rome, whether that role was played by Hercules, the god, or Evander, the famous founder of cities.

These were not the only rituals that engaged with very different and distant places within the city. The dances of the Salian priests in March also touched on many points throughout the city, but here we do not even know whether these took a fixed route across the cityscape at all. We have to acknowledge that, with the exception of Varro, none of the ancient references to such rituals displayed any interest in the systematics of topographical details of the sort attested by the monumental city map of Rome from the 3rd century CE (the *forma urbis*) and the later inventories of city quarters (the *itineraria*). This lack of interest is in clear distinction to the Roman approach taken to time, which was represented and ordered by the calendrical schemes, the *fasti*, which came to be erected in various places. Unique to the ancient Mediterranean world, these lists of every day of the year, graphically arranged in monthly columns, were invented by the Romans and still determine the graphical and experiential concept of the year on a global scale today.[14] Evidently, space was too complex to be systematised much further by ritual means or religious discourses. The exceptional attempts prove the rule. When Augustus tried to systematise a division of cities into hundreds of *vici* – blocks based around crossroads rather than quarters – the sub-units were explicitly given a priestly and ritual apparatus. Such an apparatus was, however, lacking for the fourteen regions that formed the next administrative layer. We have to wait until the time of Hadrian to identify a (probably) ritual action that brought together *vici* of different *regiones* for a common dedication. Even this ritual seems to have covered only a majority, but not all, of the regions.[15] While time is only extended in a single dimension and can be structured by the imposition of simple limits that carve out periods by marking off their beginnings and ends, space adds two more dimensions of inter-related complexity with which to grapple. It is, perhaps, unsurprising that the Romans

---

14 See Rüpke 2006i.
15 See *CIL* 6.975 and Rüpke 1998b.

found themselves less able to apply systematic distinctions to this multi-dimensional realm.

5.4 The idea of a city?

'Systematisation' in religious terms might be understood as a topographical logic applicable to the spatial and architectural management of places or ensembles such as the central Forum Romanum, the peripheral (only nowadays central) Field of Mars, the Imperial *fora*, or the Palatine hill. However, there is no common concept, no master plan, to these enterprises, which were pursued by many different agents. The principles laid out by Vitruvius in his late Republican *On architecture* are not supported by empirical evidence:

> The lanes and streets of the city being set out, the choice of sites for the convenience and use of the state remains to be decided on; for sacred edifices, for the forum, and for other public buildings. If the place adjoin the sea, the forum should be placed close to the harbour: if inland, it should be in the centre of the town. The temples of the gods, protectors of the city, also those of Jupiter, Juno, and Minerva, should be on some eminence which commands a view of the greater part of the city. The temple of Mercury should be either in the forum, or, as also the temple of Isis and Serapis, in the great public square. Those of Apollo and Father Bacchus near the theatre. If there be neither amphitheatre nor gymnasium, the temple of Hercules should be near the circus. The temple of Mars should be out of the city, in the neighbouring country. That of Venus near to the gate. According to the regulations of the Etrurian haruspices, the temples of Venus, Vulcan, and Mars should be so placed that those of the first not be in the way of contaminating the matrons and youth with the influence of lust; that those of Vulcan be away from the city, which would consequently be freed from the danger of fire; the divinity presiding over that element being drawn away by the rites and sacrifices performing in his temple. The temple of Mars should be also out of the city, that no armed frays may disturb the peace of the citizens, and that this divinity may, moreover, be ready to preserve them from their enemies and the perils of war. (2) The temple of Ceres should be in a solitary spot out of the city, to which the public are not necessarily led but for the purpose of sacrificing to her. This spot is to be reverenced with religious awe and solemnity of demeanour, by those whose affairs lead them to visit it. Appropriate situations must also be chosen for the temples and places of sacrifice to the other divinities. (Transl. Joseph Gwilt)[16]

---

16 Vitruvius, *De architectura* 1.7.1–2. The Latin original of the famous quotation is: *(1) Divisis angiportis et plateis constitutis arearum electio ad opportunitatem et usum communem civitatis est explicanda aedibus sacris foro reliquisque locis communibus. et si erunt moenia secundum mare, area ubi forum constituatur eligenda proxime portum, sin autem mediterranea, in oppido medio. aedibus vero sacris, quorum deorum maxime in tutela civitas videtur esse, et Iovi et Iunoni et Minervae in excelsissimo loco unde moenium maxima pars conspiciatur areae distribuantur.*

In this passage, Vitruvius does not so much offer a religiously coherent view of a city as underline his interpretation of specific deities by associating them with other buildings or situations. Mercury is the god of merchants and is thus located in the forum or the public square; Apollo and Bacchus are gods of dramatic performances and are thus placed near the theatre; Ceres (in a sequence that is rarely cited) is associated with the *plebs* and civil unrest and, hence, referred to a deserted location. Despite this, the text is still interesting for us as a reflection of the accentuation of specific features of cities by the positioning of religious architecture and – explicitly – corresponding ritual.

Contemporary discourses on other spatial concepts are similarly built on religious institutions or concepts. The boundary line of the *pomerium*, ideally running around the city but in fact a mostly invisible line within the settlement area of Rome, is one such concept. This served as an important juridical limit between the area 'at home' (*domi*), with all its citizen rights, and the area associated with warfare (*militiae*), in which legal rights and administrative competences might be invalidated. It was associated with a supposed founding ritual involving the drawing of an initial furrow (and thus also the creation of a symbolic wall with the plough) around a city. However, for all practical purposes the *pomerium* seems to have ceased to hold any great importance by the late Republic, with the exceptions of a few points of entry into the city that were marked by ancient gates or their imagined places. Despite the enormous growth of the city, it was not until the time of Sulla, that is to say the early 1st century BCE, that action was taken to extend the area enclosed by the *pomerium*. A similar extension was probably carried out by Caesar and certainly by Claudius and Vespasian. The Augustan author Livy is the first to make explicit the theory that the enlargement of the city requires an enlargement of the *pomerium*. In the case of the emperors of the 1st century CE, we can see the development of a justification theory that relates the enlargement of the *pomerium* to the enlargement of the empire.[17]

Mercurio autem in foro, aut etiam ut Isidi et Serapi in emporio, Apollini Patrique Libero secundum theatrum, Herculi in quibus civitatibus non sunt gymnasia neque amphitheatra ad circum, Marti extra urbem sed ad campum, itemque Veneri ad portum. id autem etiam Etruscis haruspicibus disciplinarum scripturis ita est dedicatum, extra murum Veneris Volcani Martis fana ideo conlocari uti non insuescat in urbe adulescentibus seu matribus familiarum veneria libido, Volcanique vi e moenibus religionibus et sacrificiis evocata ab timore incendiorum aedificia videantur liberari. Martis vero divinitas cum sit extra moenia dedicata, non erit inter cives armigera dissensio, sed ab hostibus ea defensa a belli periculo conservabit. (2) item Cereri extra urbem loco, quo non omnes semper homines nisi per sacrificium necesse habeant adire, cum religiose caste sanctisque moribus is locus debeat tueri. ceterisque diis ad sacrificiorum rationes aptae templis areae sunt distribuendae.

17 Livy 1.44.3 – 5. See Rüpke 1990, 2019b, 35, with further sources listed in n. 45.

Military and religious practices of disrupting continuous space were made in parallel to one another.

Similarly, the first engagement with the idea of a secret tutelary deity of the city is attested in Sulla's time, when Valerianus Soranus is said to have been killed for pronouncing the deity's name.[18] From the end of the 1st century BCE onwards, a discourse about symbolic guarantees for the continuing existence of the empire (*pignora imperii*) is attested, first in vague forms and then fully developed only in Late Antiquity.[19] These were material objects that were kept or thought to be kept in difficult-to-access places in the city centre, for instance the twelve shields in a sanctuary of Mars in the Regia on the forum that were said to have fallen from heaven or the figure of the goddess Minerva, the Palladium, transferred to the temple of Vesta from Troy. All these discussions of conceptual relations between the shape and survival of the city remained restricted, for the most part, to a few intellectuals. They could, however, occasionally translate into ritual action by individual emperors.[20] Imagined religious objects or actual ritual performances were, thus, employed to facilitate thinking about the fundamental character of the city, that is, to fuel a discourse about urbanity in the face of a quickly changing urban fabric.

5.5 Multiple appropriations

The attempt to produce encompassing religious symbols or concepts for a city was obviously restricted to certain types of communication. It cannot be compared to the impact of the architecture of several dozens of temples, hundreds of crossroad sanctuaries, thousands of domestic shrines, and tens of thousands of funerary cult places. The enormous investments put into crossroad shrines in hundreds of neighbourhoods, or the investments in highly visible tombs by noble families and upwardly mobile freedmen and freedwomen, certainly merit further analysis for the history of Rome as does comparable architecture in other cities. At Rome, it was tombs that defined for the traveller both the access roads to the city and the transition from countryside to urban space. It was neighbourhood shrines that typically served as the nearest cultural infrastruc-

---

18 Servius (auctus), *Aeneid* 1.277; see also *AE* 1977,816: *tutela*. Further sources: Pliny, *Natural History* 28.18; Macrobius, *Saturnalia* 3.9.1–9; comprehensive: Ferri 2010b, 2010a.
19 E.g. Ovd, *Fasti* 3.354; most systematically: Servius auctus, *Aeneid* 7.188.
20 See e.g. for the spear throwing on a piece of fictitiously foreign soil in the city of Rome, Rüpke 1990, 2019b, 105–8.

ture outside the home for most of the inhabitants of Rome, a topic that will be given further consideration in the next chapter.

All in all, such permanent sacralisations enabled a large number of citizens of very different means to relate to particular spaces in a publicly visible and – in principle – inalienable manner. However, practical issues had to be kept in mind. Houses needed to remain marketable and it was thus important that buyers should not be put off by burdening them with the care of the religious investments of previous owners. Thus, despite the principle of the inalienable 'property' of gods (and ancestors), domestic shrines (*sacraria*) might be demolished. The mode of appropriation was governed by rules, which themselves changed over time. Obviously, marking out a site or architecturally transforming it produced forms of self-representation, memory, and prestige, such as the erecting of a dedication or the leaving flowers or candles. And yet these latter practices, too, enabled people to relate to different places and establish a synchronic map or a diachronic memory of relations to the urban space, and to involve others in these practices. The use of inscriptions helped both with the imprinting of one's own subjectivity on the place as well as with communication with others.

From a political and, in particular, a power point of view, such individual appropriations were suspicious, even in the religious guise of relating space to transcendent powers rather than to potentially rival humans. Cicero's enterprise of formulating a sort of law of religion in the second book of his *De Legibus* identifies private religious initiative as a potential source of danger for the political order and suggests bans and sacerdotal control.[21] Imperial building programmes aimed both at monopolising large scale appropriations of urban space and at homogenising the city, for instance by making it into a city of gold or marble, if I may thus refer to the Augustan and Flavian programmes.[22] Neighbourhood shrines, as we will see in the next chapter, were products and places of contention for very different agents and agendas.

5.6 Trajectories

We can now summarise the observations collected above and relate them back to the chapter's starting hypotheses. I claimed that large urban societies need practices that craft place by means of relating people and space, disrupting continuous space, and selectively appropriating space. What I have actually shown is

---

[21] Cicero, *On laws* 2.18–20; see Rüpke 2016e, 29.
[22] Gros 1976; Boyle and Dominik 2003.

that such services *could* be provided by religion in ancient Rome. That they were important is suggested by the chronology. There is a parallelism between the extraordinary growth of the city of Rome far beyond the usual standards of the Mediterranean world and the growth of practices such as temple building, neighbourhood shrines, funerary architecture, and the use of writing in such contexts. 'Urbanising' and 'urbanised' religion are two different perspectives on the same phenomena.

Individually, it is possible to cite other causes or stimuli for each of these developments in their various phases. With a view to such counter arguments, I have paid close attention to explicit reflections on specifically urban forms of religion. These I found, in particular, in the antiquarian and technical literature of the 1st century BCE. Reflexive enterprises tend to restrict complexity and look for unifying ideas. However, at the same time they thereby attest to complexity and its lively character in the manifold practices and memories of appropriation by very different agents. Attention should be paid to these layers of practices and the resulting evidence. It may well be that it was the sum of such very localised practices and the habits thus primed that enabled Rome's improbable growth. It might be interesting to see whether the reduction of such practices had consequences as well.

6 Materiality of religion in urban space: Neighbourhoods of a metropolis

6.1 Visible and material religion

The materiality of religion is, at the same time, both an old and a new topic. When the notion of the 'sacred' dominated the thinking of historians of religion – Rudolf Otto's *Das Heilige* was already articulating widespread concerns about earlier notions in 1917 but has since become a rallying point for thinkers with related interests[1] –, the search for the holy not only investigated concepts and times but also places and objects. Following this approach, the phenomenology of religion was successful in mapping and comparing many different religions.[2] All of these phenomena were treated as simply given, to be registered and perhaps displayed by ethnographic museums or illustrated in books, usually in the form of black and white two-dimensional images.[3] In the end, the 'message' implicit in such objects was their most important feature: the objects 'spoke of' the qualities or history of some deity, or of the qualities of her or his faithful followers.[4]

By the turn of the millennium, two new perspectives had been taken up by mainstream scholarship in the field, as the analysis of 'symbols' developed into a veritable 'aesthetics of religion'. In 1982, scholars in the Netherlands with a new focus on semiotics and iconography started a journal entitled *Visible religion: Annual of religious iconography*.[5] A few years later, the first volume of the *Handwörterbuch religionswissenschaftlicher Grundbegriffe* of 1988 tried to establish a sub-discipline of 'Aesthetics of religion'. The article of the same name published in the volume[6] stressed the sensual side of all religious practices, although it retained a focus on 'signs' and construed the 'sacred' from an optical perspective that included consideration of the role of the 'ugly' in reli-

---

[1] R. Otto 1917.
[2] See Heiler 1961 as a foundational text for the 'Religionen der Menschheit' (Kohlhammer).
[3] See Bräunlein 2004b, but also Bräunlein 2004a, 2009.
[4] Stolz 1988.
[5] Founded by Hans Gerhard Kippenberg, albeit unfortunately only lasting for a few years. For contributions developing this perspective for ancient religion, see e.g. Cancik 1985; Gladigow 1986.
[6] Cancik and Mohr 1988. Taken up by, for instance, Egelhaaf-Gaiser 2002, or in different fields by Gold 2003; van den Bercken and Sutton 2005.

gions.⁷ In parallel to this, the widespread use of the concept of religious 'messages' invited theories of communication into religious studies and, ultimately, even fully-fledged 'media studies'.⁸ The University of Erfurt was one of the places where this approach was developed in the early 2000s.⁹ Still, the radical focus on the materiality of not only communication¹⁰ but our whole world-as-lived, proffered, for instance, by the sociologist Bruno Latour and, later, the archaeologist Ian Hodder, had yet to find a place in the analysis of the larger ecological and cultural contexts of religious practices.¹¹ The discovery of the scarceness of global resources in the 1970s had produced new theological concepts of 'creation' and these led Latour to demand 'a parliament of things', the parliamentary representation of the conditions and constraints of our physical and technological environment. To put it another way, our entangled co-existence with these things had not yet reached the historical study of religion. Only very recently has substantial research addressed these concerns on a larger scale,¹² bringing interests in materiality, visuality, and communication together.¹³ This has also led to a particular interest in the materiality of religion as it manifests in the complexities of urban, and, above all, public space.¹⁴ It is this particular interest that informs the present chapter.

This brief review cannot, and does not, claim to stand in for a proper report on the state of the art in the broader field. Rather, it is meant to situate the reflections on the 'materiality of religion in urban space' that follow. I start by bringing together and advancing the theories concerning how we should conceptualise religion that have been developed so far in this book in order to give material objects an appropriate place in our understanding of religion and religious communication. I will also further systematise the notion of urban space and spaces and consider their impact on religion in urban environments. The *vicomagistri* in early Imperial Rome and the specific character of *public* space will serve as a case study for this at the end of the chapter.

---

7 Cancik and Mohr 1988, 147–152.
8 Reimann 1968; Mörth 1993; Luhmann 1998; Stolz 1998; Tyrell 1998; Tyrell, Krech and Knoblauch 1998; Tyrell 2002.
9 Grözinger and Rüpke 2000; Elm von, Rüpke and Waldner 2006; H. Meyer and Uffelmann 2007; Malik, Rüpke and Wobbe 2007.
10 Gumbrecht et al. 1994.
11 See e.g. Arweck and Collins 2006; cf. Latour 1993, 2005; Hodder 2012.
12 The journal *Material Religion* was started in 2005; see, in particular, Boivin 2009; Thomas Insoll 2009; Morgan 2010; Bynum 2011; Garbin 2012; Droogan 2013; Morgan 2015; Raja and Rüpke 2015b; Wilburn 2015; Burchardt 2016; Watson and Zanetti 2016.
13 E.g. Mitchell 2005, building on his work in the 1990s.
14 Knott, Krech and Meyer 2016.

6.2 Religion and material objects

I have suggested that religion can be theorised as communication with special agents (sometimes including objects) that are accorded agency in a not unquestionably plausible way. Communication with or concerning such divine agents might reinforce or reduce human agency, create or modify social relationships, and change power relationships. Religious agency, as discussed in Chapter 1, is, on the one hand, the agency attributed to such non-human, or in this regard supra-human, agents. On the other hand, it is the agency of the human instigator of such communication, that is, an agency arrogated by the instigator by way of such religious communication as is attributed to her or him by the audience. That is to say, religious communication amounts to agentically interacting with the structure of a situation by attributing agency not primarily to the human social agents usually regarded as relevant in the situation but, rather, to agents who lie beyond the horizons of the situation.

Such communication is, thus, necessarily a spatial practice. The divine agents are either invisible – being far away – or are concealed in the interior of bodies and objects that are visibly present but do not fully contain the power of the agents to whom they play host. As such, religious action marks out the physical space in which the action takes place and, at the same time, points to a transcending of this space in the very act of communicating with such divine agents.

As a further consequence, communication is performed and stabilised by media. In the case of prayer,[15] for example, these media might consist of gestures, words, and music, but in many instances they will take the form of objects that have a material presence beyond the situation. Cities clearly offer and demand a much broader range of media. Understanding urban religion, thus, requires a closer examination of medial techniques and their material form.

In general, the materiality of religious communication needs to be interpreted from four perspectives.

1) *Relevance*. In the act of communication, objects might help to enhance the relevance of the message communicated. Relevance is a key concept for understanding communication: in the midst of noises and all kinds of simultaneous acts of communication, it is vital to win the attention of an addressee by making relevant the specific sensual and communicative impact of one's own act of communication.[16] In short, the material objects used in communication draw atten-

---

15 See Patzelt 2018.
16 See D. Wilson and Sperber 1994, 2002.

tion to the addresser and flag him or her as being focused on the act of communication and on its contents. This is not a new insight. Indeed, it is a fairly obvious interpretation of the objects used in dedications. This interpretation is easily applicable when the practice is understood in a broad sense as increasing the attention of the gods, as, for instance, when a member of the cultural and economic elite, such as Aelius Aristides, presents a silver tripod instead of just praying.[17] The same holds true within a narrower social and locative horizon, such as when a dedicant attracts the attention of other visitors to the place and thus makes them aware of something worth listening to by use of less expensive means, like gestures, noise, or a small amount of incense, even if the visitors are merely bystanders rather than full participants. Again, a silver tripod would more clearly indicate that something important is going on, thus inviting those present in or close to the situation to adjust their focus. Nevertheless, more economical means could have similar effects.

2) *Sacralisation.* Objects that are brought into the situational space of an instance of religious communication or singled out from their prior context as somehow religiously significant change their own character and the character of the place and time in which they are embedded. I have proposed above that we should use the concept of 'sacralising' not just as a synonym for 'religious' but to denote the strategy used to make the situation 'special', to mark out action and communication, spatial and temporal contexts, as 'religious'. This sacralisation can be implemented to very different degrees though, from 'just slightly different from everyday conditions' to 'strongly and permanently special'. Such scalability stands in contrast to the 'virtually absolute category' and 'kind of transcendental quality' of *the* 'sacred' as entertained by Durkheim.[18] Sacralisation can be scaled. In this sense the concept of sacralisation is akin to that of 'ritualisation' as introduced by anthropologists such as Humphrey and Laidlaw or Susan Bell,[19] although their conception focuses on objects rather than gestures. I prefer to stress the action and limited duration implied in sacralisation when compared to the rather more fixed and rigid concept of something being 'sacred'.

This terminological choice has spatial and temporal consequences. 'Sacred' is frequently used in a topographical sense, as referring to clear limits in space – a sanctuary for instance – and permanence in time. Yet within a specific situa-

---

17 Aristeides, *Hieroi logoi* 2.27.
18 Thus Pickering 1999, 11. See above 20–23.
19 Bell 1992; Humphrey and Laidlaw 1994; the notion is, thus, different from a bipolar notion of sacralisation as the rendering of the non-sacred into the sacred (see, for instance, Burkert 1984). Cf. Deuser, Kleinert and Schlette 2015; Krech 2015.

tion, the individual actor is often unable to effectively establish exclusive boundaries and instead focuses the attention of his or her audience for a limited period instead. The introduction and manipulation of objects becomes relevant here. Incense allows for a certain time to define a space through a special smell. A cake, a puppet, or spices are prepared or bought from expert producers, they are handled during a performance, or presented as a token of benevolent communication. The killing and the preparation of animals makes for an even more complex performance, if we think of pigs or even larger beasts, and also allows the involvement of a larger community. For smaller groups, a cock or dove is much quicker to prepare. If roasting or boiling an animal takes too much time, then the interest of the audience (and maybe even the addressees) might diminish. The Roman concept of *dies intercisi*, days that could be used for ordinary business *inter caesa et porrecta*,[20] between the killing of the animal and the offering of parts of the prepared meat to a deity, points towards one way of dealing with such temporal issues when carrying out large scale rituals.

3) *Sacredness.* Not all objects mobilised for the purpose of religious communication disappear at the end of communicative act. Ritual and terminological labour is sometimes invested in making sure that the product of ephemeral sacralisation is regarded as *sacer*, as the permanent property of the gods (and, as such, is withdrawn from human exchange activities).[21] This concept of permanently being sacred, beyond the period of a performance, transcends the temporal limits of religious action proper. By using the language of 'sacredness' rather than simply 'sacred' to qualify a permanently sacralised objected, my intention is to draw attention to the fact that we are dealing with an attribution, a process of sacralisation, the result of which depends on the patron's position of power as much as it does on the tying of the process into pre-existing and predominant notions.[22] Sacralised materiality has a temporal trajectory in both directions, preserving memories afterwards and raising the status of a sequence of gestures or a place by pointing to such memories at the outset of a religious action. The action and place are upgraded by memories, even if these are false ones: when seeing indicators of rituals previously carried out by others in this place, I remember a ritual in which I participated in a different place.[23] The exploitation of memory

---

20 See Varro, *On Latin language* 6.31, equated with 'morning and evening'; Rüpke 1991.
21 For details and consequences, see Wissowa 1900; Sabbatucci 1952; Prosdocimi 1988; Rüpke 2007d, 181–5.
22 For the background, see Pettenkofer 2014.
23 For the concept of memory and its application, see Halbwachs 1992; Confino 1997; Olick and Robbins 1998; Whitehouse and Laidlaw 2004; Kensinger and Schacter 2008; Erll 2011; Galinsky 2016.

requires a strategic placement of indicators for the delimitation of ritual space.[24] The agents involved are often temple personnel rather than the individual actors. They appropriate individual religious communication by, for instance, strategically placing dedications within a sanctuary, making them more or less visible, preparing for the central experience by placing indicators of earlier religious experiences along the way, or by concentrating such objects in a specific place.[25] By such means, they create what one might call the *affordances* of a place, the type of actions invited by the place proper.

4) *Traditionality*.[26] The agency approach applied so far stresses the strategic aspect of religious action. Speaking of 'strategies' points towards two dimensions of the decisions to be taken when performing a religious action. First, it is nearly always the case that 'secular' alternatives to acting religiously exist. Certain exceptions exist – there is, for instance, the famous ancient thought experiment concerning the person who utters vows while drowning: with neither a boat or rescue raft at hand, there is not much that one can do in such a situation apart from pray – but these are extremely rare in comparison to the variety of circumstances in which religious communication is in fact used. When faced with a choice, there are good reasons why one might opt for a secular alternative rather than pursuing a religious act. Acting religiously can be very risky, particularly if the religious option is, itself, regarded as socially or legally inappropriate, as, for instance, when an agent attempts to change the course of juridical proceedings by the use of secret curses.

Secondly, religious action is also strategic and risky with regard to the degree of innovation involved and the degree of connection to established traditions. Others might respond by resorting to force, questioning the initiator's religious competence, or questioning the claim that the god invoked is listening or even that it exists. The setting up of an altar to the deified Caesar in 44 BCE ultimately proved fatal to those involved in the act, who found themselves cast as enemies of the institutions of the city.[27] To minimise such reactions, the decision to pursue a religious option and the detailed choices made in following through with such a decision are usually based on previous individual experience, on the experiences of others about which the agent either knows or is told, on the

---

[24] See also Galinsky 2014 and C. Smith 2015 for strategic placing of memories in urban space.
[25] Raja 2015; Rieger 2016, 2018.
[26] For the concept of tradition, and in particular its role in religious innovation, e.g. Shils 1969, 1975; Eisenstadt 1979; Shils 1981; Hobsbawm 1983; Heesterman 1985; Marincola 1997; Wiedenhofer 2004; Lewis and Hammer 2007; Konstan 2009; Arnal 2011; Klostergaard Petersen 2012; Wischmeyer 2012; Burkhardt 2013.
[27] Appian, *Civil wars* 3.1.2–3.

agent's contributions to the sacredness of the place, on institutional patterns of plausibility, and/or on 'traditions'. To describe such cautious, but nevertheless potentially subversive action, Michel de Certeau's notion of 'tactics', understood as a level that is distinct from the strategic, is helpful.[28]

This pattern is as relevant to words and gestures as it is to material objects, albeit to differing degrees. Judging by the variations and exceptions witnessed in deposits or on the walls of sanctuaries, the choice of the object employed might have been a less risky matter than the choice of the site and much more open to individual discretion. Making such a choice involves investing one's memories and/or money in the selection of an object that was previously employed in everyday use, used on special occasions, or bought or created for the very act of religious communication. This is part of the life of the object or the 'biographies of things' that are intertwined with the users' own life.[29] The 'prehistories' of the objects create very different qualities of relationships, both with the individual who chooses the object and also with regard to later observers, thus contributing to the sacredness of a spatial context.

The high social and material investment that goes into the construction of initially less plausible addressees (or 'counterintuitive agents' in the terminology of evolutionary theories of religion),[30] into the attribution of agency to them, and into the production of relevant communication with them seems to promise increased self-stabilisation, perhaps even power, or the capacity to solve problems. At the same time, it is immediately rendered precarious and contested by any new inequality produced by success. Sacralisations within the unquestionably plausible and evident environment are elements of this sort of strategic action and frequently take material form beyond the bodies of the human agents involved. Investments can extend all the way from items as small as miniaturised objects[31] on up to the levels of grand material extravagance and monumentality. Investing in the media of religious communication could, thus, involve enormous expenditures that were focused as much or more on the size and material value of the objects used as on their aesthetic qualities and artificiality.

---

28 Certeau 1984.
29 Gosden and Marshall 1999 (speaking of objects).
30 See e.g. Boyer 1994.
31 For miniaturisation, see J. Z. Smith 1987 and Quack 2009; G. A. Fine 2010; Rüpke 2014d.

6.3 Urban space

In the last paragraphs – and in line with a long tradition of previous research – I have not further qualified the precise locations in which the communication and display of one's own body,[32] of ephemeral gestures, and of more lasting material objects, takes place. A 'geography of religion' has existed since the 1980s but the interest of this sub-discipline has primarily been focused on the imprint of a very specific form of religious mobility, that is, pilgrimage.[33] The notion of the 'sacred landscape'[34] (or sacred topography) has been used to reconstruct lasting patterns of signs (and the meaning or even identities thus produced in the eyes of the beholders), often in the form of sanctuaries or memorials, spread over and thus unifying entire regions. Semiotics and stable systems of meaning, rather than qualities of space, have been at the centre of this type of research and it has, thus, not yet been informed by the challenges posed by new approaches to spatiality. Meanwhile, spatiality itself has been intensively theorised and scholars working on the notion have identified a 'spatial turn', thus further ascribing importance to their own work.[35] The notion of religion as a spatial form of action as developed in Chapter 3.1 can be further refined.

First, contemporary studies of spatiality have rejected the Cartesian notion of homogeneous space and a historicist fixation on time, which have, taken together, long upheld the dominance of a physicalist view of space as objectively real and mappable.[36] Second, these studies have questioned the anti-spatial biases of Marxist social theory wherein space is generally viewed as a passive reflection of non-spatial social processes[37] and the spatial is seen as a static, conservative realm 'devoid of the possibility of politics'.[38] Generally speaking, it is the cross-disciplinary and cross-ideological notion of space as a blank slate for human activity, a mere 'container or stage for the human drama'[39] considered outside the realm of social practice, that spatial studies have criticised and refor-

---

[32] For the importance of the body, see Draycott and Graham 2017; Petridou 2017b, 2018.
[33] E.g. Büttner 1985; Park 1994, see Kong 2001.
[34] See Cancik 1985 for Rome.
[35] I am grateful to Asuman Lätzer-Lasar, Maik Patzelt, Emiliano Rubens Urciuoli, and Markus Vinzent (all Erfurt) and Harry O. Maier (Vancouver/Erfurt), as well as other colleagues at the Max Weber Centre for Advanced Cultural and Social Studies, for intensive discussions and suggestions concerning this paragraph in particular.
[36] Lefebvre 1974; time: Soja 1989.
[37] Thus Castells 1977.
[38] Massey 1993, 143.
[39] E. Soja 2006, xvi.

mulated in order to allow a 'science of space'[40] to emerge and to generate a full-blown spatial approach to urban life.

Space is a condition, medium, and outcome of social relations, at once expressing those relations and acting back upon them in a reciprocal manner. As such, it is neither completely opaque nor fully transparent to agents or to scientific analysis, and nor is it reducible to the explanatory power of some non-spatial determinant. That is to say, the term 'spatiality' denotes socially produced space that incorporates both the physical space of the material world (including nature) and the mental space of cognition, without being conceptually equivalent to either. The assumption that '(social) space is a (social) product'[41] implies that it consists of geographically extended, 'stretched-out' social relations,[42] the control of which is 'fundamental in any exercise of power'.[43]

In introducing a 'realm Beyond' the situation, in terms of both space and participants in communication, religious action can be understood as a specifically spatial practice. Spatial theorists have called such tactical positioning and locations 'lived space', *espace vecu* (Lefebvre), or 'Thirdspace'.[44] This labelling marks out the creative aspect and counter-hegemonic potential of such space in comparison to both commonsensically patterned, empirically measurable 'espace perçu/Firstspace' (routinised repetitions of spatial practices regarded as taking place in clearly demarcated and functionally defined places) and professionally designed 'espace conçu/Secondspace' (ideological justifications for an organisation of the socio-spatial order). Religious space is not, thus, just the Firstspace of temples, places of assembly, and processional routes that is reflected in and bolstered by Secondspace discourses, exemplified by the ancient discourse on cities or rural idylls, with its innumerable reflections on religious spaces and architectures.[45] It is also Thirdspace that is experienced and used by members of political or literary or religious elites for their specific purposes and shared by non-elite users appropriating these same spaces in ways that signal attraction, repulsion, or indifference. However, instead of the counter-cultural and utopian accent of the typical use of 'Thirdspace', I prefer the notion of 'lived space', albeit without denying that the very nature of religious prac-

---

40 Lefebvre 1974, 7–9; 404–5.
41 Lefebvre 1974, 26.
42 Massey 1984.
43 See already Foucault 1984.
44 Soja 1996.
45 Edwards 1996; Welch 2005, 2015.

tices implies the imaginative construction of alternative space beyond any given physical location.[46]

Such religious space is potentially ubiquitous. However, it seems as if, historically, it was, in many periods and regions, the city that was the locality for the development of specifically religious spaces. I am not talking here of the elitist construction of 'civic' or 'polis religion', which is, above all (as I have shown in Chapter 2 above), a) focused on the city as a conceptual space and b) a framework of all significant ancient religious practices.[47]

Cities are particular spatial constellations. Social geographers and, especially, urban planners have highlighted the behavioural and cultural consequences (that is, the development of city attitudes as a 'way of life'), the material-spatial structures, and the environments of cities.[48] In contrast, urban sociologists (admittedly hardly ever looking back to the times before the modern period) emphasise 'lived' urban space as a praxeological and thus dialectical relation between urban space, on the one hand, and, on the other, the human agent who perceives and appropriates urban space on an individual basis.[49] Cities are defined as *phenomena of density* in at least two respects. 'Density' refers to spatial functionalisation and rationalisation and to the concentration of people and buildings at certain spots in broader landscapes, as well as to the social consequences of an 'extreme increase of contact zones'.[50] Cities, hence, are spatial forms of concentration with density playing the role of the 'organizational principle by which the urban world specifically arranges itself symbolically and materially'.[51] This density is the main spatial principle by reference to which urban social relations are explained, with the complexity of the relations being increased further by the impact of social and cultural diversity.

The increasing interplay between several networks and spaces accelerates communication processes and thereby facilitates an increasing potential for *creativity* and *innovation*.[52] On this view, cities afford a variety of choices and constraints and therefore appear as sites for the production of new norms,[53] as pla-

---

46 See Maier 2013.
47 Further critique in Rüpke 2012c.
48 Manderscheid 2004, 64–69; Held 2005; Sieverts 2001; for antiquity after Kolb 1984, e. g. Cunliffe, Osborne 2005; material overview: Hanson 2016.
49 Massey 1999.
50 Berking 2008, 19–23. Fundamental: Löw 2016 (German: Löw 2001).
51 Löw 2012, 306.
52 Blum 2003; Matthiesen 2008.
53 Blum 2003, Sassen 1991.

ces that facilitate opportunity, diversity, exchange, and tolerance,[54] and, at the same time, as places that facilitate anonymity, social segregation, and intolerance. Homogenisation and differentiation are coupled processes that are constantly, and inescapably, at work in urban settings.

6.4 Religious practices and the city

What role does the materiality of religion, as outlined in the first paragraph, play in such urban contexts? What does it mean to display and experience religion in urban space? These questions can be expanded upon and developed in very different directions. From the perspective of diversity in contemporary cities, Marian Burchardt and Stefan Höhne have offered,

> the observation that the key processes that organize difference in urban life (social polarization; ethnic and cultural segregation; functional differentiation; subjective fragmentation) are always articulated with particular spatial expressions and regimes. These spatializations of difference are facilitated, shaped, and, to some extent, produced by material infrastructural formations. Transport infrastructures – roads, sideways, railways, buses – connect certain urban populations and simultaneously disconnect others.[55]

Here, the emphasis is on material infrastructure, its ownership, planning, and governance. This is an important aspect of religious communication in cities as well but it goes far beyond the medial materiality of religion in the narrower sense developed above.

Kim Knott, Vokhard Krech, and Birgit Meyer have suggested a very different approach through their development of the concept of 'iconic religion'. They, too, start from urban diversity but 'focus on specific religious sites and buildings that have been vested with either a sacrosanct or, as we call it, an iconic character'.[56] Cities are seen as 'prime arenas in which the public presence of religion—through, for instance, modes of dress, buildings, sounds, rituals and performances—is displayed and discussed'.[57] 'Icons' are treated as expressions of cultural identities, for instance of migrants, to whom 'iconic aspirations' are even ascribed.[58] But, above all, their interest is in what I have differentiated in terms of 'sacralisation', 'sacredness', and 'tradition'. They suggest,

---

54 Watson 2006; Tonkiss 2005.
55 Burchardt, Höhne; Simone 2015.
56 Knott, Krech and Meyer 2016, 125.
57 Ibid.
58 Beekers and Tamimi Arab 2016, 142.

treating 'iconic religion' as a heuristic and analytical concept in the study of religion that helps us grasp the emergence of a sense of a sacred surplus. Religious icons are not essentially given—they are not revealed nor do they appear as an epiphany—but develop as authorised socio-cultural constructs. Once established, they foster religion in all its dimensions of experience, materiality, cognition, and action. We suggest that artificial and natural objects (or sets of objects) such as buildings, pictures, places, statues, pieces of clothing, texts, gestures, and bodily behaviour can be referred to as religious icons if they trigger religious communication, including action and experience that is attributed with religious meaning.[59]

Instead of conflating these aspects, I suggest that we should, rather, bring together a wide range of perspectives on urban religion in such a way that each can cast new light on the others. The urban element is brought into focus by employing the concepts of aspiration, imagination, and appropriation. These can be brought together with those perspectives, identified above, that focus on the material dimension of religion: relevance, sacralisation, sacredness, and tradition. Putting these together provides us with the following analytical grid:

a) *Urban Aspiration.* As I have pointed out at the beginning of the volume, religion enlarges the field of agency. By invoking in specific situations agents or authorities that are held to be divine, religious agents extend their possibilities for imagining and acting. This is important with regard to a specific factor in urbanisation processes that have been called 'urban aspirations' above. Again the term 'aspirations' is taken from studies of social mobility[60] to describe the driving motifs and attitudes of immigrants as well as inhabitants. It is aspirations of this sort that drew people towards life in cities and drove both the number of cities and the growth of the individual cities, despite the fact that rates of survival in such places in the pre-modern era were significantly below the rates enjoyed by people who lived in non-urban settings. Religious aspirations for a better life, whether in a moral sense or in the hope of healing, might drive people into cities if, for instance, living in a city was part and parcel of living near an important sanctuary or other aim of pilgrimage. More frequently, however, what drove immigration was the hope of becoming a full member of a city and, thus, of fully participating in urban life. Such an urban style of life would include making use of all the services offered in a city (such as the religious services mentioned above).[61] The potential to use these services drives people to aspire to religious participation or even something like membership

---

[59] Knott, Krech and Meyer 2016, 132.
[60] Appadurai 2004b; see above, 28.
[61] For the concept of urban services, see M. E. Smith et al. 2015.

in order to find a place and allies in the multitude of urban spaces and networks. In the long run, such an initially instrumental relationship to religious practices and institutions might become co-extensive with urbanity, the feeling that one is living an urban way of life.

b) *Spatial imagination of the city.*[62] Lefebvre's notion of 'lived' space points to the fact that agents do not merely 'conceive' of or 'perceive' urban space. Whereas the notion of perceived space identifies spatial practices that reproduce a spatial order, lived space rather highlights the human capacity to imagine space differently. Even beyond Lefebvre, Urciuoli has suggested that human agents develop alternative 'representations of space', new ways of using space, and, moreover, new forms of imagining spaces beyond their material substrates, such as fictional spaces, theoretical spaces, or dreamed spaces, as modelled by philosophers, poets, and religious specialists. The city, too, is 'an imaginative object', an assemblage of views that in turn conditions particular spatial practices.[63] This concept of spatial imagination elucidates key dynamics of the dialectic between urban space and religious practice. Since religion contributes to the imagining of space, it is worth considering religious practice from the perspective of it being spatial practice that does not just reproduce existing knowledge already attached to a location but actually creates new interpretations by drawing upon extraneous religious knowledge.[64] Religious groups adapt certain spaces to the requirements of their symbolic system, just as the symbolic system affords an alternative way of using these particular spaces. Each religious group and each individual 'lives' space differently, because they imagine space differently. In doing so, they produce new forms of spatial practices and leave new objects or monumental environments which may, in turn, be appropriated by others. Since urban space is characterised in terms of social and ethnic diversity, as well as by the density of its social relations, cities are viewed as 'melting pots' in which these images and their correlative practices are shared and enhanced. Although, according to urban sociologists, both diversity and density lead to interaction and exchange between different religious networks or groups and increase the personal scale of religious choices, all these practices and the correlated imaginaries are highly contested. The competing imaginaries, whether in narrative or dramatic form, images or architecture, evoke processes of grouping

---

[62] I am grateful to Emiliano Rubens Urciuoli for his reflections on this paragraph. For further details, see Urciuoli and Rüpke 2018.
[63] Blum 2003.
[64] See, for instance, Watson and Zanetti 2016; Rüpke 2017a.

and differentiation that involve the negotiation of spatial imagining and sometimes lead to open conflicts.[65]

c) *Appropriation (and production) of urban space*.[66] The term 'appropriation' as it is used here describes both a specific transformation process involving the relations between agents (humans and things) and also the transition of a thing from being an anonymous object to a personal good.[67] With regard to cultural interaction, this conception stands in contrast to diffusion theory in that it focuses not on the producer but on the acts and practices of the recipient or consumer. Appropriation articulates cultural, social, or aesthetic differences, in so far as the relation between the participants in a given transaction or process changes through the creation of new, contingent contexts and meanings. Successful appropriation emphasises the multidimensionality of things or spaces but is, in concrete situations, conditional upon the decisions and requirements of the recipients themselves,[68] approachable again by the concepts of agency and aspirations. 'Appropriation' thus navigates between individual and collective ascriptions of meaning. Such appropriation[69] can start from mere acquisition or acceptance, that is, from the circulation of objects or knowledge between individuals within, but also outside, cities, and can extend all the way from simple exchange practices through the re-use of individual items to plunder, theft, and wanton destruction. It can include objectification and denomination, that is monumentalisation and other types of enduring reification, practices of naming locations (with or without objects), the renaming of deities or the creation of new epithets, and the enumeration and description (especially ekphrasis) of locations or deities. More radical forms of appropriation imply modifications, including the conversion of space to religious, non-religious or other religious purposes and the re-utilisation of space after an interval. Finally, traditionalisation is also a form of appropriation, that is to say a form of modification that focuses on copying processes and practices of use and re-use in order to create 'authenticity'.

---

65 See Friedrichs, Dierckx and De Boyser 2012.
66 I am grateful to Asuman Lätzer-Lasar, for the work leading to this paragraph.
67 Fundamental: de Certeau 1984.
68 Carrier 1995.
69 Following Silverstone and Morley 1992 and H.-P. Hahn 2016.

6.5 Religion at the crossroads

The grid thus developed provides us with a lens through which to view an important segment of religious practices and their materiality in the urban fabric of Rome, the data for which are available through the recent studies of Michel Tarpin, Bert Lott, and Harriet Flower.[70] Apart from the veneration of ancestors (by the end of the Republican period more and more in the form of *di manes*), religious communication that addressed *lares* was probably the most widespread form of everyday religion, not only among householders in the city of Rome but also in the Roman world beyond.[71] As Harriet Flower has stressed, this was the basic form of religious communication for many people in ancient Italy. The conceptions entertained in the process were similarly vague to those surrounding the ancestors;[72] dual and plural forms happily alternated with the singular *lar*, which was frequently understood as something like a generic title in a complex ontology, situated somewhere among gods, nymphs, heroes, demons, *manes*, and *penates*. Plautus, in the prologue to his play *Aulularia* (a drama produced for urban stages) written at the turn of the 3rd century BCE, profiles a *lar familiaris* which, residing in the hearth, comports itself as the family's observant super-ego. Two hundred years later, Dionysus of Halicarnassus, a Greek visitor to the Roman metropolis, brought together the story of the procreative, that is, fathering actor in the hearth of the royal palace and the *lares Compitales* celebrated on Roman streets, understanding them as heroes who were bound to the home but venerated at the kerbside.[73] Similarities between *lares* and *di manes* were not coincidental; the two types may have been the result of the enforced separation of home and grave as locations for communication with the dead, which contributed to the formation of a specific urbanity and the systematisation of the urban centre as far back as the royal period.[74] It is clear that, in the later periods, the *lares* no longer retained any of the characteristics of ancestors.[75]

---

[70] Tarpin 2002; Lott 2004 and H. Flower 2017b.
[71] This is attested above all for Pompeii, where a particular style developed (see H. Flower 2017b).
[72] See Rüpke 2018d, 250–5 (German original Rüpke 2016c) for the following.
[73] Plautus, *Aulularia* pr.; Dionys of Halikarnassos, *Antiquities* 4.2 and 4.14.
[74] Rüpke 2018d, 250 with further references; see above all Samter 1901, 105–28, and Boehm 1927. Flower does not follow the antiquarian suggestions. It is the overwhelming importance of the cult of the dead that invites us to take up these ancient suggestions (the knowledge basis of which is unclear from a historico-critical perspective).
[75] Rightly stressed by H. Flower 2017b, 11.

It was important for religious actors that communication with a divine agency that was associated with a particular place and its inhabitants was capable of negotiating options within the group attached to the place and solidarity between its members.[76] In first-century Pompeii, communication of this sort allowed even slaves to engage with a whole *familia*-related cult in their workplace, the kitchen.[77] Here, mural painters chose to portray these place- and group-related deities as two identical, often dancing, youths.[78] This iconography (employed also in rooms outside of the kitchen) corresponded to the linguistic collective plural and excluded any reference of these figures to a particular person. An association with a sacrificing *togatus*, and often also the purple stripes (*clavi*) that appeared on the tunics of youths, do, however, create a reference to the generic homeowner in his quality as a Roman citizen and a freeborn (usually) man. A snake clarifies the local reference: it is this particular house that is portrayed here. Portraits of an altar represent the hearth in which Plautus' *lar* was concealed. This object (sometimes added in three-dimensional form to the image) was to be revered with dedications such as wreaths, incense, and wine, but served above all as a pictorial or architectural indicator of a place of religious communication. Thus, it allowed the imagining of a transcendent relationship in such a manner as was defined at the beginning of this chapter. Even inside the house, the two- or three-dimensional material presence of such 'altars' helped in continuously sacralising a space.

However, the spatial context of the kitchen was not a necessity, a set figurative element. In Pompeii, this image that articulated the particular character of the place might be erected on a wall or in a niche in some other location, often even in a monumental fashion. Likewise, the conceptualisation and representation of the divinities as *penates* (associating the house with the place of food storage) or *lares* seems to have been merely a question of taste, both in terms of language and of fact. If one favoured and addressed a given vague collection of superhuman actors that was not closely defined or individuated, one was likely to address them as *lares*; if one preferred to favour and address a self-assembled collection of individually recognisable divine actors in the form of a collection of objects that could, availability and means allowing, actually be

---

76 See e.g. the engagement in a tomb memorial *CIL* 6.10266 = *ILS* 3606 of one or several *decur(io/nes) Larum Volusianorum* (cf. 6.10267).
77 Myth: Dionys of Halikarnassos 4.2. Pompeii: Foss 1997, 217.
78 See H. Flower 2017b, 73, who suggests Pompeian practices in the streets as a model for the painting and admonishes caution against the assumption of a standard Roman practice.

held in the hand, a mix-your-own muesli of gods rather than porridge as mother makes it, then *penates* was the word.⁷⁹

Addressing the *lares* was not confined to the interior of houses. Places marked out for this purpose could also be found on the outside of house walls and, above all, at crossroads (*compita*, 'meeting places'). The *lares Compitales* were addressed and experienced by the majority of the population of the metropolis, for whom house walls, streets, and crossroads constituted not only scenes of fleeting passage but also their main living space. They belonged to these *vici* ('neighbourhoods', 'quarters', 'groups of houses') as intensively as to a family group. 'I am from the *vicus* NN', might have been, as Flower suggests, the basic form of self-definition in encounters.⁸⁰ The *vici* appeared accordingly in the guise of puppets or heads in the festival ritual of the Compitalia – as a representation of a group rather than as a device for a census.⁸¹

Appearing in the crossroad shrines in a material form gave expression to an important fulfilment of urban aspirations, that is, being present and visible in an urban neighbourhood. The differentiation between male and female, free and slave, encoded in putting up gendered puppets or balls (for slaves) during the festival of the Compitalia,⁸² and likewise the varying placement of such figures in front of doors or on the crossroads, demonstrates the categories of and limits to such a generalised 'urban' belonging. Such a practice of self-representation was by no means the result of chance. Culturally, the use of statuettes or heads had been an established practice for centuries; in the very moment of the festival of the Compitalia, the objects, made from wool,⁸³ must have referred to or were identical with objects purchased just a few days before, during or on the *Sigillaria*, the festival of earthen puppets at the end of the Saturnalia.⁸⁴ For a few days, these images were objects kept at home and thus appropriated, perhaps interacted with or ornamented, only to leave the home a short time later to represent their owners in the public space of the street. Hanging them up or allowing them to be hung up made for a very ephemeral presence only, but one that was periodically (annually) repeated. This was an enactment, not a basis for administration.

The importance of the rituals that articulated neighbourhood is stressed by their timing. We do not know the rules that underlay the 'announcement' of this

---

79 H. Flower 2017b, 48 and 50, instead, supposes a clear-cut differentiation.
80 Ibid., 194.
81 As suggested by Flambard 1981.
82 Paulus *ex Festo* p. 273.7–12 Lindsay; cf. H. Flower 2017b, 166.
83 Thus Paulus *ex Festo* p.108.27–30 Lindsay.
84 Macrobius, *Saturnalia* 1.10.24, see Wissowa 1912, 207, n. 7.

movable feast. For the 1st century BCE, the avoidance of a collision with *nundinae* (and the day following this market day) might have been one reason.⁸⁵ This would fit with the known Compitalia dates of the 1st of January 58 BCE and the 2nd of January 50 BCE, both of which followed two days after the *nundinae* (known to have fallen on the 1st of January 52 BCE), if we postulate a regular intercalation for the years in between, although such regularity is far from certain.⁸⁶ The third known example, the 29th of December 67 BCE, would have been a day before the *nundinae*. Given the slow rise of the *kalendae Ianuariae* as a major festival, the fixing of the Compitalia to the 3rd of January, a day after a *dies postriduanus* (the day after a festival, usually kept free from important business), would fit into this scheme.

Roman *vici* of the late Republican period formed aggregations of people living in *insulae*, blocks of houses, which were bounded by certain streets. These were distinct from the even smaller door-to-door neighbourhoods of an *angiportus*, a narrow street or even a cul-de-sac where neighbours were so closely packed that they could look across into each others' windows.⁸⁷ Instead, *vici* included open spaces that made them into small local markets, where itinerant merchants could offer incense, perfumes, spices, and even paper.⁸⁸ Here, those people of the urban *plebs*, people of both free and servile status, could be found who could easily be mobilised in order to form larger urban crowds, as Cicero's speech 'For his house' attests, thus underlining the aspirations of these individuals to participate in the city as a whole.

It was for these people that the *lares Compitales* were the equivalents of the divinities of home and family. Here, a more permanent material presence is visible. The small architecturally elaborated shrines, modelled against a wall or merely depicted, were appropriations of open spaces that gave a clear point of reference for their urban aspirations as members of a segmentary aggregation that was also found in rural forms.⁸⁹ It was this spatial focus that made the *vici* comparable to the neighbourhoods that were, in rural contexts, constituted by boundary stones or, again, by crossroad markers or *termini*. The latter were subjected to a slightly different ritual treatment on the day of the Terminalia (the 23rd of February). Identical – if we take Ovid's description as an anthropological report – in both contexts was both the coronation with flowers and the

---

85 Very cautious H. Flower 2017b, 162.
86 For the underlying mechanisms, see Rüpke 1995b, 574–5 and 582–8; the dates of Compitalia are given in H. Flower 2017b.
87 See Cicero, *Pro Milone* 64.
88 Horace, *Epistels* 1.2.269f.
89 See Tarpin 2002; also Flambard 1981.

use of cakes.⁹⁰ One thing that differed in rural contexts was the role of a shared building of a fire, brought along in pots carrying flames or embers from the local hearths, and the observation of the changing of the flames after individual libations or the throwing of agricultural products into the fire, all attributing agency to households as individual centres of production instead of to the individual members of a family.⁹¹ The sacrificing of a small animal, a lamb or a piglet (Ovid stresses the lack of narrow ritual rules), the sharing of food, and the singing of songs served to produce a sense of community here. It should be stressed that a ritual involving circulating (*lustratio*) around the plot of land or the neighbourhood is attested neither for the Terminalia nor for the Compitalia.⁹² In both cases, it is the *focus* offered by a *terminus* or *compitum*, and not the marking of clear spatial (and thus also personal) borderlines, that articulates the phenomenon of grouping that was at work. *Lustrationes* as rites of aggregation stressed contested or exceptional formations.⁹³ Interestingly enough, both festivals were clearly related to the year. While the Terminalia were held at the conclusion of the year, the Compitalia were at the beginning. Perhaps the latter even *marked* the beginning of the new year, at least prior to the Imperial age with its focus on the *kalendae-Ianuariae* celebrations. In the eyes of many participants, the Compitalia must have been not just a 'midwinter festival'⁹⁴ but the most important demarcation of a new year, since dating by reference to the month of January had already begun by the 14th of December: from this day onwards all the remaining days of the month were counted as 'X days before the kalends of January' (*ante diem ... kalendas Ianuarias*).

Some of the *vici* might have, now and then, achieved incipient or temporary forms of organisation that allowed the organising of 'Compitalian festivals', although not on a common day throughout the city and not celebrated everywhere. When Marcus Agrippa tackled the reorganisation of the water supply in 33 BCE, he had the *curules aediles* appoint an individual from every *vicus*.⁹⁵ There was evidently no uniform organisation on which he could easily fall back. Nevertheless, it was diffused publics of this size that had to be reached when distributing basic goods, such as wheat or water, and that had to be addressed when mobi-

---

90 Ovid, *Fasti* 2.641–678. Cakes at the Compitalia: Dionys of Halikarnassos, *Antiquities* 4.14.4.
91 See Macrobius, *Saturnalia* 1.7.35: *pro familiarium sospitate ... pro singulorum foribus*.
92 Postulated by Lott 2004, 36 and H. Flower 2017b, 317–8 (leaving open a conceptual connection to the Compitalia, but cf. the assertion at 170).
93 See Rüpke 1990, 144–6; similar D. Baudy 1998.
94 H. Flower 2017b, 162.
95 Frontinus, *Aqaueducts* 97.8.

lising grass-roots political support.⁹⁶ Caesar drew on lists of tenants, that is to say, on private, profit-driven accounting by the owner of a house, for the eminently political task of establishing the basis for attributing the right to receive free grain. That he opted for such a procedure excludes the existence of any similar lists administered by the people who were in charge of the *vici*, running it in an association-like manner.⁹⁷

Such public spaces could also be transformed by religious gestures and material objects. Marcus Marius Gratidianus, the nephew of C. Marius and the brother-in-law of M. Tullius Cicero (and also from Arpinum like the Tullii), reached the apogee of his political career when *vicatim*, 'quarterwise', statues were set up to him and honoured by incense and candles.⁹⁸ By means of religious practices, the political options of amorphous small local groups were made smellable and visible, day and night. Sacralisation and spatial appropriation went hand in hand in this process. Gratidianus did not survive for long, however. Evidently, his cult was not as sustainable as that of the *lares Compitales*.

It was in these hard economic, political, and religious facts, and in the age-old⁹⁹ soft organisational tissue of the *vici*, that Augustus decided to intervene on a broad scale in 7 BCE. It is not fully clear whether certain later datings by individual local traditions to one, two, or even five years earlier are mistakes, invented competitive claims, or reflections of preceding test cases,¹⁰⁰ but there should be no doubt that the intervention, and investment, by Augustus occurred only once. This may have been related to a kind of *vicennalia* celebrating the emperor's assumption of the name *Augustus* in 27 BCE, as Flower suggests, or it may, rather more probably, have been part of a sequence of administrative measures. The *vici* were ordered to put up four 'magistrates' who were allowed to wear the *toga praetexta*, the official dress of Roman magistrates, even if only in their own quarter and for certain specified occasions. They were also, according to Dio, even permitted the service of two lictors.¹⁰¹ This reform was, most likely, aimed at improving the basic functioning of the city. Indeed, both Suetonius and Dio discuss the institution in the context of fire-fighting.¹⁰² That the success

---

96 See Tarpin 2002, 94–5 for the evidence.
97 See H. Flower 2017b, 224 for a discussion of the general conditions.
98 Cicero, *On duties* 3.80; also Seneca, *De ira* 3.18.1; Pliny, *Natural history* 33.132; see Dyck 1996.
99 Stressed by Lott 2004, 81–3.
100 See Tarpin 2002, 137–140.
101 Cassius Dio 55.8.7.
102 Suetonius, *Augustus* 30.1; Cassius Dio 55.5.6.

of the endeavour was limited is demonstrated by Augustus' own neglect of the matter in his autobiographical *Res gestae*. As early as 6 BCE, Augustus turned his attention to the creation of a professional fire-fighting establishment, setting up the *cohortes vigilum* to keep the city safe.[103]

If fire-fighting was a basic necessity from an urbanistic point of view, in that the stopping of fires at an early, still locally confined, stage was essential for protecting the broader urban fabric (a conflagration that the practices of a Crassus risked in bargaining for his services with owners of *insulae* that were in flames),[104] religious practices were, similarly, the basic medium of public organisation. The institutionalisation of a team of four instead of the normal duo of powerful magistrates, and the method of selection by lot rather than vote, served to significantly reduce the political agency granted to the *vici* and its *magistri*. Against the background of the undeniable political potential of the quarter publics, religion seemed to promise a less dangerous and almost unavoidable basis for self-organisation and personal advancement.[105] Thus, a set of statues, probably interpreted as two Lares and a *genius Augusti* (like the Lares, a theologically under-defined figure) were offered as an incentive.[106] It was most likely the *curatores regionum* who handed out the statuettes to those quarters and their representatives who had managed to organise themselves and find persons who were willing and able to fulfil the duties and afford the costs of the purple-broidered *toga praetexta*. The figure of 265, later reported by Pliny for his own time,[107] was likely the result of a long process of urban growth and concomitant organisation rather than of a top-down cartographic approach. It is telling that this whole statuette business is totally absent from the literary sources despite dominating the monumental evidence: from the perspective of those locals who were rich enough to finance objects that were decorated by reliefs, it was these certainly mass-produced statuettes that created a direct link with Augustus.[108]

---

[103] On the remaining responsibilities of the *vicomagistri* see Lott 2004, 168 (on Suetonius, *Claudius* 18.1).
[104] On the practices of Crassus, see Plutarch, *Crassus* 2.3–4.
[105] On the latter, see Lott 2004, 176–7.
[106] See Niebling 1956; Flambard 1981, assuming an encompassing and direct intervention of the *princeps*. For a prosopography of *vicomagistri*, see Rüpke 2008.
[107] Pliny, *Natural History* 3.66; H. Flower 2017a, 118–9 (but see again the assumption of a regular process of addition, ibid., 119).
[108] These images are imaginations, not quasi-photographic representations of a reality as suggested by H. Flower 2017a, 345.

Apart from the offer of an 'official' iconography, attempts at the regulation of grass-roots (or better cobblestone-roots) urban religious practices were focused on temporal regulations, that is, on the extension onto these practices of the calendar as encoded in the *fasti*, the primary medium of complex urban religion.[109] At least in principle, the celebration of a neighbourly solidarity had to wait for a sign from the *praetor urbanus*, a requirement that was concealed behind the definition of the Compitalia as a movable, 'mandatable' feast (*feriae conceptivae*). Likewise, a biannual decoration of the shrines with flowers was ordered,[110] continuing the mostly vegetal cult of the Lares in the narrow spaces of the quarter's streets.[111] The dates were probably May the 1st and August the 1st, the latter inviting associations with the figure of Augustus.[112]

The material and epigraphic evidence allows us to see at a microscopic level some of the mechanisms of the aspirations, imaginations, and appropriations of those who took responsibility running this cult. It also allows us to see how they attributed relevance and created permanent sacred space beyond the seasonal ritual sacralisation. First, we must take care not to over-interpret the archaeological survival of handy pieces of marble in an urban centre that was continuously inhabited. However, we can at least presume that the use of the language of loyalty to the emperor depended on an atmosphere[113] that was seen as conducive for such expressions and, *vice versa*, one that allowed the patrons to figure more prominently in the open space thus appropriated. The chronology and the form of the material objects, and the texts presented thereon by early *magistri*, demonstrate that it took some time to identify with and visibly proffer the new roles that were made prominent and identifiable by the wearing of the *toga praetexta* on one's own body. In the oldest inscription of an altar dedicated to the Lares Augusti, the patrons refer to themselves only as *magistri qui k(alendis) Augustis primi magisterium inierunt*, 'officers, who entered their term of office on the 1st of August'.[114] Proper names are lacking. On another inscription, from the second year after the institutionalisation of a *vicus*,[115] the office is not numbered (as is the case later on) and nor is the name of the dedicating

---

109 See, in general, Rüpke 2011c and Ch. 7.3 below, 120–4.
110 Suetonius, *Augustus* 31.4.
111 See Dionys of Halikarnassos, *Antiquities* 4.14.3: honey-cakes.
112 For the dates, see H. Flower 2017a, 241–2.
113 For the concept see Anderson 2009.
114 *CIL* 6,445, Vatikanische Museen, Sala delle Muse 516a. Sources are compiled by Niebling 1956.
115 *CIL* 6,763, s. ibid., 324f.

magister vici given. Only in 2 BCE, the same year in which Augustus was given the title of 'father of the fatherland' (*pater patriae*), does a change become visible. More *vicomagistri*, probably perceiving the rise of comparable displays, seem to have seen their own office as a respected one and consequently began to point to their offices in acts of public giving and self-presentation. Apart from the large inscriptions of the Via Marmorata which feature lists of the wards' magistrates, at least two large altars with elaborate reliefs were dedicated in monumentalised Compitalia shrines.[116]

The complex of inscriptions at the Via Marmorata at the foot of the Aventine demonstrates how far such imaginations could go and how local action and urban framework intertwined.[117] The large-scale marble inscriptions were material elements that served no proper ritual function. Rather, they framed ritual action[118] by creating a lasting sense of sacredness that afforded appropriation by subsequent sets of magistrates, as we will see.

The slabs feature a central calendar, the only surviving copy of *fasti* that can be assigned to the context of the shrines of the quarters.[119] A graphic representation of the year, which accommodates multiple references to Imperial achievements, Roman history, and ongoing public ritual is incorporated into the local ritual space. Adjacent, a list of Roman magistrates is engraved.[120] The list starts in the year 43 BCE, thus dating from the first consulate of Octavian (later Augustus), naming C. Iulius and Q. Pedius. In contrast to all other comparable lists, the *consules ordinarii*, Hirtius and Pansa, both killed in action, are replaced by their successors for the rest of the year, the *consules suffecti*. Evidently, a very specific imagination of Roman history, which put the present *princeps* at the very beginning, was given articulation here.

Secondly, it was within such a framework that one annual college of *vicomagistri* went even further by drawing parallels between their own office and the senior Roman political position of the consulship. I have offered a detailed analysis of this list elsewhere.[121] Probably started, like the consular list, in 2 BCE the

---

116 *CIL* 6,33 f., further altars: *CIL* 6,761; 6,36809; 6,30957; 6,449; 6,2222; 6,452 and *AE* 1964,74. For statistics concerning the annual dedication and the importance of the year 2 BCE, see Lott 2004, 124.
117 See Lott 2004 for details.
118 Rüpke 2004. For the comparable case of the priesthood of the Arval brethren and their sanctuary outside of Rome that was filled with protocols of their meetings see in detail Scheid 1990b; Broise and Scheid 1993; edition: Scheid 1998.
119 See the discussions of all copies in Rüpke 1995b.
120 *Inscr. It.* 13.2.93.
121 Rüpke 1998b.

succession of office-holders soon becomes lacunose. The persons in charge between 3 and 5 CE did not bother with, or failed to finance, the entries. The *magistri anni duodecimi* left space for supplements but did not fill it themselves. The diminishing space available forced the office-holders in 14 CE to make use of this supplemental space. Some years later, a renewed attempt to continue the list was probably instigated by somebody who had the opportunity to place his own name on the prestigious surface for a second time. The prestige involved was, evidently, a matter of opinion. Not everybody was interested in seeing his name appear on a lengthy list among dozens of other names and nor was everybody so literate as to value the urban practice of ubiquitous inscriptions. However, in some places, at least, internal recording was attributed a certain value. Several *vici* numbered their annual sets of office-holders and thus created an era of their own. The *vicus* Iovis Fagutalis was using such an era still in the early 2nd century CE, even if perhaps on a faulty base, arriving at 12 BCE as a founding date.[122] The sheer, even if minimal, divergence of the eras attests to an interest not only in a space but also in a time frame of its own, a temporal-spatiality creating a local system of reference, carefully related to the central and founding figure of Augustus – just as many later European cities claimed to be founded by Caesar. Yet a *vicus* was not an independent city but, rather, a small neighbourhood in the dense urban fabric of the overlapping spaces of *regiones*, ethnic or economic zones, social or craft-related areas.

What was the attractiveness of this everyday and at the same time precarious space? This question introduces my third observation. If we reflect upon the basic conditions of social life in the *vici* in terms of the juridical status and liberty of individuals, their relative powerlessness or power, their wealth and health, then the description of the atmosphere of the Compitalia given by Dionysios of Halicarnassos is extremely telling:

> This festival the Romans still continued to celebrate even in my day in the most solemn and sumptuous manner a few days after the Saturnalia, calling it the *Compitalia*, after the streets … And they still observe the ancient custom in connexion with those sacrifices, propitiating the heroes by the ministry of their servants, and during these days removing every badge of their servitude, in order that the slaves, being softened by this instance of humanity, which has something great and solemn about it, may make themselves more agreeable to their masters and be less sensible of the severity of their condition.[123]

---

[122] *ILS* 3620 = *CIL* 6.452, see above.
[123] Dionys of Halikarnassos, *Antiquities* 4.14.4., trsl. Ernest Cary, Loeb, 1978.

It is in the context of such religious practices that urban aspirations, the hope associated with life in the city as articulated by the nearly unanimous voice of ancient elites, are articulated in the form of material objects and are, at least temporarily, realised. It is the bodies above all – freed from attributes of servitude in the case of slaves, decorated certainly in other cases – that are on display in a space that is not just locally 'public' but also potentially open to a wider urban audience.

6.6 Conclusion: Religion and public space

Throughout the preceding chapters I have, in the first place, drawn attention to a concept of religion that focuses on religious practices as communication and on the notion of agency ascribed to the addressees of such communication. My secondary interest has been in the way in which these notions are reflected in a usually enlarged, or at least modified, agency for the instigators of these communications and their audiences. On this basis, I have suggested that we should deal with the material objects involved in religious display under the headings of relevance, sacralisation, sacredness, and traditionality. In an even more fundamental reflection on the spatial dimension of these very practices, I have argued for a focus on the materiality of religion in urban space and suggested that we should approach the practices involved by looking at them from the perspectives of aspirations, imagination, and appropriation. I will now briefly discuss an aspect of urban space that has not been made explicit so far, that is the 'public' character of some such space.

Public space is not simply given. Certainly, at Rome, in a systematic of categories of property, public space is space that is neither private property nor the property of the gods.[124] The public character in this sense is mappable. It is enforced, for instance, when permanent private usage that has encroached on such a space in the form of constructions is sanctioned because it is diminishes or blocks the original function of the space. The lament about the incorporation of sacred groves into private villas[125] or the frequent evidence of buildings blocking roads, creating dead ends and thus newly bounded spaces for private or group activities, attest to the seriousness of the problem and the precarious char-

---

124 Gaius, *Institutions* 2.2–9, especially 9.
125 See Cancik 1985.

acter of even this hard form of public space. Even the Digests are reluctant when it comes to ordering the removal of such encroaching structures.[126]

Apart from the specific juridical form of property rights, directly applicable only within the city of Rome proper, the 'public' character of space is performed by means of the presence of magistrates, for instance, or is marked out by monuments which recall memories that are ideally universally shared, or by statues (*loco dato decreto decurionum*) and buildings. The former means is temporary and ephemeral, the latter permanent but not exclusive. The route of the Roman triumph, more and more permanently marked by triumphal arches, might be used, at least partly, by other processions on other days featuring other protagonists, such as people venerating Isis or Cybele, for example. The ancient actors' opportunities for stressing the 'public' character of space, that is the belonging of space to a shared commonwealth extending beyond the property and influence zones of families and clans – the *res publica*, if we cleave to our Roman example –, were fairly limited. Public assemblies were only occasional events and were always highly regulated; few places were both suitable and allocated for such purpose while any spontaneous assembly in such a place was viewed with great suspicion. Interaction with the people was a matter of concern and strict regulation. Religious practices provided useful ways of mediating this interaction, from the performance of triumphs to funeral cortèges, from sacrificial processions to *pompae circenses*, and from the founding of temples to the annual recall of their 'birth days' (*dies natalis templi*). If religion was on display in public, we should not forget that in many instances it was above all the public that was on display in religion. Religious and urban motifs reciprocally and inseparably shaped one another.

---

126 See e.g. *Digests* 43.8.17.

7 Urban resilience and religion: Attaching time to place

7.1 Resilience and religion

In the previous chapter, the focus was on the materiality of the shaping of urban space by religious practices and the approach pursued there questioned the value of the common dichotomy of 'public and private space' for understanding the complex arrangements in Rome's neighbourhoods. The present chapter will also address the notion of intermediate space, but the focus here is less on the materiality of the religious appropriation of the one or other space and more on the conceptual relationships an individual might have to his or her own city in its spatial entirety. The specific character of such relationships is captured by the notion of 'resilience', thus relating the analysis of spatial religious practices to very different debates about the long-term history of cities. Again, the example at the core of my discussion is the ancient city of Rome, and, again, the conclusions I draw should not be understood as being limited to that city alone.

Across its three millennia of (urban) history, Rome has survived a number of disasters on greater or smaller scales. The decision of a group of people to remain at the same place after a disaster was not, however, something that was simply assumed and nor was it the only possibility available. According to its late Republican self-image, Roman historiography began with the Gallic invasion in 390/387 BCE, starting afresh after the loss of all earlier written sources (supposing that any such sources had existed). A pivotal part of the story of this catastrophe in the Roman imagination was the subsequent discussion about whether the destroyed city should be rebuilt or whether the population and its gods should instead be uprooted and moved to nearby Veii.[1] 800 years later, following the massive destruction and depopulation suffered by the city in 410 CE (by 500 CE, Rome's population had shrunk from the million inhabitants of the early 1st century CE to somewhere around 100,000), the Christian bishop Augustine could look across the Mediterranean from Hippo Regius and ridicule Rome's pagan forebears from the perspective of an even longer chronological framework. Rome itself, according to the city's history as presented, and often memorised, in the form of Vergil's epic narrative the *Aeneid*, was the successor to Troy, or even more precise, a city that was moved to its current location from

---

[1] Livy 5.52; Cancik 1995; Orlin 2011. The chapter has been published in a slightly different form in *Numen* 67 (2020), copyright Brill, Leiden.

its former place at Troy. How, Augustine asked, could the gods of Rome's founders, who had been unable to defend their home city of Troy against the devastation of its besiegers (traditionally dated to 1184/83 BCE), possibly be relied upon to protect Rome itself against another invading army now?[2] Accordingly, neither the gods nor the city[3] figure in his subsequent reflections on how to deal with the experience of plunder and rape on a massive scale, an experience that the Romans had, themselves inflicted many times on others.[4] For Augustine, what mattered when dealing with his contemporary experiences was to focus on a different god and the citizens who worshipped him. Augustine – a distant observer rather than an inhabitant of Rome, it is important to note – no longer believed in the eternity of the city but instead in the religion that was (little could he know) to go on to survive the massive de-urbanisation of the Latin West as a whole. This Latin Christianity would, ironically, later engage in a critical dialectic with the idea of a city that would shape the re-urbanization of the same area from the high middle ages onwards.

The recent apogee of urbanisation might encourage one to think that cities are the most successful and eternal form of human settlement.[5] Whether planetary urbanisation[6] is reversible or not remains to be seen. Nevertheless, it is clear that individual cities can fail. Indeed, many, if not most, historical cities are no longer inhabited. Historical and modern cities instantiate a precarious way of living together and it is against this background that the question of urban resilience has been raised. Examining the nature of urban resilience provides a way of throwing new light onto the practices and materialities of urban religions and offers another way of seeing religion as being shaped by, and as shaping, urbanity. This chapter will explore the reciprocal formation of religion and urbanity and will argue that certain religious practices in ancient Rome can be seen as stemming from and helping to constitute a pro-urban attitude and an urbanity that is aware of the need for resilience and for the development of strategies that can help to maintain it.

The 'resilient city' has been defined as one that is 'able to survive a traumatic blow to its physical infrastructure, its economy, or its social fabric'.[7] The concept

---

[2] Augustine, *De civitate dei* 1.1–7.
[3] On Augustine's shift from a spatial city to a personal community, from *urbs* to *civitas*, see Urciuoli 2019.
[4] Augustine, *De civitate dei* 1.5. See, in general, Chesnut 1992; Alroth and Scheffer 2009; Schildgen 2012. For the later memory of Rome due to Augustine, see Vessey 2012.
[5] Entertained, for example, by Campanella and Godschalk 2015, 219.
[6] Diagnosed by Brenner and Schmid 2014, for example.
[7] Campanella and Godschalk 2015, 218.

of resilience is rather recent. In the 1980s and 1990s, the notion was typically applied to materials and only occasionally also to societies, economies, and – most seriously – to individuals in the context of their physical or mental health. Before 2008/09, the notion was very rarely employed in discussions of cities and when it was used it appeared primarily in the context of the risks posed by climate change. However, in the decade that followed, 'resilience' developed into a key category in discussions of city management and urban planning,[8] modifying and partly replacing concepts such as sustainability and stability. In a similar way, resilience had some years earlier found its way into archaeology, where its relevance was fuelled by far-reaching hypotheses about the 'collapse of societies'.[9] Archaeological 'resilience theory' focuses on understanding ecosystems in terms of an adaptive cycle, positing episodic change, discontinuities, multiple equilibria, and the loss of resilience by clinging to fixed rules.[10] In these adaptive cycles, phases of remembering and returning to earlier stages are as common as revolutionary large-scale jumps to entirely new stages and the precarious ecological balances that follow from them.[11]

Such complex reasoning has done little to inform the rather loose use of the term across other disciplines and especially in Religious Studies. Resilience is usually seen as a property of social and material constellations. With regard to the ancient Mediterranean, resilience has been attributed not only to cities such as Constantinople (and to its mighty fortifications and impressive infrastructure, in particular), but also to literary genres and specific deities.[12] Religion, too, has been mentioned in passing by scholars who use the term loosely, with resilience being said to increase through the provision of an element of additional social interaction that is not strictly necessary but brings people together in a positive atmosphere. This addition to the mundane necessities of life helps bolster a society's resilience.[13] However, when considering such loose applications of the language of resilience, it is necessary to keep in mind the warning that resilience has 'to be viewed as a process and not as a fixed attribute of an individual', as Rutter puts it. His stress is on the psychological dimension of resilience and on the explicit reflection of individuals on the conditions required

---

8 Important advances or stock-tacking in Bohle 2008; Shaw and Sharma 2011; J. L. Baker 2012; Ungar 2012; Eraydin 2013.
9 Diamond 2005.
10 Redman 2005, 72.
11 Ibid., 73.
12 E.g. van Nuffelen 2012: 124 (Constantinople); D. R. Woolf 2014 (encyclopedia); Lenski 2016: 62 (late ancient sun god).
13 Hodder 2012, 200 with 188.

for retaining or regaining stability.¹⁴ In this chapter, I have chosen to treat resilience for the period between the Gallic sack of 390/387 BCE and the Germanic raid in 410 CE not as a quality belonging either to people or to social formations that can then be identified directly in such people or groups of people but, rather, as a process the existence of which can only be inferred after the fact from a history of successfully surviving physical (for instance, the flooding of Rome) and political or military traumata.

The ultimate theoretical object examined in this book is religion rather than resilience, so resilience is deployed here as a lens through which we can view religion anew. Resilience, in the sense outlined above, cannot simply be 'discovered' in religious practices, objects, or discourses. However, starting from the notion of resilience allows us to see such practices or ideas, and the ways in which they were current in Rome, from a new perspective. Which of them, we might ask, can reasonably be interpreted as reflecting upon resilience and strategies to foster resilience in the face of potential disaster? Which of them might have helped different actors to cope with a present disaster? And what was cherished afterwards as a consequence of that experience? In asking such questions we are clearly dealing with changing constellations of perceived threats, actual disasters, and memories thereof, as well as with religious practices, religious discourses, and religious material objects related to these threats, disasters, and memories.

As elsewhere in this volume, 'religious practices' are conceived of as practices related to communication with divine agents. While some of these practices might have clear material elements, even discursive practices, such as narrating the past or commenting upon ritual or speculating about divine addressees, are – whenever they are accessible to historical research – present in some mediatised form. As such, they are not only attestations of acts of communication but also material objects themselves, present in urban spaces behind the walls of libraries, for instance, or highly visible in the form of inscriptions on the walls of temples or on private or communal buildings. As 'material religion', they constitute parts of the processes by which space was claimed or marked, instigating memories or further action while indicating social, juridical, or political status, as well as religious competence.¹⁵ These media were 'sensational forms'¹⁶ that at the same time afforded experiences and expressed experiences,

---

14 Rutter 2012, 335, drawing on earlier discussions, see e.g. Rutter 1987. Cf. Redman 2005, 74, demanding the separation of 'cause from effect'.
15 Concisely Knott, Krech and Meyer 2016; B. Meyer 2008; Droogan 2013; Morgan 2015.
16 B. Meyer 2008, 129.

being formed by their users and yet also, in the long run, forming those who partook. From this perspective, the religion with which we are concerned is, again, religion 'in the making' rather than a stable resource.[17] It is changing practices and changing material forms, not fixed symbols and unchanging beliefs, that form part of the complex process that I have described as resilience above.

7.2 A wealth of practices

This chapter's interest is not in resilience and religion as such but in *urban* resilience and the religious institutions (in the widest possible sense) that might reflect and help foster it. The first type of ritual practices we can consider served as a routine strategy in the Republican period for dealing with natural or social irregularities that ranged from small-scale incidents, such as the birth of a two-headed calf, to fully-fledged disasters, such as the occurrence of a devastating earthquake. By referring to them as 'prodigies', these irregularities could be understood as signs of a divine wrath that could be propitiated by such ritual means as processions or sacrifices (*procuratio prodigiorum*).[18] This way of dealing with a small- or large-scale disaster communicated that the event was singular, that it required both redress (drowning the animal or rebuilding destroyed houses) and a ritual response, but also, most importantly, that it had no further long-term consequences. Peace with the gods could be reconstituted by taking the appropriate actions. This instrument for managing irregularities was used frequently at Rome between the 3rd and the 1st centuries BCE, allowing the Senate (and the *haruspices*, priestly experts drawn from a group of Etruscan noblemen) to deal with events not only at Rome but also, increasingly, in many other central Italian locations.[19] By the beginning of the Imperial period, these practices had fallen out of fashion, even if the institutions themselves continued on into late antiquity. When, in the second of his programmatic opening 'songs', the poet Horace reflected upon the thunderstorms, torrential rains, and floods that threatened the city of Rome over a period culminating, perhaps, in 27 BCE, the religious solution he imagined was not some ritual to the disarm the danger but, rather, the veritable epiphany of a god, realised in the figure of 'Caesar' (i.e. Augustus).[20] If the first twenty lines of this Augustan poem focus on Jupiter's

---

17 See above, 8.
18 Cf. e.g. Cicero, *De haruspicum responsu* 63; Livy 7.6.7.
19 See Ruoff-Väänänen 1972; MacBain 1982; Rosenberger 1998, 2005, 2010.
20 Horace, *Carmina* 1.2. On the discussion, see Nisbet and Hubbard 1970, 17–19; Cairns 1971, 70–76.

'threatening of the city' (*terruit urbem*, 1.2.4), the thirty-two lines that follow are much more concerned with the 'fall of the Empire' (*ruentis / imperi rebus*, l. 25–6). Consequently, the solution offered is adapted to the latter threat rather than the former.

Using the notion of resilience as a lens, further emic discourses come into focus that reflect on such processes and on strategies for the fostering of resilience. Other roughly contemporary institutions and beliefs were much more intensively concerned with threats to and the survival of the city of Rome than is Horace's song. Phenomenologically, these institutions and beliefs directly address and make themes of the eternity of the city and its divine resources, such as the fire of Vesta, the twelve heavenly shields of Mars (*ancilia*), or the hidden name of Rome.[21] These topics seem to have been particularly stressed in our sources from the late Republican and early Augustan periods, even if a focus on place was present in Roman mythology long before.[22] This points to their role in contemporary reflections on resilience in the face of aggravated social differentiation, mass immigration, and the threat of Italian and civil war. My interpretation of these institutions and beliefs through the lens of resilience is supported by the fact that many of these discourses, which may have already existed in restricted small circles of what we might call 'intellectuals', were taken up (and thus preserved) in late antique texts that post-dated the collapse of Rome and reflected on the reasons for its failure.

When drawing on the few sources that have survived by chance or through quotation, it is difficult to identify any correlations between these ideas and actual practices, or with the history of urban threats and disasters. However, in the case of the city of Rome, at least, one group of material (and frequently also monumental) objects has survived that allows us to follow developments and identify agents over a longer period. These are the Roman calendars (*fasti*). I will argue that the development of certain features of this (cross-culturally exceptional, even if it seems 'natural' to heirs of this specific form) material presence and graphic representation of a solar year and its rituals offer us a glimpse into different forms of practices that might have reflected and helped foster urban resilience. In the material form of the *fasti* and related media, memories of disasters (the massive loss of men in battle; pestilences; floods) and of the overcoming of disasters, that is, resilience, are dated to specific days within the year and are, thus, fixed and communicated. This is not an inherent feature of just any calendar but, rather, a specific characteristic of the Republican

---

21 See, for example, Groß 1935; Rüpke 1990; Ferri 2010b, 2010a.
22 Thus Beard, North and Price 1998, 1.174.

Roman development of the calendar and its medial representation, as will be shown in some detail in the two subsequent sections of this chapter.[23] In the *fasti*, the city is stressed in its structural and historical continuity.

In their material form – large-scale texts that are organised in columns and appear on walls or slabs – the *fasti* left room for additions in blank spaces within their frame or on the margins of the frame. The setting up of *fasti* and the modification of the text within or around the monthly columns allowed their authors to express through these objects their take on the city. I will demonstrate that the actual copies of the Roman calendar surviving from the early Imperial period – the only period that allows us to trace the actual distribution of *fasti* among the populace, due to the contemporary fashion of inscribing the calendars on stone – indicate not only an interest in the history of the city and in the city as political agent but also an interest in the very places that made up Rome. Such a widespread attachment to and engagement with the actual space of the city went beyond the acceptance and assertion of Rome as a symbol of power and empire. For historians of religion, calendars have been tied either to concepts of sacred time or to cultural or national identities. In both cases, arguments have typically relied on an abstract temporal scheme extracted from, or elaborated on the basis of, historical sources. However, by examining these calendars through the lens of resilience, and by setting them in the perspective of material religion, what comes into focus is the very *creating* of urban space by ancient inhabitants of the city through the erecting of large calendar ensembles and through the references in the texts of the calendars themselves to other detailed urban spaces.

7.3 Historical background: The first written Roman calendar

Like many ancient calendars, the Roman calendar, as codified in the unique form of the *fasti*, both documented and regulated local practices. The history of the calendar has been analysed in detail elsewhere,[24] so I will focus here on what is relevant from the perspective of 'urbanised religion'. The written calendar, invented in its graphical form (*fasti*) and its chronological mechanisms around 300 BCE, attributed specific legal characteristics to nearly every day. In the extant *fasti*, days are identified as *fas* or *nefas* (with various distinctions of detail), 'right' or 'not right'. This categorisation allowed or excluded specific important steps in the legal process on these days. On days labelled *nefas*, the

---

23 For the history of the Roman *fasti* in general, see Rüpke 1995b, 2006 h, 2011c.
24 Rüpke 2011c, 2012a, 2012b.

formulaic presentation of a case before the magistrate who opened and classified lawsuits was prohibited, thus closing off the 'interface' between state apparatus and citizen, the process of 'dealing with the people'. We also find *dies comitiales*, 'days for the people's political assemblies' (*comitia*). When compared with the *dies fasti*, the *dies comitiales* also functioned as days on which cases could be initiated before the *praetor*, but they differed from *dies fasti* in the fact that on days marked with a *C* the magistrates could also summon *comitia*, decision-making people's assemblies.[25] This minor differentiation was a result of developments at the beginning of the 3rd century BCE (287 BCE). Prior to this point, the central criterion by which one day was distinguished from another was the question of whether it was *fas* or not. From this point onwards, these calendars were called *fasti*.[26]

The function of the calendar was essentially to provide a sacral evaluation of non-sacral actions. The *pontifices* may have been custodians of the law but neither meetings of the people nor the legal procedures that were allowed or forbidden by the quality of the days were sacral acts. The quality of being *nefas* did not arise from the appearance of portents or from an error in performing cult activities. *Nefas* simply denoted a time-limited prohibition on certain formal actions, albeit a prohibition that was fenced in by sacral sanctions. The days were presented in columns for every month, starting from the K(alendae) Ian(uariae), the 1st of January. The days of a month were marked by letters of a recurrent week of eight days from A to H (with Z in the place of the later letter G, not yet part of the Latin alphabet). In addition to these, abbreviations of festival names – Agon(alia), Kar(mentalia), Lup(ercalia) – and of the former lunar phases of the moon – Non(ae), 'the ninth day before full moon', and Eid(us), 'full moon' – appeared in the graphical representation. Calendars of the early 3rd century BCE must have looked something like the graph on the next page.

The religious character of the *nefas* designation becomes explicit only in a sanction called *piaculum* in Latin, identifying an 'offence that needed to be dealt with ritually'. This sanction is added in the abbreviated form *NP* in the entries for the small number of days that were considered as full-scale holidays, *feriae*. The term used for the qualification of the more general *nefas* ('not allowed') character of these festive days applied equally to the offence – it *is* a *piaculum* – and to the 'expiatory offering' to which it gave rise – one has to *perform* a *piaculum*. Given the etymology from *pius* and *-culum*, we can understand

---

25 Varro, *On Latin language*. 6.29–32; Ovid, *Fasti* 1.45–54; *Inscr. It.* 13.2 (= Degrassi 1963), 111–3 (*fast. Praen.*); Macrobius, *Saturnalia* 1.16.13–14.
26 Paulus *ex Festo* p. 78.4–5 L.

the term as describing the instrument that restores the condition of being a pious person after the offence.[27]

A K IAN F	F K FEB N	B K MAR NP	A K APR F ...		Z K INT F
B F	Z N	C F	B F		H F
C F	H N	D F	C F		A F
D F	A N	E F	D F		B F
		F F			
		Z F			
E NON F	B NON N	H NON F	E NON N		C NON F
F F	C N	A F	F N		D F
Z F	D N	B F	Z N		E F
H F	E N	C F	H N		F F
A ACON	F N	D F	A N		Z F
B EN	Z N	E F	B N		H F
C KAR NP	H N	F EN	C N		A F
D F	A N	Z EQVIR	D N		B F
E EID NP	B EID NP	H EID NP	E EID NP		C EID NP
F EN	C N	A F	F N		D F
Z KAR NP	D LVP NP	B LIB NP	Z FOR NP		E F
H F	E EN	C F	H N		F F
A F	F QVIR NP	D QVIN BP	A N		Z F
B F	Z F	E F	B N		H F
C F	H F	F F	C CER NP		A F
D F	A F	Z N	D N		B F
E F	B FERA F	H TVB NP	E PARIL NP		C F
F F	C F	A QRCF	F N		D F
Z F	D TERM NP	B F	Z VIN NP		E RECIF N
H F	E RECIF N	C F	H F		F F
A F	F F	D F	A ROB NP		Z EN
B F	Z EN	E F	B F		H EQVI NP
C F	H EQVI NP	F F	C F		A F
D F	A F	Z F	D F		
E F		H F	E F		

Mid-Republican *fasti* (reconstruction)

---

27 Tromp 1921, 26–30.

The impact of the publication of this sort of list as a calendar around 300 BCE lay in its application of the calendar to the regulation of political activity. As in the case of the so-called Law of the Twelve Tables, we may assume that this codification – the collection and publication of norms – did not provide any revolutionary new design but rather confirmed an existing situation, perhaps with some minor corrective and systematising touches. In this instance, the major concern was the practical question concerning the days on which voting assemblies (*comitia*) could be held, and those on which they could not. The grounds and motives for this focus may have been many and various; the definition of genuinely sacrosanct days (the *feriae*, marked *NP*) on the basis of strict sacral law sat alongside vaguer religious considerations according to which particular cult events were accompanied by the barring of voting assemblies (that is to say, the absence of *dies comitiales*) but without the corresponding imposition of an actual religious sanction (*piaculum*) on offenders. The systematisation made in the course of the publication was also guided by very different considerations of a 'profane' nature, such as the creating of vacations for the magistrates by limiting when assemblies could be held or lawsuits opened. Simply marking days with an *N* without adding the religious sanction of *P(iaculum)* might have been the instrument used in these more mundane cases, although we simply do not know what this norm's binding power was.

Evidently, the *fasti* were the product of a line of reasoning that solved such problems not by the application of an all-pervading and consistent ratio but, rather, by the creative blurring of distinctions. The instigators of the publication marked all days as *nefas* or *fas:* this measure, which went far beyond what was justifiable on the grounds of sacral regulations or ritual practices, was legitimised by a religious code, a sacral terminology. Is it possible that it was the many distinctions the calendar introduced that led to its enduring success? The more detailed the norms it provided were, the more it supported the idea that there was a specific religious knowledge held by the pontiffs who were presented as the authors of the calendar. The extreme abbreviations of the *fasti* support this idea of an implied expert knowledge accessible, initially at least, only to the priests. The intended reader of the *fasti* must have already had an oral familiarity with the contents of this 'text', something that would not be expected of those who played no part in determining its contents. Seen from this point of view, the *fasti* must have initially been no more than an aid to memory for those who were already familiar with the contents of the calendar in detail.

Despite the in-built suggestion that the pontiffs were the privileged holders of important information, the publication of this supposed specialised knowledge in a written form was directed *against* the arbitrary exercise of pontifical power. By making the calendar public and accessible to all, the political leverage enjoyed by the pontiffs through their opportunities to intervene in the political timetable was restricted. At the same time, the laying down of the authority of the traditional rules in writing also served to safeguard that authority. For the *pontifices*, then, the development of the *fasti* may have been a double-edged sword with both welcome and unwelcome aspects.²⁸

The regulations implied in the calendar focused on urban institutions. One can plausibly argue that by limiting interactions between magistrates and the people – that is, by limiting the interactions that were the very essence of the *res publica* – these norms took account of the need of the political elite to engage in the agricultural activities that underpinned their elevated status. The elites required time to physically or conceptually cross the line that divided the city from the countryside, time to also act in their capacity as owners of plots of agricultural land, coordinating and supervising the tenants and workers who carried out the work in their fields. This land ownership was the economic foundation on which their status stood, providing them with the wealth and flexibility that allowed them to carry out their duties as senators and *magis*trates (those who were or had 'more'). The urban resilience produced by the authors of such a calendar had been identified by them as restricting urban interaction and potential conflicts to certain periods.

For more than a century we know nothing about the calendar's medial presence. It must have been accessible, perhaps inscribed on wooden or bronze plates somewhere, but it was not prominently visible in the city. In this early form, the calendar served to produce processes rather than places.

7.4 Adding urban history

A century later, Rome's growing power had survived Hannibal's assault during the Second Punic War (218–201 BCE). In the years that followed, the calendar became increasingly visible in the cityscape as it began to reflect thinking about what we would today call resilience. In the year 189 BCE, Marcus Fulvius Nobilior was consul, serving alongside one Manlius Vulso, and assumed the military command in Rome's conflict in Greece with the Aetolian League.²⁹ According to tradition, the most important event of this campaign was the siege and capture of the city of Ambracia, north of the Gulf of Actium. It was the booty taken from this city in particular that the victor displayed in his triumphal

---

28 See Rüpke 2012e.
29 Livy 37.50; 38.1–11.

procession on his return in 187.³⁰ Fulvius not only brought the treasures home but eventually put a roof over their heads, transforming a temple of Hercules into a 'museum' in the real sense of the term: a *Museion*, the first sanctuary of the Muses to be constructed in Rome.³¹ Most likely some time after 179 BCE, ³² Fulvius undertook the extension of an existing temple of Hercules, probably that of Hercules Custos, and provided it with a columned hall in which he installed the statues of the nine Muses taken from Ambracia. Hercules became *Hercules Musarum*, 'Hercules of the Muses'. This name and role signified the divine protection of the cultural production referred to by the concept of the nine Muses, a sphere of activity that was of increasing importance for the self-image of parts, at least, of the Roman elite.

Fulvius installed a calendar or *fasti* in the enlarged temple. This took the form of a wall-painting³³ and was added to the interior of an area that was set aside as a meeting place for poets and furnished with many statues or paintings from Greece. The few surviving quotations from this calendar suggest that the inscribed dedication may have run as follows:

> The consul and censor M. Fulvius Nobilior set up this calendar after the Aetolian War: Romulus had named ten months, the first in honour of his father and foremother; after having divided the people into older and younger, to ensure that one part should defend the state by advice, the other by arms, he named the third and fourth in honour of both parts; the rest was named by numbers. Numa named the two added from Janus and the Gods of the Netherworld. A thirteenth month was intercalated according to a law by the consul Acilius in the year 562.³⁴

By this time, Rome was a rapidly expanding Imperialist polity. Nevertheless, Roman armies were not always successful and nor had the dramatic threats posed to the capital just a generation earlier (*Hannibal ante portas*) been forgotten. The time-honoured names of the months were now given an interpretation that linked them to the most important military divisions of Roman society, to the founder of Rome, and to the gods of beginnings and ends.

The author of the painted text added a second element, perhaps to the right and left of the calendar proper. This was a list of the annual consuls and occasional censors, perhaps going back as far as the Gallic sack of Rome (390/387 BCE), an event construed as a second (or even a third) birth of the city. Such

---

30 Livy 39.5.14 ff.
31 Pape 1975; Östenberg 2009a.
32 Rüpke 2011c, 88–90 and the critical evaluation of the dating by Feeney 2007a, 143 n. 24.
33 Rüpke 2011c, 93–95.
34 Ibid., 95; Rüpke 2006b (also for the following).

a list must have been extracted and reworked from then-current historical narratives. Historiography was still, at that time, a literary genre exclusively written in Greek. The extract was thus a historiographical feat in its own right and probably the basis for Ennius' epic *Annales*, the first Latin annalistic account of Rome's history. Indeed, it is Ennius who was most likely the actual author of Fulvius' *fasti*.[35]

The combination of the first two elements of the calendar suggests the meaning of a third, a signal innovation of Fulvius' mural. In several spaces that had previously been left blank in the parallel columns of days, Fulvius' calendar recorded *dies natales templorum*, the foundation days of urban temples. The construction of temples financed by war booty had proliferated at Rome in the half-century that followed the end of the war against Hannibal. These were donations to the gods that had given victory to the Romans in many of the individual battles of the war: they commemorated military success – and success only. Temple foundations rank highly in the list of those historical events that were retained in the most precise manner in Rome's ritually performed memory.[36] In these temples, the Romans could see history in tangible terms, having already seen, heard, and smelled the victories in the lavish processions of triumphs and games. The recording of these important foundations was a novel calendrical feature that coincided with Fulvius' installation of his public calendar. It was paralleled by brief references to the games: the *Loed(i) Apol(lini)* on the 13th of July and *(Ludi) M(agni)* held from the 8th to the 10th of September. Just as in the case of the foundation of temples, the context for these games was the investment of booty and the commemoration of victories.

Fulvius' ensemble was clearly an attempt at constructing a history of continuity and self-identity despite the intermittent disasters that Rome had endured. Condensing and unifying into a coherent list the most important and eponymous agents of Roman history, the consuls whose names were used to date events during their year of office, underlined a sense of orderliness that cut across all vicissitudes of the past. At the same time, the graphic ensemble presented an open-ended history, as it left empty space for the annual addition of consular names henceforth. There is good reason to assume that the list of temples in the painted calendar on the wall of the *Museion* was complete up to the date of its production and that it was intended that additions referring to temples built after that date would be made, and the calendar thus kept up to date, just as in the case of the consular lists. Despite the fact that Rome's mili-

---

[35] Rüpke 2006e.
[36] Rüpke 2006b.

tary actions had been performed on a grand Mediterranean scale, of which the very building that housed the calendar was itself a primary witness, the documentary or narrative focus in the text was on the city itself. A reflection of the very fact of and the future need for urban resilience seems to have buttressed the whole project and its reinterpretation of political and religious practices. These were presented as a subject suitable for re-narration in other genres as well; the location of the calendar in a space in which writers would assemble was guaranteed to generate further impact.

If the wall calendar is concurrent with, and thus contextualised by, the beginning of the Latin historiography that reflected upon the necessity of resilience and provided a reassuringly repetitive narrative, it also stands at the beginning of an even more space-related material practice: the erecting of similar calendars elsewhere in the city and in other places in the Roman world. The oldest surviving copy is the so-called *Fasti Antiates maiores* of c. 70 BCE, found at Antium. The presence of *fasti* in a Latin town, even one that is close to Rome, strongly suggests that copies would have existed elsewhere in Rome itself at an earlier date. With a width of some 4 meters and a height of 1.16 meters (if we accept these *fasti* as representative), they created a space of their own, not for ritual but, rather, for practices of reading and (probably) re-narrating the successes of Roman history, a practice that might have contributed to Rome's resilience during the period in which civil war blighted the Roman polity. The *fasti* reflected and multiplied those religious practices referred to in the calendar, the monthly calling out of festivals, the formal taking up of office by the consuls, the many local celebrations of temple dedications throughout the year. At the same time, the rituals themselves were now performed within interpretive frameworks suggested by the *fasti*, such as the long-term continuity of the city represented by the list of annual consuls.

7.5 Negative history

Religious practices (and the calendrical representation of such practices) that reflected and fostered urban resilience in segments of Roman society, and in places both within and beyond the city, did more than just stress the fitness of Rome's basic social structures, its long list of military victories, and the continuous lines of successive consuls. A closer look at the text of the *fasti* reveals the inclusion of an exceptional date in the list, establishing a subsequent practice. This is the *dies Alliensis*, the commemoration on the 18th of July, on which date the Romans had suffered a defeat by the Gauls at the river Allia in 390/387 BCE.[37] This inclusion set a precedent for the subsequent practice of creating 'unlucky days' (*dies atri*), the negative character of which became apparent only over the course of time, mostly by the repetition of military defeats on the same dates.

At issue was not just the preservation of the memory of a historical event. Granted, the *dies Alliensis* points to the historically exceptional dimension of the Gallic attack in 390/387 BCE, a day that appears to have become established in tradition by the beginning of the 2nd century BCE.[38] More important, however, was the accumulation of unlucky events on the same date. While the Augustan poet Ovid associated the well-known annihilation of three hundred and six Fabians on the Cremera with the 13th of February,[39] others placed the event on the same day as the Gallic catastrophe commemorated by the *dies Alliensis*.[40] A peculiarly Roman point of view developed in this context which found its evidence for the unluckiness of a day in the confirmation of that day's bad luck by repeated events: in the case of the 11th of June, for instance, Ovid notes two defeats on the same day of the year in his commentary on the calendar.[41] A tendency towards accumulation and intensification can also be found when it comes to military success, as in his notes on the 1st and 2nd of August.[42]

The mechanism at work here, clearly attested for the middle of the 2nd century BCE by the historiographer Cassius Hemina and intensified in the Augustan period, *pace* Ovid, is the conjunction of a new event with an infelicitous element that has been repeated frequently enough to become an *omen*. Infelicitous elements of this type were not solely restricted to dates. The necessary basis for an *omen* could be provided even by the more contingent details of political decision-making processes. In the historiographic narrative of the year 310 BCE, for instance, the beginning of polling on a new law by the Faucian *curia* was deemed a bad omen. The reason given is that this was the very same *curia*

---

[37] *Inscriptiones Italiae* 13.2.189 (F. Amit.); *Inscr. It.* 13.2.15 (F. Ant. mai.); see also Lucan 7.409 and Ovid, *Remedia amoris* 219f. Verrius Flaccus provides considerable detail in Gellius 5.17.2; Livy 6.1.1–2 and Macrobius, *Saturnalia* 1.16.21–24.

[38] Radke 1990a, 43. See Cassius Hemina (c. mid-2nd cent. BCE) fr. 20 Peter = 23 Beck/Walter = Macrobius, *Saturnalia* 1.16.21–24; Lucan 7.409: *Et damnata diu Romanis Allia fastis*. On antique speculations on the date and the following day, cf. G. J. Baudy 1991, especially 16–18 (for critique, see Rüpke 1994c).

[39] Ovid, *Fasti* 2.193–6.

[40] *Inscr. It.* 13.2.208 (F. Ant. min.). Cf. Livy 6.1.11 f. and Plutarch, *Life of Camillus* 19.1; Macr. *Sat.* 1.16.23.

[41] Ovid, *Fasti* 6.563–8.

[42] Horace, *Carmen* 4.14.34–38; *Inscr. It.* 13.2.191 (F. Amit. 2nd August); Plutarch, *Caesar* 56 (Liberalia).

that had also led the ballot in the year of the Gallic conquest of Rome and the defeat at the Caudine Forks. This tradition was stressed by Livy, who combined it with Licinius Macer's account, citing the catastrophe on the Cremera and thus adding to this *curia*'s discredit.[43]

In order to come to terms with extraordinary negative events, the contingency of the disaster is interpreted in intangible terms that become inevitable in hindsight. This is evident in nearly all contemporary sources that date Nero's great fire of Rome in CE 64 to the 19th of July, a date which is said to coincide with the Gallic capture and burning of Rome centuries earlier.[44] This sort of discourse tries to come to terms with a present disaster by understanding it as an event that does not cast doubt on one's own or one's city's abilities in principle and that does not, thus, forestall the possibility of a better future. The literary sources allow us to see how strategies for fostering urban resilience were developed when dealing with catastrophes against a backdrop of traditions about the auspicious or inauspicious quality of dates. Military catastrophes, for example, were frequently explained by reference to the quality of the date on which they took place, thus removing the blame from the commanding general or the military forces. Repetition of similar catastrophes in future could be avoided by not giving battle on the same ill-starred dates. The Roman example shows just one of the many ways in which cultural and religious resources could be deployed in processes that supported resilience. In certain other societies, for example in ancient China,[45] the execution of a defeated general (and maybe even some of his troops as well) served to remove fear and foster resilience.

The Roman way of dealing with historical dates gave a certain air of empiricism to those involved and implied a rational ability to control the actions and effects to which an individual or state was subject. Nevertheless, when set alongside Babylonian attempts to provide thorough and systematic documentation of *omina*, the Roman approach can seem somewhat haphazard and opportunistic. The documents on ritual dealings with prodigies, forewarnings or indications of disaster which were written down in the *commentarii* of the supreme pontiffs, noted only very few 'defeats'. With the exception of the *dies Alliensis*, the dates of military defeats were not noted in the calendars; only very few traditions concerning dates were actually tangible.[46] Others, as Ovid demonstrated, were

---

43 Livy 9.38.15–16. The dates in question are 477, 387, 321, and – the event cited – 310 BCE.
44 Tacitus. *Annals* 15.41.2.
45 Franke 1970.
46 E.g. the defeat in the battle of Lake Trasimene, dated the 22nd of June (Ovid, *Fasti* 6.763–8), and the battle of Cannae, dated the 2nd of August (Gellius 5.17.5). See also Grafton and Swerdlow 1988.

open to re-interpretation. The Roman aristocracy developed no ritual nor other institutional form of documentation of defeat.[47] What we can detect instead is a broader discourse about the existence of a whole group of unlucky days, the *dies postriduani*, the days following Kalends, Nones, and Ides, which were typically marked as *fas* in the *fasti*. This discourse suggests a necessary frequency in the production of days of bad luck in order to generate a substantial list of calendar dates that were thus qualified. This is not confirmed by the *fasti*. There is a disproportion between historical events of this type and their selective representation in the calendar: within the whole calendar year only one single fixed date, the Battle of the Allia, was actually noted in the *fasti*. Furthermore this very date – not one but three days after the Ides – fitted so uncomfortably with the speculation on *dies postriduani* that it had to be reconceptualised as being intimately linked not to the actual battle but to a sacrifice two days before, thus producing an event that actually fell on the day directly after the Ides (as the theory of the *dies postriduani* would demand).[48] Talking about further cases without being able to specify these events demonstrates that the ancient writers fully endorsed the claim that all these were 'empirical facts', without being able to reconcile them with substantiated historical argument.[49]

This specifically Roman form of fostering resilience by taming and overcoming negative events through the use of the calendar had an application that went beyond cases of military defeat. In 30 BCE, in the aftermath of the victory at Actium and Antony's final defeat at Alexandria, the Senate declared his birthday, the 14th of January,[50] *dies vitiosus*.[51] The intention behind this act is perfectly clear: the day was qualified as a 'day of misfortune' by the Senate's declaration. This is our first (and last) encounter with the concept of *dies vitiosus* and no sources survive to tell us anything about what consequences were implied by the term. In augural discourses, *vitium* denoted an error that rendered an act, such as an election, invalid.[52] But we know of no augural rule that would provide justification for applying such a categorisation to a day. *Dies vitiandi*, 'days to be avoided', are mentioned on one occasion only, in a letter written by Cicero in

---

47 Rosenstein 1990. For the lack of monuments in the city: Östenberg 2009b, 258.
48 See Livy 6.1.11–22 and Gellius 5.17.1–2.
49 Cf. Plutarch's critique in *Roman questions* 25.
50 For the pre-Julian nonexistence of *a. d. XIX Kal. Febr.* (as the month of January had only 29 days and the date for the day after the Ides would have been *XVII K. Febr.*), see Suerbaum 1980; problematical: Feeney 2007a, 155–6. The dating points to a tradition of defining important dates also by distance *back* to Ides.
51 Cassius Dio 51.19.3; *Inscr. It.* 13.2.72.
52 Linderski 1986, 2159. 2162–77.

55 BCE. Significantly, according to this source it was the people's tribunes who let it be known by way of rumour that they wished to use this particular obstructive measure against the political moves of other magistrates. Unfortunately, we are left in ignorance as to what the designation meant in practice. Indeed, it is even unclear as to whether Cicero is really using the term here in its technical sense.[53] In the absence of a clear understanding of the words on the part of the augurs, the senators may have had the *dies religiosi* in mind, days upon which religiously motivated prudence (*religio*) advised refraining as far as possible not only from sacral actions but also from any other kind of activity. *Dies religiosi* as such were not indicated in the calendar either, although they were determined on its basis.

Despite its well-defined motivation, the initiative taken by the senators was something entirely new. Drawing for aid upon the augural metaphor of *vitium*, for the purpose of labelling a single day they created and introduced a new category of days into the *fasti*.[54] This development could only have been instituted in a legitimate fashion by the pontiffs or the Senate in the form of a declaration of *religio*. Examining these events through the lens of urban resilience draws attention to the threats to Rome implied here. Three stand out. Caesar was already credited with reflections on transferring the base for future operations in the East to Alexandria or Ilium[55] – contemporaries had no concept of 'shifting the capital'. Antonius was likewise seen as shifting weight to Alexandria, as when he held his triumph in 34 in the Egyptian city instead of Rome.[56] Oracles in Greek language, collected in the *Sibylline Oracles* (not to be confused with the collection of Sibylline books hosted at Rome), went much further and announced the destruction of Rome.[57] In the face of such perspectives, avoiding the birthday of a potential threat may well have reflected thinking about resilience. For the more than three centuries prior to Constantine the Great's foundation of Constantinople, the idea of establishing 'another Rome' remained a mere object of imagination. Challenges such as floods or fires were much more present.[58]

---

53 Cicero, *Letters to Atticus* 4.9.1.
54 Attested in, for instance, the Fasti Maffeiani, *Inscr. It.* 13.2.72: *ex s(enatus) c(onsulto)*.
55 Suetonius, *Iulius* 79.4.
56 Plutarch, *Antonius* 50.6–7; Cassius Dio 49.40.3.
57 *Oracula Sibyllina* 3, see (Schäfer 2006): 192–4.
58 See Aldrete 2018, 365–371.

7.6 Urban practices in the face of empire building

My reading of the representation of religious practices and discourses in the calendar as a reflection of discourses on and processes of resilience conflicts with a recent approach taken by Sacha Stern. In his comparative study of ancient calendars, Stern argues that the rationalisation of the calendar in the form of solar – instead of luni-solar – years at Rome (as earlier in Egypt and Persia) primarily served the purposes of Imperial administration and identity.[59] It was not only provincial administrators and generals who could abstract a calendar *system*, a 'Julian year', from the material representations of this calendar. A solar year of 365 days and just one intercalary day could also be used by provincials throughout the empire and could be translated into local calendars, as we will see below. If Stern is correct, then the *fasti* might not have served simply as an instrument of daily business but also as tools by which Imperial resilience (to use my terminological framework) was fostered. I will argue that the contents and materiality of the Roman *fasti* provide good reasons to doubt the assumption of an Imperial re-orientation of the calendar. I will then go on to offer some brief reflections on early Imperial practices that fostered *urban* resilience.

We can begin by making a fundamental observation. The urban calendar that was developed from the 3rd century BCE onwards was never used as an actual instrument for the coordination of cult. For a city of the size that Rome had reached by the early 2nd century BCE, this was simply not an option. The graphic layout and material form of the *fasti* spread beyond the city. Only half of the more than fifty *fasti*, or rather fragments of *fasti*, discovered so far have been found in or can be attributed to the city of Rome, with most of the others belonging to Latium, Etruria, and Campania. The southernmost example, the Fasti Tauromenitani, was found at Tauromenium, an Augustan colony in Sicily, and is the only copy yet to be discovered outside the Italian peninsula. Such a limited geographical distribution hardly supports the idea that the *fasti* had a function in the broader Imperial administration.

The geographical limitation to the city of Rome and a few middle Italian townships orientating themselves towards Rome[60] reflects the urban form and contents of the *fasti*. All the dates in our surviving copies refer to urban events, from the types of dates we have considered so far to traditional and new Imperial festivals. The same holds true for a new type of holidays that appear from the

---

59 S. Stern 2012; contrasting are separatist agendas, which promoted different calendar systems, luni-solar above all: S. Stern 2001, 2002; S. Stern and Burnett 2014 (Jews); Daviet 1965; Olmsted 1992; Monard 1999; Gschaid 2003 (Gaul).
60 For the mechanisms, see Rüpke 1995a.

Augustan period onwards. These were established by the senate in order to commemorate Imperial victories, important births, or the accession of emperors to power (*feriae ex senatus consulto, quod eo die* …, 'holidays by decree of the Senate, because on that day …'). These new holidays referred to urban Roman rituals, even if the days to which they were assigned were more and more also taken as points of reference for the days on which courts were closed and legal settlements prohibited in the provinces.[61] With the unique exception of a single date in the exceptional and learned *fasti* from Praeneste,[62] local dates were never integrated into the graphical form of the *fasti*. The list of festivals reproduced on the *fasti* from Urbinum Metaurense in northern Umbria was identical to the list on the *fasti* from Venusia. At the same time, we can exclude the possibility that any obscure Italian *municipia* reproduced the cultic variety of the capital by means of ritual performances. The dates of the festivals reproduced everywhere were urban dates specific to the locale of the city of Rome. The *fasti* did not even incorporate local Italian festivals or cultic events in the other cities in which they were displayed. Can the concept of resilience help us to understand this fact?

As far as the length of the year and the structure of just twelve months adding up to 365 days is concerned, the technical shape of the Julian calendar was an instrument suitable for an empire.[63] Judging from dated inscriptions,[64] the technical system of the Roman calendar was adopted in Italy and in many parts of the Western Empire in particular during the 2nd and 3rd centuries CE. It has reasonably been assumed that the Feriale Duranum, a list of festivals and commemorative dates translated into performances at the Mesopotamian garrison of Dura Europos in the second quarter of the 3rd century, represents an Augustan order that obliged the whole military apparatus to perform standard rituals on a number of days that were celebrated at Rome in quite different ways.[65] This was exceptional and restricted to military units. Only a few festivals seem to have been celebrated on a larger geographical scale outside of Rome. The local festival list wrongly called Fasti Guidizzolenses[66] attests as local festivals the Apollinaria (13th of July), Neptunalia (23rd of July), Diana (Ides of Au-

---

61 See Rüpke 2017c.
62 The local character of the *dies vern(arum)* of the Fasti Antiates ministrorum is doubtful, see Rüpke 1995b, 144f.
63 Thus S. Stern 2012.
64 Herz 1975.
65 Edition and commentary: Fink, Hoey and Snyder 1940; on the local context, see Dirven 1999; Kaizer 2006, 2015, 2016.
66 *Inscr. It.* 13,2, p. 235.

gust), Volkanalia (23rd of August), the Septimontium (11th of December), the Saturnalia (17th of December), and then a festival for the Gallic deity Epona (18th of December) on the very next day. The positions of the festivals within the calendar year and the names of the festivals were derived from the calendar of the capital, even if it is hard to imagine a festival as firmly related to the topography of Rome as was the Septimontium (the 'feast of the seven hills') being performed in Northern Italy or Carthage. Even here, school holidays in North Africa were, according to Tertullian, mandated on the same occasion.[67] As in the case of the Saturnalia and the New Year festivals of the 1st of January, which were observed throughout the Mediterranean world, the quality of general merry-making would be a central factor for the proliferation and diffusion of Roman dates. The personnel of the provincial governor, merchants, and soldiers might have been responsible for the spread of an attractive custom in an anarchic process of copying, modifying, and rejecting.[68]

The only regulations strictly related to the calendar are found formulated in a city law at the end of the 1st century CE. These calendrical regulations, found among the norms concerning juridical procedure from the Spanish city of Irni (*lex Irnitana*), codified provisions forbidding any juridical or legal activity on the days of Imperial festivals, which were not fixed by local political bodies but evidently taken from the calendar of Rome itself. The sanction was harsh: even if all parties consented to deal with their legal problem on such a day, the results would not be valid (c. 92). Social consensus, the need to demonstrate loyalty, and the potentially positive sanction of a recourse to the central, i.e. Imperial, authority by the defeated party would be the most effective guarantees for the universal observation of central calendrical decisions in a still thinly bureaucratised Imperial state in all its precarious statehood. To conclude, the provinces of the Imperium Romanum drew on the figure of the Augustus (or later Augusti) while central Italian townships drew on the nearby mega-city as resources for the creation of order and politico-religious identities. The former was materialised in statues (and occasionally temples) while the latter took the form of monumental stone calendars. Both were precarious. The statues of emperors served as the primary points of attack on the Imperial order in several instances; the practice of putting up marble calendars had been discontinued already by the end of the Claudian period, as they did not convincingly serve their purpose. Permanent corrections, suppressions of old dates, and the addition of new dates did partner well with the carving letters into marble. Technically, the abstract struc-

---

67 Tertullian, *On idolatry* 10.3.
68 For a more detailed analysis, see Rüpke 2007e.

ture of the Roman calendar was a 'second' calendar throughout the empire, just as Latin was a second (and sometime third) language in many places. For the functioning of the empire and the cooperation of Imperial and regional communication it was sufficient to have tools for translating between different regional calendars and also between dates formulated in terms of local and Imperial calendars. Such synopses were produced on the basis of parchment or papyrus forms of the *fasti*. Stone calendars were not necessary.

7.7 Attachment to urban places

The emperor did not plant marble calendars, neither in the provinces nor at Rome itself. So how can the bottom-up practices of setting up *fasti* and modifying their text have been a strategy to foster urban resilience? It is important to view this phenomenon from below, from the perspective of the unknown individuals or traceable colleges that erected calendars, as the challenges to the urban ways of life in the city of Rome were obviously different in different social strata. Massive urban growth may have appeared as a marker of the strength of the city when observed from a bird's eye view but it also placed great stress on the urban fabric at the same time.[69] The danger of 'provincialising Rome', de-centering the Imperial capital, was countered by the major topographical refashioning of the city, as exemplified by the construction of the new *fora*, vast monumentalised urban spaces, of Caesar and Augustus, and by the restoration of various older buildings by their generals.[70] Incipient intellectual reflection on urban space, exemplified by figures such as Varro and Vitruvius, is observable around the middle of the 1st century BCE.[71] But what about the social strata below?

The medium of the *fasti* did not allow the mapping of all the religious locations and practices mentioned. It did, however, allow the location of spaces in a piecemeal fashion. Across the (mostly fragmentary) copies, precise locations are given for many temples, although these are highly selective in each individual copy and never aim at completeness. The 2nd century BCE Fulvio-Ennian calendar as represented by the 1st century copy of the Fasti Antiates maiores seems not to be have been very interested in the actual location of rituals and, hence, temples. Judging on the basis of the fragmentary text, many 'opportunities' to locate the deities 'to whom on these days temples were dedicated' were left out. Only five

---

69 Overview: Claridge 2018.
70 Gros 1976.
71 See Rüpke 2017a.

locations are preserved: two deities named Juno are differentiated by the location *in Arce* and *in Campo* (1st of June and 23rd of December); Concordia and Vediovis are located *in Capitolio* (5th of February and 7th of March); Maia is venerated *supra Comitium* (23rd of August). All of these instances refer to busy and central dates – Kalends, Nones, and major festivals – or to multiple dedications on the 23rd day of *Sextilis* and *December*. If we look for differences between this Republican tradition and the Augustan and Tiberian calendars, one important distinction is found in the presence of topographical indications in the latter group and their relative absence in the former. Distinctions can also be made when comparing individual specimens of Augustan-Tiberian calendars in terms of the presence or absence of specific topographical indications, which may appear in one calendar but not the other. This is true for calendars used both inside and just outside of Rome. I will start with those from inside Rome, treating them in chronological order.

The small surviving fragments of the *fasti* put up for the priesthood of the Arval Brethren on the outskirts of Rome (the Fasti fratrum Arvalium), probably the earliest calendar in Italy that is both monumental and made from marble,[72] preserve locations for eighteen different temples and their rituals. The large size and the general degree of detail (both did not always go together)[73] are certainly a major factor accounting for the preservation of so many locations. Nevertheless, a clear deviance from the earlier tradition remains. Another early calendar, the Fasti Pinciani from about 20 BCE, is much smaller but is similarly detailed with regard to place-names.[74] The Fasti Maffeiani, probably still Augustan and nearly completely known from surviving early sketches, offers a different selection, providing detailed information for only a small set of dates. For such dates in this particular calendar, a place-name is nearly always given.[75] It is possible that the selection of festivals included here might be due to their relevance for the members of the college that was responsible for this particular calendar, all of whom were less than elite.[76] The suburban Fasti viae Ardeatinae, dating from perhaps as early as the first years of the 1st century CE, only survives in fragmentary form but these fragments preserve mentions of a number of locations that find no parallel elsewhere.[77] The same holds true on a much larger scale for the so-called Fasti Vallenses, one of the largest marble calendars. At the

---

72 Rüpke 1995b, 178–9.
73 Ibid., 167.
74 Ibid., 52. See *Inscr. It.* 13.2.47–48.
75 *Inscr. It.* 13.2.72–83.
76 Rüpke 1995b, 54–5.
77 Ibid., 65, see *Inscr. It.* 13.2.154–5.

same time, this calendar often does *not* mention any second or further temple dedication named by other calendars for the same day;[78] locations were important for this monumental text but details far less so. Further unparalleled locations can be found on a small surviving fragment of the undoubtedly large Fasti viae Principe Amedeo[79] and on the similarly sized Fasti Farnesiani, although the latter's urban provenance is not certain.[80] Unlike the Fasti Vallenses, the Fasti viae dei Serpenti, inscribed sometime after 23 CE, errs on the side of the inclusion of detail, even going so far as to risk obscuring the overall graphic layout.[81] An otherwise unrecorded location is again given by the Fasti viae Graziosa, a calendar that is again of Tiberian date.[82] It is interesting to note that the only calendar that might have been related to a public temple, the Fasti aedis Concordiae, includes almost no details at all. This strongly supports the idea that the inclusion of locations was not a formal requirement demanded by some authority.

It bears repeating that details and detailed locations are also given in examples of calendars found outside of Rome, even if the interest in antiquarian details and the history of the Roman calendar displayed in the exceptional Fasti Praenestini need not imply a similar interest in other urban locales.[83] Nevertheless, it is interesting to see in this period that not only that old rival of Rome, Praeneste, but also a mountain village like Allifae might choose to invest in a thoroughly detailed calendar.[84] From these data and dates we can infer the development of strategies to foster urban resilience as well as thinking about urban resilience in broader terms. By giving them a monumental stone form, calendars were also given high and continuous visibility. These were not, however, a geographically isolated phenomenon but must rather be seen as part of a larger suburban and regional network, which shared an interest in knowing about and referring to details of an urban topography articulated in religious practices.

Putting up calendars could serve another purpose, which also had a relevance for resilience. In the form of large steles or tables, the calendar copies were themselves instrumental in creating specific spaces, in appropriating urban space, and in attaching individuals to this space. The pieces were massive and often, as we have seen, made of marble, a material that had only recently

---

78 Ibid., 69–70, see *Inscr. It.* 13.2.147–151.
79 Ibid., 76, see *Inscr. It.* 13.2.223.
80 Ibid., 76–7, see *Inscr. It.* 13.2.225.
81 Ibid., 81–82; Degrassi 1963, 193 and 381–2.
82 Rüpke 1995b, 83–4.
83 See *Inscr. It.* 13.2.111–140.
84 On the *Fasti Allifani*, Rüpke 1995b, 129–30.

been made available in larger quantities from Luni but which still exceptional and very decorative.[85] They were highly visible due to their areas of two to four square meters, with widths that were typically two metres or more. In those cases where clear indications of the original settings are available – as in the Fasti fratrum Arvalium, Maffeiani, Esquilini, magistrorum vici, and Vallenses – colleges or broader associations are identifiable as initiators. The re-use of marble plates from the calendars for burial purposes might suggest suburban locations in some cases but need not exclude the possibility that at least some of the calendars were originally erected at the meeting places of organised groups.

It is not a given that Roman voluntary associations[86] invested in an exclusively owned meeting space in order to meet just a few times per year.[87] In Greek cities, many groups used meeting spaces that were part of sanctuaries and were equipped with cooking facilities and further infrastructure for accommodating the assemblies of such associations.[88] Other groups, however, used architecture or large-scale inscriptions of their own to lay claim to a place.[89] Roman calendars articulated a similar tradition of claiming and appropriating place in a particular way.[90] On the one hand, *fasti* were instrumental in the making of exclusive space, set apart for a group to cultivate its own identity. The sublime genre and the spectacular size and degree of detail of the newly fashionable media of inscriptions on stone produced a highly visible focus and conveyed the idea of high status.[91] Each calendar had a headline running above the monthly columns which would typically refer to the association and those of its 'magistrates' who had taken the initiative and provided the necessary funds. Lists of the annually elected magistrates would sometimes also be added, paralleling rather than replacing the lists of consuls which were a frequent part of the ensemble. Such an arrangement afforded space for the self-representation of future

---

85 Schneider 1999, 929. See also Bradley 2006.
86 For the concept, see Kloppenborg and Wilson 1996; Bendlin 2011a; Eckhardt and Leonhard 2018.
87 For the architecture of such *scholae*, see Bollmann 1998 and (with occasionally problematic classifications and generalisations) Nielsen 2014.
88 See Steinhauer 2014.
89 Harland 2003.
90 For the conceptual pair of space and place, see Tuan 1977.
91 See Rüpke 2003b.

magistrates and thus offered an incentive for those who filled such offices to do so in an active manner.[92]

At the same time, the very material object and its contents referred to a larger spatial and social framework, namely urban space and the city's history. The ensemble of calendar, list of consuls, headline, and list of the association's magistrates mutually integrated these spatial and temporal imaginaries. They thus both reflected earlier strategies for fostering urban resilience and manifested another such strategy themselves. They also paralleled the effects, if not the intentions, of ritual performances – processions for instance – organised by closed groups but performed in public space, insofar as monumental calendars like rituals provided for high visibility and claimed urban space. Again, this is not an inherent quality of the *fasti* but a consequence of the spatial and medial practices in which they were employed in the city (and suburbs) of Rome. One of the very few calendars that can be attributed to a private setting, the Fasti viae Graziosa, was a painting on the wall of an interior room. This calendar was spatially associated with large paintings showing scenes from the Odyssey on other walls.[93] Here, the religious, historical, and spatial references of the *fasti* seem to be commodified and to signal the cultural distinction of the house owner in a manner similar to the spatial and historical references to Greek mythology and Eastern Mediterranean space. Thus, it is not the existence of calendars *per se*, but the practice of associations putting up and modifying calendars in topographical detail, that seems to point to a process of awareness of the need for resilience and of strategies for fostering it. This awareness had built up in the period that followed Rome's civil wars and its subsequent focus on the building of an empire, which demanded a moving emperor rather than a stable capital.

7.8 Spatial interest and attachment to place in contemporary literary texts

It is interesting to note that it was the spatial dimension of the *fasti* that was central to Ovid's poetic commentary on the calendar in the late Augustan period. Ovid exploits urban space, terrestrial as well as celestial, the window onto the

---

92 See the analysis in Rüpke 1998b. The epigraphic ensemble of the Fasti magistrorum vici demonstrates that this offer was not always taken up, the affordance of an empty space for inscribing one's own names could be neglected.
93 On the latter, see Woermann 1876; Biering 1995.

sky as seen from the city, to move through time by taking up the historical associations of places. His text may not be representative of associations and reflections of his contemporaries. Nevertheless, from its success at Rome we can infer that the view it presents was shared in at least some respects by many others.

In generic terms, Ovid's *Libri fastorum* is a commentary on the calendar.[94] In other, less talented, hands it might well have been just as bureaucratic as Augustus' nearly contemporary *Res gestae*, consisting of lists upon lists and unleavened by anything more worthy of literary esteem. The *fasti* proper, however, already had a second level of meaning beyond their apparent list-like character. They did not name temples as part of an urban landscape but, rather, as places of religious action, that is, of rituals performed on the 'birthdays' of the sanctuaries. In inscribing reminders of such actions, the calendars served as an instrument of urban memory. In his commentary, Ovid takes this dynamic even further. Just as he represents himself as an author who is busy with his writing tablets in his own home when the god Janus enters (*fast.* 1.93 f.), so his text presents people and gods respectively going from and coming to places: *eunt, itur*, 'one goes', the imperative *i* (1.249), 'go!', joined by *venire* etc. appear frequently in the work. By adding stories about stars and including the morning and evening risings and settings – an inclusion he explicitly justifies (1.295–310) despite these features not being registered in the *fasti* –, he deliberately increases the dynamic to suggest continuous motility and flow.

Despite the length of many of Ovid's entries, sometimes extending to more than two hundred lines for a single date, the text offers no descriptions of temple architecture. The interior of a temple is occasionally mentioned as the setting of ritual action (e.g. 1.587) and the access route to the place, an ascent for instance, is sometimes briefly described (1.79, 638). But the viewer is no *flaneur* and Ovid's work no ancient *Baedeker*. It is ritual agents who move. The very first description is a model in many respects (the 1st of January, 1.63–88). People move properly dressed (*uestibus intactis*), decked in festive colours (*concolor*). Optical effects are more important than architectural features, here the flickering of the flames and their reflections in the temple's gilding (1.77 f.). But the focus is more on the god's eye view of the scene than on humans looking at religious objects or on the participants' exchange of glances.[95] Time and again gods 'look out', not in a controlling manner or as irreproachable actors from a privileged vantage-point,[96] but as entities who take pleasure in what they see. The deity looking

---

94 Rüpke 1994b.
95 See Urry 2013, referring to Simmel.
96 Ibid.

out might be a statue, even a bust being carried along, but such things are not the focus of the text.

Despite this, it is worth stressing that the visual does not dominate in Ovid's writing. Religious events were truly multi-sensorial and he depicts them as such. This is clear, again, from the very first ritual that Ovid narrates, with the text pointing to both the smell and the sound of the event (e.g. *odoratis ignibus ... sonet spica*, 1.74 f.). These are not merely mentioned in passing. To concentrate on smell and scents for a moment, at 1.341–44 the narrator himself describes how laurel and Sabine herbs have now been replaced by Syrian incense, Indian costus, and saffron oil from eastern Asia Minor. Strong scents of course had a pragmatic role, for urban effluvia were also an ancient problem: Cicero, for example, thought architects should take great care to keep bad smells away from the proprietor of a house.[97] Where does this multi-sensory depiction lead Ovid?

All in all, Ovid is less interested in buildings, objects, and routes than in integrating interior spaces and open places with the dynamic motion of events. Even statues or images figure very rarely in his narratives.[98] Of course, Ovid knows about inscriptions. They figure prominently in his prefaces but are hardly ever mentioned in the main text or quoted as a source. Even where administrative information is available in the form of membership lists of the *curiae* on the Forum Romanum, dull people make no use of such inscriptions, as Ovid tells us in the context of the *feriae stultorum*, the 'holidays of the dull people' who do not know to which unit they belong (2.531 f.). Knowing the limitations of the information that inscriptions provide,[99] the narrator draws instead on authentic informants, above all the gods but often also the appropriate religious specialists (passim). Moreover, the method of participant observation is recommended to amateurs of ancient religion: 'If you like the old rituals, stand beside the one praying' (1.631).

Ovid's interest in space is in lived and embodied space, peopled by ordinary participants, occasionally religious specialists, and – in a different way – by gods. This space cannot adequately be captured by maps, GIS data, or digital reconstructions. Ovid's bird's-eye-view gods are many; they fly at different heights and are not bound by laws, whether those be human, avian, or even optical. The Mars who looks out on the people scattered over the Field of Mars *might* be a

---

[97] Cicero, *On the nature of gods* 2.141.
[98] After the introduction of the peculiar statue of Janus, 1.95. 111. 231, only in 4.21, 317 and – human – 6.583, 613.
[99] Cf. Augustus, *Res gestae* 19 and 20, where Augustus tells the reader that he is behind a number of dedications, the inscriptions of which do not mention him – by his own (benevolent) consent. At the end of his life, however, in the inscriptional *Res gestae*, he is willing to share.

statue but he surveys the whole like a hovering drone (2.857–60). The Jupiter on the Capitol gazes out to the limits of the empire (1.85f.). It is quite irrelevant here to object that nearby hills would have made such a view impossible. The imaginary of the urban space extends beyond the city and is indifferent to lines of sight. The narrator indeed reflects this claim in the text itself: *Quid uetat*, what forbids us to refer to external origins, he asks (1.423).[100] It is references of this kind that register the difference between Romans and others, and their constant entanglement. And it is the topic of the dead that registers the difference between the urban and the non-urban. To neglect caring for the dead, cremated on 'suburban pyres' (2.550), endangers the security offered by the city and allows its streets to be haunted by deformed souls (2.553f.).

All in all, the perspective is not a top-down approach to the rulers' politics of memory (in itself clearly attested in Ovid's preface to the second book of the *Libri fastorum*),[101] but an intelligent observer's take on the calendar. The text of the calendar, present in many people's hands as a book roll, invites the individual appropriation of diverse urban spaces – an attachment to place so clearly visible in Ovid's own longing for Rome during his subsequent exile at Tomis on the Black Sea.

7.9 Conclusion

The interpretations and modifications of the calendar described in the last paragraphs for the Augustan and Tiberian periods were lost in the course of time. The Fasti porticus, by contrast, large wall-paintings found under Santa Maria Maggiore at Rome and painted before the end of the 2nd century, interspersed the monthly columns with frescoes that offered a bird's eye view of agricultural activities.[102] By forcing the observers to look up at the frescoes in order to see an image that looks downwards, the distance between the observer and the rural world is accentuated. Nevertheless, despite some indications within the textual elements of the calendar of games that were held in the city, time is framed as rural time in this calendar, not as an urban quality. In the luxury codex calendar of the 4th century (the 'Chronographer of 354') produced by the calligrapher Furius Dionysius Filocalus, topographical indications are lacking completely; the

---

100 See also Ovid, *Fasti* 1.359: *adde peregrinas causa* and passim.
101 Rüpke 2009c.
102 A short analysis in Rüpke 1995b, 86–90; publication: Magi 1972. The graphical arrangement might point to the contemporary existence of calendars in the form of codices, offering two pages for every month.

work as a whole has an Imperial frame of reference.[103] It is only in the last copy of a *fasti*-like calendar, produced in mid-5th century Gaul by Polemius Silvius for the bishop of Lyon, that spatial indications return. But these reference single dates, or, rather, the recurrent procedures, to Rome *in toto*, in difference to other places. The Gallic bishop was neither interested in topographical detail nor in Rome's resilience.

There is no reason to suggest a causal relationship between these observations and the demographic decline of post-plague Rome at the end of the 2nd century CE or the 'fall of Rome' in 410 CE. The additional list of the birthdays of martyrs in the Chronographer of 354, reflecting the connection of Peter and Paul, as well as martyrs from Carthage, with urban Roman space, demonstrates the ongoing use of religious practices related to the calendar as strategies for fostering urban resilience, even if the concept of that particular *urbs* was changing and the idea of Rome's historical mission was spelt out very differently in Christian narratives and identities than it had been in its earlier representations.

Focusing on resilience also helps us to identify nuances in religious practices and material religion, as well as changes over time. This perspective provides an antidote to the notion of calendars as timeless expressions of 'a' religion and of 'Roman religion' in particular. Resilience ties in with conceptualisations of religion as lived, material, and urban practices and communication by serving as a concept that relates people, practices, and material and spatial infrastructures to catastrophic events. This concept also comprehends the anticipation of such catastrophes and the anxieties produced thereby, as well as the 'steeling' of individuals and societies against these events and the provision of quick responses in the aftermath. From such a perspective, changes in the practices of qualifying and representing temporal and spatial religious practices in the form of calendars can also be seen in a new light and in more detail.

To sum up, practices relating to, and memories of, divine help and military victory (which were bound to and moulded into specific urban places) were given a long-term visibility by the erection of *fasti*, a materialised invitation to re-narrate past strengths. By identifying disasters as the consequence of an inherent quality of time, that is of particular days, rather than as the consequence of the abilities of the actors involved, the participants in this discourse seem to have entertained the hope that continuation in the face of disasters might be fa-

---

103 The one exception is the awkward, and semantically not indubitably topographical, phrase *equus ad nixas fit* (15th of October), referring to the killing of the October horse on the campus Martius; see Rüpke 2009. On this assemblage of calendar and chronographic texts, see Mommsen 1850; H. Stern 1953; Salzman 1990; Burgess 2012; Rüpke 2015d.

cilitated. The possibility of writing oneself into the calendar was clearly beyond the power of most people and groups. Even in the calendar of Filocalus, written by one of the foremost calligraphers of the time and dedicated to somebody who also had to navigate the religious divide of the 4th century,[104] large-scale modifications were not thought admissible. Martyrs' dates were not integrated into the rather traditional *fasti* of this work but were instead presented in the form of a separate list. We have to wait another century before we find a surviving work that overcomes this dichotomy, namely that created by Polemius Silvius in the mid-5th century CE. But by that time, the *fasti* had become more repositories of historiographic knowledge than they were of contemporary urban life.

If we look back to Augustus' era, matters could hardly be more different. At that time, against the background of an already flourishing interest in and production of calendars, further practices had been developed. People were using calendars as means by which to claim places as much as means for relating themselves to urban space more generally. By communicating about urban religious practices through the media of inscribed *fasti*, small groups carved out spaces for their own religious and sociable practices.

We do not know whether any of these practices actually helped to render Rome a 'resilient city' that was 'able to survive a traumatic blow to its physical infrastructure, its economy, or its social fabric', as defined at the beginning of this chapter. However, the very prominence of the calendrical practices, their material presence, and the effort invested into literary aesthetics or textual visibility, suggest that the people involved tacitly or explicitly assumed that such practices fostered an urban way of living and of framing one's life that could survive natural and military disasters. At the very least, these practices might reflect the participation in such discourses of those involved. Reflecting on such religious practices has brought to light some of the peculiar ways in which Romans dealt with the fear of disaster, as well as its actual occurrence. Looking for signs of resilience helps us to historicise religious practices at Rome. If we keep this history of memories, fears, and changing presents in mind, we will be able to better understand these practices as an outcome of their relationship with urban space.

---

104 Rüpke 2015d.

8 Urban Selves: Individualisation in urban space

8.1 The problem

At this point it is necessary to turn our attention from religious practices and discourses to the very agents of urban religion and their constitution. At several points, this book has hinted at the role played by urban ways of life, the role of the number and character of encounters in internal and external flows, in shaping the subjects of urban life and their social relationships. Families and neighbourhoods are not alternatives to but, rather, co-present with transient exchanges and lasting alliances reaching far beyond the immediate social space. Family bonds might be severed by processes of immigration and supplemented by new strategies of grouping, such as ethno-genesis. Religious practices are instrumental in all of this. The two chapters of the final section of this book will explore these issues, starting with the nature of the individual subjects in the present chapter before turning to processes of grouping in Chapter 9. Previous research has helped to historicise processes of subjectivisation and, above all, to develop a historical perspective on religious individualisation.[1] Initial findings for the Mediterranean world of the Imperial age suggest that processes of urbanisation were a significant factor for developments that can be clustered together under the concept of 'individualisation'.[2] It is these suggestions to which I now turn.

8.2 The concept of the self

Terms such as 'subject', 'self', and 'subjectivity' all share a common conceptual root. Underpinning this conceptual vocabulary is the idea of discrete individual agents who act based on their lived experiences and with at least some degree of autonomy. A further essential component is that these agents are conscious, to at least a minimal extent, of their individuality and autonomy. It is this inwardly directed awareness that we typically call the 'self' and the accompanying consciousness of it that we term 'self-reflection'.

The concept of the self – *autòs* in Greek and *ipse* in Latin – is a central concern of the ancient philosophical tradition from Plato in the 4th century BCE onwards. Significantly, theorising about the self is closely connected to theories

---
1 Joas and Rüpke 2013; for antiquity: Rüpke 2013b.
2 Rüpke and Woolf 2013; Rüpke 2018e; Fuchs et al. 2019.

about the nature of the soul, which is identified as the most important part of the individual, responsible for overseeing and governing the body. In a number of key ancient philosophical traditions, the soul is also responsible for connecting the human with the divine, either by aligning the whole soul with that of God or by bringing the best and leading part of the soul into a harmonious relationship with the higher power.[3] The *real* self, stripped of its more base and earthly elements, tends to be identified with the divine intellect, as a microcosm stands to the macrocosm.[4]

The nature of the connection between human and divine was fertile ground for philosophical writers and was analysed in a wide variety of ways by these thinkers. One major school, the Stoics, placed great emphasis on the importance of self-analysis, drawing on their concept of *oikeiosis*, often translated as 'appropriation', to show how internal reflection is both a natural part of the development of the individual and also a central goal in one's personal development. In its earliest stage, *oikeiosis* is driven by the natural force of self-preservation, which motivates the young individual to appropriate the surrounding environment to the self and, reciprocally, the self to the surrounding environment. As the individual grows and develops, deeper levels of inquiry into the nature of the self are necessitated by one's consciousness of being embedded within an expanding social and physical world to which one must stand in an appropriate relationship. The ideal individual develops in incremental steps until his whole soul is brought into a harmonious relationship with the divinely ordered cosmos, achieving the end of living 'a life in agreement with nature'. It is this that constitutes a good, and thus happy, life. This same process of self-analysis also leads the individual to identify the 'duties' (*officia*) one must fulfil, both for one's own sake and for the sake of the society to which one belongs.[5] The appropriate way

---

3 The foundational text for this tradition is Plato's *Timaeus*. Here, the physical human soul is constructed as an imperfect copy of the divine world soul. The ethical goal for humans is identified as the 'healing' of their imperfections by modelling themselves on the structure of the divine and, thus, bringing themselves into harmony with the macrocosm. Plato's approach informed not just the views of later Platonists and Neo-Platonists but also the naturalistic ethics and metaphysics of the Stoics, the dominant philosophical school of the Hellenistic period. On the relationship between nature and the soul in Plato, see, for example, Gill 2004a. For examples of the burgeoning literature on the Platonic background to Stoicism, see Reydams-Schils 1999, Gill 2004b, and the papers collected in Long 2013. See also briefly Setaioli 2007, 350; for the problems faced by Jewish thinkers in adapting the concept and for Philo's creative solutions, see Dillon 2009; van Kooten 2009 (I am grateful to Paul Scade for these additions and references); Niehoff 2018, 192–208.
4 Trapp 2007, 99–109.
5 Ibid., 109–14.

of living, and one's corresponding duties, thus vary according to one's gender, age, and juridical and social status.[6] As both a part of and a microcosmic reflection of the divine intellect, the highest aim and capacity of the human soul and/or mind is participating in rational thought and raising one's cognitive standards to the impersonal level of the divine cosmos.[7] Deviations from this perfect rationality are considered to be psychic or physical illnesses, structural disharmonies that mark the individual as being out of tune with the divine. Through the pursuit of philosophical or other healing therapies, the human soul can be cured of these defects and brought back into a proportionate relationship with that of God.[8]

Philosophers in the Platonic and Stoic traditions reflected on the precise position of the individual in the world and made both the soul and the self key concepts in their thought. However, it is only in the works of Seneca the Younger, in the 1st century CE, that we can first discern an explicit and increasing interest in the specifically biographical dimension of the self.[9] The philosophical schools of the Hellenistic period[10] offered what amounted to a training course in self-reflection, to an extent that found no parallel in the religious practices of the era.[11] However, this reflection did not emphasise the notion of the self as an individual. The ultimate goal of Stoic self-examination was to achieve consistency in the conduct of one's own life[12] – internal consistency, consistency with the society to which one belongs, and, more broadly, consistency with the cosmos of which the individual is a part.[13] This was far from a form of enhanced individualism. On the contrary, the Roman Stoics emphasised the interdependent nature of all the parts of the cosmic structure and stressed the obligations owed by the individual towards others.[14] Indeed, an important theme underlying much Stoic thought is the limited relevance of apparent individuals: in the coherent Stoic cosmos, the idea that anything is separate from everything else is an illusion grounded in the limitations of the microcosmic perspective.[15] To understand

---

6 Ibid., 115 f.
7 Ibid., 109.
8 Ibid., 116–122.
9 Gill 2009, 82. See Reydams-Schils 2019, §3. However, Roller 2019 convincingly argues that the Ciceronian technique of situationally shaping and re-shaping examples already points to a conceptual, even if not a terminological, interest in such differences.
10 Sellars 2004.
11 Fowden 2005, 528.
12 Gill 2009, 77–8; see Graver 2019.
13 This also applies to Plotinus: Kühn 2008, 140.
14 Richter 2011, 82–5; Reydams-Schils 2005, 53–63, 140–1, 174–6.
15 On Stoic thought concerning the relationship between parts and wholes, see Scade 2013.

human nature fully is, ultimately, to understand that there are no distinct individuals at all, only differentiated parts of a greater unified whole. However, this fundamental integration of the parts of the whole does not deny individual difference. The notion of preferred indifferents – objects of choice that do not matter normatively (that is, are 'indifferent') but are, rather, subject entirely to the choice of the individual (that is, 'preferred') – points to the fact that some choices matter in everyday life, even if such differences have no relevance in the larger picture, from the perspective of the cosmos as such.[16]

The topography of the inner self, and the figurative language used to describe it, remained complex in all its varied formulations across different genres and philosophical schools.[17] In the various Platonic traditions, in particular, the figure of the demon provided a lens through which to discover the other (or plural others) that delineated the innermost essence of the human. This discovery was achieved by bringing oneself into the proper relationship with the inner, or innermost, aspect of that self, which was held to be responsible for thought and rational action.[18]

Philosophical approaches place a clear emphasis on the essential underlying similarity of human selves, which differ from one another only in their deviation from an ideal model and which should, ideally, all strive for cosmic uniformity. Individual differences in social and physical situations within the world are noted and accounted for but are not further theorised, since the ultimate goal is precisely the transcendence of such variations.[19] The concept of *persona*, for instance, is not brought to bear in discussions of this kind of worldview.[20] This term was important in ancient grammar, as later in Christology, denoting a role in a theatrical production, law court, or administration. However, it was used neither in an elaborated role theory nor in discussions about the attribution of responsibility or about holders of rights. This lack needs to be spelt out, as the concept had wider potential. In Cicero's discussion of *oikeiosis*, of the task of the individual to determine his or her own precise place in the larger social and natural world, *persona* had already been used as a tool. Similarly, arguments from the life and character of a person (*de vita*) did not play a major role

---

16 See Reydams-Schils 2019.
17 See Markschies 1997.
18 Ildefonse 2008, 233; Aubry 2008. Cf. Song 2009.
19 Cf. e.g. Sorabji 2007, 87 and 97 on Epictetus. The tendencies of an individual's rational decisions, identified by Epictetus as *prohairesis*, could differ widely between individuals. However, every individual is admonished to turn to oneself (*epistrephein*) in order to search for the 'true innate preconceptions about the good' (Epict. 3.22.38–39, quoted ibid., 97).
20 Trapp 2007, 120.

in the Roman rhetorical system that trained students for advocacy.[21] In short, the concept of the individualised self is, despite the description of empirical differences, comparatively under-theorised in our ancient sources.

In this chapter, I would like to offer a different perspective on historical constructions of the self, one based on sociology and history, and, particularly, on studies of urbanity. I will employ a term, 'individualisation', which can help to bring out further nuances of selfhood. My concern here is not with the specific historical example of 'individualisation' in the ancient Mediterranean world but, rather, with the potential the concept has for helping us to analyse and map out both the transfer of ideas within and across different periods and regions of urbanisation and changes in the practices and processes involved in the institutionalisation of increased selfhood and individuality. Here, 'individualisation' offers more than just a window into our own 'individualistic' modern era: the term as I use it is unbundled from the concept of 'modernity' and, thus, can freely be applied to our understanding of other periods as well. [22] But its value is not restricted to the study of any specific past society or historical moment. Concepts such as 'self', 'agency', 'subject', 'personhood', 'individuation', and 'personal identity' can all be illuminated and understood in a more fine-grained way by considering them under the umbrella of individualisation as an urban process. [23]

Such an approach allows us to identify institutional structures that prompt and strengthen processes of individualisation. This might, at first, seem counter-intuitive, for it seems natural to assume that institutions limit or threaten individuality in various ways by hemming in the individual and restricting freedom of expression and choice. However, I argue that rather than playing a limiting role, institutions in antiquity actually created significant spaces for shaping individuality. By taking a closer look at processes of individualisation in cities, we can come to appreciate the potential multiple personalities open to or taken up by individuals and recognise in a new way the salience of personal as well as collective identities. My goal in this chapter is to show that such processes became so deeply ingrained in the fabric of urban experience that they also shaped the *imaginaire* of religious texts. I study the test-case of the *Shepherd of Hermas*,

---

21 See *Rhetorica ad Herennium* 2.5.
22 Fuchs, Linkenbach and Reinhard 2015; Fuchs and Rüpke 2015b; Rüpke 2011a, 2012f, 2012 h, 2012 g, 2013b, 2014c, 2015b, 2015e, 2016e; Rüpke and Spickermann 2012; Vinzent 2011; Vinzent 2014.
23 See Fuchs and Rüpke 2015a; Lichterman 2013; Rebillard and Rüpke 2015; Rüpke 2012c, 2015c, 2016b; Rüpke and Woolf 2013.

a second-century text from Rome, and point to the role played in this text by distinct cities that symbolise opposite poles of individuation.

In the Hellenistic and Imperial periods, individualisation was furthered by processes of urbanisation.[24] These processes increased both the quantity and the scope of social and geographical mobility, made migration more common, and, ultimately, helped develop what I have called 'practical individuality' or 'being on one's own'.[25] Practical individuality (as opposed to moral, competitive, representative, or reflexive individuality) is generated by the need for people to act on their own account instead of simply following the dictates of tradition. It arises from, and points towards, situations of disembeddedness that are a consequence of the temporary rupture of social bonds (as in the cases of migrants, travellers, or survivors of natural or man-made disasters) or of a sharp division of labour. Being on one's own is rarely reflected in written or learnt instructions but it could be prepared for by reference to them, for instance by drawing on texts that reflect upon the journey of the soul after death.

In the context of the present volume, this leads naturally to the question of how practices of self-reflection in the Hellenistic and Imperial periods are related to cities or to notions of cities. I will argue that urbanisation and urbanity, urban ways of living and thinking, are related to processes of individualisation that employ notions of the self in three different ways: cities created a market for such practices; cities offered citizenships, a comprehensive notion of identity, which could be employed to sharpen notions of the self; and cities furthered the formation of urban identities by building on notions of belonging to or striving towards such places. This is because cities were as much characterised by internal complexity as they were by their entanglement in networks consisting of other cities and, thus, by urban thinking that refers to places outside of the city (as when the city-dweller compares his or her own urbanity with life in a different city or even in a rural idyll).

8.3 An urban market for the shaping of the self[26]

The surviving evidence does not suggest that the self was a typical focus for early Greco-Roman religious practices, with the exception of some limited indications in marginal phenomena such as the 'Orphic gold tablets' and their related nar-

---

24 Rüpke 2018e.
25 Rüpke 2013c, 13.
26 The following text is based on Rüpke 2018d, 289–292.

ratives.²⁷ The philosophical schools provided important sources for the systematic acquisition of techniques for self-reflection, offering these techniques up as methods for pursuing the ultimate end (*telos*) in life. Whilst the field of religious communication also embraced practices directed towards self-reflection, in doing so it followed a radically different logic. One telling example is offered by practices using the symbol of 'Asclepius'. Important actors in this field were able to work within a widespread institutional framework in the form of the network of sanctuaries dedicated to Asclepius, which spread from Epidaurus to the furthest limits of the Hellenistic world. Those who lived and worked in these places of healing treated illnesses as individualised phenomena that were more than just disruptions of a natural social order or of the procession of generations.²⁸ In the *Hieroi Logoi*, the invalid rhetorician Aelius Aristides describes his dreams, pilgrimages, and personal encounters with Asclepius. He not only plumbs the depths of his own self in these accounts but also extols its excellence as the most important evidence of the power of his god, despite the frightful illnesses from which he suffers.²⁹ Even in the wider world beyond the bounds of the healing sanctuaries, deities were regularly asked for assistance in recovering from an illness or to help maintain current good health.³⁰ However, despite the connection between healing and the divine, and the individualised relationship between man and god, illness was not generally treated as indicative of a flawed or deviant self.

The kinds of dreams recounted by Aristides were an important form of individualised experience, inaccessible to other observers unless narrated but taken seriously at all social levels.³¹ Manuals were written and read to assist in the interpretation of the symbols that appeared and the events that took place in dreams.³² Unsurprisingly, the divinities who appeared most frequently were also among the most widespread, with Asclepius and Silvanus regularly attending the slumbers of worshippers and, thus, instigating religious activities.³³

The Imperial period also saw the revival and spread of small, local oracles, which were available for individual consultation and were, thus, accessible on a

---

27 Marginal: J. N. Bremmer 1994, 2011.
28 Sfameni Gasparro 2007; Israelowich 2015.
29 Harris and Holmes 2008; Petridou 2015; see also Fields 2008; Petsalis-Diomidis 2010.
30 Petridou 2017a.
31 See, for example, Pliny, *Letters* 7.27 (I owe the suggestion to the late Veit Rosenberger).
32 Athanassiadi 1993; Harris 2009; Renberg 2010; Pizzone 2013. On Artemidorus, see also G. Weber 1999; Brakke, Satlow and Weitzman 2005; du Bouchet and Chandezon 2012; Downie 2015.
33 Renberg 2015, 257.

personal level to a significant portion of the population.[34] Ready-made portions of text, short and variably applicable answers to a multitude of potential questions written, for instance, on tablets of wood, were used in divination by lot, making the procedure both straightforward and cheap. This combination of accessibility and affordability meant that the practice of consulting oracles became democratised, as it ceased to be restricted primarily to members of the land-owning and monied elites. Even in contexts in which the individual self did not become the central locus for direct communication with, or manifestations of, the divine, it still became an object of significant interest. The ability to enter into direct religious communication with addressees who could be accessed in specific sanctuaries and sites provided a valuable, individualised complement to the centralised forms of communication.

As should be clear from the arguments advanced in the preceding chapters, ancient religion was no more a unified phenomenon than was ancient philosophy. For cities, certain common ideas present in specific areas were important, such as the complementary yet conflicting ideas and practices clustering around kinship and citizenship in the Italian towns.[35] The interest of this chapter, however, is in the practices of instrumental religion, religious practices dealing with specific mundane problems in order to achieve a solution, such as the practices of economic agents set free by Roman law.[36] The economic dimensions of production, consumption, and exchange concentrated in urban settlements are vital in this context; healing, oracles, dream interpretation, and philosophical training were not services offered up for free. Group membership involved costs, in the form of fees or payment in kind, just as did the acquisition of religious services sold by individuals. We can, thus, draw no hard distinction between collective religious practice and individual practice on the grounds of economic exchange. The borderlines between the two were evidently permeable.

Cicero's attempt in his *Laws* to regulate the economic dimension of religion by sanctioning separated private cults (*separatim*)[37] was one of a number of failed attempts to conceptualise this area. Religious choices offered to selves were driven by immigration, markets, and the differentiation of growing cities at the same time.

---

[34] Bendlin 2006; Stoneman 2011, 174–89; Kindt 2015. See also Eidinow 2007, 42–55.
[35] See Cliff Ando 2019 on the inalienability of these aspects. Cf. Rüpke 2018d, 250 vs. H. Flower 2017b.
[36] See again Ando, ibid. Thus, the range of religious entrepreneurs could extend beyond traditional definitions of religious competence.
[37] Cicero, *On laws* 2.19.

8.4 Urban identities

The resultant 'urban selves' did not simply identify with their cities. On the contrary, I suggest that there must have been a growing sense of individuality in the civic context of the crowded city described by Georg Simmel[38] and that this, in turn, provoked the institutionalisation of alternative options.[39] In the ancient Mediterranean, those who dwelt in cities were always a minority of the total population. Nevertheless, a steady influx of migration brought enough newcomers into the cities not only to keep up with the high mortality rates caused by poor sanitation[40] but also, in a number of regions and across a range of periods, to drive processes of urbanisation, as has been pointed out in the Introduction. Migrants were drawn in by 'urban aspirations' as defined in Chapter 1: hopes, and optimistic ideas shaped by images and representations of life in the cities. At the same time, cities 'trapped' their inhabitants, holding them in the cage constructed by the densely organised framework characteristic of urbanisation both across the ancient world and beyond.[41] Urban identities served both as a 'pull factor' and as one of a number of forces that acted on residents to persuade them to remain. Despite their power, these notions of collective identity were not all-encompassing and we have no reason to suppose that they created an enduring and exclusive sense of belonging in those who shared them.[42] Rather, collective identities captured the dynamics of the relationship between the individual and the others with whom they were in a real or imaginary relationship. As such, they supplemented self-referential individual identities instead of replacing them.

My general analysis of collective identities here mirrors my understanding, based on recent psychological research, of religious collective identities more particularly. Group membership, I suggest, is defined primarily by self-classification, that is by the individual's personal assessment of his or her group affiliation. This assessment is, itself, influenced by the individual's perception of how they are classified by others; the meaning the individual and others place on group affiliation; emotional connectedness to, and dependence on, the inter-relationship between personal and collective identities, which can, in

---

38 Simmel 1917.
39 In this context, we can think of the substantial number of migrants, often young males, for whom family traditions of ancestor cult were neither locally available nor easily reproducible; see Scheidel 2001b, 2003 on demography and Tacoma 2016 for Roman migration in general.
40 This point is based on the urban graveyard theory, see Scobie 1986.
41 For the concept, see Mann 1986, 211 (pages according to the German edition of 1994).
42 See Rebillard 2012, 2–5, who opts for the term 'salient identity'.

some cases, completely overlap; the degree to which individual group members are embedded in everyday collective routines and the level of impact this embeddedness has on individual behaviour; and, finally, the cognitive dimension of group membership, or the way in which shared stories and imaginaries reveal the values, characteristics, and history of the group.[43]

When thinking about religious groups, or even entire religions, in the Roman Empire, for example,[44] it is important to bear in mind that these terms do not identify strictly demarcated associations of people. Rather, a religious group or a religion consists of a situationally specific group of actors, which may include non-humans, to which a rational individual believes him- or herself to belong. A consequence of this is that highly complex collective identities can develop, comprised of a multiplicity of affiliations and/or conscious acts of distancing.[45]

In the case of cities and discourses about 'the city', the situation is even more complex. Here, it is not groups but places that provide the points of reference for the construction of collective identities. As Alexia Petsalis-Diomidis has observed in her study of spatial imaginaries, Judaism, Christianity, and the cult of Mithras all share an important trait in the Severan period, in that each places great significance on a distant, holy landscape (a 'sacred landscape') and each does so without giving up its universalist claims.[46] This is not simple coincidence and nor is it an isolated phenomenon. The Severan architectural programme in Rome and North Africa, as well as the expansion of citizenship through the *Constitutio Antoniniana*, points towards 'a re-casting of geographical centres and perspectives, followed by a shift in what constituted local and universal Imperial culture'.[47] Petsalis-Diomidis draws on travel diaries and epiphany narratives to explain the 'sacred landscape' phenomenon, using these texts to introduce new manners of seeing and perceiving difference. She argues that these new modalities of perception go hand in hand with a growing individual desire for a personal relationship with the divine.[48]

Many other examples of this phenomenon can be identified during the 2nd and 3rd centuries.[49] Reimagined and idealised views of Jerusalem may be something of a special case due to the very real political crises, as well as the crises of

---

43 Ashmore, Deaux and McLaughlin-Volpe 2004.
44 See Rüpke 2010b, 2010a; Rüpke 2011e, 2011b.
45 See Ashmore, Deaux and McLaughlin-Volpe 2004, 84.
46 Petsalis-Diomidis 2007, 252.
47 Ibid.
48 Ibid., 289.
49 Rüpke 2017b.

imagination, the city faced as a result of its destruction. However, we should not think that it belongs in a category by itself. Throughout the empire, people in a given place looked to other locations to both define and differentiate themselves. As an example, we can note the enactments of episodes from Egyptian mythology by the cult of Isis in the early Imperial Period, or the construction of capitol structures in the provinces with direct reference to comparable buildings at Rome in the 1st and 2nd centuries CE.[50]

Perhaps the most important factor in motivating this phenomenon was the process of 'empire creation' itself. By 'empire creation', I mean not the formation of the territorial Roman state but, rather, the systematic co-opting of local and regional political elites in order to make them part of a loosely coordinated administrative structure; the development of a single market system, even while local taxation remained in place; and the centralising of local military commands. The goal of this process was to establish centralised authority over these key domains across the vast area of the empire.[51] While the fulfilment of these goals opened up new possibilities for action and prestige for the local elites, the creation of the empire nevertheless also diminished their earlier monopolies on local power. Where once local elites could enjoy near complete control in their own areas, now the emperor and his provincial governors became mediating authorities whose influence was strongly manifested at the local level through the minting of coins, the construction of statues and buildings, and the disbursement of charitable funds. And yet, external flows and looking beyond one's own city walls to other cities and their distinct urbanities had been a hallmark of urbanisation processes around the Mediterranean Sea since the 'Great Colonisation' of the Greeks. In this sense, what the Roman Empire brought about was, above all, an enlargement of the relevant horizons, and new meanings and different degrees of significance attributed to particular sites.

The considerable level of migration to the cities from a world of primarily local economies, knowledge, religion, and identities had a further important impact. On the one hand, the variety of immigrants from a diverse range of regions brought with them a new religious plurality that reflected the differences amongst the incomers and increasingly began to crystallise in personal experience.[52] On the other hand, immigrants who had chosen to leave behind their

---

50 See, for example, Kuhfeldt 1882; Lomas 1997; Lackner 2013. Older interpretations, which claimed that these buildings reflected the status of a city, have been invalidated, as their construction was often only initiated a decade or century after the change in status.
51 Cf. G. Woolf 2012, 26f.; Ando 2012, 186–200.
52 Rüpke 2001a, 2009d.

old homes rarely acted on the basis of nostalgic attachment to childhood cults. Instead they demanded a certain 'branding',[53] packages of recognisable symbolic systems they had engaged with before. Iconographic schemes, pattern books, and other widely circulated texts that were produced to satisfy these demands created the kind of recognisability that tempts some modern scholars to speak of homogenised 'cults'.[54] In fact, religious practices and their corresponding imaginaries remained, first and foremost, local. Nevertheless, they necessarily laid claim to something trans-local, as was implicit in the uniformity they developed and the relevance they maintained in urban centres far distant from their origins.

In the world of multi-layered and often ambiguous political identities that arose as a result of the Imperial project, the idea of the Roman Empire itself, represented in its foremost cities rather than in a cartographical imagination, became a crucial instrument for the creation of collective identities and networks on the local level. This reflects the fact that the more quickly and thoroughly religious symbols and practices are able to replace the comprehensive framework for engaging with the world that was previously provided by local political identities and institutions, the more victorious and successful they emerge. The sooner reflective exercises and community formation can be integrated into these practices and symbols, the more likely they are to survive.

It is in this context that trans-regional linkages – the idea of a site of worship that lies beyond the boundaries of the individual's everyday urban experience – become significant. Such sites have the power to secure the global (on the Imperial scale) presence and importance of a deity that also continues to remain effective on the local level. Whilst such a 'global' stature might seem to be a self-evident characteristic for henotheistic or monotheistic deities such as Isis, Mithras, or the nameless *ho theos*, it can also be detected in appeals to more localised divinities, such as the Nemesis of Smyrna or the Victoriae of the Balkan provinces.

All these processes for linking one's own city with other cities of the network that formed the empire required both visual didactics and a comprehensive rhetoric. The template for this may have been the emperor himself, whose claim to a unique and universal power was propagated throughout the empire with great intensity, using a variety of media, ranging from coins to the penal code, and taking in such things as busts, calendars, and buildings. The emperor represented the most widely recognised god of the Imperium Romanum, his image identified

---

[53] On religious branding, see also Ch. 3.2, 51 above.
[54] See, for example, Rüpke 2005.

with the faraway city of almighty Rome.[55] While the emperor might be seen as a marker of a local identity from outside the borders of the empire, within its boundaries the ruler-deity could no longer serve this role. Precisely because he transcended the local and the particular, the figure of the emperor was unable to facilitate the existence of the specific, distinct collective identities that expressed the social and geographical affiliations of particular individuals and groups. Yet, at the same time, this god truly raised the bar: for a deity to be competitive in the religious 'marketplace' it would now have to somehow 'outdo', out-perform, or otherwise go beyond the god that occupied the symbolic centre of the world. One response to the need to surpass Rome itself was the introduction of cult sites with transcendental locations beyond this world – I think here of the epistle to the Hebrews and its heavenly, but urban-sized, temple cult[56] – but other tactics were exploited as well. Ultimately, religious sites that inspire identity formation need not be real cult locations, nor even real locations of any sort. In fact, as the example of the divine emperor demonstrates, human beings can themselves serve as a *locus* or *topos* for this purpose.

Of course, the choice of such sites, which were usually cities, was never random. From the 1st century CE to at least the early 3rd century, the Imperium Romanum had its intellectual and symbolic centre at Rome. Every school of thought and every social network sought to be represented in Rome in some way because validation in the centre conferred status, indeed reality, at the periphery. Ideas and values travelled to Rome over vast distances and at great speed, moving across boundaries of cultural communication that proved to be as porous as those that we can identify from the Hellenistic period to Late Antiquity at Alexandria, in the workshops of the translators of the Septuagint or in the schools bringing together Neoplatonist, Jewish, and Christian thoughts and thinkers.[57] It is for just this reason that Rome itself was the subject of polemics and attempts at confinement. The *Sibylline Oracles*, for instance, condemns Rome. Hermetic texts, meanwhile, argue that it is Egypt that stands as the 'temple of the whole world' (*templum totius mundi*), exploiting Juvenal's framing of Rome's centrality with the image of the Syrian Orontes flowing into the Tiber.[58]

So, exactly what effect did these far-away cities have on those people who employed depictions and imagery of them in their own city? In order to answer this question, we are forced to fall back on our very limited textual evidence. We can begin by noting that acts of self-classification are simplified and clarified by

---

55 As forcefully argued by Ando 2008, 119.
56 Rüpke 2012i.
57 For the latter, see e.g. Stefaniw 2011, 2019.
58 *Asclepius* 24; Juvenal, *Satires* 3,62.

cultic sites, in the sense that participation in activities in these cities allows for a clear-cut procedural division between those who belong to a group and those who do not. Given the rather fuzzy boundaries between the various manifestations of Isis or Sol Invictus, or between the various expressions of Jupiter, *ho theos*, and *theos Hypsitos*, the clear differentiations offered at specific locations – from Alexandria, Delphi, and Smyrna to Jerusalem and Rome – will surely have been advantageous. Of course, as the degree of competition increased, and the demands for identifiability and differentiation became stronger, the number of viable alternatives was reduced.

In most cases, we know very little about how people evaluated their own group membership. We might assume that they perceived their affiliations positively, given that they were voluntary. Yet, at the same time, individual group members would have been aware of positive or negative external evaluations of their group, and these might have an impact on their own views. There was certainly no uniform desire for high visibility across groups, even if, for many, urban density called for iconic distinctiveness, as discussed at the end of Chapter 1. Even in the case of groups that did seek a highly visible position in certain social and geographical contexts, in other places and among other company the focus was on minimising negative interactions. We can think here of the contrast between the visibility sought by Judaism in Jerusalem, or by the cult of Isis in Alexandria, and the comparatively low-key presence of their adherents in the provincial areas of the empire. Visibility was, then, a situational rather than an absolute goal.

The significance accorded by individuals to group membership can hardly be overestimated. Being part of a group involves acceding to a hegemonic, asymmetrical classification, or, to put it more simply, to a very black and white depiction of one's position relative to others. Those outside the group are not just different in specific regards but are 'others' in a quite general and almost entirely negative sense as well. This kind of identity construction could become particularly acrimonious in contexts involving Imperial disdain or colonial resistance.[59] In texts such as the Apocalypse of John, being a Roman becomes a kind of totalising identity that carries a highly negative moral evaluation with it. A more complex dynamic comes into play when reading a text such as the early 3rd century *Commentary on the Book of Daniel*, one of the earliest Judeo-Christian texts transmitted from the city of Rome.[60] In Daniel, we read of four successive earthly kingdoms which will then be followed by the Kingdom of God. This succession pro-

---

[59] Momigliano 1992b; Frankfurter 1998; cf. Webster and Cooper 1996; Chakrabarty 2008.
[60] See Bracht 2014.

vides a framework for interpreting history by locating given periods at specific points within the sequence. The identity of the first kingdom, Babylon, is a fixed and negative point of reference determined by the original text, so to describe someone as Babylonian is, once again, to label them with a totalising identity. However, the commentary identifies the final earthly kingdom with the contemporary Roman Empire, the empire at a specific moment in time. To label someone as a Roman in this context is not to say something timeless about Rome but, rather, to say something about the Roman identity at a given moment in time, a necessary, even if transitional, period. This kind of approach to collective identity contrasts with the totalising approach but, as the commentary makes clear, can happily co-exist with it in the same work.

The idea that the individual's felt emotional connection to, and dependence on, a collective identity could, at times, lead to an almost complete overlap between personal and group identity is impossible to confirm with the sources available to us. Nevertheless, scholars often demand precisely this kind of evidence in support of such claims. While conclusive proof may not be available, the eleventh book of Apuleius' *Metamorphoses* does indicate this kind of thoroughgoing overlap in relation to a specific deity. The same is true in the writings of Aelius Aristides, for whom we have strong evidence of an almost complete identification with Asclepius at Pergamum. By contrast, none of our evidence suggests any similar kind of complete identification in relation to a religious site.

Taken together, the preceding points suggest that the degree of embeddedness into everyday activities implied by membership of a group that is tied to a specific place is negligible. The same is probably true for the extent to which an individual's own behaviour was influenced by his or her place-related group membership. In this case, the majority of examples are individuals who would be considered extremists in today's world: authors and readers of apocalyptic texts, as well as martyrs (albeit not quite in the modern sense of the word ...). Stories about such individuals were particularly prominent in Christianity in the post-Constantine era.

However, things look rather different when we consider the cognitive dimension of such place-related stories and reflect upon the ideas that shed light on the values, characteristics, and histories of such groups. Even a group without a sharply defined profile could have a wealth of stories tying it to a particular site, which is to say that these groups in no way lack in rich mythologies. This richness is perhaps least tied to specific locations in the case of the cult of Mithras, although here we do not have enough textual evidence to allow for a comparison with our body of iconographic evidence.[61] Still, we cannot ignore the fact that location-bound traditions are usually ambivalent in the associations they evoke: Persia can be both source of ancient wisdom and arch-enemy of civilisation; Egypt can be the fount of tradition and authority but also a den of decadence and corruption. We need only consider the defeat at Carrhae or the death of Valerian at Edessa to see how a variety of positive and negative associations can accrete to a place. Even Rome does not appear in an entirely unproblematic light, given its long history of civil wars. Similarly, Jerusalem appears in negative historic-religious traditions from at least the time of the prophet Amos.[62]

Here the city comes into focus again. The idea that one's own city is the centre of the world may well be a feature of urban imaginaries but it is a feature that has been significantly overemphasised in some of the earlier scholarship on the topic.[63] Just as important are the bounds that separate the city from the rest of the world, the limits that define it and mark it off from what lies outside. These limits both identify the city as *this* city and form the basis for comparisons with other cities. Religious communication, in both ritual and verbal forms, seems to have been a central medium for constructing and framing such imaginaries. Religions transcend the boundaries of the local, directing attention to the importance of places beyond and thus shaping identity, both positively and negatively, by forcing individuals to look outwards when considering who they are.[64] Their views of urbanity are formulated in the easily distinguishable form of the names of gods and names of places. These are marks of distinction, no matter whether one looks inside or outside the city.

Specifically city-based religion adds a further momentum to this direction of travel. My claim is that urban selves not only have access to media – writing, first and foremost – that allow them to identify their self-reflection but that they also have much readier access to other forms of artistic expression than do non-urban selves. The close association of such expressive media with cities seems to have been characteristic of many types of urbanisation across a wide range of periods.[65] From this we can conclude that it is the fascination with other, distant cities that is the peculiar feature both of urban imaginaries and of the religiously

---

61 For information on the iconographic tradition of the Mithras cult, see Clauss 1990; Gordon 2009, 2012.
62 On the image of Jerusalem, see Walker 1990; Collins 2000; Friedheim 2010b; Capes 2011; Häusl 2011; K. R. Jones 2011b.
63 For example, Rykwert 1976.
64 See Rüpke 2015c.
65 See Law et al. 2015.

articulated (or instigated) selves characteristic of the urban context. Urban diversity, and the density of interactions that occur when large numbers of people live in close proximity, sparks grouping processes that produce both homologous and competing forms of institutionalisation. However, the same conditions also have other results. The diversity and density of urban encounters lead not just to institutionalisation but also, as Simmel pointed out over a hundred years ago, to individualisation as well.[66]

8.5 Citizenship and imagined cities

Attempts at stabilising one's own self need not be individualistic, in the sense of fully disembedding the agent from its social context. The second-century[67] text *Pastor Hermae,* the *Shepherd of Hermas,* shows just how fluid could be the boundaries between individual and group practice. This text is usually left aside in narratives of the history of religion from a 'Roman', 'Jewish', or 'Christian' perspective, but it is an important source when considering the broader problem of urban selves. On the one hand, its author was an individual producer of religion while, on the other, he produced texts intended for circulation within groups. This is reflected in the metaphors offered for self-reflection.

The *Pastor Hermae,* written in Greek by a Jewish author at Rome shortly before the middle of the 2nd century CE, does not provide a general theory of the soul. Rather, it attempts to locate its author, Hermas, at the heart of contemporary society and within a process of religious grouping. The autobiographical sketch with which the work opens claims that it was Hermas' everyday style of life that made him a particularly appropriate vehicle for a special form of contact with the divine. However, the author's composition of this dynamic, growing text was not solely directed at the production of a visionary work. Hermas' goal was, rather, to provide a means by which the self could be fashioned, primarily through the practice of reading and engaging with the text.[68] The reciting of the text by a range of groups in a variety of distinct types of communal gathering was a practice aimed at the institutionalisation of situations that were designed to lead members of the audience to reflect on their own inner moral states. The problem of sins of the mind, with which the earliest layer of the text opens,[69] is a

---

66 Simmel 1917.
67 See in detail, Rüpke 2013a, 2013d. The possibility of an earlier dating is stressed by Gregory 2002.
68 Cf. Inwood 2009 for the Senecan authorial self.
69 *Pastor Hermae* 1 (*vis* 1,1), 8; cf. 2 (*vis* 1,2), 1.

case in point. In order to detect such inner problems, one must be suitably motivated or provoked by an external source, such as the female revelatory figure in the text. The goal of the work was the fashioning of a specific religious self through self-reflective practices. Such practices held out the possibility of changing the individual's position in the *ekklesia* through *metanoia*, the changing of oneself and one's behaviour. As such, this kind of care of the self had the potential to 'democratise' the visionary experience.

Hermas' revelation is presented as a sequence of encounters with male and female revelatory figures who lead Hermas on to a further encounter with the Shepherd and an angel. The book serves as an externalisation of the safe imaginative space within which the reader or listener can witness the struggle between angels and spirits. Two opposing angels serve as the most important protagonists in the text. They are part of a demonology, or rather an angelology, that in other texts provides space for further divine figures, Christ included.[70]

In Hermas' text, the motif of two contrasting cities – one base and associated with earthly powers, the other truly real and associated with the divine – provides the central object of a technique for reflecting on the self. By imagining these two distinct cities and then putting them into motion by carrying out thought experiments concerning behaviour within them, beyond them, and directed towards them, a practitioner creates an instrument for reflecting on his or her own self and its place in relation to others. This reflective individuality, as I call it,[71] treats the individual self not as a free-floating and completely malleable soul but, rather, as a part of the person that is fully integrated within local contemporary society. This motif is most evident in the very first parable of the work[72] but the depiction of the city is developed further by the image of the tower used in parables 8 and 9.

Hermas certainly does not create something entirely new here, when a specific urbanity is used for religious purposes. The lines of thought he takes up can ultimately be traced back to the Jewish personifications of the cities of Jerusalem and Babylon following the destruction of the First Temple. However, Hermas' text was both written and read by its audience within a quite different political and social context, that of the Roman Empire, and this context is inseparable from its content. Core concepts, such as the laws or constitution of a city, or the notion of citizenship as including the particular 'civic way of life' (*politeues-*

---

[70] See Longenecker 1970, 26–32; Bucur 2009; again, such figures are part of a long tradition of prophetic calls for repentance.
[71] See the typology in Rüpke 2013c, 12–14.
[72] Osiek 1999, 157.

thai) of a given city,⁷³ underpin the way in which the soul is conceived. The discussion of the 'fatherly laws' (*patrioi nomoi*) of a minority group is as old as the Hellenistic empires and can be found, for instance, at 2 Maccabees 6.⁷⁴ The same condition of living under an empire similarly suggested to the Roman citizens of other Italian municipalities the motif of dual fatherlands (*patriae*), as Cicero discusses in his *Laws*.⁷⁵ In these cases, the types of citizenship nest within each other, rather than being exclusive.⁷⁶

It is clear, then, that the general outlines of Hermas' imagery were common currency. So how exactly does he fit into the broader picture? At least some Jews, and particularly those taken to Rome as slaves, viewed the Flavian destruction of Jerusalem as part of a duel between two cities⁷⁷ rather than a clash between two distinct peoples.⁷⁸ The idea that there was a degree of symmetry between the two cities may have been reinforced by the contemporaneous rebuilding of the Roman temple to Capitoline Jupiter. This temple was the seat of the Capitoline triad, whom Tacitus, most likely drawing on an actual formula used in prayer, refers to as the leading tutelary deities of the empire (*praesides imperi*).⁷⁹ Against such a backdrop, Hermas' renewed elaboration of the idea of a more perfect city takes on a clear contemporary meaning with strong political overtones.

According to Hermas, many people have already decided that it is not the Roman city but its more divine counterpart to which they truly belong. However, they have come to this conclusion without thinking the matter through clearly.⁸⁰ When confronted with the actual choice of minimising their commitments to and engagement with the earthly city, they are much more reluctant to exchange their present urban community for the imagined city. Hermas offers up a thought experiment concerning how to find accommodation in 'the tower', which serves, I argue, as another symbol of the city. The comparison is embedded in the thought experiments of architectural competition, of the tower as an architectural miracle, an ongoing process of construction that resolves all the problems implied by its human building material. Hermas' 'cities' are not compared to each

---

73 Lieu 2004, 243.
74 See ibid. and Kippenberg 1986.
75 Cicero, *Laws* 2.5. Cf. the discussion on Jews in Alexandria in Iosephus, *c. Apion* 2.6.
76 In these cases, the types of citizenship nest within each other, rather than being exclusive. The need to balance such nested identities, and the concomitant legal obligations involved, is discussed in the *Letter to Diognetus* 5–6.
77 See Iosephus, *bell. Iud.* pr. 3–4 with § 9.
78 See Barclay 2007, 362–9 on Josephus' view of the Romans.
79 Tacitus, *Histories* 4.53.3.
80 *Pastor Hermae* 47.5.

other by reference to their walls. The points of reference used are the fields, which symbolise sustenance and wealth, and the houses, the primary focus of social self-representation. At the end of parable 1 (50.8–10), it is made clear that the construction of oneself is not merely a matter of leaving the earthly city behind. Rather, there are things that can be done here and now that instantiate the values of the other city to which one already belongs: caring for widows and orphans and winning souls in the earthly city are equated with purchasing fields and houses in the other city. This approach to constructing oneself is clearly confrontational or polemical: the self is distinguished from other possible selves by identifying it with a contingent choice. The city-like tower imagined by the text is intimately tied to this kind of boundary construction.

Rome, however, was more than just a city. As Pliny the Elder claimed in the early 70s CE, Rome had a universalised status, standing as a common home for the whole world (*una cunctarum gentium in toto orbe patria*).[81] In such a context, it is not entirely surprising that some residents of the city reacted by creating identities that were not primarily local.[82] In doing so, they were able to stress the negative aspect of universality, the loss or lack of any local home. This is the strategy followed in the slightly earlier *Letter to Diognetus*, a Greek text that, like the *Shepherd*, came from a Jewish background.[83] A different but related idea can be found in the apocalyptic literature, in which the claim is proffered that there exists a categorically different place, a heavenly town to which one's loyalties should belong.

While Rome undoubtedly provided a vital context for Hermas, the Shepherd's discourse is not directed towards the empire but towards the self: in the text, the stones used to construct the tower are alive. Indeed, according to the same *Letter to Diognetus*, the intended readers live in just the same way as everyone else.[84] The transcendent tower is, above all, an instrument for the shaping of the self, a tower in the making. This important image offers institutionalised frameworks within a discourse that we can understand as just one element in a greater process of individualisation. This process is characterised by the practice of reading, by communal meetings of the select few, and by constant reflection on oneself and one's place in society.[85] This sort of individualisation is not opposed to institutionalisation. Citizenship was, after all, a collectivising and

---

81 Pliny, *Natural History* 3.39; see Perkins 2009, 33 for further references from the early empire.
82 See Nasrallah 2008 on the *Acta apostolorum* as creating an empire-like network of cities.
83 Perkins 2009, 32 on *Letter to Diognetos* 5.1. In Chapter 6, the author of the letter compares the Christians to the all-pervading (Stoic) soul, in order to explain difference and local presence.
84 In particular 5.4–5.
85 For this concept, see Rüpke 2013c; Fuchs et al. 2019.

homogenising institution as well as an engine for individualisation. It both informed individuals and hung over them in the form of the oppressive and increasingly pervasive presence of the Roman Empire, which compelled the adoption of its values through a combination of forceful coercion and alluring, attractive benefits. The manifest presence of the empire helped provoke the emphasis on the individual and collective selves by distancing groups and drawing boundaries.[86]

8.6 Conclusion

Certain religious traditions may possess or develop practices of self-reflection that are able to foster individuality. The institutionalisation of such tendencies, however, and its conceptualisation as 'individuality' is a matter of historical contexts and social location; it is contingent and requires a descriptive frame beyond the self. 'Individualisation' has the potential to fulfil this role and can even embrace processes of de-individualisation. Since processes of religious individualisation are closely connected to the formation of institutions and traditions, the interactions among them must be taken into account in a systematic way. Institutional protection of individual practices, such as self-reflection and auto-inspection, creates at the same time an awareness of the possibilities for heteropraxis or heterodoxy, and the tools to counteract it through standardisation.

In the cities of the Roman Empire, the formation of diverse forms of religious individualism (from elective-membership groups to hermits) was associated in a reciprocal process with self-reinforcing tendencies toward normalisation, whether in the criminal law of the Codex Theodosianus or in Mishnaic texts. Throughout this period, religious communities pressed, through their conduct and their stated commitments, for appropriate conduct from group members. But such communities were not a natural given. As this chapter has shown, it was urban diversity and density of interaction, the growth of a religious market, and the concepts and semantics of urban and trans-urban discourses that would have sparked the homologous, as well as competing, institutionalisations that attempted to regulate religious practices, collective identities, and urban religious selves.

---

86 For the notion of boundaries, see Lamont and Molnár 2002.

9 Urbanity and multiple religious identities

9.1 Introduction

The formation of new religious traditions, identities, and groups is at the heart of many histories of religion. Processes of formation are clearly developments that take place over time and it has been claimed by some scholars that such pluralisation of religious *options* was a process that was radicalised up to the point of creating different religious *organisations* in Late Antiquity.[1] At the same time, research on 'urban religion' has claimed that many of the phenomena identified in this context are the outcome of a development that falls outside that of traditional religions and constitutes a reaction to the inability of classical traditions to deal with the new conditions of urban life.[2] Is it the case, then, that religions (in the traditional sense) come to an end in cities? Such a conclusion would be in clear contrast to the suggestions I have made at several points throughout the course of this book. The development of a plurality of specifically religious identities is, I claim, directly related to urbanity. In other words, what are typically seen as 'religions' are a product of the urban. This historical claim will be argued for in this final chapter on the basis of concrete historical data, focusing again on the ancient Mediterranean. The claim is supported from two perspectives. I will start from observations by ancient authors concerning cultural and religious plurality in cities and will then move on to voices that reflect on the urban context and character of religious distinctions from within such emergent religious traditions. The available evidence suggests that we can build on observations made in the previous chapter by focusing on emergent Judaism, paying attention to practices and discourses, as well as to religious stereotypes ascribed from the outside just as much as to reflection on the urban from within.

I start by distinguishing three very different (and *consequentially* different) meanings of 'religious identity'. First, 'religious identity' might mean a form of personal identity achieved through self-reflection in dialogue with the 'divine' or some divine addressee. I take this to be a synonym for the 'religious selves' dealt with in the previous chapter. Multiple religious identities belonging to the same person would then point towards different threads of self-reflection, employing different ideas or techniques, either in parallel to each other or in a biographical sequence. 'Conversion' would be the dramatising narrative of some significant shift undergone by the person.

---

1 See Rüpke 2010b.
2 See above, Ch. 3.

Secondly, 'religious identity' might mean a person's 'collective identity', that is an individual's occasional, repeated, or even frequent entertaining or acceptance of the idea of being part of a religious collective. It does not matter whether this collective is an imagined community or a group that might be encountered directly and be able to confirm the idea that the individual belongs. What is important and consequential for one's way of life, attitudes, and even knowledge is one's own perception of membership. Typically, such collective identities become salient in specific situations. Multiple religious identities, that is, one's ideas of belonging to several different religious collectives, might be compartmentalised and kept separate from one another, without any one identity 'knowing' the others or reflecting on possible connections, interferences, or problems. This would be something like a 'balkanisation of the brain', to use Paul Veyne's political metaphor.[3] However, it is also possible that such multiple identities might be entertained consciously, with the individual reflecting upon them together and considering the ways in which each collective identity conforms to or conflicts with rules about inclusiveness or exclusiveness known or supposed to be present in the other identities.

Finally, 'religious identity' might mean the ascription by others of somebody's belonging to a religious collective, from inside or outside of that collective. Such acts of ascription typically add stereotypes or explicit norms about conforming behaviour. What is being applied in such a case in historical thinking as much as in today's research praxis is a container model. With regard to the characteristics of the group, everybody is predictable and alike. Or at least should be. Here, multiple religious identities are affirmed or bemoaned with strong normative undertones. The focus is, above all, on distinction. Being a member of that group renders the member different from all non-members. This is basic and helpful, for instance, in communicating about the others, that is, about those who are not members of the group, or in gaining political support against some others. Internal coherence, the likeness of all inside the group, comes only in second place. All in all, such discourse has importance in processes of institutionalisation and grouping, and in monitoring boundaries.

9.2 Religious identities as seen by urban observers

As a city, Rome was just one of many foundations in a longer lasting Mediterranean and particularly central-Italian wave of urbanisations. It is pointless to dis-

---

3 Veyne 1983.

cuss whether the urban settlements that developed in this process were Latin, Etruscan, or Greek cities – in many respects these were all conglomerations in peripheral late ancient oriental cultures and parasites of an East to West cultural diffusion. At Rome, an important template for urbanisation was *Greek*, the overlords felt related to other *Etruscan*-speaking elites, while the populace spoke *Latin*. The Latin language was closely related to other central Italian languages, such as Faliscan and, more distantly, Oscan or Umbrian. Rome was a river crossing and a port settlement, and it was the intense exchange along and across the regionally important river Tiber – passing through, keeping one's presence as a merchant or enterprise, settling down – that accounted for urban growth. In the 6th century BCE, the rulers of the city were in close contact with urban elites in other central-Italian cities who defined themselves as 'Etruscans' in a decisively different language (and in inscriptions in this language). The removal of these rulers, called 'kings' or *reges*, sometime around 500 BCE was the achievement of a different segment of the local elite, predating similar events in other Italian towns. For the next two centuries, regional warfare as a pursuit by Rome was directed as much against towns and tribes of Etruscan language as it was against settlements of Italic or Latin languages.

What we might call 'ethno-genesis' at Rome was a process that is visible above all in our sources for the 3rd to the 1st centuries BCE, parallel to the building of an empire of ever more distant Roman 'provinces', from Sicily to Spain, Asia Minor, and Syria. Religion, the ascribing of agency to non-human powers and the creating of special space for communicating with these powers, was an important tool for the process of ethno-genesis.[4] This can be seen, for instance, in the evolving distinction between the *ritus patrius*, or 'Roman ritual manner', and the *ritus Graecus*, or the 'Greek ritual manner'.[5] The difference between the two essentially boiled down to the question of whether or not one covered one's head during the ritual act. This distinction turned on the creation of an artificial foreignness: both rites were, in fact, equally a part of the local political elite's religious repertoire. That the forging of a Roman 'identity' took place in a multi-cultural space can be seen in a text from the middle of the 1st century CE:

> ... My friends, I can't stand
> A Rome full of Greeks. Yet few of the dregs are Greek!
> For the Syrian Orontes has long since polluted the Tiber,
> Bringing its language and customs, pipes and harp-strings,

---

4 Orlin 2010.
5 Scheid 1995; Orlin 2002; Sterbenc Erker 2013.

> And even their native timbrels are dragged along too,
> And the girls forced to offer themselves in the Circus.
> Go there, if your taste's a barbarous whore in a painted veil.[6]

'Greek' here is a synonym for 'skilled non-Romans', and also a stereotype, as the subsequent verses demonstrate. It conceals the reality of a multi-linguistic empire in which the dominance of Greek over the Aramaic that was developing into Syrian was a product of hindsight only. Linguistically, Gauls and Celts were quickly Latinised, despite the fact that, even in the 2nd century BCE, Gauls and Greeks were both religiously identified as 'others'. This is evident from the fact that couples (male and female) of each were buried alive in the city of Rome in a ritual of expiation.[7]

Rome was not unique in its othering and integrating of foreigners but was, rather, building on an older practice of Mediterranean *poleis*. In the second book of his *The Peloponnesian War*, the Greek historiographer Thucydides gives the Athenian politician Pericles a speech in the winter of 431 or 430 BCE which offers insight into Athenian self-images in this regard. The question of the importance of the city is discussed with regard to those who lost their lives for Athens in the war. After praising the rule of the people, equality, and laws, Pericles continues:

> Then our way of thinking also created the most rest from work: competitions and sacrifices, which are customary, year in, year out, and the most beautiful domestic facilities, whose daily delight in use frightens away the bitterness. And because of the size of the city, everything comes in from all over the world. So we can say about ourselves, we reap just as intimate a pleasure from the goods that thrive here as from those of the rest of mankind.[8]

Pericles paints a picture here of an attractive cosmopolitan 'city'. As is the case with other Greek texts, one needs to be careful, however, about assuming that the word 'polis' as it is used in the original should be understood as equivalent to 'city'. The concept of the polis was, rather, employed to obscure the differences and dependencies between the city and its hinterland (a difference which could have been highlighted by the use of *astu*, the 'capital' of a territory). Pericles then immediately goes on to explain why, even in times of war, Athens could afford not to carry out expulsions of foreigners (2,39): apparently not only 'the goods … of the other people' had come in but also the people themselves. As dedicatory inscriptions or sanctuaries that were newly erected in the 4th and 3rd centuries BCE indicate, the urban space became an increasingly diverse cultural space

---

6 Juvenal 3.60–66 (my translation).
7 See e.g. Perl 1982; Schultz 2010.
8 Thukydides, *Peloponnesian War* 2.38, my translation.

through regional and supra-regional migration and marriage, through slave imports and the activities of established long-distance traders. This diversity was concentrated in Piraeus, Athens' port, but could also be grasped in Athens itself.

Despite this cultural diversity, the import of foreign gods by non-Greek ethnic groups was not common; since the middle of the 5th century BCE, only the Thracians had done so, bringing in their goddess Bendis. It was, rather, cosmopolitans who were the primary driving force behind the addressing of new deities and, thus, behind making them at home in Athens.[9] In the 4th, 3rd, or 2nd centuries BCE, the introduction of new gods sometimes occurred in parallel with the re-energising of older cults, as seen, for example, in Lycurgus' reforms of the Ephebeia in the second half of the 4th century.[10] The introduction of the veneration of Asklepios, the formation of Dionysian associations, and the proliferation of admirers of Isis provide prominent examples of the pull of the new in this epoch. For today's research, it is fundamental to recognise the principle that religious diversity was rarely an expression of other social or ethnic cleavages and was usually not even the result of some old fundamental religious difference. This recognition is more important than the compiling of lists of the novel deities who suddenly appeared in the religious actions of urban inhabitants.

Here we must note an important historical difference when comparing the ancient world to our contemporary situation. This is that long-distance migration was very limited in earlier eras simply because the low capacity of ancient shipping made the transportation of large numbers difficult, if not impossible. This capacity limited the numbers who could be carried across the Mediterranean before the Imperial age to just a few tens of thousands of people per year, according to Greg Woolf's calculations.[11] The same limitations also applied in the subsequent Imperial period, but due to the increasing integration of the cities into the now Roman-dominated empire, other forms of mobility and their visibility were enhanced. Urban density and religious diversity as such need not be consequential. But in what circumstances and periods did they become important? On what terms? And where were religious differences seen or produced?

The characteristics of religions was certainly a *topos* of ancient ethnography, even if it was not a dominant one. In Pomponius Mela's mid-1st century CE description of the world as seen from a navigator's perspective, religious characteristics show up only occasionally, perhaps when other powerful distinctions were not available to him from the earlier texts he used as sources. Of all the people

---

[9] Parker 1996, 152–187.
[10] Dazu Mikalson 1998, 292–3.
[11] See G. Woolf 2017.

living around the Black Sea, only the Colchi and their city of Phasis are credited with anything religious, namely the temple of Phrixus.[12] Exceptionally, in the case of Ireland the total lack of religion is mentioned:

> On the far side of Britain, Iuverna is more or less equal in area, but it is oblong with equally extended lateral coastlines. Its climate is hideous for ripening seeds, but the island is so luxuriant with grass – not only abundant but sweet – that sheep stuff themselves in a fraction of the day, and, unless they are kept from the pasture, they burst from feeding too long. Its inhabitants are undisciplined and ignorant of all virtue, to a greater degree than any other nation, and they are very much inexperienced in piety.[13]

Despite the broad lack of focus on the subject, religious differences could still be important in specific contexts. In his proposal for a sort of constitution in his mid-1st century BCE treatise *On laws*, Cicero turns his attention to the problem of religious separatism in the second paragraph of his religious laws, writing that 'No-one should have his own new cult, or foreign cults'.[14] He 'resolves' the problem by reconstructing it in terms of a – clearly precarious – dichotomy between the private and the public, and at the same time assigns control over the private realm to the public priesthoods.[15] External boundaries are not reflected in more detail in here and internal differences are not seen as solely the result of importation from other places. However, such differences between the city and external others are reflected elsewhere in Cicero's writings. Just as the Romans had their public *religio* (in the singular), so others also had theirs: 'Every community has its religion, and we have ours, Laelius'.[16]

Cicero's distinction between what is 'ours' and 'theirs' provides no scope for the possibility of either choice or cooperation. Moreover, it also fails to reflect the complex composition of the Roman population itself,[17] which was precisely the source of his initial problem: the choice of new and imported gods over or alongside the traditional gods of Rome. Cicero, as other texts demonstrate, was primarily concerned about the combination of human and animal forms in religions with an Egyptian origin. However, other, even more sinister, images could also raise suspicions.

A touchstone for how serious the problem was considered to be and how it was framed at Rome is offered by the periodically attested persecutions and ex-

---

12 Pomponius Mela 1.107, cf. 1.102–17.
13 Pompon. 3.53, trsl. Romer 1998.
14 Cicero, *Laws* 2.19: *Separatim nemo habessit deos neve novos neve advenas [...]*.
15 Cicero, *Laws* 2.20.
16 Cicero, *Pro Flacco* 69: *sua cuique civitati religio, Laeli, est, nostra nobis*.
17 See Noy 2000, 2004, 2010.

pulsions of people who worshipped gods that were deemed, at various times, to be beyond the pale. These negative reactions took two distinct forms. The first focused on and sought to reverse processes of institutionalisation. The destruction of cult places of Bacchus and the regulation of the Bacchanalia in the early 2nd century BCE, the destruction of temples dedicated to the Egyptian gods Sarapis and Isis, and the interdiction of the local crossroad festivals in mid-1st century BCE, are all examples of this sort of response. These reactions seem to be connected to crack-downs on priesthoods and on any form of permanent association that had not been licensed by the Roman Senate. The second type of reaction is narrated in terms of the expulsion of peoples, primarily the Jews and Chaldeans but our sources also mention the expulsion of Greek philosophers and astrologers at various times. It has been convincingly shown that even the Jews on the list do not refer to a group that was identified at Rome as an ethnic group but, rather, to providers of religious services, rites, objects, and knowledge.[18] Such specialists offered religious services or divination and used, or were seen as using, *Iudaei* as a label of quality and superior knowledge, just as the *Chaldaei* did. The provision of astrological knowledge and horoscopes was given a superior aura by referring to distant Eastern arts and sciences in the form of a geographical adjective (implying cities like Babylon or Jerusalem). In both cases, ethnic terms were closely associated with bodies of knowledge in written form and provided valuable labels for those selling services. In one of the earliest Roman sources, Horace's satire *Ibam forte via sacra*, 'By chance I walked down the Via Sacra',[19] from the end of the 1st century BCE, there is a reference to such a person which, while it remains enigmatic, clearly demonstrates that the close association of a contemporary Roman with such a character was within the bounds of the imagination, at least as far as the rendering of special services or the sharing of observations was concerned.

The ethnic label, frequently used in our sources, was as much a stereotype used by others as a marketing strategy exploited by small entrepreneurs who wished to associate themselves with a far distant, ancient, and, thus, proven source of knowledge. The misogynist polemics of Juvenal's satires allow us to see not only an instance of such a usage ('Phrygian', a region in Asia Minor frequently associated both with Troy and with elaborate ritual), but also the social and economic context of such classification and competition. The urban market for divinatory services was differentiated, featuring very different suppliers and

---

18 Wendt 2015a, see also Wendt 2015b, 2016.
19 Horace, *Satires* 1.9.

services according to the social standing (and economic possibilities) of the female clients:

> If she's middle-class she'll try the fortune-tellers at the Circus,
> Select the cards, or offer her hand and brow to the prophet
> Who demands of her lots of clicking sounds with the tongue.
> Rich women obtain their readings from Phrygian soothsayers,
> Or someone expert in star-signs and the cosmos, or the elder
> Who publicly purifies the places where lightning buries itself.
> Plebeian fates are decided in the Circus or on the Embankment,
> Where those displaying a long gold chain hung on a bare neck,
> Ask advice at the foot of the Circus towers or the dolphin columns,
> About whether to leave the tradesman and marry the inn-keeper.[20]

In Apuleius' mid-2nd century CE *Metamorphoses*, the first-person narrative of Lucius as he travels around transfigured into the form of a donkey adds further facets to the image of such practices. Apuleius depicts a bunch of rough men who carry about a statue of Dea Syria and earn their living from offering rituals to city-dwellers. These men are shown entering a city and attracting a venerator of the deity by playing a form of music that is typically associated with the goddess.[21] Priests of Isis are later described as carrying their deity in a procession through a Greek port city, accompanied again by music that is typical for her temple.[22] In the dense urban streets, it is sound rather than sight that guides people in until they are close enough for direct visual contact. Under these conditions, we can conclude, a diversity of ethnic identities from within the Roman Empire was actively construed rather than fought. This diversity could, however, be exploited and dramatised in situations of conflict, allowing radical measures up to and including expulsions framed in terms of ethnic identification.

These examples also allow us to shift from considering differences conceptualised in terms of ethnic groups to individuals and their very varying relationships to any such groups. The examples are helpful in so far as they assist us in grasping the breadth of the wide range of different forms of interaction and grouping in which individuals might participate, from being occasional clients, through permanent supporters (but infrequent participants), to full-time followers or even professionals. The institutionalisation of 'associations' in a legal sense (*collegia*) is only occasionally invoked, probably whenever property is in-

---

20 Juvenal 6.582–591, trsl. King 1991.
21 Apuleius, *Golden Ass* 8.24.2, 26–5, 30.4; s.a. 8.27–29; 9.8.
22 Ibid., 11.10.6.

volved.²³ On the one hand, this could take the form of relatively 'static' assets, such as a foundation, a lasting fund of capital, and/or a building. On the other hand, capital could also be raised through monthly fees, for instance with an eye on providing for the future burial expenses of members and/or for an annual party. Typically, social interactions in such *collegia* were restricted to very few days each year. Tertullian, in his defence of the practices of Christian grouping, not only mention their peaceful purposes – for instance that they come together to pray for the emperor and civil rest, literally, 'the quietness of the affairs' – but also stresses that fees are not raised more frequently than once a month.²⁴ Whatever the actual temporal rhythms and percentages of presence of the different forms of meetings, such groups hardly provided the blueprint for Christian churches, neither in terms of frequency of interaction – here one should look rather to synagogal meetings – nor in terms of network building. Across religious orientations, such groups were strictly local.

Nevertheless, institutions such as associations, cult-sites, or trans-local *personal* networks could serve as 'bridgeheads' for people moving to a city for the first time or from one city to another. Again, Apuleius' protagonist Lucius, now no longer a donkey, provides details that are equally salient whether they are imagined or historical. Having been initiated into the worship of Egyptian gods, Lucius moves for professional reasons to Rome in order to find success as a lawyer. These urban aspirations are accompanied by his ongoing association with a temple of Isis, in which he describes himself as a permanent venerator, an immigrant to the temple, yet indigenous in his religious practice.²⁵ The goddess shows a reciprocal regard for Lucius and ensures that he receives a more than comfortable flow of legal fees.²⁶ Religion serves as a bridgehead here rather than as a nostalgic refuge. Similar observations can be made in relation to a number of other groups. Through a personal network, the cult of Syrian deities in the Trastevere quarter of Rome, for instance, seemingly peripheral in terms of gods as well as location, provided access to figures as central as the priesthood of the Vestal Virgins.

Religious identities in all these cases were manifold. The multiple and uncoordinated layers of urban religion, from the festivals of a deity associated with Asia Minor such as Cybele, to neighbourhood rites at the crossroad shrines,

---

23 See Kloppenborg and Wilson 1996; Harland 2003; Jaccottet 2003; Ustinova 2005; Bendlin 2011a; Steinhauer 2014; for strategies of attraction, Rüpke 2018d, 313–9.
24 Tertullian, *Apology* 39.5.
25 Apuleius, *Golden Ass* 11.26.3: *eram cultor denique adsiduus, fani quidem aduena, religionis autem indigena*.
26 Ibid., 11.30.2.

were easily compatible with one another, so long, at least, as no theological specialist with differing views decided to argue the contrary. Even when incompatibilities were pointed out and attempts to stir up conflicts made, the specialists responsible were rarely successful over anything longer than a very short-term window, as the ongoing lamentations and exhortations of Christian homilies demonstrate.

All such activities were embedded in a correspondingly incoherent, but frequently shared and overlapping, layer of stories, narratives told or performed in intimate or open spaces. These stories allowed for different uses of 'We', that is to say the acceptance or celebration of one's identity as an inhabitant of the city of Rome, an inhabitant of the Roman empire, as an individual trained in Hellenistic culture, as a non-barbarian, philosopher, traveller, and/or descendant of some more ancient people through one or another (often very complicated) line of genealogical descent. Above all, these stories made it easy to opt into those identities, whether by merely listening to recitals or by viewing dramatic pieces at the scene of some public entertainment.[27]

'Entertainment' is, of course, a problematic term here. Usually, at Rome as much as at Sabratha in Libya, these performances were presented to the gods and the quality of the production honoured them as much as it drew larger audiences. In Greek, Oscan, Etruscan, and Latin cities, as well as at Rome, the institutionalisation and multiplication of competitions, in the form of horse races as much as dramatic performances, was a significant change in urban religion throughout the second half of the 1st millennium BCE.[28] This change created temporary religious spaces that brought together the gods, large parts of the populace (sometimes only male), and the political elites who sponsored this form of religious communication. Distinction by innovation and the permanent adding of new stories were hallmarks of these institutions.

Stories, however, could also divide. Instead of competing for and bolstering popular support through the distribution of meat, that is by animal sacrifice, as the landed aristocracy did, urban intellectuals drew much smaller, but more stable, groups of adherents together by means of different stories, new interpretations, and the championing of new ways of life.[29] Alphabetic writing – increasingly indispensable not only for palace households but also for the administration of growing cities in the region – enabled more complex and less public forms of communication.[30] Here, the proposal of radical changes in

---

27 E.g. Apuleius, *Golden Ass* 10.29.4; 34.2.
28 Bernstein 1998, 2007; Manuwald 2011; Rüpke 2012f, 35–50.
29 Rüpke 2018d, 329–348.
30 Petsalis-Diomidis 2006; Corbier 2013; Law et al. 2015; Howley 2017.

how to live one's everyday life, from caring for one's self and one's own body by way of rituals and specific forms of nourishment, became ever more present in the course of the 1st to 3rd centuries CE. This growing market witnessed fierce competition in which nuances were decisive. The import or immigration of proponents of the schools of Hellenistic philosophy was joined by a rapidly differentiating field of thinkers who built on the Greek translations of Hebrew Scripture, leading to Jewish and, in particular, Christian schools and networks.

9.3 Semantics

The terminology used in the preceding sentences needs to be supplemented by the notion of 'religious identities'. As we have seen before, even 'collective identity' is not identical with existing collectives, whether those be nations, groups, or networks. In order to deal with the problem of pluralisation and diversity, and, in particular, with the problem of a single person's multiple identities, the semantics of such imaginations are as important as the frequency and form of social interactions or knowledge and the stories related to such collectives.[31]

The most consequential identity for an individual was that of *civitas*, 'citizenship'. This identity entailed not only a topographical belonging, often but not necessarily urban, but also a whole bundle of civic rights, from marriage and contracting, through legal and military protection, to political participation.[32] Above all, it guaranteed personal liberty in the face of servitude or marginality. Such a citizenship was not built on ethnicity and nor was it exclusive. Cicero argued for the granting of citizenship to the Greek poet Archias by pointing to the many other citizenships he had already been granted by other cities.[33] Cicero himself, stemming as he did from the Italian countryside outside of Rome, spoke already in this context of his *two fatherlands*.[34] The model of the Imperium Romanum, that overarching political super-structure which sat above all the cities of the empire and employed their administrative institutions in its running, made dual citizenship – unthinkable in the model of Fustel de Coulanges, discussed in Chapter 2 – a standard.

Religious preferences could occasionally be thought of as being part of citizenship, as is evident from Cicero's views cited above. Likewise, religious be-

---

[31] See the discussion in Rüpke and Degelmann 2015; Rüpke 2016f.
[32] Ando 2017.
[33] Cicero, *Pro Archia poeta* 10.
[34] Cicero, *Laws* 2.5.

longing *could* itself be conceptualised as a form of citizenship. Judaeo-Christian authors of the Imperial period played around with reflections concerning the potentially conflicting loyalties involved in holding dual citizenships and the problems of priority, as I will discuss in more detail below. Despite such reflections, many religious practices were never and could not be related to concepts of citizenship. Roman neighbourhood festivals, the Compitalia, explicitly transgressed the boundaries between the free, freedmen, and slaves, and between men and women, in the performance of prayers at street-corners and the competitions of the *ludi compitalicii* in the streets. The same holds true for the urban pursuits of watching the games and other publicly or privately financed spectacles, from horse-races and dramatic productions to gladiatorial shows. The common and frequent engagement with such pursuits need not be thought to entail that one was obliged to participate. Cicero, for example, looked forward to taking long walks with visiting friends on the days of the neighbourhood festival while Seneca objected to visiting the amphitheatre.[35] Religious identities could vary, but so too could the obligations that individuals felt were implied in such imaginations of belonging.

9.4 Construing identity boundaries in hindsight

My argument is not restricted to ancient 'cults' and their embedment in the city. My claim is, rather, that the findings about religious plurality discussed above are equally relevant for what are usually addressed as separate 'religions'. Separate religious groups and traditions are not the basic form of religious activity but, rather, the outcome of specific, and above all urban, processes. To substantiate this claim, it will be necessary to shift my perspective somewhat and turn my focus towards shared religious practices, rather than beginning with differences. Practices shared across religious identities (or better, practices pursued without the involvement of such identities), were inseparable from the rise of the cities of the Hellenistic and Imperial Mediterranean world. My argument thus focuses again on religion in the making rather than on fixed systems of local civic religions and elective cults.

In order to make the argument stronger, I test it against what is seen as the strongest form of religious identity and groupness in the ancient world, Judaism. Even Jews can easily be shown to have participated in shared religious practices, that is practices that were performed by Roman citizens (all free-born or manu-

---

35 Cicero, *Letters to Atticus* 2.3.4; Seneca, *Letters* 7.

mitted people after the *Constitutio Antoniniana* of 212 CE) or slaves, regardless of their ethnic relationship with Judaea, allegiances to Jewish synagogues, regular or irregular participation in associated rituals, or veneration of the one god propagated by the Scriptures. The mapping of such a field is not a completely new endeavour but the process is hindered by the basic assumption that the behaviour being described is, in some way, deviant.[36] Against the background of a historiography of religion that takes 'religions' as their natural units,[37] such a description can hardly avoid taking a normative stance, no matter how critical of, or sympathetic with, these deviances we happen to be. With regard to Jewish actors, the term 'assimilation' has been used to describe this behaviour and, regardless of whether this language is understood as having a positive or negative connotation, the underlying concept always claims to identify a process of change and deviance.

Another conceptual framework to deal with participation in shared religious practices seemingly deviant from the actors' primary religious allegiance is the language of 'popular' or 'folk religion'. Such a language allows to make such behaviour irrelevant for a more general account of (in this instance) 'Judaism' by projecting deviance onto social (and sometimes spatial: 'pagan' or 'rustic') differences. The deviant practices are thus attributed to marginal or inferior agents. Louis H. Feldman, for instance, in his substantial treatment of *Jew and Gentile in the Ancient World*, summarises a sub-chapter on what he calls 'syncretism among the Jews' with a remark on the wide range of divinities named on amulets used by those who he classifies as Jews: 'And yet this was all at the level of folklore and hardly diminished the loyalty to Judaism of the Jewish possessors of these amulets'.[38]

'Folklore' does not, as a framework, aim at explanation or understanding but, rather, at bracketing facts that do not fit into the 'big picture'. My own approach is rather different. By setting aside a large number of documented individual religious activities, studies of distinct ritual traditions, I claim, overlook a vast field of religious practices performed by those agents who are the very subjects of those studies. This field of ritual practices consists, above all, of innovations in urban contexts and is an important legacy of the urbanisation processes in the Mediterranean basin. In order to demonstrate that this claim is plausible, I will show to just how great a degree much of the Judaism of the Imperial period is city-based and city-focused, and, thus, is urbanised and urbanising religion.

---

36 For the notion of religious deviance with regard to the Imperial period, see Rüpke 2016e.
37 See Rüpke 2018a. The following is based on Rüpke 2018f.
38 Feldman 1993, 69.

In pursuit of this goal, I will focus on polemics concerning issues that have been overlooked and, in particular, on Rabbinic attempts to regulate life in the Mishnah.

9.5 Mapping differences

My analysis starts by focusing on Latin voices, many, but not all, of which come from the city of Rome. Here, *Iudaei* appear from the second half of the 1st century BCE onwards in antiquarian, historiographical, lyric, ethnographic, and satiric texts. If we disregard the narrative details of the extended historiographical account given by Tacitus, written to prepare his readers for his description of the Jewish rebellion from 66 to 70 CE, the construction of difference boils down to a very restricted number of topics and thus *topoi*, a consequence, I suggest, of the fact there was neither pressing danger nor sufficient intellectual interest to motivate a deeper study. The Judeans (*Iudaei; Hebraei* is much rarer, although also understood in geographical terms)[39] are presented as a geographically defined group, culturally characterised by a few clearly distinguishing traits. These include food, circumcision, and regulated behaviour on a specific day of the astrological week (a concept familiar in Italy from the 1st century BCE onwards), namely Saturn's day. They are said to venerate the sky instead of gods (Cornelius Tacitus) or just one (philosophical) god (M. Terentius Varro). In sum, the description is, as Erich Gruen has pointed out, rather friendly, amused, and sometimes amazed.[40]

This broad characterisation is confirmed by, for example, the administrative measures taken by the Romans to enable access to food distribution in order to compensate for the observance of Sabbath regulations on movement, as pointed out by Philo.[41] A historiography formatted by the business of keeping Judaism and Christianity distinct cannot, by definition, cite voices that reflect the other perspective. Rather, it must rely on contemporary voices stemming from Alexandria, such as Philo, or from Judea, such as Josephus, as well as Rabbinic texts from the Mishnah, a product of the advanced Imperial age. I will return to this line of argument shortly but will begin with observations on roughly contemporary texts by Roman Jews that were excluded from the later historiography, large-

---

39 See e.g. Tacitus, *Histories* 5.2.
40 Gruen 2002, 53; see also Gruen 1990, 1992, 1998 for the Roman and Jewish background.
41 *Legatio ad Gaium*. In general see Goldenberg 1979.

ly because their authors, while clearly from a Jewish background, were seen as taking an interest in the figure of Christ.

The anonymous *Tractate to the Hebrews* and the *Shepherd of Hermas* demonstrate the embeddedness of the religious fellows of the authors in the urban and economic fabric of Rome. I start with the latter text, already introduced in Chapter 8.5. In Hermas' view, it is easy to listen to stories about the God, to be persuaded of their importance, and to come to believe in their underlying message. The easy access to such stories being read out suggests an urban context, as does his assumption that (as a consequence of the easiness of listening) all the people first share belief and community.[42] Hermas never claims that these Jews form the majority of Roman citizens but this is not presented as the major problem. Hermas is not concerned with the character of the external borderline between Jews and Gentiles but, rather, with the more difficult problems that arise *within* the borders due to the behaviour of those who do not act in accordance with their supposed identity. This leads to the question of who is truly within and who is outside?[43] Hermas' foremost intention is to bring firmly within the boundaries all of those who currently reside in the grey area, that is to bring them to conversion (*metanoia*).[44]

However, Hermas remains remarkably silent about the theoretical differences between the 'peoples' and the believers. The very few statements that refer to this distinction remain vague. In the discussion of marriage and separation, 'to do the same as the peoples' is regarded as equivalent to adultery, leading to the pollution of the flesh.[45] Whether 'pollution of the flesh' is related to sacrificial meals is far from clear.[46] With regard to Israel's relationship to Yahweh, while idolatry is regarded as adultery in the Tanakh, there is no clue suggesting such an association in Hermas' text.[47] Idolatry is, however, mentioned in another context: it is equated with taking counsel from a professional diviner and diagnosed even among members of Hermas' own community.[48]

A central notion of the text is that of the laws or constitution of a city, with citizenship including the particular 'civic way of life (*politeuesthai*)' of a given

---

42 *Pastor Hermae* 94.
43 E.g. *Pastor Hermae* 75.
44 Osiek 1999, 29.
45 *Pastor Hermae* 29.9.
46 See *Pastor Hermae* 60.
47 Such a reference is assumed by Brox 1991, 208, pointing to passages like *Hosea* 2:4; 3:1, Jeremiah and Ezekiel.
48 *Pastor Hermae* 43.4.

city.[49] But that is not all. Hermas also adds to the imagery of the city found in several apocalyptic texts composed at least a little earlier. Hermas, however, stands out from these texts with their typically provincial concerns.[50] Hermas places a great deal of emphasis on the imagery of the city and its most notable feature, a tower, described in more detail Chapter 8 above. The tower recalls the prominent and representative *acropoleis* or *Capitolia* of Greco-Roman cities, already featured in the oppositional collection of anti-Roman oracles found in the Fifth Sibylline Oracle. The tower, at the same time, takes up an important biblical and postbiblical image.[51] The rewards allotted in *sim* 8 regulate admittance to a tower[52] which is at once both differentiated from the wall[53] and also its central feature, directly accessed by the gates, as the later *sim* 9 makes clear.[54] For Hermas, the inhabitant of Rome and visionary of a new *ecclesia*, this is not the old Jerusalem, which has been destroyed, but a Jerusalem which has to be re-imagined from scratch. For Hermas' readers, Rome is not an imaginary opponent, as is the case in the other apocalyptic texts. Hermas' readers are confronted with the real Rome, the marble city of Flavian and Trajanic-Hadrianic times.[55] Hermas is aware of the enormous attraction of the city and its society and social rules;[56] his personal presence at Rome (probably shared by the author of Hebrews, who had to design an alternative priesthood that could challenge the splendour and power of the emperor as supreme pontifex) only strengthens this factor. Following another trend in the post-70s apocalyptic literature, Hermas turns inward. The alternative to an incommensurable, eschatological, imagined city would be a distant one, an image so radical that it does not fit with the problems of daily life.

I have presented an analysis of the sacerdotal imagery of *Hebrews* elsewhere and will only summarise the results here.[57] Against the backdrop of an intensive appropriation of priestly offices and roles by the Flavian emperors, from Vespasian through Titus to Domitian, the author mobilises the dimly-lit figure of Melchizedek. He uses this figure in order to create the image of a heavenly high priest, Jesus. The author maps onto Melchizedek many details or polemical alter-

---

49 Lieu 2004, 243.
50 See K. R. Jones 2011a, 277 f. for such 'local Jewish concerns'.
51 See Busi 1999, 235–9.
52 *Pastor Hermae* 68.1.
53 *Pastor Hermae* 72.6; 73.3.
54 *Pastor Hermae* 79 f.
55 On the latter, see Boyle and Dominik 2003.
56 Stressed for the author of Hebrews by Maier 2015.
57 Rüpke 2012i.

ations of the role of the supreme Roman pontiff, so eagerly proffered by the contemporary emperor. If Gelardini is right in assuming that the homily of *Hebrews* was read on the day of commemoration of the destruction of the Second Temple,[58] it would have helped to bring out differences between the group being addressed and its Roman environment (Roman certainly in a political sense and perhaps even in a geographical sense as well). The recipients originally targeted were an audience that was in danger of losing its religious zeal. It has been rightly observed that *Hebrews* addresses 'a certain weariness in pursuing the Christian goal'[59] rather than fear about the impact of persecution. Apostasy – or we should, less dramatically, say: total neglect of obligations – was considered a real danger by the author.[60] The rhetorical strategy aimed not at radical dichotomy and incompatibility but, rather, at concurrence on equal terms, taking seriously the religious dimension of the non-Jewish environment. The message is: We have a sort of *pontifex maximus*, too (*echein archierea*, 8.1), but a better one, sworn by god, eternal and present – the son remains the son and will not be replaced by his brother (as Domitian replaced Titus). Given our knowledge of the slow development of an understanding of the figure and the 'name' of Christ, son-ship is here not any early theological claim about of the son[61] but, rather, a contemporary pun.

Hebrews and Hermas demonstrate the great attraction of not only Rome but its specific urbanity, the urban lifestyle of this city and the high degree of embeddedness of the Greek speakers and their audiences.[62] In the view of the Latin-writing authors, there seem to be no threatening differences. For intellectual boundary work on the ground, closeness is threatening and this closeness is created above all by the shared urban contexts.

9.6 Prescribing differences in the Mishnah

The description of Jews in Roman sources is not generally hostile and the same holds true for the description of Romans or the Roman administration in the Mishnah (if we disregard depictions of the military, a topic of fear for civilians in general, and corresponding regulations in Roman law, too, which were intended to give at least some protection to civilians). This is not to say that the Mishnah

---

58 Gelardini 2005, 123.
59 Ellingworth 1993, 78.
60 Ellingworth 1993, 79; see also DeSilva 1996.
61 Cf. Dunnill 1992, 188–226.
62 See *Hebrews* 2.2 and 2.3.

ignores differences between Jews and Romans. On the contrary, these differences are emphasised. However, what is important is that the differences that are recognised are not necessarily construed in a negative light and are, indeed, presented as being possibly advantageous in certain circumstances. For instance, we learn that a Jew can jump into a well-heated bath run by a non-Jew immediately after the end of Sabbath, whereas if the customer were to visit a bath run by a Jew instead they would have to allow some hours for the water to be heated up.

The rabbis ultimately focus on idolatry, mirroring Roman concerns about Judaism having just one god or no proper god at all, and explore the topic in all its details (in particular, but not exclusively, in Avodah Zarah). This discussion is extended to take in even very indirect forms of co-operation, such as the aiding and abetting of the construction and veneration of images. Indirect forms of benefit, derived from the acts of others, are said to be much less problematic, even to the point of allowing the use of skin resulting from acts of sacrifice or the eating of meat intended for the same purpose.[63]

There is a lacuna in the boundary work that is clearly going on in the Mishnah. Visiting theatres, something done regularly by Philo, is hardly ever mentioned in Rabbinic sources and not at all in the Mishnah. It is, however, attested later in the Babylonian Talmud and referred back to an old saying[64] that Rabbi Meir provides arguments which parallel Tertullian's concerns in his early 3rd-century treatise *On spectacles:* ultimately, theatrical performances are conceived of as parts of rituals that involve idols. This diagnosis is not only correct but also draws attention to the reality that the viewing of the ritual elements involved was practically unavoidable for all spectators. This fact makes it all the more surprising that there is a lack of criticism directed at visiting theatrical performances. Instead we find positive attestations of regular visits, for instance in discussions of the marking out of special seats at Milet.[65] Circuses or amphitheatres were accessible. Processions, or rather the witnessing of processions and participation in them as a spectator, are never mentioned, as far as I can see. The use of bathhouses is simply taken for granted.[66] Why?

With Caesarea being the only metropolis in Palestine, the Rabbis might simply not have concerned themselves with such issues, which would not have been at all relevant to Jews living in most other places. Nevertheless, theoretical boundary work need not be restricted to the realm of day-to-day experience. I would, thus, like to offer an alternative explanation. An important proportion of the

---

63 *Avodah Zarah* 2:3–4.
64 *bT Avodah Zarah* 18: *baraita.*
65 For some further details see Feldman 1993, 61–63; Milet: Reynolds 1982, 54.
66 E. g. *Avodah Zarah* 5:4.

many shared ritual practices were not thematised as illegitimate crossings of boundaries because they were regarded as part and parcel of an urban way of life that transcended religious divides. It is the very hallmarks of urbanity, even if clearly conceptualised using Greco-Roman religious semantics, that are exempted from aggressive criticism. I base this claim on the positive view of cities that is visible in the Mishnaic tractates on even the most cursory of readings.

9.7 Urbanity in the Mishnah

I propose that the lack of critique of urbanised religion in the Mishnah should be read as part and parcel of the urban aspirations[67] that were shared by the Rabbinic authors in the same way as by those others who also lived or aspired to live in cities. Even if the Mishnah, taken as a whole, reflects the rural setting of a clear majority of those it addresses (in common with probably more than ninety percent of the population of the Roman world), urban life is not only viewed with sympathy but is seen as a preferred form of life that cannot be reduced or given up. Not even parts of cities, we read, should be surrendered back to the rural way of life.[68]

Terms for 'city' or 'town' appear several hundred times in the tractates of the Mishnah. It is impossible to review these passages here in any detail but the overall impression given by these uses is of a significant degree of coherence across very different fields of regulation. Starting from basic economics, we can reflect on the fact that onions from towns were supposed to be of a higher quality than those from villages.[69] Likewise, transport into towns raises the value of goods and might necessitate further tithing.[70]

Regardless of its structural complexity, a town can be treated as a unit and can even act as a unit.[71] The tractate *Eruvim* takes particular care in constituting towns as spatial units with regard to Sabbath regulations.[72] People who come from a big city are permitted to roam a smaller town in its entirety, even if it

---

[67] For this concept in contemporary urban studies see Goh and van der Veer 2016, drawing on Appadurai.
[68] *Arakhin* 9:8.
[69] *Terumot* 2:5.
[70] *Maaser Sheni* 4:1.
[71] For instance, in sending contributions, *Sheqalim* 1:7.
[72] *Eruvim* 5, 8, and 9.

is larger than two thousand steps (a privilege not granted people from smaller towns coming into bigger cities).[73]

Solidarity within towns (and among 'Jews') takes many different forms, from allowing the usage of somebody's house if he has left for Sabbath,[74] through the renouncing of taxes for 'shekel' given to fellow-townsmen,[75] to the inclusion of all animals that stay at night in the town as domestic beasts.[76] Betrothal and marriage regulations offer further evidence. If one marries a woman from one's own town (ʿir) and that town has a bath house, one cannot then later argue for divorce on the basis of 'secret defects', since these would have been publicly visible.[77] After the military occupation of a smaller town, one should presume that all women in the town have been raped; in a larger city, the benefit of the doubt is granted.[78] Size is also a limit to credibility. One need not believe the statement of a single inhabitant of a large city, because it might not be representative of the community as a whole, while those who live in smaller towns are more likely to be trustworthy when it comes to representing the community.[79]

The tractate *Megillah* adapts the dates for reading the scroll of Esther to the regular assembly dates in villages (*kepharim*) but insists on specified dates for larger towns (ʿ*ayaroth gedoloth*).[80] It is also concerned with the loss of sacralised space due to the conversion of public space, asking for profits from the selling of streets to be directed into the building of synagogues, and not *vice versa*.[81] But above all, as noted above, cities themselves should not be allowed to shrink.[82]

There is a clear hierarchy in the presentation of the quality of life when comparing life outside towns, life in smaller towns, and the lives of those who reside in larger cities. For example, one cannot move one's wife from a city into a town without her consent,[83] a recognition that this would be an intolerable degradation of her living standards if she were not to agree to the move. Similarly, priests should take their brides only from cities, implying that the women who live in cities are superior in some way.[84]

---

73 *Eruvim* 5:8. See in detail C. M. Baker 2002; Fonrobert 2004; Klein 2006, 2017.
74 *Erubin* 8:5.
75 *Sheqalim* 1:7.
76 *Betzah* 5:7.
77 *Ketuboth* 7:8.
78 *Ketuboth* 2:9.
79 *Demai* 4:6–7.
80 *Megillah* 1:1–2.
81 *Megillah* 3:1.
82 *Arakhin* 9:8.
83 *Ketuboth* 13:10.
84 *Ketuboth* 4:8.

Even with regard to the presence of idols and, hence, to indirect participation in idolatry, regulations show an awareness of the dense interactions that occur in towns and cities. This comes to the fore in discussions of the possibility of selecting shops without idols[85] or the possibility of rebuilding on a smaller footprint a damaged house that shares a wall with a temple by withdrawing the new wall into the interior of one's property.[86] Likewise, the free use of wine is granted in towns of mixed populations.[87]

Religion, too, is seen as, above all, a spatial practice: to seduce somebody is to point out to him that 'There is a god in such a place, who eats thus, drinks thus, does good in one way, and harm in another' (*Sanhedrin* 7:10 A).[88] The division of labour among a polytheistic constellation of deities is seen in terms of the location of different gods in different spaces. To ask everybody who can hear this to 'go and perform an act of service to an idol' is to lead a whole town astray (7:10 O).[89]

To sum up, cities, and above all cities that are walled and feature a court,[90] are places of great value that were sought after by people. Those who lived in such places gained citizenship after a period of twelve months, thus also conferring on them the duty to participate in wall building.[91] Cities are presented as complex places but they are not particularly full of idols[92] and nor are they characterised as the primary sphere of activity for sorcerers, sorceresses, and diviners, religious agents who are presented throughout the Mishnah as also performing in rural contexts.[93]

Evidently, the authors and users of the Mishnah, that is to say, the Rabbinic movement, shared the positive outlook on urban life that was characteristic of the political and cultural elites of the Roman empire.[94] Complexity and opportunities are stressed rather than dangers, despite the ambivalent (to say the least)

---

85 *Avodah Zarah* 1:4.
86 *Avodah Zarah* 3:6.
87 *Avodah Zarah* 4:11.
88 *Sanhedrin* 7:10 A.
89 *Sanhedrin* 7:10 O.
90 *Kelim* 1:7; *Sotah* 9:2.
91 *Baba Batra* 1:5.
92 See *Avodah Zarah* 3:5 G.
93 See Murray 2007.
94 See e.g. Edwards 1996, Eshleman 2012, and also S. Fine 2005 and Miller 2010 for the evidence from material Jewish culture. For the formation of the Rabbis, see Lightstone 2002 (and Dohrmann 2013), Friedheim 2010a, Lapin 2012, Cohn 2013; For differences between Palestinian and Babylonian thinking on the political and spatial context, see e.g. Hodkin 2014.

character of the city of Rome[95] and the lack of a contemporary model of an urban Jerusalem not reduced to the location of the Temple.[96] This balanced view of the urban sits comfortably alongside scholarly views that Rabbis often had an urban base from the earliest period.[97]

Such a positioning was not for want of alternatives. In the long process by which two 'religions' were mutually constituted (to follow the model of Daniel Boyarin),[98] an anti-urban strand in the developing Christian churches, in particular those of the Eastern part of the Mediterranean, developed despite the thorough urban transformation of many local Christianities.[99] This strand was characterised by an explicit withdrawal from cities in the form of the monastic movement, on the one hand, and the tacit shift of authority from urban self-administration to episcopal authority, on the other. Focusing on the individual believer rather than on the mutual constitution of political bodies and urban spaces (such as city councils and *agorai*), in this context the city was valued above all as the residence of a bishop.[100] Such bishops' 'palaces' could also easily be built outside the walls of cities, thus weakening rather than strengthening the function of the cityscape as a central place.

9.8 A particular and a general conclusion

The problematising of rigid notions of identity raises important questions about the nature of shared religious practices. The answers to these questions are rather surprising. The result is not a list of activities, similar to those used to categorise 'popular religion' or 'folklore', such as beliefs and practices transmitted in families or neighbourhoods or by marginal practitioners like female rhizomatists.[101] Shared religious practices turn out, rather, to be related to shared spaces, and shared urban spaces in particular. From the point of view of normative traditions, this might be conceptualised as a consequence of the complexity of the urban, leading to spaces and attractions that are beyond the social control of one's own group.

---

95 For the latter, see Stemberger 1979; Hodkin 2014.
96 See Stemberger 2016.
97 Hezser 1997, 157–165, criticising the idea in Levine 1989 of a urbanisation from the 3rd century onwards.
98 E.g. Boyarin 2001, 2004b, 2004a, 2006.
99 I am grateful to Emiliano Urciuoli for stressing this parallel development.
100 Alston 2002, 366 for Egyptian cities.
101 On whose importance see Gordon 2007, 2013b.

The course of the inquiry followed in this book leads to a more radical view taken from the perspective of the city. What we discover in the city is an 'urbanised religion' with practices adapted to, or even developed in and for, cities. These practices allow the boundaries of small neighbourhoods to be transgressed due to the enormous investments put into the creation of specific spaces (circuses, theatres, amphitheatres) or spatially far-ranging rituals, above all processions. These are supplemented by the many religious services, such as divination, healing and cursing, that are offered due to the enormous economic possibilities enabled by the urban marketplace or, better, by numerous market corners. This was a feature not stressed in the Mishnah but one that was evidently a niche intensively used by *Iudaei* themselves in the city of Rome.

If such services were part of an urbanised religion, we have to acknowledge the urban character of changes in the use of specifically religious identities and the driving forces behind such changes. Observations in previous chapters have pointed towards urbanisation and urban growth as the most important dynamic factors for religious change. Such factors include urban aspirations that triggered migration, identification, and ethnogenesis, but also include the density and diversity of living quarters and the political interests involved in administering and dominating urban space. A closer inspection of these combined factors has highlighted their role in the development of intermittent and multiple religious identities as forms of urbanity that combined rather than mutually excluded choice and control. Collective religious identities and, hence, religious plurality, in the sense of a plurality of such imagined or interacting groups, were a phenomenon triggered by migration to and between cities and furthered by urban conditions of density, confirming the usefulness of the definition employed in the beginning of this inquiry.[102]

In the face of these overlapping personal and material networks, the necessary boundary work, performed by urban intellectuals in the role of religious specialists, can be identified even in the case of ancient Judaism in the world of Imperial cities.

Such religious practices and ideas are as much the outcome of urban conditions, that is to say urbanised religion, as a factor in the formation of cities, that is to say urbanising religion. Taken together, this 'urban religion' is neither the invention of locals or immigrants in the megacities of a globalised modernity nor the creation of some central agency or the political authorities of ancient cities. Instead, the phenomena are a composite of different, often competing, agents in competition for social and religious prestige, or simply for the appro-

---

[102] Robinson, Scott and Taylor 2016, 5, quoted above, 26.

priate means by which to make a living. They take the form of 'confessionalised' (or religionificated) religion as much as that of an underlying and encompassing 'third' confession, the relation of which to the others is a matter of contingent constellations. Sometimes and for some, living this urban religion was the essence of urban life.

Conclusion: Religion and urbanity

The phenomena of the urban and religion must be thought together. This interrelationship can already be found in very old religious texts, although the relationship in these works is tense. The 'Tower of Babel' (Gen 11.1–9) is a symbol for the urban in that it stands for the hubris of the inhabitants of cities. The conglomeration of actors, their cooperation, their architecture would otherwise, according to the underlying fear, allow people to reach heaven. In the Jewish Bible and in its Christian interpretation, the urban is a suspicious place, a place of sin and godlessness. God can be found in the desert, in solitude, at Mount Sinai. This West Asian and then European tradition finds its equivalent in South Asia: Buddha finds his enlightenment under a tree, outside the city. It is the village that offers the ideal image of social community and religious division of labour.

But the authors of these texts are, themselves, to be found in urban spaces. The art of writing itself, the invention and use of writing as it developed into the production of extensive texts and, thus, into 'writing religion', was an urban art. 'Religions of the book' are therefore first and foremost urban phenomena. Urban consciousness cannot be detached from notions about the non-urban. It is characteristic of urbanity to think of oneself as being different from others, different from an opposite, from the non-urban, from the 'rural'. At the same time, this opposite can serve as a counter-image, the basis for wishful thinking about the rural idyll or for critiques of the urban. When Rome, probably the first city in history to reach a population of a million inhabitants, wanted to be ruled by a truly religious and incorruptible ruler, it had to tear Cincinnatus from the field, from the plough – or it did at least as the traditional Roman historiography has it.

Cincinnatus' reluctance can be readily understood. After all, living in urban settlements is not a walk in the park. Viewed from below, urban life can look extremely attractive, with all its promises of security and the potential for prosperous livelihoods, of new internal and external networks, new friends and partners in business. At the same time, what is at stake is not megalomania, as in the story of the Tower of Babel, but survival, not the reaching of a state of divinity, as in biblical history, but the enabling of humanity. The actors' view of the topic is marked by the ambivalence of the man-made urban space and the way of life actually prevailing there. Urban life and urban space is 'heaven and hell' at the same time: it is a place of innovation but also a place of social and ecological crises. Religion is not only an observer but also an important actor in this setting.

Conclusion: Religion and urbanity — 191

The current problems and opportunities of planetary urbanisation and religious change cannot be addressed without looking at the long history of each in relation to the other. Only a detailed investigation with great historical depth and a broad outlook on the present will show just how entangled are the mutual formations of religion and urbanity. It will show to what extent urbanity and urban ways of life have been shaped by religious forms of action or religious social structures. It will also show to what extent what we know today as 'religion' was also a result of urbanity, of living in spaces that were perceived as urban and that, by this very fact, became qualified as 'cities' by their inhabitants and visitors. This book offers an attempt to argue for these claims on the basis of a series of observations and analyses, mostly concerning ancient Mediterranean cities.

But what is the 'religion' addressed here? If one wishes to understand religion in its urban settings, one needs to find a suitable conceptual language with which to frame it and through which to view it. Religion is best seen, I have suggested, as a collective term for religious practices, ideas, and institutions that serve the purpose of communicating with superhuman addressees, with deceased humans, with spirits, or with gods. The fact that communication and its contents are attributed to the existence of these superhuman addressees generates power and relevance for the religious actions and situations of the speakers and their audiences. It thus becomes a resource for them, a resource from which to draw power as well as one that motivates critique, a resource that encourages the view of other inhabitants as equal as well as one which stabilises the differences between the people who live in the same city.

Previous research on 'urban religion' has examined such religion from the perspective of how it changes, how it finds its place, and how it reinvents itself in the globalised cities of modernity, as has been shown in Chapter 3. However, a fuller grasp of urban religion requires that we go well beyond this research, and not just in terms of time and space. Religion is not merely some age-old tool that is used in and adapted to life in urban spaces. As a cultural technique, religion itself is space-relevant, as we saw in Chapter 1. Religious practices are spatial practices in two respects. On the one hand, religious practices appropriate space or construct it: houses, streets, or markets, when used for prayers, hymns, dances, processions, and performances of sacrifices or dramatic performances, temporarily become ritual spaces – and then return to their former status. In the longer run, such spaces can be sacralised through the use of media – trees, flagpoles, steles, altars, panels, walls, or even more extensive architecture – whether for occasional remembrance and religious re-use or even to mark them out exclusively and permanently. Such media thus mark out present spaces for religious actions that can compete with other actors or purposes, in particular when space is scarce (as it almost always is in urban contexts). On the other hand, religious practices also deal with absent spaces. They refer to locations beyond the respective concrete space and even beyond the space of the urban settlement at hand. They refer to 'transcendent' addressees, to their spatial associations with other places or to inaccessible virtual places: heavens or underworlds. Chapter 8 has offered some examples of such views.

There are plentiful examples of religious action that pre-existed any form of urban settlement by millennia, and some of these have been hinted at in the second and third chapters of this book. There is no doubt that religion precedes urbanisation, whether in East Asia, South and West Asia, Africa, or Meso-America. As a space-constituting and space-transcending practice, religion was and is important for many, but not all, urbanisation processes. Where did religious space markings form crystallisation points for new urban settlements? Where did they deepen the division of labour? Where did they create coherence in the countless exchange processes, in the internal and external flows that constitute cities? Where did they enable differentiation that made spatial confinement and the pressure of social interaction bearable and thus stabilised urban settlements? Or where, on the contrary, did they push processes of disintegration into bloody and self-destructive conflicts? Case studies with interests in such topics abound and the final chapters of the present volume have adduced further material of relevance to these questions. However, they have also argued for a change of perspective, for a new historical view not only on the fate of the cities but also on religion.

Evidently, being space-dependent, religious practices and ideas cannot have remained unaffected by such developments. They must have been repeatedly transformed by urban factors such as forms of domination, cultural techniques, and interdependencies that were internal and external to the urban settlements. This volume has offered ample evidence for such transformations as they took place on different levels and across different social and spatial dimensions. Using Cicero's dialogue *On the nature of the gods* as an example, the Chapter 4 has shown how the urban can become a tacit prerequisite as for open religious discourse. Urbanity is seen here not only as the highest form of life but also as the only appropriate space for religious reflection – even if one might need to retire to the tranquillity of the rural villas of the urban elite in order to pursue it. The urban, however, is not only a prerequisite but also the topic of discourses. Systematised worldviews and their concepts of space must deal with urban space. This also influences, as the fifth chapter and its analysis of texts by Varro and Vitruvius have made clear, religious practices or the interpretation of religious practices. The results include processional paths as well as norms for the placement of temples.

The confrontation between religion and urbanity does not only take place in intellectual discourses and from a top-down bird's-eye view. On the contrary, religion and urbanity are something that is also 'done' at the level of smaller urban spaces, of quarters and neighbourhoods. The Chapter 6 has analysed religious institutions at such a level and reconstructed their changes through interventions by municipal administrations and local actors. In the Chapter 7, the intensive appropriation of urban space traced in the previous chapters led to the question of how religious practices changed through their interaction with the city as a whole, dealing in particular with the common problem of survival, that is of urban resilience. Despite the problem of reconstructing causal relationships, it can be shown that the interest in what we today call resilience led to new religious practices of appropriation of space. These included both narrative and performative practices. The design and order of time, the calendar, is a classic field of religious competence, and one in which urban religious concerns have often been felt – not only at Rome. It is precisely in this area and its media that a close connection with urban space is inscribed.

Religious change in interaction with the urban environment is not restricted to piecemeal practices and modifications. Reflecting on resilience has suggested taking a further step forward to consider even longer-term processes that have frequently been associated with urbanisation, namely individualisation and pluralisation. The Chapter 8 followed on from extensive recent research on historical constellations and processes of religious individualisation. Already here it had become obvious that the development of different forms of religious individuality, reflexive as well as institutional, might be connected with processes of urbanisation. The closer examination showed to what extent such institutional and reflexive practices of individualisation (and at times de-individualisation) led to a specifically urban subjectivity in the processes of Hellenistic and Roman urbanisation. Part of such individualisation was the development of various religious options and identities, some of which were even supported and stabilised by processes of grouping. The formation of institutionalised difference as institutionally separated 'religions' may have been the result of such processes, as the last chapter argues. For Judaism, for example, it can be shown that this institutionalisation goes hand in hand with its own religious discourse on urbanity.

The reciprocal formation of religion and urbanity is not a specific feature of Mediterranean antiquity, despite this geographical and historical area providing the starting point for this book and remaining an ever-present horizon. However, the present volume has only been able to show that the connection between the urban and religion was highly relevant for this particular epoch and that it is reflected in the religious changes of this period and geographical space. In this respect, the book is, above all, an invitation, an invitation to not only engage with the arguments presented here about the ancient Mediterranean world but to review and modify its research hypothesis for other periods and spaces as well. There can be no doubt that such an enterprise will hold some surprises in store. It will change our own view of religions *and* of the urban.

References

Albrecht, Janico et al. 2018, 'Religion in the Making: The Lived Ancient Religion Approach', *Religion* 48 (4), 568–93.

Aldrete, Gregory S. 2018, 'Hazards of Life in Ancient Rome: Floods, Fires, Famines, Footpads, Filth, and Fevers', in: Amanda Claridge and Claire Holleran (eds.), *A Companion to the City of Rome*, Hoboken, NJ: Wiley-Blackwell, 365–81.

Alexander, Jeffrey C., Giesen, Bernhard and Mast, Jason L. (eds.) 2006, *Social Performance: Symbolic Action, Cultural Pragmatics, and Ritual* (Cambridge Cultural Social Studies), Cambridge: Cambridge University Press.

Alroth, Brita and Scheffer, Charlotte (eds.) 2009, *Attitudes towards the Past in Antiquity: Creating Identities. Proceedings of an International Conference held at Stockholm University, 15–17 May 2009* (Stockholm Studies in Classical Archaeology 14).

AlSayyad, Nezar 2011, 'The Fundamentalist City?', in: Nezar AlSayyad and Mejgan Massoumi (eds.), *The fundamentalist city? Religiosity and the remaking of urban space*, London: Routledge, 3–26.

AlSayyad, Nezar and Massoumi, Mejgan (eds.) 2011, *The fundamentalist city? Religiosity and the remaking of urban space*, London: Routledge.

Alston, Richard 2002, *The city in Roman and Byzantine Egypt*, London: Routledge.

Altini, Carlo 2015, *Progresso – definitivo*, Pisa.

Ammerman, Nancy T. 1997, 'Golden Rule Christianity: Lived Religion in the American Mainstream', in: David D. Hall (ed.), *Lived Religion in America: Toward a History of Practice*, Princeton: Princeton University, 196–216.

Anderson, Ben 2009, 'Affective atmospheres', *Emotion, Space and Society* 2 (2), 77–81.

Ando, Clifford 2001, 'The Palladium and the Pentateuch: towards a sacred topography of the later Roman empire', *Phoenix* 55, 369–411.

Ando, Clifford 2008, *The Matter of the Gods: Religion and the Roman Empire* (Transformation of the Classical Heritage 44), Berkeley: University of California Press.

Ando, Clifford 2011, *Law, Language, and Empire in the Roman Tradition*, Philadelphia: University of Pennsylvania Press.

Ando, Clifford 2012, *Imperial Rome AD 193–284: The critical century* (Edinburgh History of Ancient Rome), Edinburgh: Edinburgh University Press.

Ando, Clifford 2015, *Roman social imaginaries: Language and thought in contexts of empire* (The Robson classical lectures), Toronto: University of Toronto Press.

Ando, Clifford 2017, 'City, village, sacrifice: The political economy of religion in the early Roman empire', in: Richard Evans (ed.), *Mass and Elite in the Greek and Roman World: From Sparta to Late Antiquity*, New York: Routledge, 1–43.

Ando, Clifford 2019, 'Citizenship and self', in: Maren R. Niehoff (ed.), *The Self in Antiquity*, Leiden: Brill.

Ando, Clifford and Rüpke, Jörg (eds.) 2015, *Public and Private in Ancient Mediterranean Law and Religion* (Religionsgeschichtliche Versuche und Vorarbeiten 65), Berlin: de Gruyter.

Appadurai, Arjun 2004a, 'The Capacity to Aspire: Culture and the Terms of Recognition', in: Vijayendra Rao and J. Michael Walton (eds.), *Culture and Public Action*, Palo Alto: Stanford University Press, 59–84.

Arnal, William 2011, 'The Collection and Synthesis of "Tradition" and the Second-Century Invention of Christianity*', *Method & Theory in the Study of Religion* 23 (3–4), 193–215.

Arnhold, Marlis 2015, 'Sanctuaries and Urban Spatial Settings in Roman Imperial Ostia', in: Rubina Raja and Jörg Rüpke (eds.), *A Companion to the Archaeology of Religion in the Ancient World*, Malden: Wiley, 293–303.

Arweck, Elisabeth and Collins, Peter Jeffrey (eds.) 2006, *Reading religion in text and context: Reflections of faith and practice in religious materials* (Theology and religion in interdisciplinary perspective series), Aldershot: Ashgate.

Ashmore, Richard D., Deaux, Kay and McLaughlin-Volpe, Tracy 2004, 'An Organizing Framework for Collective Identity: Articulation and Significance of Multidimensionality', *Psychological Bulletin 130, No. 1*, 80–114.

Aspinall, P. J. and Song, M. 2013, 'Is race a "salient …" or "dominant identity" in the early 21st century: The evidence of UK survey data on respondents' sense of who they are', *Soc Sci Res 42* (2), 547–61.

Assmann, Aleida and Assmann, Jan (eds.) 1987, *Kanon und Zensur* (Archäologie der literarischen Kommunikation 2), München: Fink.

Assmann, Jan 2006, 'Kulte und Religionen: Merkmale primärer und sekundärer Religion(serfahrung) im Alten Ägypten', in: Andreas Wagner (ed.), *Primäre und sekundäre Religion als Kategorie der Religionsgeschichte des Alten Testaments* (Beihefte zur Zeitschrift für die alttestamentliche Wissenschaft 364), Berlin: de Gruyter, 269–80.

Assmann, Jan and Stroumsa, Guy G. 1999, *Transformations of the inner self in ancient religions* (Studies in the history of religions ; 83), Leiden: Brill.

Athanassiadi, Polymnia 1993, 'Dreams, Theurgy and Freelance Divination: The Testimony of Iamblichus', *JRS 83*, 115–30.

Aubry, Gwenaelle 2008, 'Démon et intériorité d'Homère à Plotin : esquisse d'une histoire', in: Gwenaelle Aubry (ed.), *Le moi et l'intériorité* (Textes et traditions 17), Paris: Vrin, 255–68.

Auffarth, Christoph 1995, 'Gaben für die Götter – für die Katz? Wirtschaftliche Aspekte des griechischen Götterkults am Beispiel Argos', in: Hans G. Kippenberg and Brigitte Luchesi (eds.), *Lokale Religionsgeschichte*, Marburg: diagonal, 259–72.

Augé, Marc 1992, *Non-lieux: Introduction à une anthropologie de la surmodernité* (La librairie du XXe siècle), Paris: Seuil.

Baines, John et al. 2015, 'Cities as performance arenas', in: Norman Yoffee (ed.), *The Cambridge world history 3: Early cities in comparative perspective, 4000 BCE–1200 CE*, Cambridge: Cambridge Univ. Press, 94–109.

Baird, J. A. 2013, 'Religon and Ritual', in: Peter Clark (ed.), *The Oxford Handbook of Cities in World History* (Pb. 2016 edn.), Oxford: Oxford University Press, 181–96.

Baker, Cynthia M. 2002, *Rebuilding the house of Israel: Architectures of gender in Jewish antiquity* (Divinations), Stanford, Calif.: Stanford University Press.

Baker, Judy L. (ed.) 2012, *Climate change, disaster risk, and the urban poor: Cities building resilience for a changing world* (Urban development series), Washington, DC: World Bank.

Barchiesi, Alessandro 2006, 'Mobilità e religione nell'Eneide: Diaspora, culto, spazio, identità locali', in: Dorothee Elm von, Jörg Rüpke and Katharina Waldner (eds.), *Texte als Medium und Reflexion von Religion im römischen Reich*, Stuttgart: Franz Steiner, 13–30.

Barclay, John M. G. 2007, *Flavius Josephus, Against Apion: translation and commentary*, Leiden Brill.

Baudy, Dorothea 1998, *Römische Umgangsriten: Eine ethologische Untersuchung der Funktion von Wiederholung für religiöses Verhalten* (Religionsgeschichtliche Versuche und Vorarbeiten 43), Berlin: de Gruyter.
Baudy, Gerhard J. 1991, *Die Brände Roms: Ein apokalyptisches Motiv in der antiken Historiographie* (Spudasmata 50), Hildesheim: Olms.
Baumhauer, Otto A. 1997, 'Diskursnormen', *Neuer Pauly 3*, 695–6.
Beard, Mary 1985, 'Writing and Ritual: A Study of Diversity and Expansion in the Arval Acta', *Papers of the British School at Rome 53*, 114–62.
Beard, Mary 1991, 'Writing and religion: Ancient Literacy and the function of the written word in Roman religion', in: *Literacy in the Roman world*, Ann Arbor, Mi.: Journal of Roman Archaeology, 35–58.
Beard, Mary, North, John and Price, Simon 1998, *Religions of Rome. 1: A History. 2: A Sourcebook*, Cambridge: University Press.
Becci, Irene and Burchardt, Marian 2013, 'Introduction: Religon Takes Place: Producing Urban Locality', in: Irene Becci, Marian Burchardt and Jose Casanova (eds.), *Topographies of Faith: Religion in Urban Spaces*, Leiden: Brill, 1–21.
Becci, Irene, Burchardt, Marian and Casanova, Jose (eds.) 2013, *Topographies of Faith: Religion in Urban Spaces* (International Studies in Religion and Society), Leiden: Brill.
Becker, Eve-Marie 2012a, 'Antike Textsammlungen in Konstruktion und Dekonstruktion: Eine Darstellung aus neutestamentlicher Sicht', in: Eve-Marie Becker and Stefan Scholz (eds.), *Kanon in Konstruktion und Dekonstruktion: Kanonisierungsprozesse religiöser Texte von der Antike bis zur Gegenwart. Ein Handbuch*, Berlin: de Gruyter, 1–29.
Becker, Eve-Marie 2012b, 'Literarisierung und Kanonisierung im frühen Christentum: Einführende Überlegungen zur Entstehung und Bedeutung des neutestamentlichen Kanons', in: Eve-Marie Becker and Stefan Scholz (eds.), *Kanon in Konstruktion und Dekonstruktion: Kanonisierungsprozesse religiöser Texte von der Antike bis zur Gegenwart. Ein Handbuch*, Berlin: de Gruyter, 389–97.
Becker, Eve-Marie and Rüpke, Jörg 2019, 'Autor, Autorschaft und Autorrolle in religiösen literarischen Texten: Zur Betrachtung antiker Autorkonzeptionen', in: Eve-Marie Becker and Jörg Rüpke (eds.), *Autoren in religiösen literarischen Texten der späthellenistischen und der frühkaiserzeitlichen Welt: Zwölf Fallstudien* (Culture, Religion, and Politics in the Greco-Roman World 3), Tübingen: Mohr Siebeck, 1–17.
Becker, Jochen et al. (eds.) 2014, *Global prayers: Contemporary manifestations of the religious in the city* (MetroZones 13), Zürich: Müller.
Beekers, Daan and Tamimi Arab, Pooyan 2016, 'Dreams of an Iconic Mosque: Spatial and Temporal Entanglements of a Converted Church in Amsterdam', *Material Religion 12* (2), 137–64.
Bell, Catherine 1992, *Ritual Theory, Ritual Practice*, New York: Oxford University Press.
Bellah, Robert N. 2011, *Religion in Human Evolution: From the paleolithic to the Axial Age*, Cambridge, Mass.: Harvard Univ. Press.
Bendlin, Andreas 2002, 'Vates', *Neuer Pauly 12/1*, 1150–1.
Bendlin, Andreas 2006, 'Vom Nutzen und Nachteil der Mantik: Orakel im Medium von Handlung und Literatur in der Zeit der Zweiten Sophistik', in: Dorothee Elm von, Jörg Rüpke and Katharina Waldner (eds.), *Texte als Medium und Reflexion von Religion im römsichen Reich*, Stuttgart: Franz Steiner, 159–207.

Bendlin, Andreas 2011a, 'Associations, Funerals, Sociality, and Roman Law: The collegium of Diana and Antinous in Lanuvium (CIL 14.2112) Reconsidered', in: Markus Öhler (ed.), *Aposteldekret und antikes Vereinswesen: Gemeinschaft und ihre Ordnung*, Tübingen: Mohr Siebeck, 207–96.

Bendlin, Andreas 2011b, 'On the Uses and Disadvantages of Divination: Oracles and their Literary Representations in the Time of the Second Sophistic', in: J.A. North and S.R.F. Price (eds.), *The Religious History of the Roman Empire: Pagans, Jews, and Christians.*, Oxford: Oxford University Press, 175–250.

Berking, Helmuth 2006, 'Contested Places and the Politics of Space', in: Helmuth Berking et al. (eds.), *Negotiating Urban Conflicts: Interaction, Space and Control*, Bielefeld: transcript Verlag, 29–39.

Berking, Helmuth 2008, 'Städte lassen sich an ihrem Gang erkennen wie Menschen': Skizzen zur Erforschung der Stadt und der Städte', in: Helmuth Berking and Martina Löw (eds.), *Die Eigenlogik der Städte. Neue Wege für die Stadtforschung*, Frankfurt a.M., 15–31.

Berking, Helmuth et al. (eds.) 2006, *Negotiating Urban Spaces: Interaction, Space and Control*, Bielefeld: transcript Verlag.

Berking, Helmuth and Löw, Martina (eds.) 2008, *Die Eigenlogik der Städte: Neue Wege für die Stadtforschung* (Interdisziplinäre Stadtforschung 1), Frankfurt/Main: Campus Verlag.

Bernabé Pajares, Alberto 2008 *Instructions for the Netherworld: The Orphic Gold Tablets* (Religions in the Graeco-Roman world 162), Leiden: Brill.

Bernstein, Frank 1998, *Ludi publici: Untersuchungen zur Entstehung und Entwicklung der öffentlichen Spiele im republikanischen Rom* (Historia Einzelschriften 119), Stuttgart: Steiner.

Bernstein, Frank 2007, 'Complex rituals: Games and processions in Republican Rome', in: Jörg Rüpke (ed.), *A Companion to Roman Religion*, Oxford: Blackwell, 222–34.

Beyer, Peter 2013, 'Questioning the secular/religious divide in a postWestphalian world', *International Sociology* 28 (6), 663–79.

Biering, Ralf 1995, *Die Odysseefresken vom Esquilin* (Studien zur antiken Malerei und Farbgebung 2), [Ennepetal]: Biering & Brinkmann.

Blum, Alan 2003, *The imaginative structure of the city*, Montreal: McGill-Queen's University Press.

Boehm 1927, 'Lustratio', *RE 13,2*, 2029–39.

Bohle, Hans-Georg (ed.) 2008, *Megacities: Resilience and social vulnerability. Outcomes of the 2nd UNU EHS Summer Academy of the Munich Re Chair on Social Vulnerability, 22–28 July 2007, Hohenkammer, Germany* (Studies of the university: research, counsel, education ; No. 10), Bonn: UNU EHS.

Boivin, Nicole 2009, 'Grasping the Elusive and Unknowabel: material Culture in Ritual Practice', *Material Religion* 5, 266–87.

Bollmann, Beate 1998, *Römische Vereinshäuser: Untersuchungen zu den Scholae der römischen Berufs-, Kult- und Augustalen-Kollegien in Italien*, Mainz: Zabern.

Bowern, Claire and Evans, Bethwyn 2015, *The Routledge handbook of historical linguistics* (Routledge handbooks in linguistics), London: Routledge.

Boyarin, Daniel 2001, 'Justin Martyr Invents Judaism', *Church History* 70 (3), 427–61.

Boyarin, Daniel 2004a, *Border lines: The partition of Judaeo-Christianity* (Divinations), Philadelphia, Pa.: University of Pennsylvania Press.

Boyarin, Daniel 2004b, 'The Christian Invention of Judaism: The Theodosian Empire and the Rabbinic Refusal of Religion', *Representations* 85, 21–57.
Boyarin, Daniel 2006, 'Twenty-Four Refutations: Continuing the Conversations', *Henoch: Studies in Judaism and Christianity from Second Temple to Late Antiquity* 28 (1), 30–45.
Boyer, Pascal 1994, *The naturalness of religious ideas: A cognitive theory of religion*, Berkeley University of California Press.
Boyle, A.J. and Dominik, J. W. (eds.) 2003, *Flavian Rome: Culture, Image, Text*, Leiden: Brill.
Bracht, Katharina 2014, *Hippolyts Schrift In Danielem: Kommunikative Strategien eines frühchristlichen Kommentars* (Studien und Texte zu Antike und Christentum 85), Tübingen: Mohr Siebeck.
Bradley, Mark 2006, 'Colour and Marble in Early Imperial Rome', *Cambridge Classical Journal* 52, 1–22.
Brakke, David, Satlow, Michael L. and Weitzman, Steven (eds.) 2005, *Religion and the self in antiquity*, Bloomington, Ind.: Indiana Univ. Press.
Bräunlein, Peter 2004a, 'Bildakte: Religionswissenschaft im Dialog mit einer neuen Bildwissenschaft', in: Brigitte Luchesi and Kocku von Stuckrad (eds.), *Religion im kulturellen Diskurs: Festschrift für Hans G. Kippenberg zu seinem 65. Geburtstag* (Religionsgeschichtliche Versuche und Vorarbeiten 52), Berlin: de Gruyter, 195–231.
Bräunlein, Peter (ed.) 2004b, *Religion und Museum: zur visuellen Repräsentation von Religion/en im öffentlichen Raum* (Kultur- und Museumsmanagement), Bielefeld: transcript.
Bräunlein, Peter 2009, 'Ikonische Repräsentation von Religion', in: Hans G. Kippenberg, Jörg Rüpke and Kocku von Stuckrad (eds.), *Europäische Religionsgeschichte: ein mehrfacher Pluralismus*, Göttingen: Vandenhoeck & Ruprecht, 774–7.
Bremmer, Jan N. 1987, *"Romulus, Remus and the Foundation of Rome."* (University of London Inst. of Classical Studies: Bulletin Suppl. 52), London: Institute of Classical Studies.
Bremmer, Jan N. 1994, 'The Soul, Death and the Afterlife in Early and Classical Greece', in: J. M. Bremer, Th P. van den Hout and R. Peters (eds.), *Hidden Futures: Death and Immortality in Ancient Egypt, Anatolia, the Classical, Biblical and Arabic-Islamic World*, Amsterdam: Amsterdam University Press, 91–106.
Bremmer, Jan N. 2011, 'Tours of hell: Greek, Jewish, Roman and Early Christian', in: Walter Ameling (ed.), *Topographie des Jenseits – Studien zur Geschichte des Todes in Kaiserzeit uns Spätantike* (Altertumswissenschaftliches Kolloquium), Stuttgart: Franz Steiner, 13–34.
Bremmer, Jan N. 2016, 'The Construction of an Individual Eschatology: The Case of the Orphic Gold Leaves', in: Katharina Waldner, Richard Gordon and Wolfgang Spickermann (eds.), *Burial Rituals, Ideas of Afterlife, and the Individual in the Hellenistic World and the Roman Empire* (Potsdamer altertumswissenschaftliche Beiträge 57), Stuttgart: Steiner, 31–51.
Brenner, Neil and Schmid, Christian 2014, 'The "Urban Age" in Question', *International Journal of Urban and Regional Research* 38 (3), 731–55.
Bridge, Gary and Watson, Sophie (eds.) 2013, *The New Blackwell Companion to the City* (rev. ed. edn., Wiley-Blackwell Companions to Geography), Malden, Mass.: Wiley-Blackwell.

Bridge, Gary and Watson, Sophie 2013, 'Reflections on Affect', in: Gary Bridge and Sophie Watson (eds.), *The New Blackwell Companion to the City* (rev. ed. edn., Wiley-Blackwell Companions to Geography), Malden, Mass.: Wiley-Blackwell, 277–87.

Brinton, Laurel J. 2017, *English historical linguistics. Approaches and perspectives*, Cambridge: Cambridge University Press.

Broise, Henri and Scheid, John 1993, 'Etude d'un cas: le lucus deae Diae à Rome', *Les bois sacrés: Actes du colloque international de Naples*, 145–57.

Brox, Norbert 1991, *Der Hirt des Hermas* (Kommentar zu den Apostolischen Vätern / Ergänzungs-Reihe zum kritisch-exegetischen Kommentar über das Neue Testament ; 7), Göttingen: Vandenhoeck & Ruprecht.

Bruit Zaidman, Luoise and Schmitt Pantel, Pauline 1992, *Religion in the ancient Greek city*, trans. Paul Cartledge, Cambridge: University Press.

Brunt, P. A. 1987, *Italian Manpower 225 B. C.–A. D. 14*, Oxford: Clarendon.

Bucur, Bogdan Gabriel 2009, *Angelomorphic pneumatology : Clement of Alexandria and other early Christian witnesses* (Supplements to Vigiliae Christianae 95), Leiden Brill.

Burchardt, Marian 2016, 'Infrastrutture del religioso: materialità e disposizioni d'ordine urbano', *Historia Religionum 8*, 67–77.

Burchardt, Marian and Wohlrab-Sahr, Monika 2013, '"Multiple Secularities: Religion and Modernity in the Global Age" – Introduction', *International Sociology 28* (6), 605–11.

Burchardt, Marian; Höhne, Stefan; Simone, AbdouMaliq 2015, 'The Infrastructures of Diversity: Materiality and Culture in Urban Space', *New Diversities 17* (2).

Burgess, R. W. 2012, 'The Chronograph of 354: Its Manuscripts, Contents, and History', *Journal of Late Antiquity 5* (2), 345–96.

Burkert, Walter 1984, *Die Anthropologie des religiösen Opfers: Die Sakralisierung der Gewalt* (C. F. v. Siemens Stiftung. Themen 40), München: Siemens Stiftung.

Burkert, Walter 2011, *Griechische Religion der archaischen und klassischen Epoche* (2. überarb. u. erw. Aufl. edn., Die Religionen der Menschheit 15), Stuttgart: Kohlhammer.

Burkhardt, Nadin 2013, 'Zwischen Tradition und Modifikation. Kulturelle Austauschprozesse in den Bestattungsriten der griechischen Kolonien in Unteritalien und Sizilien vom 8. bis zum 5. Jh. v. Chr.'.

Busi, Giulio 1999, *Simboli del pensiero ebraico: lessico ragionato in settanta voci*, Torino: Einaudi.

Büttner, M. (ed.) 1985, *Grundfragen der Religionsgeographie: Mit Fallstudien zum Pilgertourismus* (Geographia Religionum 1), Berlin: Reimer.

Bynum, Caroline Walker 2011, *Christian Materiality: An Essay on Religion in Late Medieval Europe*, New York: Zone Books.

Cairns, Francis 1971, 'Horace, Odes 1. 2', *Eranos 69*, 68–88.

Campanella, Thomas J. and Godschalk, David R. 2015, 'Resilience', in: Rachel Weber and Randall Crane (eds.), *The Oxford Handbook of Urban Planning*, Oxford: Oxford University Press, 218–36.

Cancik, Hubert 1978, 'Die republikanische Tragödie', in: Eckard Lefèvre (ed.), *Das römische Drama*, Darmstadt: Wissenschaftliche Buchgesellschaft, 308–47.

Cancik, Hubert 1979, 'Römische Rationalität: Religions- und kulturgeschichtliche Bemerkungen zu einer Frühform des technischen Bewußtseins', *Eicher 1979*, 67–92.

Cancik, Hubert 1985, 'Rome as Sacred Landscape: Varro and the End of Republican Religion in Rome', *Visible Religion* 4/5, 250–65.
Cancik, Hubert 1995, 'Militia perennis: Typologie und Theologie der Kriege Roms gegen Veji bei T. Livius', in: Heinrich von Stietencron and Jörg Rüpke (eds.), *Töten im Krieg*, Freiburg: Alber, 197–212.
Cancik, Hubert 1997, 'Kanon, Ritus, Ritual – Religionsgeschichtliche Anmerkungen zu einem literaturwissenschaftlichen Diskurs', in: Maria Moog-Grünewald (ed.), *Kanon und Theorie*, Heidelberg: Winter, 1–19.
Cancik, Hubert 1998, *Antik – modern: Beiträge zur römischen und deutschen Kulturgeschichte*, Stuttgart: Metzler.
Cancik, Hubert 2006, '"Götter einführen": Ein myth-historisches Modell für die Diffusion von Religion in Vergils Aeneis", in: Dorothee Elm von, Jörg Rüpke and Katharina Waldner (eds.), *Texte als Medium und Reflexion von Religion im römischen Reich*, Stuttgart: Franz Steiner, 31–40.
Cancik, Hubert and Mohr, Hubert 1988, 'Religionsästhetik', *HrwG*, 121–56.
Cancik, Hubert and Rüpke, Jörg (eds.) 1997, *Römische Reichsreligion und Provinzialreligion*, Tübingen: Mohr.
Cancik, Hubert and Rüpke, Jörg (eds.) 2003, *Römische Reichsreligion und Provinzialreligion: Globalisierungs- und Regionalisierungsprozesse in der antiken Religionsgeschichte*, Erfurt: Universität.
Capes, David B. 2011, '"Jerusalem" in the Gabriel Revelation and the Revelation of John', in: Matthias Henze (ed.), *Hazon Gabriel: New Readings of the Gabriel Revelation* (SBL Early Judaism and Its Literatur 29), Atlanta: Society of Biblical Literature, 173–88.
Carrier, James G. 1995, *Gifts and commodities exchange and Western capitalism since 1700* (First issued in paperback edn., Material cultures: interdisciplinary studies in the material construction of social worlds), London.
Caseau, Beatrice 1999, 'Sacred Landscapes', in: G. W. Bowersock, Peter Brown and Oleg Grabar (eds.), *Late Antiquity: A Guide to the postclassical World*, Cambridge, Mass.: Belknap Press, 21–59.
Castells, Manuel 1977, *The urban question a marxist approach* (Social structure and social change 1), Cambridge, Mass.: MIT Press.
Ceccarelli, Letizia 2008, 'Religious Landscape. A case – study from Latium Vetus', in: M.L. Di Marzio and D. Fossataro O. Menozzi (ed.), *SOMA 2005: Proceedings of the IX Symposium on Mediterranean Arcaeology Chieti (italy), 24–26 February 2005*, Oxford: BAR International Series 1739, 333–9.
Certeau, Michel de 1984, *The practice of everyday life*, Berkeley: University of California Press.
Certeau, Michel de 2007, *Arts de faire* (Nouvelle ed. par Luce Giard edn.), Paris: Gallimard.
Chakrabarty, Dipesh 2008, *Provincializing Europe: Postcolonial thought and historical difference* (Reissue, with a new preface by the author. edn.), Princeton, NJ Princeton Univ. Press.
Chaniotis, Angelos (ed.) 2011, *Ritual dynamics in the ancient Mediterranean: Agency, emotion, gender, representation* (Heidelberger althistorische Beiträge und epigraphische Studien 49), Stuttgart: Steiner.
Chaniotis, Angelos 2013, 'Processions in Hellenistic cities. Contemporary discourses and ritual dynamics', in: Richard Alston, Onno M. Van Nijf and Christina G. Williamson (eds.),

Cults, Creeds and Identities in the Greek City after the Classical Age (Groningen-Royal Holloway Studies on the Greek City after the Classical Age), Leuven; Paris; Walpole, Ma: Peeters, 21–48.

Chesnut, Glenn F. 1992, 'Eusebius, Augustine, Orosius, and the Later Patristic and Medival Christian Historians', in: Harold W. Attridge and Gohei Hata (eds.), *Eusebius,Christianity and Judaism* (Studia Post-Biblica 42), Köln: E.J.Brill, 687–713.

Citroni, Mario 2006, 'The Concept of the Classical and the Canons of Model Authors in Roman Literature', in: James I. Porter (ed.), *Classical pasts: the classical traditions of Greece and Rome*, Princeton, NJ Princeton University Press, 204–34.

Claridge, Amanda 2018, 'The Development of the City: An Archaeological Perspective', in: Amanda Claridge and Claire Holleran (eds.), *A Companion to the City of Rome*, Hoboken, NJ: Wiley-Blackwell, 71–136.

Clauss, Manfred 1990, *Mithras: Kult und Mysterien*, München: Beck.

Clemen, Carl 1930, 'Die Tötung des Vegetationsgeistes in der römischen Religion', *RhM NF 79*, 333–42.

Cohn, Naftali S. 2013, *The memory of the temple and the making of the Rabbis* (Divinations: Rereading late ancient religion), Philadelphia: University of Pennsylvania Press.

Collins, John Joseph 2000, *Between Athens and Jerusalem: Jewish Identity in the Hellenistic Diaspora* Caambridge Eerdmans Publishing Company.

Confino, Alon 1997, 'Collective Memory and Cultural History: Problems of Method', *The American Historical Review 102* (5), 1386–403.

Connor, W R 1987, 'Tribes, Festivals and Processions: Civic ceremonial and political manipulation in archaic greece', *Journal of Hellenic Studies 107*, 40–50.

Corbier, Mireille 2013, 'Writing in Roman Public Space', in: Gareth Sears, Peter Keegan and Ray Laurence (eds.), *Written space in the Latin West, 200 BC to AD 300*, London: Bloomsbury, 13–48.

Cunliffe, Barry and Keay, Simon (eds.) 1995, *Social Complexity and the Development of Towns in Iberia from the Copper Age to the Second Century*, Oxford: University Press.

Davies, Douglas 2008, 'Cultural Intensification: A Theory for Religion', In: Abby Day (ed.), *Religion and the Individual: Belief, Practice, Identity*, Bodmin, Cornwall: MPG Books, 7–18.

Daviet, R 1965, 'La mesure du temps en Gaule: Essai d'interprétation du calendrier de Coligny', *RAE 16*, 295–300.

Day, Katie 2017, 'Space and Urban Religion in the United States', *Oxford Encyclopedia of Religion*, online.

de Cazanove, Olivier 2000, 'I destinatari dell'iscrizione di Tiriolo e la questione de campo d'applicazione del senatoconsulto De Bacchanalibus', *Athenaeum 88*, 59–69.

de Cazanove, Olivier 2015, 'Water', in: Rubina Raja and Jörg Rüpke (eds.), *A Companion to the Archaeology of Religion in the Ancient World*, Malden: Wiley, 181–93.

De Ligt, Luuk 2012, *Peasnats, Citizens and Soldiers: Studies in the Demographic History of Roman Italy 225 BC-AD 100*, Cambridge: Cambrdige Unviersity Press.

Degrassi, Attilio (ed.) 1963, *Inscriptiones Italiae 13: Fasti et elogia. Fasciculus 2: Fasti anni Numani et Iuliani, accedunt ferialia, menologia rustica, parapegmata*, Roma: Libreria dello stato.

DeSilva, David A. 1996, 'Exchanging Favor for Wrath: Apostasy in Hebrews and Patron-Client Relationship', *Journal of Biblical Literature 115* (1), 91–116.

Detienne, Marcel 2002, 'The Art of Founding Autochthony: Thebes, Athens, and Old-Stock French', *ARION*, 46–55.

Deuser, Hermann 2014, '"A feeling of objective presence": Rudolf Ottos Das Heilige und William James' Pragmatismus zum Vergleich', in: Jörg Lauster et al. (eds.), *Rudolf Otto: Theologie – Religionsphilosophie – Religionsgeschichte*, Berlin de Gruyter, 319–33.

Deuser, Hermann, Kleinert, Markus and Schlette, Magnus (eds.) 2015, *Metamorphosen des Heiligen: Struktur und Dynamik von Sakralisierung am Beispiel der Kunstreligion* (Religion und Aufklärung 25), Tübingen: Mohr Siebeck.

Dey, Hendrik 2014, 'Urban Armatures, Urban Vignettes: The Interpermeation of the Reality and the Ideal of the Late Antique Metropolis', in: Stine Birk, Troels Myrup Kristensen and Birte Poulsen (eds.), *Using Images in Late Antiquity*, Oxford: Oxbow, 190–208.

Diamond, Jared M. 2005, *Collapse: How societies choose to fail or succeed*, New York, NY: Viking.

Dillon, John M. 2009, 'Philo of Alexandria and Platonist Psychology', in: Maha Elkaisy-Friemuth and John M. Dillon (eds.), *The afterlife of the platonic soul. Reflections of platonic psychology in the monotheistic religions* (Studies in platonism, neoplatonism, and the platonic tradition 9), Leiden: Brill, 17–24.

Dirven, Lucinda 1999, *The Palmyrenes of Dura-Europos: A Study of Religious Interaction in Roman Syria* (Religions in the Graeco-Roman World 138), Leiden: Brill.

Dohrmann, Natalie B. 2013, 'Law and Imperial Idioms: Rabbinic Legalism in the Roman World', in: Natalie B. Dohrmann and Annette Yoshiko Reed (eds.), *Jews, Christians, and the Roman Empire. The poetics of power in late antiquity* (Jewish culture and contexts), Philadelphia, Pa.: Univ. of Pennsylvania Press, 63–78, 272–88.

Downie, Janet 2015, 'Narrative and divination: Artemidorus and Aelius Aristides', *Archiv für Religiongeschichte 15*, 97–116.

Draycott, Jane and Graham, Emma-Jayne (eds.) 2017, *Bodies of evidence: Ancient anatomical votives past, present, and future*, London: Routledge.

Droogan, Julian 2013, *Religion, material culture and archaeology* (Bloomsbury advances in religious studies), London ; New York: Bloomsbury.

du Bouchet, Julien and Chandezon, Christophe (eds.) 2012, *Études dur Artémidore et l'interprétation des rêves*, Paris: Presses universitaires du Paris Ouest.

Dumont, Jean Christian 2000, 'L'espace plautinien: de la place publique à la ville', *Pallas 54*, 103–12.

Dunnill, John 1992, *Covenant and sacrifice in the Letter to the Hebrews*, Cambridge: Cambridge University Press.

Dupont, Florence 1986, *L'acteur-roi: le théatre dans la Rome antique*, Paris: Belles Lettres.

Durkheim, Émile 1947, *The Elementary Forms of the Religious Life: A Study in Religious Sociology*, trans. Trsl. from the French by Joseph Ward Swain, Glencoe, Ill.: Free Press.

Dyck, Andrew R. 1996, *A commentary on Cicero, De officis*, Ann Arbor: University of Michigan Press.

Eckhardt, Benedikt and Leonhard, Clemens 2018, *Juden, Christen und Vereine im römischen Reich* (Religionsgeschichtliche Versuche und Vorarbeiten 75), Berlin: deGruyter.

Edmonds III, Radcliffe G. 2013, *Redefining Ancient Orphism: A Study in Greek Religion*, Cambridge: Cambridge University PRess.

Edmonds, Radcliffe G. (ed.) 2011, *The "Orphic" gold tablets and Greek religion: further along the path*, Cambridge: Cambridge Univ. Press.

Edwards, Catharine 1996, *Writing Rome: Textual approaches to the city*, Cambridge: Cambridge University Press.

Egelhaaf-Gaiser, Ulrike 2002, 'Religionsästhetik und Raumordnung am Beispiel der Vereinsgebäude in Ostia', in: Alfred Schäfer and Ulrike Egelhaaf-Gaiser (eds.), *Religiöse Vereine in der römischen Antike. Untersuchungen zu Organisation, Ritual und Raumordnung* (Studien und Texte zu Antike und Christentum), Tübingen: Mohr Siebeck, 123–63.

Eidinow, Esther 2007, *Oracles, Curses, and Risk among the Ancient Greeks*, Oxford: Oxford University Press.

Eisenstadt, Samuel N. 1979, *Tradition, Wandel und Modernität*, trans. Suzanne Heintz, Frankfurt a. M.: Suhrkamp.

Eliade, Mircea 1961, *The sacred and the profane the nature of religion: The significance of religious myth, symbolism, and ritual within life and culture*, trans. Willard R. Trask (Harper torchbooks 81), New York: Harper & Brothers.

Ellingworth, Paul 1993, *The Epistle to the Hebrews: a commentary on the Greek text* (The New international Greek Testament commentary), Grand Rapids, Mich.: Eerdmans.

Elm von, Dorothee, Rüpke, Jörg and Waldner, Katharina (eds.) 2006, *Texte als Medium und Reflexion von Religion im römischen Reich* (Potsdamer Altertumswissenschaftliche Beiträge 14), Stuttgart: Franz Steiner.

Emberling, Geoff, Clayton, Sarah C. and Janusek, John W. 2015, 'Urban landscapes: Transforming spaces and reshaping', in: Norman Yoffee (ed.), *The Cambridge world history 3: Early cities in comparative perspective, 4000 BCE–1200 CE*, Cambridge: Cambridge Univ. Press, 300–16.

Eraydin, Ayda (ed.) 2013, *Resilience thinking in urban planning* (GeoJournal library 106), Dordrecht: Springer.

Erdkamp, Paul 2013, 'Urbanism', in: Walter Scheidel (ed.), *The Cambridge Companion to Roman Economy*, Cambridge: Cambridge University Press, 241–65.

Erll, Astrid 2011, *Memory in culture*, Houndmills, Basingstoke: Palgrave Macmillan.

Erskine, Andrew 2001, *Troy between Greece and Rome: Local Tradition and Imperial Rome*, Oxford: University Press.

Eshleman, Kendra 2012, *The social world of intellectuals in the Roman Empire: Sophists, philosophers, and Christians* (Greek culture in the Roman world), Cambridge: Cambridge University Press.

Fantham, Elaine 1997, 'Images of the city: Propertius' new-old Rome', in: Thomas Habinek and Alessandro Schiesaro (eds.), *The Roman Cultural Revolution*, Cambridge: Cambridge University Press, 122–35.

Feeney, Denis 1998, *Literature and Religion at Rome: Cultures, Contexts, and Beliefs*, Cambridge: Cambridge University Press.

Feeney, Denis 2007a, *Caesar's calendar: ancient time and the beginnings of history* (Sather classical lectures 65), Berkeley: University of California Press.

Feeney, Denis 2007b, 'On Not Forgetting the "Literatur" in "Literatur und Religion": Representing the Mythic and the Divine in Roman Historiography', in: Anton Bierl, Rebecca Lämmle and Katharina Wesselmann (eds.), *Literatur und Religion 2: Wege zu einer mythisch-rituellen Poetik bei den Griechen*, Berlin: de Gruyter, 173–202.

Feldman, Louis H. 1993, *Jew and Gentile in the Ancient World: Attitudes and Interactions from Alexander to Justinian*, Princeton: University Press.

Ferri, Giorgio 2010a, *Tutela segreta ed evocatio nel politeismo romano* (Mos maiorum 4), Roma: Bulzoni Ed.
Ferri, Giorgio 2010b, *Tutela urbis : il significato e la concezione della divinità tutelare cittadina nella religione romana* (Potsdamer altertumswissenschaftliche Beiträge 32), Stuttgart: Steiner.
Fields, Dana 2008, 'Aristedes and Plutarch on Self', in: William V. Harris and Brooke Holmes (eds.), *Aelius Aristides between Greece, Rome, and the Gods*, Leiden: Brill, 151–72.
Filppula, Markku et al. (2017), 'Changing English. Global and local perspectives', in English Changing and Mouton De Gruyter (eds.), *Topics in English linguistics ; volume 92* (Berlin: De Gruyter Mouton), xiii, 347 Seiten.
Fine, Gary Alan 2010, 'Sociology of the Local: Action and its Publics', *Sociological Theory* 28 (4), 355–76.
Fine, Steven 2005, *Art and Judaism in the Greco-Roman world. Toward a new Jewish archaeology*, Cambridge: Cambridge Univ. Press.
Fink, Robert O, Hoey, Allan S and Snyder, Walter F 1940, 'The Feriale Duranum', *Yale Classical Studies* 7, 1–222.
Fish, Stanley Eugene 1995, *Professional correctness: Literary studies and political change*, Oxford: Clarendon Press.
Flambard, Jean-Marc 1981, 'Collegia Compitalicia: phénomène associatif, cadres territoriaux et cadres civiques dans le monde romain à l'époque républicaine', *Ktema* 6, 143–66.
Fless, Friederike and Moede, Katja 2007, 'Music and Dance: Forms of Representation in Pictorial and Written Sources', in: Jörg Rüpke (ed.), *A Companion to Roman Religion*, Oxford: Blackwell, 249–62.
Flower, Harriet 2002, 'Rereading the Senatus Consultum de Bacchanalibus of 186 BC: Gender Roles in the Roman Middle Republic', in: Vanessa B. Gorman and Eric W. Robinson (eds.), *Oikistes: Studies in Constitutions, Colonies, and Military Power in the Ancient World. Offeres in Honor of A.J. Graham*, Leiden: Brill, 79–98.
Flower, Harriet 2017b, *The Dancing Lares and the Serpent in the Garden: Religion at the Roman Street Corner*, Princeton: Princeton University Press.
Folkert, Kendall W. 1989, 'The 'Canons' of 'Scripture'', in: Miriam Levering (ed.), *Rethinking Scripture: Essays from a Comparative Perspective*, New York: State University of New York Press, 170–9.
Fonrobert, Charlotte Elisheva 2004, 'From Separatism to Urbanism: The Dead Sea Scrolls and the Origins of the Rabbinic Eruv', *Dead Sea Discoveries* 11 (1), 43–71.
Foss, Pedar 1997, 'Domestic space in the Roman world: Pompeii and beyond', *Journal of Roman Archaeology Supplementary Series Number* 22, 196–240.
Foucault, Michel 1984, 'Space, Knowledge, and Power', in: P. Rabinow (ed.), *The Foucault Reader: An Introduction to Foucault's Thought*, London, 239–56.
Fowden, Garth 2005, 'Late Polytheism', in: Alan K. Bowman, Averil Cameron and Peter Garnsey (eds.), *The Cambridge Ancient History 12: The Crisis of Empire, A.D. 193–337*, Cambridge Cambridge University Press, 521–72.
Franke, Herbert 1970, *Zum Militärstrafrecht im chinesischen Mittelalter* (Sitzungsberichte Bayerische Akademie der Wissenschaften, Phil.-hist. Kl. 1970,5), München: Verlag der Bayerischen Akademie.
Frankfurter, David 1998, *Religion in Roman Egypt: Assimilation and Resistance*, Princeton: University Press.

Freitag, Ulrike and Oppen, Achim von 2010, "Introduction: 'Translocality': An Approach to Connection and Transfer in Area Studies", in: Ulrike Freitag and Achim von Oppen (eds.), *Translocality: The Study of Globalising Processes from a Southern Perspective* (Studies in Global Social History 4), Leiden: Brill, 1–21.

Friedheim, Emmanuel 2010a, 'Entre normativité et dissidence: Les écrits rabbiniques et la société juive en terre d'Israel au temps de la Mishna et du Talmud ', *Les Cahiers du judaïsme 28*, 32–6.

Friedheim, Emmanuel 2010b, 'Quelques remarques sur l'évocation de Jérusalem dans la littérature gréco-latine non Chrétienne', *Revue d'histoire et de philosophie religieuses 90* (2), 161–78.

Friedrichs, Jürgen, Dierckx, Danielle and De Boyser, Katrien 2012, *Between the Social and the Spatial. Exploring the Multiple Dimensions of Poverty and Social Exclusion*, Farnham: Ashgate Publishing Ltd.

Fuchs, Martin et al. (eds.) 2019, *Religious Individualisations: Comparative Perspectives*, Berlin: de Gruyter.

Fuchs, Martin, Linkenbach, Antje and Reinhard, Wolfgang (eds.) 2015, *Individualisierung durch christliche Mission?* (Studien zur außereuropäischen Christentumsgeschichte (Asien, Afrika, Lateinamerika)/Studies in the History of Christianity in the Non-Western World 24), Wiesbaden: Harrassowitz.

Fuchs, Martin and Rüpke, Jörg 2015a, 'Religion: Versuch einer Begriffsbestimmung', in: Christoph Bultmann and Antje Linkenbach (eds.), *Religionen übersetzen: Klischees und Vorurteile im Religionsdiskurs* (Vorlesungen des Interdisziplinären Forums Religion der Universität Erfurt 11), Münster: Aschendorff, 17–22.

Fuchs, Martin and Rüpke, Jörg 2015b, 'Religious Individualization in Historical Perspective', *Religion 45* (3), 323–9.

Furseth, Inger 2011, 'Why in the city? Explaining urban fundamentalism', in: Nezar AlSayyad and Mejgan Massoumi (eds.), *The fundamentalist city? Religiosity and the remaking of urban space*, London: Routledge, 27–50.

Fustel de Coulanges, Numa Denis 1864, *La cité antique, étude sur le culte, le droit, les institutions de la Grèce et de Rome*, Paris, Strasbourg.

Fustel de Coulanges, Numa Denis 1956, *The ancient city. A study on the religion, laws, and institutions of Greece and Rome*, Garden City: Doubleday Anchor Books.

Galinsky, Karl (ed.) 2014, *Memoria Romana: Memory in Rome and Rome in Memory* (Memoirs of the American Academy at Rome), Ann Arbor: Univ. of Michigan Press.

Galinsky, Karl (ed.) 2016, *Memory in Ancient Rome and Early Christianity*, Oxford: Oxford University Press.

Galvao-Sobrinho, Carlos R. 2008, 'Claiming places: Sacred dedications and public space in Rome in the Principate', in: John Bodel and Mika Kajava (eds.), *Dediche Sacre nel mondo greco-romano: Religious Dedications in the Greco-Roman World* (Acta Instituti roman Finlandia), Rome: Institutum Romanum Finlandiae 127–59.

Garbin, David (ed.) 2012, *Believing in the city: Urban cultures, religion and (im)materialitay* (Culture and religion), Abingdon: Routledge.

Garbin, David and Strhan, Anna (eds.) 2017, *Religion and the Global City* (Bloomsbury Studies in Religion, Space and Place), New York: Bloomsbury.

Gelardini, Gabriella 2005, 'Hebrews, an Ancient Synagogue Homily for Tisha be-Av: Its Function, its Basis, its Theological Interpretation', in: Gabriella Gelardini (ed.), *Hebrews*.

Contemporary methods, new insights (Biblical interpretation series ; 75), Leiden: Brill, 106 – 27.
Giesecke, Annette Lucia 2007, *The epic city: Urbanism, utopia, and the garden in ancient Greece and Rome* (Hellenic studies 21), Washington, DC/Cambridge, Mass.: Center for Hellenic Studies/Harvard Univ. Press.
Gill, Christopher 2004a, 'Plato, Ethics and Mathematics', in: Maurizio Migliori, Linda M. Napolitano Valditara and Davide Del Forno (eds.), *Plato Ethicus: Philosophy is Life*, St. Augustin: Academia Verlag, 165 – 76.
Gill, Christopher 2004b, 'The Stoic Theory of Ethical Development: in What Sense is Nature a Norm?', in: Jan Szaif and Matthias Lutz-Bachmann (eds.), *Was is das für den Menschen Gute? Menschliche Nature und Güterlehre. What is Good for a Human Being? Human Nature and Values*, Berlin: deGruyter, 101 – 25.
Gill, Christopher 2009, 'Seneca and selfhood: Integration and disintegration', in: Shadi Bartsch and David Wray (eds.), *Seneca and the Self*, Cambridge: Cambridge University Press, 65 – 83.
Gladigow, Burkhard 1986, 'Präsenz der Bilder – Präsenz der Götter: Kultbilder und Bilder der Götter in der griechischen Religion', *Visible Religion 4/5 (1985/6)*, 114 – 33.
Goh, Daniel P. S. and van der Veer, Peter 2016, 'Introduction: The sacred and the urban in Asia', *International Sociology 31* (4), 367 – 74.
Gold, Daniel 2003, *Aesthetics and analysis in writing on religion. Modern fascinations*, Berkeley: University of California Press.
Goldberg, Sander 2007, 'Comedy and society from Menander to Terence', in: Marianne McDonald and J. Michael Walton (eds.), *The Cambridge companion to Greek and Roman theatre*, Cambridge: Cambridge Univ. Press, 124 – 38.
Goldenberg, Robert 1979, 'The Jewish Sabbath in the Roman World up to the Time of Constantine the Great', *ANRW II.19,1*, 414 – 47.
Gordon, Richard 2007, 'The coherence of magical-herbal and analogous recipes ', *MHNH 7*, 115 – 46.
Gordon, Richard 2009, 'The Roman Army and the Cult of Mithras: A critical view', in: Catherine Wolff and Yan LeBohec (eds.), *L'armée romaine et la religion sous le Haut-Empire romain*, Paris: CEROR, 397 – 450.
Gordon, Richard 2012, 'Mithras', *Reallexikon für Antike und Christentum 24*, 964 – 1009.
Gordon, Richard 2013a, 'Cosmology, Astrology, and Magic: Discourse, Schemes, Power, and Literacy', in: Laurent Bricault and Corinne Bonnet (eds.), *Panthée: Religious Transformations in the Graeco-Roman Empire* (Religions in the Graeco-Roman World 177), Leiden: Brill, 85 – 111.
Gordon, Richard 2013b, 'The Religious Anthropology of Late-Antique 'High' Magical Practice', in: Jörg Rüpke (ed.), *The Individual in the Religions of the Ancient Mediterranean*, Oxford: Oxford University Press, 163 – 86.
Gordon, Richard 2014, 'Charaktêres Between Antiquity and Renaissance: Transmission and Re-Invention', in: Véronique Dasen and Jean-Michel Spieser (eds.), *Les savoirs magiques et leur transmission de l'Antiquité à la Renaissance* (Micrologus' Library 60), Firenze: Sismel, 253 – 300.
Gordon, Richard 2016, 'Negotiating the Temple-Script: Women's Narratives among the Mysian-Lydian 'Confession-Texts'', *Religion in the Roman Empire 2* (2), 227 – 55.

Gosden, Chris and Marshall, Yvonne 1999, 'The Cultural Biography of Objects', *World Archaeology 31* (2), 169–78.
Grafton, A T and Swerdlow, N M 1988, 'Calendar Dates and Ominous Days in Ancient Historiography', *Journal of the Warburg and Courtauld Institutes 51*, 14–42.
Graver, Margaret 2019, 'Interiority and Freedom in Seneca's De beneficiis: Acts of Kindness and the Perfected Will', in: Maren R. Niehoff (ed.), *The Self in Antiquity*, Leiden: Brill.
Gregory, Andrew 2002, 'Disturbing Trajectories: 1 Clement, the Shepherd of Hermas and the Development of Early Roman Christianity', in: Peter Oakes (ed.), *Rome in the Bible and the Early Church*, Carlisle: Paternoster Press, 142–66.
Grimes, Ronald L. 2011, *Ritual, media, and conflict*, New York: Oxford Univ. Press.
Gros, Pierre 1976, *Aurea Templa: Recherches sur l'architecture religieuse de Rome à l'époque d'Auguste* (Bibliothèque des écoles françaises d'Athènes et de Rome 231), Rome: École française.
Groß, Karl 1935, *Die Unterpfänder der römischen Herrschaft* (Neue Deutsche Forschungen 41), Berlin: Junker & Dünnhaupt.
Grözinger, Karl E. and Rüpke, Jörg 2000, *Literatur als religiöses Handeln* (Religion, Kultur, Gesellschaft 2), Berlin: Berlin Verlag.
Gruen, Erich S. 1990, *Studies in Greek culture and Roman policy* (Cincinnati classical studies ns 7), Leiden: Brill.
Gruen, Erich S. 1992, *Culture and National Identity in Republican Rome* (Cornell Studies in Classical Philology 52), Ithaca, NY: Cornell University Press.
Gruen, Erich S. 1998, *Heritage and Hellenism: The Reinvention of Jewish Tradition*, Berkeley: University of California Press.
Gruen, Erich S. 2002, *Diaspora: Jews amidst Greeks and Romans*, Cambridge, Mass.: Harvard University Press.
Gschaid, Max 2003, 'Ein keltischer Kalender: Der Bronzekalender von Coligny', in: *Gold und Kult der Bronzezeit*, Nürnberg, 267–70.
Gumbrecht, Hans Ulrich et al. (eds.) 1994, *Materialities of communication* (Writing science), Stanford, Calif.: Stanford Univ. Press.
Guthrie, W. K. 1966, *Orpheus and Greek Religion: A Study of the Orphic Movement*, New York: Norton.
Gutiérrez, Gerardo, Terrenato, Nicola and Otto, Adelheid 2015, 'Imperial cities', in: Norman Yoffee (ed.), *The Cambridge world history 3: Early cities in comparative perspective, 4000 BCE–1200 CE*, Cambridge: Cambridge Univ. Press, 532–45.
Haas, Christopher 1997, *Alexandria in Late Antiquity: Topography and Social Conflict* (Pb ed. 2006 edn.), Baltimore: Johns Hopkins University Press.
Hahn, Alois 1987, 'Kanonisierungsstile', in: Aleida Assmann and Jan Assmann (eds.), *Kanon und Zensur* (Beiträge zur Archäologie der literarischen Kommunikation 2), München: Fink, 28–37.
Hahn, Hans-Peter 2016, 'Aneignung und Domestikation: Handlungsräume der Konsumenten und die Macht des Alltäglichen', in: Dirk Hohnsträter (ed.), *Konsum und Kreativität* (Konsumästhetik 1), Bielefeld, 43–60.
Hahn, Johannes 2008, *From Temple to Church: Descruction and Renewal of Local Cultic Topography in Late Antiquity*, Leiden: Brill.
Halbwachs, Maurice 1992, *On collective memory*, trans. Lewis A. Coser, Chicago: University of Chicago Press.

Hall, David D. 1997, 'Introduction', in: David D. Hall (ed.), Princeton: Princeton University Press, VII-XIII.
Harders, Ann-Cathrin 2014, 'Eine Frage von Herrschaft: Religion und Geschlecht im alten Rom', in: Barbara Stollberg-Rilinger (ed.), *Als Mann und Frau schuf er sie* (Religion und Politik 7), Würzburg: Ergon Verlag, 17–45.
Harland, Philip A. 2003, *Associations, Synagogues, and Congregations. Claiming a place in Ancient Mediterranean Society*, Minneapolis: Fortress Press.
Harris, William V. 2009, *Dreams and experience in classical antiquity*, Cambridge, Mass.: Harvard University Press.
Harris, William V. and Holmes, Brooke (eds.) 2008, *Aelius Aristides between Greece, Rome, and the Gods* (Columbia Studies in classical Tradition 33), Leiden: Brill.
Häusl, Maria (ed.) 2011, *Tochter Zion auf dem Weg zum himmlischen Jerusalem: Rezeptionslinien der "Stadtfrau Jerusalem" von den späten alttestamentlichen Texten bis zu den Werken der Kirchenväter*, Leipzig: Universitätsverlag.
Heesterman, J. C. 1985, *The Inner Conflict of Tradition: Essays in Indian Ritual, Kingship, and Society*, Chicago: University of Chicago Press.
Heiler, Friedrich 1961, *Erscheinungsformen und Wesen der Religion* (Die Religionen der Menschheit 1), Stuttgart: Kohlhammer.
Henderson, John 2006, 'From ΦΙΛΟΣΟΦΙΑ into Philosophia: Classicism and Ciceronianism', in: James I. Porter (ed.), *Classical pasts: the classical traditions of Greece and Rome*, Princeton, NJ Princeton University Press, 173–203.
Herz, Peter 1975, *Untersuchungen zum Festkalender der römischen Kaiserzeit nach datierten Weih- und Ehreninschriften*, Diss. Mainz.
Hezser, Catherine 1997, *The social structure of the rabbinic movement in Roman Palestine* (Texte und Studien zum antiken Judentum 66), Tübingen: Mohr Siebeck.
Hill, Andrew 2013, 'The City, the Psyche, and the Visibility of Religious Spaces', in: Gary Bridge and Sophie Watson (eds.), *The New Blackwell Companion to the City* (rev. ed. edn., Wiley-Blackwell Companions to Geography), Malden, Mass.: Wiley-Blackwell, 367–75.
Hillard, Tom 2013, 'Graffiti's Engagement: The Political Graffiti of the Late Roman Republic', in: Gareth Sears, Peter Keegan and Ray Laurence (eds.), *Written space in the Latin West, 200 BC to AD 300*, London: Bloomsbury, 105–22.
Hin, Saskia 2013, *The Demography of Roman Italy: Population Dynamics in an Ancient Conquest Society (201 BCE–14 CE)*, Cambridge: Cambridge University Press.
Hirschauer, Markus 2014, 'Un/doing Differences: Die Kontingenz sozialer Zugehörigkeiten/ Un/doing Differences: The Contingency of Social Belonging', *Zeitschrift für Soziologie* 43 (3), 170–91.
Hobsbawm, Eric J. 1983, *The invention of tradition*, Cambridge: Cambridge University Press.
Hodder, Ian 2012, *Entangled: An Archaeology of the Relationships between Humans and Things*, Chichester: Wiley-Blackwell.
Hodkin, Bernie 2014, 'Theologies of Resistance: A Re-examination of Rabbinic Traditions About Rome', in: Dan Batovici and John Anthony Dunne (eds.), *Reactions to Empire: Sacred Texts in their Socio-Political Contexts* (Wissenschaftliche Untersuchungen zum Neuen Testament II/372), Tübingen: Mohr, 161–74.
Hooke, Samuel Henry (ed.) 1958, *Myth, Ritual and Kingship: Essays on the Theory and Practice of Kingship in the Ancient Near East and Israel*, Oxford.

Howley, Joseph A. 2017, 'Book-Burning and the Uses of Writing in Ancient Rome: Destructive Practice between Literature and Document', *Journal of Roman Studies 107*, 213–36.

Humphrey, Caroline and Laidlaw, James 1994, *The Archetypal Actions of Ritual: A Theory of Ritual Illustrated by the Jain Rite of Worship*, Oxford: Clarendon.

Hüsken, Ute and Brosius, Christiane 2010, *Ritual matters: Dynamic dimensions in practice*, London: Taylor & Francis.

Ildefonse, Frédérique 2008, 'Questions pour introduire à une histoire de l'intériorité', in: Gwenaelle Aubry (ed.), *Le moi et l'intériorité* (Textes et traditions 17), Paris: Vrin, 223–39.

Insoll, Thomas 2009, 'Materiality, Belief, Ritual-Archaeology and Material Religion: An Introduction', *Material Religion 5*, 260–4.

Insoll, Timothy (ed.) 2001, *Archaeology and world religion*, London: Routledge.

Insoll, Timothy 2011, *The Oxford handbook of the archaeology of ritual and religion*, Oxford: Oxford Univ. Press.

Inwood, Brad 2009, 'Seneca and self assertion', in: Shadi Bartsch and David Wray (eds.), *Seneca and the Self*, Cambridge: Cambridge University Press, 39–64.

Israelowich, Ido 2015, *Patients and healers in the High Roman Empire*, Baltimore: Johns Hopkins University Press.

Jaccottet, Anne-Françoise 2003, *Choisir Dionysos: Les associations dionysiaques ou la face cachée du dionysisme*, Kilchberg: Akanthus.

Jackson, Peter 2016, 'The Arrival of the Clients: Technologies of Fame and the Prehistory of Orphic Eschatology', *Historia Religionum 8*, 169–94.

Jacobs, Andrew 2014, 'Temples and Civic Representation in the Theodosian Period', in: Stine Birk, Troels Myrup Kristensen and Birte Poulsen (eds.), *Using Images in Late Antiquity*, Oxford: Oxbow, 132–49.

Jehne, Martin 2006, 'Who attended roman assembles? Some remarks on political participation in the roman republic', in: Francisco Marco Simón, Francisco Pina Polo and José Remesal Rodríguez (eds.), *Repúblicas y Ciudadanos: Modelos de Participación Cívica en el Mundo Antiguo*, Barcelona: Universitat de Barcelona, 221–34.

Joas, Hans 1996, *Die Kreativität des Handelns*, Frankfurt a. M.: Suhrkamp.

Joas, Hans 2017, *Die Macht des Heiligen: Eine Alternative zur Geschichte von der Entzauberung*, Frankfurt a. M.: Suhrkamp.

Joas, Hans and Rüpke, Jörg (eds.) 2013, *Bericht über die erste Förderperiode der Kolleg-Forschergruppe "Religiöse Individualisierung in historischer Perspektive" (2008–2012)*, Erfurt: Max-Weber-Kolleg.

Jones, Kenneth R. 2011a, *Jewish reactions to the destruction of Jerusalem in A.D. 70: Apocalypses and related pseudepigrapha* (Supplements to the Journal for the study of Judaism 151), Leiden: Brill.

Jones, Kenneth R. 2011b, *Jewish Reactions to the Destruction of Jerusalem in A.D. 70: Apocalypses and Related Pseudepigrapha* (Suppl. tot he Journal for the Study of Judaism 151), Leiden: Brill.

Jones, Robert Alun 1993, 'Durkheim and La cité antique: An essay on the origins of Durkheim's sociology of religion', in: Stephen P. Turner (ed.), *Emile Durkheim: Sociologist and moralist*, London: Routledge, 23–49.

Jung, Matthias 2005, '"Making us explicit": Artikulation als Organisationsprinzip von Erfahrung ', in: *Anthropologie der Artikulation: Begriffliche Grundlagen und transdiziplinäre Perspektiven* Würzburg: Königshausen and Neumann 103–41.
Kaizer, Ted 2006, 'A note on the Fresco of Iulius Terentius from Dura-Europos', in: Robert Rollinger and Brigitte Truschnegg (eds.), *Altertum und Mittelmeerraum: Die antike Welt diesseits und jenseits der Levante: Festschrift für Peter W. Haider zum 60. Geburtstag* (Oriens et occidens 12), Stuttgart Steiner, 151–9.
Kaizer, Ted 2015, 'Dura-Europos under Roman Rule', in: Juan Manuel Cortés Copete, Elena Muñiz Grijalvo and Fernando Lozano Gómez (eds.), *Ruling the Greek World: Approaches to the Roman Empire in the East* (Potsdamer altertumswissenschaftliche Beiträge 52), Stuttgart: Steiner, 91–102.
Kaizer, Ted (ed.) 2016, *Religion, society and culture at Dura-Europos* (Yale classical studies 38), Cambridge, United Kingdom: Cambridge University Press.
Keller, Rudi 1994, *On language change: The invisible hand in language*, trans. Brigitte Nerlich, London: Routledge.
Kensinger, Elizabeth A. and Schacter, Daniel L. 2008, 'Memory and Emotion', in: Michael Lewis et al. (eds.), *Handbooks of Emotions*, New York: Guilford Press, 601–17.
Kindt, Julia 2015, 'Oracular Shrines as Places of Religious Experience', in: Rubina Raja and Jörg Rüpke (eds.), *A Companion to the Archaeology of Religion in the Ancient World*, Malden: Wiley, 268–78.
King, Richard 1999, *Orientalism and Religion. Postcolonial Theory, India and 'The Mystic East'*, London, New York: Routledge.
Kippenberg, Hans G. 1986, 'Die jüdischen Überlieferungen als 'patrioi nomoi'', in: Richard Faber and Renate Schlesier (eds.), *Die Restauration der Götter: Antike Religion und NeoPaganismus*, Würzburg: Königshausen + Neumann, 45–60.
Klein, Gil P. 2006, 'The Topography of Symbol: Between Late Antique and Modern Jewish Understanding of Cities', *ZRGG 58* (1), 16–28.
Klein, Gil P. 2017, 'Squaring the City: Between Roman and Rabbinic Urban Geometrya', in: Herniette Steiner and Maximilian Sternberg (eds.), *Phenomenologies of the City: Stduies in teh History and Philosphy of Architecture*, London: Ashgate, 33–48.
Kloppenborg, John S. and Wilson, Stephen G. (eds.) 1996, *Voluntary Associations in the Graeco-Roman World*, London: Routledge.
Klostergaard Petersen, Anders 2012, '"Invention" and "Maintenance" of Religious Traditions: Theoretical and Historical Perspectives', in: Jörg Ulrich, Anders-Christian Jacobsen and David Brakke (eds.), *Invention, Rewriting, Usurpation – Discursive Fights over Religious Traditions in Antiquity* (Early Christianity In The Context Of Antiquity), Frankfurt am Main: Peter Lang, 129–60.
Knott, Kim 2005, *The location of religion: A spatial analysis*, London: Equinox.
Knott, Kim 2008, 'Spatial Theory and the Study of Religon', *Religion Compass 2* (6), 1102–16.
Knott, Kim 2015, 'Walls and Other Unremarkable Boundaries in South London: Impenetrable Infrastructure or Portals of Time, Space and Cultural Difference?', *New Diversities 17* (2), 15–34.
Knott, Kim, Krech, Volkhard and Meyer, Birgit 2016, 'Iconic Religion in Urban Space', *Material Religion 12* (2), 123–36.
Kolb, Frank 1984, *Die Stadt im Altertum*, München: Beck.

Kong, Lily 2001, 'Mapping "New" Geographies of Religion: Politics and Poetics in Modernity', *Progress in Human Geography* 25 (2), 211–33.
Konstan, David 2009, 'Cosmopolitan Traditions ', in: Ryan K. Balot (ed.), *A companion to greek and roman political thought*, Chichester: Wiley-Blackwell, 473–84.
Krech, Volkhard 2012, 'Dynamics in the History of Religions – Preliminary Considerations of Aspects of a Research Programme', in: Volkhard Krech and Marion Steinicke (eds.), *Dynamics in the history of religions between Asia and Europe: encounters, notions, and comparative perspectives* (Dynamics in the history of religions 1), Leiden: Brill, 15–70.
Krech, Volkhard 2015, 'Beobachtungen zu Sakralisierungsprozessen in der Moderne – mit einem Seitenblick auf die Kunstreligion', in: Hermann Deuser, Markus Kleinert and Magnus Schlette (eds.), *Metamorphosen des Heiligen: Struktur und Dynamik von Sakralisierung am Beispiel der Kunstreligion* (Religion und Aufklärung 25), Tübingen: Mohr Siebeck, 411–25.
Krostenko, Brian A. 2000, 'Beyond (Dis)belief: Rhetorical Form and Religious Symbol in Cicero's de Divinatione', *Transactions and proceedings of the American Philological Association 130*, 353–91.
Kuhfeldt, Oskar 1882, *De Capitoliis imperii Romani*, Berlin: Pormetter.
Kühn, Wilfried 2008, 'Se connaître soi-même : la contribution de Plotin à la compréhension du moi', in: Gwenaelle Aubry (ed.), *Le moi et l'intériorité* (Textes et traditions 17), Paris: Vrin, 127–49.
Lackner, Eva-Maria 2013, 'Arx und Capitolinischer Kult in den Latinischen und Bürgerkolonien Italiens als Spiegel römischer Religionspolitik', in: Martin Jehne, Bernhard Linke and Jörg Rüpke (eds.), *Religiöse Vielfalt und soziale Integration: Die Bedeutung der Religion für die kulturelle Identität und politische Stabilität im republikanischen Italien* (Studien zur Alten Geschichte 17), Heidelberg: Verlag Antike, 163–201.
Lamont, Michèle and Molnár, Virág 2002, 'The Study of Boundaries in the Social Sciences', *Annual Reviews of Sociology 28*, 167–95.
Lange, Carsten Hjort and Vervaet, Frederik Juliaan (eds.) 2014, *The Roman Republican triumph: Beyond the spectacle* (Analecta Romana Instituti Danici Supplementum 45), Roma: Ed. Quasar.
Lanz, Stephan 2014, 'Assembling Global Prayers in the City: An Attempt to Repopulate Urban Theory with Religion', in: Jochen Becker et al. (eds.), *Global prayers: Contemporary manifestations of the religious in the city* (MetroZones 13), Zürich: Müller, 16–47.
Lapin, Hayim 2012, *Rabbis as Romans: The Rabbinic Movement in Palestine, 100–400 CE*, New York: Oxford University Press.
Latour, Bruno 1993, *We have never been modern*, Cambridge, Mass.: Harvard University Press.
Latour, Bruno 2005, *Reassembling the Social: An Introduction to Actor-Network-Theory*, Oxford: Oxford University Press.
Latte, Kurt 1960, *Römische Religionsgeschichte* (Handbuch der Altertumswissenschaft 5,4), München: Beck.
Law, Danny et al. 2015, 'Writing and record-keeping in early cities', in: Norman Yoffee (ed.), *The Cambridge world history 3: Early cities in comparative perspective, 4000 BCE-1200 CE*, Cambridge: Cambridge Univ. Press, 207–25.
Lefebvre, Henri 1974, *La production de l'espace* (Collection société et urbanisme), Paris: Éd. Anthropos.

Lenski, Noel Emmanuel 2016, *Constantine and the cities: Imperial authority and civic politics* (Empire and after), Philadelphia: University of Pennsylvania Press.
Leonhard, Clemens 2017, 'Establishing Short-Term Communities in Eucharistic Celebrations of Antiquity', *Religion in the Roman Empire 3* (1), 50–65.
Levine, Lee I. 1989, *The rabbinic class of Roman Palestine in late antiquity*, Jerusalem: Yad Izhak Ben-Zvi.
Lewis, James R. and Hammer, Olav 2007, *The Invention of Sacred Tradition*, Cambridge: Cambridge University Press.
Lichterman, Paul 2013, 'Studying Public Religion: Beyond the Beliefs-Driven Actor', in: Courtney Bender et al. (eds.), *Religion on the Edge: De-Centering and Re-Centering the Sociology of Religion*, Oxford: Oxford University Press, 115–23; 32–35.
Lieu, Judith M. 2004, *Christian identity in the Jewish and Graeco-Roman world*, Oxford: Oxford Univ. Press.
Lightstone, Jack N. 2002, *Mishnah and the Social Formation of the Early Rabbinic Guild: A Socio-Rhetorical Approach* (Studies in Christianity and Judaism 11), Waterloo, Ont.: Wilfrid Laurier University Press.
Linders, Tullia and Nordquist, Gallög (eds.) 1987, *Gifts to the Gods: Proceedings of the Uppsala Symposium 1985* (Acta Universitatis Upsaliensis: Boreas 15), Uppsala: Universitet.
Linderski, Jerzy 1986, 'The Augural Law', *ANRW II.16,3*, 2146–312.
Lomas, Kathryn 1997, 'The idea of a city: Élite ideology and the evolution of urban form in Italy, 200 BC–AD 100', in: Helen M. Parkins (ed.), *Roman Urbanism: Beyond the Consumer City*, London: Routledge, 21–41.
Long, Alex G. (ed.) 2013, *Plato and the Stoics* Cambridge: Cambridge University Press.
Longenecker, Richard N. 1970, *The Christology of early Jewish Christianity*, London: SCM Press.
Lott, John Bert 2004, *The neighborhoods of Augustan Rome*, Cambridge: Cambridge Univ. Press.
Löw, Martina 2001, *Raumsoziologie* (Wissenschaft 1506), Frankfurt am Main: Suhrkamp.
Latour, Bruno 2008, *Soziologie der Städte*, Frankfurt am Main: Suhrkamp.
Latour, Bruno 2012, 'The intrinsic logic of cities: Towards a new theory on urbanism', *Urban Research and Practice 5*, 303–15.
Latour, Bruno 2016, *Sociology of space. Materiality, social structures, and action* (Cultural sociology), New York: Palgrave Macmillan.
Luhmann, Niklas 1998, 'Religion als Kommunikation', in: Hartmann Tyrell, Volkhard Krech and Hubert Knoblauch (eds.), *Religion als Kommunikation*, Würzburg: Ergon, 135–45.
MacBain, Bruce 1982, *Prodigy and Expiation: A Study in Religion and Politics in Republican Rome* (Collection Latomus 177), Bruxelles: Latomus.
MacCormack, Sabine G. 1990, 'Loca sancta: the organization of sacred topography in late antiquity', in: R. Ousterhout (ed.), *The blessings of pilgrimage* (7–40).
MacMullen, Ramsay 2017, 'Roman Religion: The Best Attested Practice', *Historia 66* (1), 111–27.
Magi, Filippo 1972, *Il calendario dipinto sotto Santa Maria Maggiore. Con appendici sui graffiti del vano XVI a cura di Paaro Castrén 69–87* (Atti della Pontificia Accademia Romana di Archeologia ser. 3: Memorie 11,1), Citta del Vaticano: Tipografia Poliglotta Vaticana.

Maier, Harry O. 2013, 'Soja's Thirdspace, Foucault's Heterotopia and de Certeau's Practice: Time- Space and Social Geography in Emergent Christianity.', *Historical Social Research – Historische Sozialforschung 38 (2013) 3* (145), 76–93.

Maier, Harry O. 2015, 'From Material Place to Imagined Space: Emergent Christian Community as Thirdspace in the Shepherd of Hermas', in: Mark R. C. Grundeken and Joseph Verheyden (eds.), *Early Christian Communities between Ideal and Reality*, Tübingen: Mohr Siebeck, 143–60.

Malik, Jamal, Rüpke, Jörg and Wobbe, Theresa 2007, *Religion und Medien. Vom Kultbild zum Internetritual* (Vorlesungen des Interdisziplinären Forums Religion der Universität Erfurt 4), Münster: Aschendorff.

Manderscheid, Katharina 2004, *Milieu, Urbanität und Raum: Soziale Prägung und Wirkung städtebaulicher Leitbilder und gebauter Räume*, Wiesbaden: Verlag für Sozialwissenschaften.

Mann, Michael 1986, *The sources of social power 1: A history of power from the beginning to A. D. 1760*, Cambrigde: Cambridge Univ. Press.

Manuwald, Gesine 2011, *Roman republican theatre*, Cambridge: Cambridge Univ. Press.

Marincola, John 1997, *Authority and Tradition in Ancient Historiography*, Cambridge: Cambridge University Press.

Markschies, Christoph 1997, 'Innerer Mensch', *Realenzyklopädie für Antike und Christentum 18*, 266–312.

Marshall, Ruth 2009, *Political spiritualities: The Pentecostal revolution in Nigeria*, Chicago.: University of Chicago Press.

Massey, Doreen H. 1984, *Spatial Divisions of Labour: Social Structures and the Geography of Production*, London.

Massey, Doreen H. 1993, 'Politics and Space/Time', in: M. Keith and Steve Pile (eds.), *Place and Politics of Identity*, London, 141–61.

Massey, Doreen H. 1999, *Power-geometries and the politics of space-time* (Hettner-Lectures 2), Heidelberg: Department of Geography.

Matthiesen, Ulf 2008, 'Eigenlogiken städtischer Wissenslandschaften: Zur Koevolutionsdynamik von Stadt- und Wissensentwicklungen in urbanen KnowledgScapes', in: Helmuth Berking and Martina Löw (eds.), *Die Eigenlogik der Städte. Neue Wege für die Stadtforschung*, Frankfurt a. M., 95–152.

McGuire, Meredith B. 2008, *Lived Religion: Faith and Practice in Everyday Life*, Oxford: Oxford University Press.

Meyer, Birgit 2008, 'Media and the senses in the making of religious experience: an introduction', *Material Religion 4*, 124–35.

Meyer, Birgit 2009, *Aesthetic formations. Media, religion and the senses* (Religion, culture, critique), New York: Palgrave Macmillan.

Meyer, Holt and Uffelmann, Dirk (eds.) 2007, *Religion und Rhetorik* (Religionswissenschaft heute 4), Stuttgart: Kohlhammer.

Michaels, Axel (ed.) 2010, *Ritual Dynamics and the Science of Ritual*, Wiesbaden: Harrassowitz Verlag.

Mikalson, Jon D. 1998, *Religion in Hellenistic Athens* (Hellenistic Culture and Society 29), Berkeley: University of California Press.

Millar, Fergus 1998, *The Crowd in Rome in the Late Republic* (Thomas Spencer Lectures 22), Ann Arbor: University of Michigan Press.

Miller, Stuart S. 2010, "Stepped Pools, Stone Vessels, and other Identity Markers of 'Complex Common Judaism'", *Journal for the Study of Judaism 41* (2), 214–43.
Mitchell, William J. Thomas 2005, *What do pictures want? The lives and loves of images*, Chicago: Univ. of Chicago Press.
Momigliano, Arnaldo 1992a, 'From the Pagan to the Christian Sibyl: Prophecy as History of Religion', *Nono contributo alla storia degli studi classici e del mondo antico*, 725–44.
Momigliano, Arnaldo 1992b, 'Some preliminary Remarks on the 'Religious Opposition' to the Roman Empire', *Nono contributo alla storia degli studi classici e del mondo antico*, 681–99.
Mommsen, Theodor 1850, 'Über den Chronographen vom J. 354', *Abhandlungen der Königlich-Sächischen Gesellschaft der Wissenschaften, phil.-hist. Cl. 1*, 547–693.
Monard, Joseph 1999, *Histoire du calendrier gaulois: le calendrier de Coligny*, Vannes: Editions Burillier.
Morgan, David (ed.) 2010, *Religion and Material Culture: The Matter of Belief*, London: Routledge.
Morgan, David 2015, 'Religion and Embodiment in the Study of Material Culture', *Oxford Research Enxclopedias: Religion 1*, online.
Morstein-Marx, Robert 2012, "Political Graffiti in the Late Roman Republic: 'Hidden Transcripts' and 'Common Knowledge'", in: Christina Kuhn (ed.), *Politische Kommunikation und öffentliche Meinung in der antiken Welt*, Stuttgart: Franz Steiner Verlag, 191–217.
Mörth, Ingo 1993, 'Kommunikation', in: Hubert Cancik, Burkhard Gladigow and Karl-Heinz Kohl (eds.), *Handwörterbuch religionswissenschaftlicher Grundbegriffe*, Stuttgart: Kohlhammer, 392–414.
Moser, Sara 2013, 'New Cities in the Muslim World: The Cultural Politics of Planning an 'Islamic' City', in: Peter Hopkins, Lily Kong and Elizabeth Olson (eds.), *Religion and place: Landscape, politics and piety*, Dordrecht: Springer, 39–55.
Müller, Werner 1961, *Die heilige Stadt: Roma quadrata, himmlische Jerusalem und die Mythen vom Weltnabel*, Stuttgart: Kohlhammer.
Mumford, Lewis 1961, *The city in history: Its origins, its transformations, and its prospects*, New York: Harcourt.
Murray, Michele 2007, 'Th e Magical Female in Graeco-Roman Rabbinic Literature', *Religion & Theology 14*, 284–309.
Nagy, Blaise 1985, 'The Argei Puzzle', *American Journal for Ancient History 10*, 1–27.
Narayanan, Yamini 2015, *Religion, heritage and the sustainable city: Hinduism and urbanisation in Jaipur* (Routledge research in religion and development), Abingdon: Routledge.
Nasrallah, Laura 2008, 'The Acts of the Apostles, Greek cities, and Hadrian's Panhellenion ', *Journal for Biblical Literature 127* (3), 533–66.
Neudecker, Richard 2015, 'Gardens', in: Rubina Raja and Jörg Rüpke (eds.), *A Companion to the Archaeology of Religion in the Ancient World*, Malden: Wiley, 220–34.
Niebling, Georg 1956, 'Laribus Augustis Magistri Primi: Der Beginn des Compitalkultes der Lares und des Genius Augusti', *Historia 5*, 303–31.
Niehoff, Maren R. 2018, *Philo of Alexandria: An Intellectual biography*, New Haven: Yale University Press.

Nielsen, Inge 2014, *Housing the Chosen: The Architectural Context of Mystery Groups and Religious Associations in the Ancient World* (Contextualizing the Sacred 2), Turnhout: Brepols.
Nisbet, R. G. M. and Hubbard, Margeret 1970, *A Commentary on Horace: Odes I, II*, Oxford: Clarendon Press.
Nissinen, Martti and Carter, Charles E. (eds.) 2009, *Images and prophecy in the ancient eastern Mediterranean* (Forschungen zur Religion und Literatur des Alten und Neuen Testaments 233), Göttingen: Vandenhoeck & Ruprecht.
Norenzayan, Ara 2013, *Big gods: How religion transformed cooperation and conflict*, Princeton: Princeton University Press.
Noy, David 2000, *Foreigners at Rome: citizens and strangers*, London: Duckworth.
Noy, David 2004, 'Being an Egyptian in Rome: Strategies of Identity Formation', in: Jürgen Zangenberg and Michael Labahn (eds.), *Christians as a religious minority in a multicultural city: Modes of interaction and identity formation in early Imperial Rome* (Journal for the study of the New Testament Supplement series 243), London: T&T Clark International, 47–54.
Noy, David 2010, 'Immigrant and Jewish Families at Rome in the 2nd-5th Centuries', in: Éric Rebillard and Claire Sotinel (eds.), *Les frontières du profane dans l'antiquité tardive* (Collection de l'école francaise de Rome 428), Rome: Ecole Française de Rome, 199–211.
Nygaard, Simon 2016, 'Sacral rulers in pre-Christian Scandinavia: The possibilities of typological comparisons within the paradigm of cultural evolution', *Temenos 52* (1), 9–35.
Obbink, Dirk 1997, 'Cosmology as Initiation vs. the Critique of Orphic Mysteries', in: *Studies on the Derveni Papyrus*, Oxford: Clarendon Press, 39–54.
Olick, Jeffrey K. and Robbins, Joyce 1998, "Social Memory Studies: Fom 'Collective Memory' to the Historical Sociology of Mnemonic Practices", *Annual Review of Sociology 24*, 105–40.
Olmsted, Garrett 1992, *The Gaulish Calendar: A reconstruction from the bronze fragments from Coligny with an Analysis of its Function as a Highly Accurate Lunar/Solar Predictor as well as an Explanation of its Terminology and Development*, Bonn: Habelt.
Orlin, Eric M. 2002, 'Foreign Cults in Republican Rome: Rethinking the Pomerial Rule', *Memoirs of the American Academy in Rome 47*, 1–18.
Orlin, Eric M. 2010, *Foreign Cults in Rome – Creating a Roman Empire*, Oxford: Oxford University Press.
Orlin, Eric M. 2011, 'Augustan Religion: from Locative to Utopian', in: Jeffery Brodd and Jonathon L. Reed Reed (eds.), *Rome and Religion: A Cross-Disciplinary Dialogue on the Imperial Cult*, Atlanta: Society of Biblical Literature, 49–59.
Orsi, Robert A. 1985, *The Madonna of 115th Street: Faith and community in Italian Harlem, 1880–1950*, New Haven: Yale Univ. Press.
Orsi, Robert A. 1997, 'Everyday Miracles: The Study of Lived Religion', in: David D. Hall (ed.), *Lived Religion in America: Toward a History of Practice*, Princeton: Princeton University Press, 3–21.
Orsi, Robert A. 1999, *Gods of the city: Religion and the American urban landscape* (Religion in North America), Bloomington, Ind.: Indiana Univ. Press.
Osiek, Carolyn 1999, *Shepherd of Hermas: A Commentary* (Hermeneia), Minneapolis: Fortress Press.

Östenberg, Ida 2009a, *Staging the world: Spoils, captives, and representations in the Roman triumphal procession*, Oxford: Oxford Univ. Press.
Östenberg, Ida 2009b, 'War and Remembrance: Memories of Defeat in Ancient Rome', in: Brita Alroth and Charlotte Scheffer (eds.), *Attitudes towards the Past in Antiquity: Creating Identities* (Stockholm Studies in Classical Archaeology 14), Stockholm.
Otto, Bernd-Christian, Rau, Susanne and Rüpke, Jörg (eds.) 2015, *History and religion: Narrating a religious past* (Religionsgeschichtliche Versuche und Vorarbeiten 68), Berlin: de Gruyter.
Otto, Rudolf 1917, *Das Heilige: Über das Irrationale in der Idee des Göttlichen und sein Verhältnis zum Rationalen*, Breslau: Trewendt u. Granier.
Otto, Rudolf 2014, *Das Heilige: Über das Irrationale in der Idee des Göttlichen und sein Verhältnis zum Rationalen. Mit einer Einf. zu Leben und Werk Rudolf Ottos von Jörg Lauster und Peter Schüz und einem Nachw. von Hans Joas* (Erw. Neuausg. edn., Beck'sche Reihe 328), München: Beck.
Pailler, Jean-Marie 1988, *Bacchanalia: La répression de 186 av. J.-C. à Rome et en italie: vestiges, images, tradition* (Bibliothèque des écoles françaises d'Athène et de rome 270), Rome: École Française.
Pape, Magrit 1975, *Griechische Kunstwerke aus Kriegsbeute und ihre öffentliche Aufstellung in Rom: Von der Eroberung von Syrakus bis in augusteische Zeit*, Diss. Hamburg.
Park, Chris C. 1994, *Sacred worlds: an introduction to geography and religion*, London: Routledge.
Parker, Robert 1996, *Athenian Religion: A History*, Oxford: Clarendon.
Patzelt, Maik 2018, *Über das Beten der Römer: Gebete im spätrepublikanischen und frühkaiserzeitlichen Rom als Ausdruck gelebter Religion* (Religionsgeschichtliche Versuche und Vorarbeiten 73), Berlin: deGruyter.
Pauketat, Timothy R., Killebrew, Ann E. and Micheau, Françoise 2015, 'Imagined cities', in: Norman Yoffee (ed.), *The Cambridge world history 3: Early cities in comparative perspective, 4000 BCE – 1200 CE*, Cambridge: Cambridge Univ. Press, 455–65.
Pease, Arthur Stanley (ed.) 1955, *M. Tullii Ciceronis De natura deorum*, Cambridge, Mass.: Harvard University Press.
Peirce, Charles S. 1986, *Semiotische Schriften*, edited and translated by Christian J. W. Kloesel, 3 vols., Frankfurt am Main: Suhrkamp.
Peirce, Charles S. 1991, *Peirce on signs: Writings on semiotic*, Chapel Hill, NC: Univ. of North Carolina Press.
Perkins, Judith 2009, *Roman imperial identities in the early Christian era* (Routledge monographs in classical studies), London: Routledge.
Perl, G 1982, 'Gallus et Galla', *Klio* 64, 413–20.
Petridou, Georgia 2015, 'Emplotting the Divine: Epiphanic Narratives as Means of Enhancing Agency', *Religion in the Roman Empire* 1 (3), 321–42.
Petridou, Georgia 2017a, 'Contesting religious and medical expertise: The therapeutai of Pergamum as religious and medical entrepreneurs', in: Georgia Petridou, Richard Gordon and Jörg Rüpke (eds.), *Beyond Priesthood: Religious Entrepreneurs and Innovators in the Roman Empire* (Religionsgeschichtliche Versuche und Vorarbeiten 66), Berlin: de Gruyter, 185–214.
Petridou, Georgia (ed.) 2017b, *Embodying religion: Lived ancient religion and medicine*, Tübingen: Mohr Siebeck.

Petridou, Georgia 2018, '"One Has To Be So Terribly Religious To Be An Artist": Devine Inspiration and *theophilia* in Aelius Aristides' *Hieroi Logoi*", *Archiv für Religionsgeschichte 20* (1), 257–71.

Petridou, Georgia and Thumiger, Chiara (eds.) 2016, *Homo patiens – approaches to the patient in the ancient world* (Studies in ancient medicine 45), Leiden: Brill.

Petsalis-Diomidis, Alexia 2006, 'Sacred Writing, Sacred Reading: The Function of Aelius Aristides' Self-Presentation as Author in the Sacred Tales', in: Brian McGing and Judith Mossman (eds.), *The Limits of Ancient Biography*, Swansea: The Classical Press of Wales, 193–211.

Petsalis-Diomidis, Alexia 2007, 'Landscape, transformation, and divine epiphany', in: Simon Swain, Stephen Harrison and Jaś Elsner (eds.), *Severan culture*, Cambridge: Cambridge Univ. Press, 250–89.

Petsalis-Diomidis, Alexia 2010, *Truly beyond wonders: Aelius Aristides and the cult of Asklepios*, Oxford: Oxford Univ. Press.

Pettenkofer, Andreas 2014, 'Sakralisierung und Abweichung: Das Collège de Sociologie, Marcel Mauss und die Aktualität der Durkheim-Schule', *Mittelweg 36 23* (4), 95–110.

Pickering, W.S.F. 1999, *Locating the Sacred: Durkheim, Otto and some Coemporary Issues* (British Association for the Study of Religions: Occasional Papers 12), London: Routledge & Kegan Paul.

Pizzone, Aglae Massima Valeria 2013, 'The Tale of a Dream: Oneiros and Mythos in the Greek Novel', in: Marilia P. Futre Pinheiro, Anton Bierl and Roger Beck (eds.), *Intende, Lector – Echoes of Myth, Religion and Ritual in the Ancient Novel* (MythosEikonPoiesis 6), Berlin: de Gruyter, 67–81.

Potter, David S. 1990, *Prophecy and History in the Crisis of the Roman Empire: A Historical Commentary on the Thirteenth Sibylline Oracle* (Oxford Classical Monographs), Oxford: Clarendon.

Prosdocimi, Aldo 1988, 'Sacerdos "qui sacrum dat": sacrum dare and sacre ! facere in ancient Italy', in: Mohammad Ali Jazayery and Werner Winter (eds.), *Languages and Cultures: Studies in Honor of Edgar C. Polomé*, Berlin: Mouton de Gruyter, 509–23.

Quack, Joachim Friedrich 2009, 'Miniaturisierung als Schlüssel zum Verständnis römerzeitlicher ägyptischer Rituale?', in: Olivier Hekster, Sebastian Schmidt-Hofner and Christian Witschel (eds.), *Ritual dynamics and religious change in the Roman Empire: Proceedings of the Eighth Workshop of the International Network Impact of Empire (Heidelberg, July 5–7, 2007)* (Impact of Empire 9), Leiden Brill, 349–66.

Rackham, Harris 1933, *Cicero, On the Nature of the Gods. Academics (Cicero XIX)* (Loeb Classical Library 268), Cambridge, Mass.: Harvard University Press.

Radke, Gerhard 1990a, *Fasti Romani: Betrachtungen zur Frühgeschichte des römischen Kalenders* (Orbis antiquus 31), Münster: Aschendorff.

Radke, Gerhard 1990b, 'Gibt es Antworten auf die 'Argeerfrage'?', *Latomus 49*, 5–19.

Raja, Rubina 2015, 'Complex Sanctuaries in the Roman Period', in: Rubina Raja and Jörg Rüpke (eds.), *A Companion to the Archaeology of Religion in the Ancient World*, Malden: Wiley, 307–19.

Raja, Rubina and Rüpke, Jörg 2015a, 'Appropriating Religion: Methodological Issues in Testing the 'Lived Ancient Religion' Approach', *Religion in the Roman Empire 1* (1), 11–9.

Raja, Rubina and Rüpke, Jörg 2015b, 'Archaeology of Religion, Material Religion, and the Ancient World', in: Rubina Raja and Jörg Rüpke (eds.), *A Companion to the Archaeology of Religion in the Ancient World*, Malden: Wiley, 1–25.

Raja, Rubina and Rüpke, Jörg (eds.) 2015c, *A Companion to the Archaeology of Religion in the Ancient World*, Boston: Wiley-Blackwell.

Rau, Susanne 2014, *Räume der Stadt. Eine Geschichte Lyons 1300–1800*, Frankfurt am Main: Campus.

Rautman, Alison E. 1998, 'Hierarchy and Heterarchy in the American Southwest: A Comment on Mcguire and Saitta', *American Antiquity 63* (2), 325–33.

Rebillard, Éric 2012, *Christians and their many identities in late antiquity, North Africa, 200–450 CE*, Ithaca: Cornell University Press.

Rebillard, Éric and Rüpke, Jörg (eds.) 2015, *Group Identity and Religous Individuality in Late Antiquity* (CUA Studies in Early Christianity), Washington, DC: Catholic University of America Press.

Redman, C.L. 2005, 'Resilience theory in archaeology', *American Anthropologist 107* (1), 70–7.

Reimann, Horst 1968, *Kommunikations-Systeme: Umrisse einer Soziologie der Vermittlungs- und Mitteilungsprozesse* (Heidelberger Sociologica 7), Tübingen: Mohr.

Renberg, Gil 2010, 'Dream-Narratives and Unnarrated Dreams in Greek and Latin Dedicatory Inscriptions', in: Emma Scioli and Christine Walde (eds.), *Sub imagine somni: Nighttime Phenomena in the Greco-Roman World* (Testi e studi di cultura classica 46), Pisa, 33–61.

Renberg, Gil 2015, 'The Role of Dream-Interpreters in Greek and Roman Religion', in: Gregor Weber (ed.), *Artemidor von Daldis und die antike Traumdeutung: Texte – Kontexte – Lektüren* (Colloquia Augustana 33), Berlin: de Gruyter, 233–62.

Revell, Louise 2009, *Roman imperialism and local identities*, Cambridge: Cambridge Univ. Press.

Revell, Louise 2014, 'Urbanism and imperialism: Living an urban ideal', in: Tønnes Bekker-Nielsen (ed.), *Space, place and identity in Northern Anatolia* (Geographica historica 29), Stuttgart: Steiner, 87–97.

Rexine, John E. 1968, *Religion in Plato and Cicero*, New York: Greenwood.

Reydams-Schils, Gretchen J. 1999, *Demiurge and Providence: Stoic and Platonist Readings of Plato's Timaeus*, Turnhout: Brepols.

Reydams-Schils, Gretchen J. 2005, *The Roman Stoics: Self, responsibility, and affection*, Chicago: University of Chicago Press.

Reydams-Schils, Gretchen J. 2019, 'How to Become Like God and Remain Oneself', in: Maren R. Niehoff (ed.), *The Self in Antiquity*, Leiden: Brill.

Reynolds, Jocye 1982, *Aphrodisias and Rome: Documents from the excavation of the theatre at Aphrodisias conducted by Professor Kenan T. Erim, together with some related texts* (JRS Monographs 1), London: Society for the Promotion of Roman Studies.

Richter, Daniel S. 2011, *Cosmopolis: Imagining community in late classical Athens and the early Roman Empire*, Oxford: Oxford University Press.

Rieger, Anna-Katharina 2016, 'Waste matters: Life cycle and agency of pottery employed in Graeco-Roman sacred spaces', *Religion in the Roman Empire 2* (3), 307–39.

Rieger, Anna-Katharina 2018, 'Approaches to an interpretation of visual and material cultural remains from the cave sanctuary at Caesarea Philippi/Bania (Gaulantis)', in: Marlis Arnhold, Harry O. Maier and Jörg Rüpke (eds.), *Seeing the Gods*, Tübingen: Mohr, ##-##.

Rizos, Efthymios 2017, *New Cities in Late Antiquity: Documents and archaeology* (Bibliothèque de l'antiquité tardive 35), Turnhout, Belgium: Brepols.

Robinson, Jennifer, Scott, Allen J. and Taylor, Peter J. 2016, *Working, Housing: Urbanizing: The International Year of Global Understanding – IYGU* (SpringerBriefs in Global Understanding), Berlin: Springer.

Roller, M. 2019, 'Selfhood, exemplarity, and Cicero's four personae: On fashioning your self after your model and your model after your self', in: Maren R. Niehoff (ed.), *The Self in Antiquity*, Leiden: Brill.

Romer, Frank E. 1998, *Pomponius Mela's description of the world*, Ann Arbor: University of Michigan Press.

Rosenberger, Veit 1998, *Gezähmte Götter: Das Prodigienwesen der römischen Republik* (HABES 27), Stuttgart: Steiner.

Rosenberger, Veit 2005, 'Prodigien aus Italien: geograophische Verteilung und religiöse Kommunikation', *Cahiers Glotz 16*, 235–57.

Rosenberger, Veit 2010, 'Strange Signs, Divine Wrath, and the Dynamics of Rituals. The Expiation of Prodigies in the Roman Republic', in: Axel Michaels (ed.), *Ritual Dynamics and the Science of Ritual*, Wiesbaden: Harrassowitz Verlag, 247–59.

Rosenstein, Nathan 1990, *Imperatores victi: Military Defeat and Aristocratic Competition in the Middle and Late Republic*, Berkeley: University of California Press.

Ruoff-Väänänen, Eeva 1972, 'The Roman prodigia and the ager Romanus', *Arctos 7*, 139–55.

Rüpke, Jörg 1990, *Domi militiae: Die religiöse Konstruktion des Krieges in Rom*, Stuttgart: Steiner.

Rüpke, Jörg 1991, 'Dies endotercisi?', *ZPE 86*, 212–4.

Rüpke, Jörg 1993, 'Krieg', in: Hubert Cancik, Burkhard Gladigow and Karl-Heinz Kohl (eds.), *Handbuch religionswissenschaftlicher Grundbegriffe*, Stuttgart: Kohlhammer, 448–60.

Rüpke, Jörg 1994a, 'Der späte Norden (1925–1941): Die Entstehung der "Altrömischen Priesterbücher" als biographischer Schlüssel', in: Bernhard Kytzler, Kurt Rudolph and Jörg Rüpke (eds.), *Eduard Norden (1868–1941): Ein deutscher Gelehrter jüdischer Herkunft*, Stuttgart: Steiner, 129–50.

Rüpke, Jörg 1994b, 'Ovids Kalenderkommentar: Zur Gattung der libri fastorum', *Antike und Abendland 40*, 125–36.

Rüpke, Jörg 1994c, 'Rez. Gerhard J. Baudy, Die Brände Roms ... 1991', *Gnomon 66*, 40–4.

Rüpke, Jörg 1995a, 'Fasti: Quellen oder Produkte römischer Geschichtsschreibung?', *Klio 77*, 184–202.

Rüpke, Jörg 1995b, *Kalender und Öffentlichkeit: Die Geschichte der Repräsentation und religiösen Qualifikation von Zeit in Rom* (RGVV 40), Berlin: de Gruyter.

Rüpke, Jörg 1996, 'Quis vetat et stellas ...? Les levers des étoiles et la tradition calendaire chez Ovide', in: Béatrice Bakhouche, Alain Moreau and Jean-Claude Turpin (eds.), *Les astres 1: Les astres et les mythes, la description du ciel* (Publications de la Recherche Université Paul Valéry), Montpellier: Séminaire d'Étude des Mentalités Antiques, 293–306.

Rüpke, Jörg 1997, 'Kognitive Einheit ritueller Sequenzen? Zur kommunikativen Funktion kalendarischer Gattungen in Rom', in: Gerhard Binder and Konrad Ehlich (eds.), *Stätten* und Formen der Kommunikation im Altertum 6: Religiöse Kommunikation: Formen und Praxis vor der Neuzeit, Trier: Wissenschaftlicher Verlag Trier, 191–223.

Rüpke, Jörg 1998a, 'Kommensalität und Gesellschaftsstruktur: Tafelfreu(n)de im alten Rom', Saeculum 49, 193–215.

Rüpke, Jörg 1998b, 'Les archives des petits collèges: Le cas des vicomagistri', La mémoire perdue: Recherches sur l'administration romaine, 27–44.

Rüpke, Jörg 2001a, 'Polytheismus und Pluralismus: Überlegungen zur religiösen Konkurrenz in der römischen Kaiserzeit', in: Andreas Gotzmann et al. (eds.), Pluralismus in der europäischen Religionsgeschichte (Europäische Religionsgeschichte 1), Marburg: Diagonal 17–34.

Rüpke, Jörg (ed.) 2001b, Von Menschen und Göttern erzählen: Formkonstanzen und Funktionswandel vormoderner Epik (Potsdamer altertumswissenschaftliche Beiträge 4), Stuttgart: Steiner.

Rüpke, Jörg 2003a, 'Acta aut agenda: Text-Performanz-Beziehungen in der römischen Religionsgeschichte', in: Benedikt Kranemann and Jörg Rüpke (eds.), Das Gedächtnis des Gedächtnisses: Zur Präsenz von Ritualen in beschreibenden und reflektierenden Texten, Marburg: Diagonal, 11–38.

Rüpke, Jörg 2003b, 'L'histoire des fasti romains : aspects médiatiques', Revue historique de droit francais et étranger 81, 125–39.

Rüpke, Jörg 2004, 'Acta aut agenda: Relations of Script and Performance', in: Alessandro Barchiesi, Jörg Rüpke and Susan Stephens (eds.), Rituals in Ink: A Conference on Religion and Literary Production in Ancient Rome held at Stanford University in February 2002 (Potsdamer altertumswissenschaftliche Beiträge 10), Stuttgart: Steiner, 23–43.

Rüpke, Jörg 2005, 'Buchreligionen als Reichsreligionen? Lokale Grenzen überregionaler religiöser Kommunikation', Mittellateinisches Jahrbuch 40, 197–207.

Rüpke, Jörg 2006a, 'Communicating with the Gods', in: Robert Morstein-Marx and Nathan Rosenstein (eds.), The Blackwell Companion to the Roman Republic, Oxford: Blackwell, 215–35.

Rüpke, Jörg 2006b, 'Ennius' fasti in Fulvius' Temple: Greek Rationality and Roman Tradition', Arethusa 39 (3), 489–512.

Rüpke, Jörg 2006c, 'Holy War', The Brill Dictionary of Religion 2, 877.

Rüpke, Jörg 2006e, 'Tempel, Daten, Rituale: die Götter als Langzeitgedächtnis der Gesellschaft', in: Elke Stein-Hölkeskamp and Karl-Joachim Hölkeskamp (eds.), Erinnerungsorte der Antike: Die römische Welt, München: Beck, 554–69.

Rüpke, Jörg 2006f, 'Triumphator and ancestor rituals between symbolic anthropology and magic', Numen 53, 251–89.

Rüpke, Jörg 2006 g, 'War / Armed Forces', The Brill Dictionary of Religion 4, 1960–3.

Rüpke, Jörg 2006 h, Zeit und Fest: Eine Kulturgeschichte des Kalenders, München: Beck.

Rüpke, Jörg 2006i, Zeit und Fest. Eine Kulturgeschichte des Kalenders, München: Beck.

Rüpke, Jörg (ed.) 2007a, Antike Religionsgeschichte in räumlicher Perspektive: Abschlussbericht zum Schwerpunktprogramm 1080 der Deutschen Forschungsgemeinschaft "Römische Reichsreligion und Provinzialreligion", Tübingen: Mohr Siebeck.

Rüpke, Jörg 2007b, 'Religio and Religiones in Roman Thinking', Études Classiques 75, 67–78.

Rüpke, Jörg 2007c, 'Religion medial', in: Jamal Malik, Jörg Rüpke and Theresa Wobbe (eds.), *Religion und Medien: Vom Kultbild zum Internetritual* (Vorlesungen des Interdisziplinären Forums Religion der Universität Erfurt 4), Münster: Aschendorff, 19 – 28.

Rüpke, Jörg 2007d, *Religion of the Romans*, trans. Trsl. and ed. by Richard Gordon, Cambridge: Polity Press.

Rüpke, Jörg 2007e, 'The role of the roman calendar for the formation of the Imperium Romanum and for the confessional states of the XVI. century', in: Jean-Philippe Genet (ed.), *Rome et l'état moderne européen*, Rome: Ecole française, 43 – 63.

Rüpke, Jörg 2008, *Fasti sacerdotum. A prosopography of Pagan, Jewish, and Christian Religious officials in the city of Rome, 300 BC to AD 499*, trans. David M. B. Richardson, Oxford: Oxford University Press.

Rüpke, Jörg 2009a, 'Antiquar und Theologe: systematisierende Beschreibung römischer Religion bei Varro', in: Andreas Bendlin and Jörg Rüpke (eds.), *Römische Religion im historischen Wandel*, Tübingen: Mohr Siebeck, 73 – 88.

Rüpke, Jörg 2009b, 'Equus October und ludi Capitolini: Zur rituellen Struktur der Oktoberiden und ihren antiken Deutungen', in: Uelli Duell and Christine Walde (eds.), *Antike Mythen: Medien, Transformationen und Konstruktionen: FS Fritz Graf zum 65. Geburtstag*, Berlin: de Gruyter, 97 – 121.

Rüpke, Jörg 2009c, 'Properz: Aitiologische Elegie in Augusteischer Zeit', in: Andreas Bendlin and Jörg Rüpke (eds.), *Römische Religion im historischen Wandel. Diskursentwicklung von Plautus bis Ovid* (Potsdamer altertumswissenschaftliche Beiträge 17), Stuttgart: Steiner, 115 – 42.

Rüpke, Jörg 2009d, 'Religiöser Pluralismus und das Römische Reich', in: Hubert Cancik and Jörg Rüpke (eds.), *Die Religion des Imperium Romanum: Koine und Konfrontationen*, Tübingen: Mohr Siebeck, 331 – 54.

Rüpke, Jörg 2010a, 'Early Christianity in, and out of, context', *Journal of Roman Studies 99*, 182 – 93.

Rüpke, Jörg 2010b, 'Hellenistic and Roman Empires and Euro-Mediterranean Religion', *Journal of Religion in Europe 3*, 197 – 214.

Rüpke, Jörg 2011a, *Aberglauben oder Individualität? Religiöse Abweichung im römischen Reich*, Tübingen: Mohr Siebeck.

Rüpke, Jörg 2011b, 'Reichsreligion? Überlegungen zur Religionsgeschichte des antiken Mittelmeerraums in römischer Zeit', *Historische Zeitschrift 292*, 297 – 322.

Rüpke, Jörg 2011c, *The Roman Calendar from Numa to Constantine: Time, History and the Fasti*, trans. David M.B. Richardson, Malden, MA: Wiley-Blackwell.

Rüpke, Jörg 2011d, 'Roman Religion and the Religion of Empire: Some Reflections on Method', in: John A. North and Simon R.F. Price (eds.), *The Religious History of the Roman Empire: Pagans, Jews, and Christians*, Oxford:: Oxford University Press, 9 – 36.

Rüpke, Jörg 2011e, *Von Jupiter und Christus: Religionsgeschichte in römischer Zeit*, Darmstadt: Wissenschaftliche Buchgesellschaft.

Rüpke, Jörg 2012a, 'Calendars III. Greco-Roman Antiquity and New Testament', *Encyclopedia of the Bible and its Reception 4*, 789 – 92.

Rüpke, Jörg 2012b, 'Calendars V. Christianity', *Encyclopedia of the Bible and its Reception 4*, 803 – 7.

Rüpke, Jörg 2012c, 'Lived Ancient Religion: Questioning 'Cults' and 'Polis Religion'', *Mythos ns 5 (2011)*, 191 – 204.

Rüpke, Jörg 2012d, 'Public and publicity: long-term changes in religious festivals during the Roman republic', in: Johan Rasmus Brandt and Jon Wikene Iddeng (eds.), *Greek and Roman Festivals: Content, Meaning, and Practice*, Oxford: Oxford Univ. Press, 305–22.

Rüpke, Jörg 2012e, 'Rationalizing Religious Practices: The Pontifical Calendar and the Law', in: Olga Tellegen-Couperus (ed.), *Law and Religion in the Roman Republic* (Mnemosyne Supplement 336), Leiden: Brill, 85–106.

Rüpke, Jörg 2012f, *Religion in Republican Rome: Rationalization and Ritual Change*, Philadelphia: University of Pennsylvania Press.

Rüpke, Jörg 2012g, 'Religion und Individuum', in: Michael Stausberg (ed.), *Religionswissenschaft*, Berlin: de Gruyter, 241–53.

Rüpke, Jörg 2012h, 'Religiöse Individualität in der Antike', in: Bernd Janowski (ed.), *Der ganze Mensch: Zur Anthropologie der Antike und ihrer europäischen Nachgeschichte*, Berlin: Akademie-Verlag, 199–219.

Rüpke, Jörg 2012i, 'Starting sacrifice in the beyond: Flavian innovations in the concept of priesthood and their repercussions in the treatise 'To the Hebrews'', *Revue d'histoire des religions 229*, 5–30.

Rüpke, Jörg 2013a, 'Fighting for differences: Forms and limits of religious individuality in the "Shepherd of Hermas"', in: Jörg Rüpke (ed.), *The Individual in the Religions of the Ancient Mediterranean*, Oxford: Oxford University Press, 315–41.

Rüpke, Jörg (ed.) 2013b, *The Individual in the Religions of the Ancient Mediterranean*, Oxford: Oxford University Press.

Rüpke, Jörg 2013c, 'Introduction: Individualisation and individuation as concepts for historical research', in: Jörg Rüpke (ed.), *The Individual in the Religions of the Ancient Mediterranean*, Oxford: Oxford University Press, 3–28.

Rüpke, Jörg 2013d, 'Two cities and one self: Transformations of Jerusalem and reflexive individuality in the Shepherd of Hermas', in: Jörg Rüpke and Greg Woolf (eds.), *Religious Dimensions of the Self in the Second Century CE* (Studien und Texte zu Antike und Christentum 76), Tübingen: Mohr Siebeck, 49–65.

Rüpke, Jörg 2013e, 'Was ist ein Heiligtum? Pluralität als Gegenstand der Religionswissenschaft', in: Afe Adogame, Magnus Echtler and Oliver Freiberger (eds.), *Alternative Voices: A Plurality Approach for Religious Studies. Essays in Honor of Ulrich Berner* (Critical Studies in Religion/Religionswissenschaft 4), Göttingen: Vandenhoeck & Ruprecht, 211–25.

Rüpke, Jörg 2014a, 'Historicizing Religion: Varro's Antiquitates and History of Religion in the Late Roman Republic', *History of Religions 53* (3), 246–68.

Rüpke, Jörg 2014b, 'Is history important for a historical argument in religious studies', *Religion 44* (4), 645–8.

Rüpke, Jörg 2014c, *Religion: Antiquity and its Legacy*, London/New York: Tauris/Oxford University Press.

Rüpke, Jörg 2014d, 'Religiöses Handeln: Kommunikation mit göttlichen Mächten', in: Badisches Landesmuseum (ed.), *Imperium der Götter: Isis – Mithras – Christus. Religionen im römischen Reich*, Stuttgart: Theiss, 32–9.

Rüpke, Jörg 2015a, 'Historians of religion and the space of law', in: Salvo Randazzo (ed.), *Religione e Diritto Romano: La cogenza del rito*, Tricase: Libellula, 43–9.

Rüpke, Jörg 2015b, 'Individual Choices and Individuality in the Archaeology of Ancient Religion', in: Rubina Raja and Jörg Rüpke (eds.), *A Companion to the Archaeology of Religion in the Ancient World*, Malden: Wiley, 437–50.
Rüpke, Jörg 2015c, 'Religious Agency, Identity, and Communication: Reflecting on History and Theory of Religion', *Religion 45* (3), 344–66.
Rüpke, Jörg 2015d, 'Roles and Individuality in the Chronograph of 354', in: Éric Rebillard and Jörg Rüpke (eds.), *Group Identity and Religous Individuality in Late Antiquity* (CUA Studies in Early Christianity), Washington, DC: Catholic University of America Press, 247–69.
Rüpke, Jörg 2015e, *Superstition ou individualité ? Déviance religieuse dans l'Empire romain*, trans. Ludivine Beaurin, Bruxelles/Leuven: Latomus/Peeters.
Rüpke, Jörg 2016a, 'Knowledge of Religion in Valerius Maximus' Exempla: Roman Historiography and Tiberian Memory Culture', in: Karl Galinsky (ed.), *Memory in Ancient Romne and Early Christianity*, Oxford: Oxford University Press, 89–111.
Rüpke, Jörg 2016b, *On Roman Religion: Lived Religion and the Individual in Ancient Rome* (Townsend Lectures/Cornell studies in classical philology), Ithaca, NY: Cornell University Press.
Rüpke, Jörg 2016c, *Pantheon: Geschichte der antiken Religionen* (Historische Bibliothek der Gerda-Henkel-Stiftung), München: Beck.
Rüpke, Jörg 2016e, *Religious Deviance in the Roman World: Superstition or Individuality*, trans. David M. B. Richardson, Cambridge: Cambridge University Press.
Rüpke, Jörg 2016f, 'The Role of Texts in Processes of Religious Grouping during the Principate', *Religion in the Roman Empire 2* (2), 170–95.
Rüpke, Jörg 2017a, 'Crafting complex place: Religion, antiquarianism, and urban development in late republican Rome', *Historia Religionum 9*, 109–17.
Rüpke, Jörg 2017b, 'Cult and Identity', *Politica antica 7*, 1–17.
Rüpke, Jörg 2017c, 'Doubling Religion in the Augustan Age: Shaping Time for an Empire', in: Jonathan Ben-Dov and Lutz Doering (eds.), *The Construction of Time in Antiquity: Ritual, Art and Identity*, Cambridge: Cambridge University Press, 50–68.
Rüpke, Jörg 2017d, '[Review] The Horologium of Augustus ... ed. L. Haselberger ... 2014', *American Journal of Archaeology 121* (3).
Rüpke, Jörg 2018a, 'Creating Religion(s) by Historiography', *Archiv für Religionsgeschichte 20*, 3–6.
Rüpke, Jörg (ed.) 2018b, *Creating Religion(s) by Historiography = Archiv für Religionsgeschichte 20*, Berlin: de Gruyter.
Rüpke, Jörg 2018c, 'Gifts, votives, and sacred things: Strategies, not entities', *Religion in the Roman Empire 4* (2), 207–36.
Rüpke, Jörg 2018d, *Pantheon: A New History of Roman Religion*, Princeton: Princeton University Press.
Rüpke, Jörg 2018e, *Religiöse Transformationen im römischen Reich: Urbanisierung, Reichsbildung und Selbst-Bildung als Bausteine religiösen Wandels* (Hans-Lietzmann-Vorlesungen 16), Berlin: deGruyter.
Rüpke, Jörg 2018f, 'Living urban religion: Blind spots in boundary work', *Historia religionum 10*, 53–36.
Rüpke, Jörg 2019a, 'Lived Ancient Religion', *Oxford Research Encyclopedia, Religion*, online.

Rüpke, Jörg 2019b, *Peace and War at Rome: The Religious Construction of Warfare. With a afterword by Federico Santangelo*, trans. David M. B. Richardson, Stuttgart: Steiner.
Rüpke, Jörg 2019c, 'Religion als Urbanität: Ein anderer Blick auf Stadtreligion', *Zeitschrift für Religionswissenschaft 27*. 174–195.
Rüpke, Jörg and Degelmann, Christoph 2015, 'Narratives as a lens into lived ancient religion, individual agency and collective identity', *Religion in the Roman Empire 1* (3), 289–96.
Rüpke, Jörg and Spickermann, Wolfgang (eds.) 2012, *Reflections on Religious Individuality: Greco-Roman and Judaeo-Christian Texts and Practices* (Religionsgeschichtliche Versuche und Vorarbeiten 62), Berlin: de Gruyter.
Rüpke, Jörg and Woolf, Greg (eds.) 2013, *Religious Dimensions of the Self in the Second Century CE* (Studien und Texte zu Antike und Christentum 76), Tübingen: Mohr Siebeck.
Russo, Manfred 2016, *Projekt Stadt: Eine Geschichte der Urbanität*, Basel: Birkhäuser.
Rutter, Michael 1987, 'Psychosocial resilience and protective mechanisms', *American Journal of Orthopsychiatry 57*, 316–31.
Rutter, Michael 2012, 'Resilience as a dynamic concept', *Development and Psychopathology 24* (2), 335–44.
Rykwert, Joseph 1976, *The Idea of a Town: The Anthropology of Urban Form in Rome, Italy and the Ancient World*, Princeton: UP.
Sabbatucci, Dario 1952, 'Sacer', *Studi e materiali della storia delle religioni 23 (1951/52)*, 91–101.
Salzman, Michele Renee 1990, *On Roman Time: The Codex-Calendar of 354 and the Rhythms of Urban Life in Late Antiquity* (The Transformation of the Classical Heritage 17), Berkeley: University of California Press.
Samter, Ernst 1901, *Familienfeste der Griechen und Römer*, Berlin: Reimer.
Sassen, Saskia 1991, *The Global City*, Princeton, NJ: Princeton University Press.
Sassen, Saskia 2013, 'Analytic Borderlands: Economy and Culture in the Global City', in: Gary Bridge and Sophie Watson (eds.), *The New Blackwell Companion to the City* (rev. ed. Wiley-Blackwell Companions to Geography), Malden, Mass.: Wiley-Blackwell, 210–20.
Schalles, Hans-Joachim and Hesberg, Henner von 1992, 'Ausblick', in: Hans-Joachim Schalles (ed.), *Die römische Stadt im 2. Jahrhundert n. Chr.: Der Funktionswandel des öffentlichen Raumes* (Xantener Berichte 2), Köln: Rheinland-Verl., 391–8.
Scheid, John 1990a, 'Rituel et écriture à Rome', in: Anne-Marie Blondeau and Kristofer Schipper (eds.), *Essais sur le rituel*, Louvain: Peeters, 1–15.
Scheid, John 1990b, *Romulus et ses frères: Le collège des frères arvales, modèle du culte public dans la Rome des empereurs* (Bibliothèque des Écoles françaises d'Athènes et de Rome 275), Rome: École française.
Scheid, John 1995, 'Graeco ritu: A typically Roman way of honouring the gods', *HSCPh 97*, 15–31.
Scheid, John 1998, *Commentarii fratrum Arvalium qui supersunt: Les copie épigraphiques des protocoles annuels de la confrérie arvale (21 av.–304 ap. J.-C.)*. (Roma antica 4 – Recherches archéologiques à La Magliana), Roma: École française de Rome/ Soprintendenza archeologica di Roma.
Scheid, John 2001, *Religion et piété à Rome*, Paris: Michel.
Scheid, John 2003, *An introduction to Roman religion*, Edinburgh: Edinburgh Univ. Press.
Scheidel, Walter (ed.) 2001a, *Debating Roman Demography*, Leiden: Brill.
Scheidel, Walter 2001b, 'Roman Age Structure: Evidence and Models', *JRS 91*, 1–26.

Scheidel, Walter 2003, 'Germ for Rome', in: Catherine Edwards and Greg Woolf (eds.), *Rome The Cosmopolis* Cambridge Cambridge University Press, 158–76.
Schildgen, Brenda Deen 2012, *Divine providence. A history: The Bible, Virgil, Orosius, Augustine, and Dante*, London: Continuum.
Schmidt, Klaus 2006, *Sie bauten die ersten Tempel: Das rätselhafte Heiligtum der Steinzeitjäger. Die archäologische Entdeckung am Göbekli Tepe*, München: Beck.
Schmidt, Klaus 2013, 'Die Steinmetze vom Göbekli Tepe', *Archäologie Weltweit 1*, 18–23.
Schneider, Rolf Michael 1999, 'Marmor', *Neuer Pauly 7*, 928–38.
Schultz, Celia E. 2010, 'The Romans and ritual murder ', *Journal of the American Academy of Religion 78* (2), 515–41.
Scobie, A. 1986, 'Slums, sanitation, and mortality in the Roman world', *Klio 68*, 399–433.
Sear, Frank 2006, *Roman theatres: An architectural study*, Oxford: Oxford Univ. Press.
Sellars, John 2004, *The art of living: The Stoics on the nature and function of philosophy*, Burlington, VT: Ashgate.
Setaioli, Aldo 2007, 'Seneca and the Divine: Stoic tradition and personal developments', *International Journal of the Classical Tradition 13*, 333–68.
Sfameni Gasparro, Giulia 2007, 'ΘΕΘΣ ΣΩΤΗΡ: Aspetti del culto di Asclepio dell'eta ellenistica alla tarda antichita', in: Hugo Brandenburg, Stefan Heid and Christoph Markschies (eds.), *Salute e guarigione nella tarda antichità: atti della giornata tematica dei Seminari di Archeologia Cristiana, Roma, 20 maggio 2004* (Sussidi allo studio delle antichità cristiane 19), Città del Vaticano: Pontificio Istituto di Archeologia Cristiana, 245–71.
Shaw, Rajib and Sharma, Anshu (eds.) 2011, *Climate and Disaster Resilience in Cities* (Community, Environment, and Desaster Management 6).
Shils, Edward 1969, 'Tradition', in: *Wörterbuch der Soziologie*, Stuttgart: W. Bornsdorf, 1182–4.
Shils, Edward 1975, 'Tradition', in: Edward Shils (ed.), *Center and Periphery: Essays in Macrosociology*, Chicago: University of California Press, 182–218.
Shils, Edward 1981, *Tradition*, London: Faber.
Short, John Rennie 2013, 'The Liquid City of Megalopolis', in: Gary Bridge and Sophie Watson (eds.), *The New Blackwell Companion to the City* (rev. ed. edn., Wiley-Blackwell Companions to Geography), Malden, Mass.: Wiley-Blackwell, 26–37.
Silverstone, Roger and Morley, D. 1992, 'Information and Communication Technologies and the Moral Economy of the Household', in: Roger Silverstone and Eric Hirsch (eds.), *Consuming Technologies: Media and Information in Domestic Space*, London.
Simmel, Georg 1917, 'Individualismus', *Marsyas* (1), 33–9.
Sinha, Vineeta 2016, 'Marking spaces as 'sacred': Infusing Singapore's urban landscape with sacrality', *International Sociology 31* (4), 467–88.
Sinopoli, Carla M. 2015, 'Ancient South Asian cities in their regions', in: Norman Yoffee (ed.), *The Cambridge world history 3: Early cities in comparative perspective, 4000 BCE-1200 CE*, Cambridge: Cambridge Univ. Press, 319–42.
Sinopoli, Carla M. et al. 2015, 'The distribution of power: Hierarchy and its discontents', in: Norman Yoffee (ed.), *The Cambridge world history 3: Early cities in comparative perspective, 4000 BCE–1200 CE*, Cambridge: Cambridge Univ. Press, 381–93.

Smith, Christopher 2015, 'Urbanization and Memory', in: Rubina Raja and Jörg Rüpke (eds.), *A Companion to the Archaeology of Religion in the Ancient World*, Malden: Wiley, 362–75.

Smith, Jonathan Z 2001, 'The History of the History of Religions' History', *Numen* 48 (2), 131–46.

Smith, Jonathan Z. 1987, *To Take Place: Toward Theory in Ritual* (Chicago Studies in the History of Judaism), Chicago: University of Chicago Press.

Smith, Jonathan Z. 2003, 'Here, There, and Anywhere', in: Scott B. Noegel, Joel Thomas Walker and Brannon M. Wheeler (eds.), *Prayer, magic, and the stars in the ancient and late antique world* (Magic in history), University Park, Pa: Pennsylvania State Univ. Press, 21–36.

Smith, Michael E. et al. 2015, 'Conceptual approaches to service provision in cities throughout history', *Urban Studies*, 1–17.

Smith, Monica L. 2019, *Cities: The First 6,000 Years*, London: Simon & Schuster.

Soja, Edward W. 1989, *Postmodern Geographies*, London: Verso.

Soja, Edward W. 1996, *Thirdspace: Journeys to Los Angeles and Other Real-and-Imagined Places*, Oxford: Blackwell.

Soja, Edward W. 2000, *Postmetropolis: Critical studies of cities and regions*, Oxford: Blackwell Publishers.

Soja, Edward W. 2006, 'Cityspaces as Cityspaces', in: C. Lindner (ed.), *Urban Spaces and Cityscapes: Perspectives from Modern and Contemporary Culture*, New York, xv–xviii.

Soja, Edward W. 2013, 'Regional Urbanization and the Ende of the Metropolitan Era', in: Gary Bridge and Sophie Watson (eds.), *The New Blackwell Companion to the City* (rev. ed. edn., Wiley-Blackwell Companions to Geography), Malden, Mass.: Wiley-Blackwell, 679–89.

Song, Euree 2009, *Aufstieg und Abstieg der Seele : Diesseitigkeit und Jenseitigkeit in Plotins Ethik der Sorge* (Hypomnemata 180), Göttingen Vandenhoeck & Ruprecht.

Sorabji, Richard 2007, 'Epictetus on prohairesis and Self', in: Theordore Scaltas and Andrew S. Mason (eds.), *The Philosophy of Epictetus*, Oxford: Oxford University Press, 87–98.

Stackelberg, Katharine T. von 2009, *The Roman Garden: Space, sense, and society*, London: Routledge.

Stärk, Ekkehard 1996, 'Afranius 4, L.', *Neuer Pauly 1*, 215–6.

Stausberg, Michael 2010, *Religion and tourism: Crossroads, destinations,and encounters*, London: Routledge.

Stausberg, Michael 2014, 'Bellah's Religion in Human Evolution: A Postreview', *Numen* 61 (2–3), 281–99.

Stavrianopoulou, Eftychia 2015, 'The Archaeology of Processions', in: Rubina Raja and Jörg Rüpke (eds.), *A Companion to the Archaeology of Religion in the Ancient World*, Malden: Wiley, 349–60.

Stefaniw, Blossom 2011, *Mind, text, and commentary: Noetic exegesis in Origen of Alexandria, Didymus the Blind, and Evagrius Ponticus* (Early Christianity in the context of antiquity 6), Frankfurt a. M.: Lang.

Stefaniw, Blossom 2019, *Christian Reading: Language, Ethics, and the Order of Things*, Oakland: University of California Press.

Steger, Florian 2016, *Asklepios: Medizin und Kult*, Stuttgart: Franz Steiner.

Steinhauer, Julietta 2014, *Religious Associations in the Post-Classical Polis* (PawB 50), Stuttgart: Steiner.
Steinsapir, Ann Irvine 2005, *Rural sanctuaries in Roman Syria. The creation of a sacred landscape* (BAR international series 1431), Oxford: Hedges.
Stemberger, Günther 1979, 'Die Beurteilung Roms in der rabbinischen Literatur', *ANRW II.19,2*, 338–96.
Stemberger, Günter 2016, 'Die Bedeutung des Jerusalemer Tempels für die Identität des rabbinischen Judentums', in: Martina Böhm (ed.), *Kultort und Identität: Prozesse jüdischer und christlicher Identitätsbildung im Rahmen der Antike* (Biblisch-theologische Studien 155), Neukirchen: Neukirchener Theologie, 167–88.
Sterbenc Erker, Darja 2013, *Religiöse Rollen römischer Frauen in "griechischen" Ritualen* (Potsdamer Altertumswissenschaftliche Beiträge 43), Stuttgart: Steiner.
Stern, Henri 1953, *Le calendrier de 354: Étude sur son texte et ses illustrations* (Institut français d'archéologie de Beyrouth: Bibliothèque archéologique et historique 55), Paris: Impr. Nationale.
Stern, Sacha 2001, *Calendar and Community: A History of the Jewish Calendar Second Century BCE-Tenth Century CE*, Oxford: University Press.
Stern, Sacha 2002, 'Jewish calendar reckoning in the Graeco-Roman cities', in: John R. Bartlett (ed.), *Jews in the Hellenistic and Roman cities*, London: Routledge, 107–16.
Stern, Sacha 2012, *Calendars in Antiquity: Empires, States, and Societies*, New York: Oxford University Press.
Stern, Sacha and Burnett, Charles (eds.) 2014, *Time, Astronomy, and Calendars in the Jewish Tradition* (Time, Astronomies, and Calendars 3), Leiden: Brill.
Stolz, Fritz 1988, *Grundzüge der Religionswissenschaft*, Göttingen: Vandenhoeck & Ruprecht.
Stolz, Fritz 1998, 'Effekt und Kommunikation: Handlung im Verhältnis zu anderen Kodierungsformen von Religion', in: Hartmann Tyrell, Volkhard Krech and Hubert Knoblauch (eds.), *Religion als Kommunikation*, Würzburg: Ergon, 301–22.
Stoneman, Richard 2011, *The ancient oracles: Making the gods speak*, New Haven, CT: Yale University Press.
Storper, Michael 1997, *The regional world: Territorial development in a global economy* (Perspectives on economic change), New York: Guilford Press.
Suerbaum, Werner 1980, 'Merkwürdige Geburtstage: Der nicht-existierende Geburtstag des M. Antonius, der doppelte Geburtstag des Augustus, der neue Geburtstag der Livia und der vorzeitige Geburtstag des älteren Drusus', *Chiron 10*, 327–55.
Sulzbach, Carla 2013, 'From Urban Nightmares to Dream Cities: Revealing the Apocalyptic Cityscape', in: C.M. Maier, G. Prinsloo (eds), *Constructions of Space V*, New York: Bloomsbury, 226–243.
Sun, Anna Xiao Dong 2013, *Confucianism as a world religion: Contested histories and contemporary realities*, Princeton: Princeton Univ. Press.
Tacoma, Laurens Ernst 2016, *Moving Romans: Migration to Rome in the Principate* (First edition edn.), Oxford: Oxford University Press.
Tarpin, Michel 2002, *Vici et pagi dans l'occident romain*, Paris: Ecole française de Rome.
Taves, Ann 2009, *Religious experience reconsidered: A building block approach to the study of religion and other special things*, Princeton, NJ: Princeton University Press.
Taves, Ann 2010, 'Experience as site of contested meaning and value: The attributional dog and its special tail', *Religion 40* (4), 317–23.

Tellegen-Couperus, Olga (ed.) 2012, *Law and Religion in the Roman Republic* (Mnemosyne Supplement 336), Leiden: Brill.
Thomassen, Einar 2010, *Canon and Canonicity: the formation and use of scripture* Copenhagen: Museum Tusculanum Press.
Tonkiss, Fran 2005, *Space, the city and social theory social relations and urban forms*, Cambridge: Polity.
Trapp, Michael 2007, *Philosophy in the Roman Empire: ethics, politics and society* (Ashgate ancient philosophy series), Aldershot: Ashgate.
Tromp, Sebastian Petrus 1921, *De Romanorum piaculis*, Diss. Leiden.
Tuan, Yi-Fu 1977, *Space and place: The perspective of experience*, Minneapolis, Minn.: Univ. of Minnesota Press.
Tweed, Thomas A. 2006, *Crossing and dwelling: A theory of religion*, Cambridge, Mass.: Harvard University Press.
Tweed, Thomas A. 2011, 'Space', *Material Religion* 7, 116–23.
Tyrell, Hartmann 1998, 'Handeln, Religion und Kommunikation: Begriffsgeschichtliche und systematische Überlegungen', in: Hartmann Tyrell, Volkhard Krech and Hubert Knoblauch (eds.), *Religion als Kommunikation*, Würzburg: Ergon, 83–134.
Tyrell, Hartmann 2002, 'Religiöse Kommunikation. Auge, Ohr und Medienvielfalt', in: Klaus Schreiner (ed.), *Frömmigkeit im Mittelalter: Politisch-soziale Kontexte, visuelle Praxis, körperliche Ausdrucksformen*, München: Fink, 41–93.
Tyrell, Hartmann, Krech, Volkhard and Knoblauch, Hubert 1998, 'Religiöse Kommunikation: Einleitende Bemerkungen zu einem religionssoziologischen Forschungsprogramm', in: Hartmann Tyrell (ed.), *Religion als Kommunikation*, Würzburg: Ergon, 7–29.
Uehlinger, Christoph 2006, 'Visible Religion und die Sichtbarkeit von Religion(en): Voraussetzungen, Anknüpfungsprobleme, Wiederaufnahme eines religionswissenschaftlichen Forschungsprogramms', *Berliner Theologische Zeitschrift* 23 (2), 165–84.
Umemoto, Karen and Zambonelli, Vera 2015, 'Cultural Diversity', in: Rachel Weber and Randall Crane (eds.), *The Oxford Handbook of Urban Planning*, Oxford: Oxford University Press, 197–217.
Ungar, Michael (ed.) 2012, *The social ecology of resilience: A handbook of theory and practice*, New York: Springer.
Urban, Hugh B. 2003a, 'Sacred Capital: Pierre Bourdieu and the Study of Religion', *Method & Theory in the Study of Religion* 15 (4), 354–89.
Urban, Hugh B. 2003b, 'Sacred Capital: Pierre Bourdieu and the study of religion', *Method & Theory in the Study of Religion* 15, 354–89.
Urciuoli, Emiliano Rubens 2020, 'A tale of no cities: Searching for city-spaces in Augustine's City of God', *Forthcoming*.
Urciuoli, Emiliano Rubens and Rüpke, Jörg 2018, 'Urban Religion in Mediterranean Antiquity: Relocating Religious Change', *Mythos* 12, 117–35.
Urry, John 2013, 'City Life and the Senses', in: Gary Bridge and Sophie Watson (eds.), *The New Blackwell Companion to the City* (rev. ed. Wiley-Blackwell Companions to Geography), Malden, Mass.: Wiley-Blackwell, 347–56.
Ustinova, Yulia 2005, 'Voluntary cult associations in the Greek law', in: Véronique Dasen and Marcel Piérart (eds.), *Les cadres "Privés" et "publics" de la religion grecque antique*, Liége: Centre International d'Ètude de la Religion Grecque Antique, 177–90.

Van Andringa, William 2015, 'The Archaeology of Ancient Sanctuaries', in: Rubina Raja and Jörg Rüpke (eds.), *A Companion to the Archaeology of Religion in the Ancient World*, Malden: Wiley, 29–40.

van den Bercken, Wil and Sutton, Jonathan (eds.) 2005, *Aesthetics as a Religious Factor in Eastern and Western Christianity* (Eastern Christian Studies), Leuven/Paris/Dudley: Peeters.

van der Veer, Peter 2015a, *Handbook of religion and the Asian city. Aspiration and urbanization in the twenty-first century*, Oakland, Calif.: Univ. of California Press.

van der Veer, Peter 2015b, 'Introduction: Urban Theory, Asia and Religion', in: Peter van der Veer (ed.), *Handbook of religion and the Asian city. Aspiration and urbanization in the twenty-first century*, Oakland, Calif.: Univ. of California Press, 1–17.

van Kooten, George H. 2009, 'St Paul on Soul, Spirit and the Inner Man', in: Maha Elkaisy-Friemuth and John M. Dillon (eds.), *The afterlife of the platonic soul. Reflections of platonic psychology in the monotheistic religions* (Studies in platonism, neoplatonism, and the platonic tradition 9), Leiden: Brill, 25–44.

van Nuffelen, Peter 2012, 'Playing the Ritual Game in Constantinople (379–457)', in: Lucy Grig and Gavin Kelly (eds.), *Two Romes: Rome and Constantinople in late antiquity* (Oxford studies in late antiquity), Oxford: Oxford Univ. Press, 183–200.

van Straten, F. T. 1981, 'Gifts for the Gods', in: H. S. Versnel (ed.), *Faith, Hope and Worship: Aspects of Religious Mentality in the Ancient World*, Leiden: Brill, 65–151.

Versnel, Hendrik S. 1996, 'Argei', *Neuer Pauly 1*, 1057–9.

Vessey, Mark 2012, 'The History of the Book: Augustine's *City of God* and Post-Roman Cultural Memory', in: James Wetzel (ed.), *Augustine's City of God: A Critical Guide* (Cambridge Critical Guides), Cambridge: Cambridge University Press, 14–32.

Veyne, Paul 1983, *Les Grecs ont-ils cru à leurs mythes?*, Paris: Seuil.

Vinzent, Markus 2011, *Christ's Resurrection in Early Christianity and the Making of the New Testament*, Farnham: Ashgate.

Vinzent, Markus 2014, *Marcion and the Dating of the Synoptic Gospels* (Studia patristica suppl. 2), Leuven: Peeters.

Waghorne, Joanne Punzo Jh (ed.) 2017, *Place/No-Place in Urban Asian Religiosity* (ARI – Springer Asia Series), Singapore: Springer.

Walker, P. W. 1990, *Holy City, Holy Places? Christian Attitudes to Jerusalem and the Holy Land in the Fourth Century* (Oxford Early Christian Studies), Oxford: Clarendon.

Wallraff, Martin 2013, *Kodex und Kanon: Das Buch im frühen Christentum* (Hans-Lietzmann-Vorlesungen 12), Berlin: de Gruyter.

Watson, Sophie 2006, *City publics the (dis)enchantments of urban encounters* (Questioning Cities), London: Routledge.

Watson, Sophie and Zanetti, Oliver 2016, 'Religion as practices of attachment and materiality: the making of Buddhism in contemporary London', *Culture and Religion* 17 (3), 257–78.

Weber, Gregor 1999, "Artemidor von Daldis und sein 'Publikum'", *Gymnasium 106*, 209–29.

Weber, Max 1922, *Wirtschaft und Gesellschaft: Grundriss der verstehenden Soziologie* (5., rev. Aufl. 1985 edn.), Tübingen: Mohr.

Weber, Max 1972, *Wirtschaft und Gesellschaft*, Tübingen: Mohr.

Weber, Max 2014, *Gesamtausgabe I,9: Asketischer Protestantismus und Kapitalismus: Schriften und Reden 1904–1911*, Tübingen: Mohr.

Weber, Rachel and Crane, Randall (eds.) 2015, *The Oxford Handbook of Urban Planning* (Pb. edn.), Oxford: Oxford University Press.

Webster, Jane and Cooper, Nicholas J. (eds.) 1996, *Roman Imperialism: Post-Colonial Perspectives: Proceedings of a Symposium held at Leicester University in November 1994* (Leicester Archaeology Monographs), Leicester: School of Archaeological Studies University of Leicester.

Weinfurter, Stefan 1992, 'Idee und Funktion des Sakralkönigtums bei den ottonischen und salischen Herrschern (10. und 11. Jahrhundert)', in: Rolf Gundlach and Hermann Weber (eds.), *Legitimation und Funktion des Herrschers: Vom ägyptischen Pharao zum neuzeitlichen Diktator*, Stuttgart: Steiner, 99–127.

Welch, Tara S. 2005, *The Elegiac Cityscape: Propertius and the Meaning of Roman Monuments*, Columbus: Ohio State University Press.

Welch, Tara S. 2015, *Tarpeia: Workings of a Roman myth*, Columbus: Ohio State University Press.

Weltecke, Dorothea 2016, 'Space, Entanglement and Decentralisation: On How to Narrate the Transcultural History of Christianity (550 to 1350 CE)', in: Reinhold F. Glei and Nicolas Jaspert (eds.), *Locating religion: Contact, Diversity and Translocality* (Dynamics of religion 9), Leiden: Brill, 315–44.

Wendt, Heidi 2015a, 'Iudaica Romana: A Rereading of Judean Expulsions from Rome', *Journal of Ancient Judaism 6*, 97–126.

Wendt, Heidi 2015b, 'A Rereading of Judean Expulsions from Rone', *Journal of Ancient Judaism 6*, 97–126.

Wendt, Heidi 2016, *At the temple gates: The religion of freelance experts in the Roman empire*, New York: Oxford University Press.

Wengrow, David 2013, "'Fleshpots of Egypt': rethinking temple economy in the ancient Near East', in: Elizabeth Frood and A. McDonald (eds.), *Decorum and experience: Essays in ancient culture for John Baines*, Oxford: Griffith Institute.

Whitehead, Alfred North 1926, *Religion in the making* (Lowell lectures), New York: Macmillan.

Whitehead, Alfred North 1990, *Wie entsteht Religion?*, trans. Hans Günter Holl (Suhrkamp-Taschenbuch Wissenschaft 847), Frankfurt am Main: Suhrkamp.

Whitehouse, Harvey and Laidlaw, James (eds.) 2004, *Ritual and Memory: Toward a Comparative Anthropology of Religion* (Cognitive science of religion series), Walnut Creek: AltaMira Press.

Wiedenhofer, Siegfried 2004, 'Tradition, Traditionalismus', in: Otto Brunner, Werner Conze and Reinhart Koselleck (eds.), *Geschichtliche Grundbegriffe – Historisches Lexikon zur politisch-sozialen Sprach in Deutschland*, Stuttgart: Klett-Cotta, 607–49.

Wifstrand Schiebe, Marianne 1999, 'Lactanz, Varro und die Tradition des Argeer-Ritus', *Rheinisches Museum 142*, 189–209.

Wilburn, Drew 2015, 'Inscribed Ostrich Eggs at Berenike and Materiality in Ritual Performance', *Religion in the Roman Empire 1* (2), 263–85.

Wilson, Deirdre and Sperber, Dan 1994, 'Outline of Relevance Theory', *Links & Letters 1*, 85–106.

Wilson, Deirdre and Sperber, Dan 2002, 'Relevance Theory', *UCL Working Papers in Linguistics 14*, 249–90.

Wilson, R. R. 1980, *Prophecy and Society in Ancient Israel*, Philadelphia.

Wirth, Louis 1938, 'Urbanism As A Way of Life', *American Journal of Sociology 44*, 1–24.

Wirth, Louis 1964, *Louis Wirth on cities and social life: Selected papers* (The Heritage of sociology), Chicago: University of Chicago Press.

Wischmeyer, Oda 2012, '"Invented Traditions" and "New Traditions" in Earliest Christianity', in: Jörg Ulrich, Anders-Christian Jacobsen and David Brakke (eds.), *Invention, Rewriting, Usurpation – Discursive Fights over Religious Traditions in Antiquity* (Early Christianity In The Context Of Antiquity), Frankfurt am Main: Peter Lang, 177–89.

Wiseman, Timothy P. 1992, 'Lucretius, Catiline, and the Survival of Prophecy', in: Timothy P. Wiseman (ed.), *Historiography and imagination: eight essays on Roman culture*, Exeter University of Exeter Press, 49–67.

Wissowa, Georg 1900, 'Consecratio', *RE 4,1*, 896–902.

Wissowa, Georg 1912, *Religion und Kultus der Römer* (2. edn., Handbuch der Altertumswissenschaft 5,4), München: Beck.

Woermann, Karl 1876, *Die antiken Odyssee-Landschaften vom esquilinischen Hügel zu Rom: In Farben-Steindruck*, München: Ackermann.

Woolf, Daniel R. 2014, *A Global Encyclopedia of Historical Writing*, Hoboken: Taylor & Francis.

Woolf, Greg 2012, *Rome: An empire's Story*, Oxford: Oxford Univ. Press.

Woolf, Greg 2013, 'Ritual and the Individual in Roman Religion', in: Jörg Rüpke (ed.), *The Individual in the Religions of the Ancient Mediterranean*, Oxford: Oxford University Press, 136–60.

Woolf, Greg 2015, 'Movers and Stayers', in: Luuk de Ligt and Laurens Ernst Tacoma (eds.), *Migration and Mobility in the Early Roman Empire*, Leiden: Brill, 438–61.

Woolf, Greg 2017, 'Moving Peoples in the Early Roman Empire', in: Elio Lo Cascio, Laurens Ernst Tacoma and Miriam J. Groen-Vallinga (eds.), *The impact of mobility and migration in the Roman Empire: Proceedings of the Twelfth Workshop of the International Network Impact of Empire (Rome, June 17–19, 2015)* (Impact of Empire 22), Leiden: Brill, 25–41.

Wunn, Ina 2005, *Die Religionen in vorgeschichtlicher Zeit* (Religionen der Menschheit 2), Stuttgart: Kohlhammer.

Yoffee, Norman 2015, *The Cambridge world history 3: Early cities in comparative perspective, 4000 BCE–1200 CE*, Cambridge: Cambridge Univ. Press.

Yoffee, Norman and Terrenato, Nicola 2015, 'Introduction: a history of the study of early cities', in: Norman Yoffee (ed.), *The Cambridge world history 3: Early cities in comparative perspective, 4000 BCE–1200 CE*, Cambridge: Cambridge Univ. Press, 1–24.

Ziolkowski, Adam 1992, *The Temples of Mid-Republican Rome and their Historical and Topographical Context* (Saggi di Storia antica 4), Roma: Bretschneider.

Ziolkowski, Adam 1998, 'Ritual Cleaning-Up of the City: From the Lupercalia to the Argei', *Ancient Society 29*, 191–218.

Zuiderhoek, Arjan 2017, *The ancient city* (Key themes in ancient history), Cambridge: Cambridge University Press.

Index

Academic 2, 20, 30, 66 f.
addressee 18–20, 47–49, 56, 59, 90, 92, 94, 112, 117, 152, 166, 191 f.
Aelius Aristides 91, 151, 159
aesthetic 6, 17, 29, 43, 88, 94, 101, 144
affordance 65, 93, 139
agency 18, 21–23, 26, 29, 40, 45, 47 f., 50, 53, 70 f., 82, 90, 93 f., 99, 101, 106, 108, 112, 149, 168, 188
agent 3, 18–21, 47–49, 56, 58, 90, 93 f., 96, 101, 140, 145, 178
– divine agent 20–22, 90, 117
– human agent 18, 21, 33, 44, 48, 94, 97, 100
agriculture 26, 65, 67
Alexandria 30, 59, 130 f., 157 f., 163, 179
alliance 45, 79, 145
alluvial plain 26, 42
altar 22, 32 f., 35, 69, 93, 103, 109 f., 191
amphitheatre 28, 83, 177, 183, 188
ancestor 18, 33, 47, 55 f., 74, 86, 102
ancestor cult 38, 56, 153
angel 47, 162
Antioch 59
Apollo 83 f.
appropriation 3, 12, 27, 48 f., 56, 61, 85–87, 101, 107, 142, 146
architecture 27 f., 49, 57–59, 68, 73, 83–85, 87, 96, 100, 138, 140, 190 f.
Argei 81 f.
aristocracy 130, 175
articulation 19 f., 110
Asclepius 60, 151, 157, 159
ascription 21, 40, 47, 98, 101, 112, 166 f.
aspiration 3, 14, 25, 28, 37, 44, 57, 98 f., 101, 104 f., 109, 112, 153, 174, 184, 188
association 6, 8, 35, 37, 39, 49, 56, 81, 84, 103, 107, 109, 138–140, 154, 160, 170, 172–174, 180, 192
astronomy 71
Athens 28, 31, 59, 72, 169 f.
attachment 13, 49, 120, 135, 139, 142, 156
attraction 63, 96, 174, 181 f., 187

attractiveness 25, 46, 111
Augé, Marc 50
Augustine 114 f.
Augustus, Roman emperor 24, 60, 80, 82, 107–111, 118, 134 f., 140 f., 144
author 7 f., 74, 120, 124–126, 159, 161, 190
authority 24, 28, 36, 40, 49, 74, 124, 134, 137, 155, 160, 187

Bacchus 83 f., 172
Baghdad 42
belief 2, 4, 10 f., 14, 17, 30, 34, 36, 38, 63 f., 76, 118 f., 180, 187
Bellah, Robert N. 7, 19
Beyond 27, 36, 50, 61, 65, 77, 90, 96 f., 100, 155, 192
body 19, 21, 28, 65, 72, 95, 109, 146, 160, 176
boundary 14, 55, 84, 105, 164, 182 f., 188
bride 185
bridge 1, 62, 81
Buddhism 17
building 22, 43, 83 f., 87, 98 f., 135, 141, 155 f., 174, 185 f.

Cahokia 42
calendar 11, 13, 23, 35, 49, 55, 57, 67, 69, 71, 80 f., 109 f., 119–121, 123–140, 142–144, 156, 193
canon 10, 17, 23 f., 28 f.
canonicity 23
Capitoline 30, 68, 163
Carthage 57, 59, 134, 143
cave 28, 53 f.
centralisation 27, 39, 42, 49, 152, 155
Christian 29, 51 f., 60, 114, 143, 157 f., 161, 164, 174–177, 182, 187, 190
Christianity 17, 56, 115, 154, 159, 179
Cicero, Marcus Tullius 11 f., 24, 39, 62–76, 79, 86, 105, 107, 118, 130 f., 141, 148, 152, 163, 171, 176 f., 192
circus 9, 28, 83, 169, 173, 183, 188

https://doi.org/10.1515/9783110634426-014

citizenship   6, 35, 150, 152, 154, 161–164, 176 f., 180, 186
city-space   9, 29 f., 76
civic religion   6, 10, 30, 177
cognitive studies   12
collective identity   153, 159, 167, 176
collegia   173 f.
communication   8, 18–20, 41, 47–49, 77, 85 f., 89–92, 94–97, 102 f., 112, 117, 135, 143, 152, 157, 175, 191
compita   104
Compitalia   104–106, 109–111, 177
conceptualisation   50 f., 59, 103, 143, 165
conflict   22, 24, 26, 34, 101, 124, 132, 167, 173, 175, 192
Constantinople   59, 116, 131
consumption   152
control   12, 14, 24, 37, 41, 51, 65, 73, 77, 86, 96, 129, 155, 171, 187 f.
co-production   7
Corinth   59
cosmopolitan   26, 169 f.
counterpublic   28
counting   58
countryside   51, 66, 85, 124, 176
court   25, 66, 133, 148, 186
creativity   38 f., 97
crowd   59, 65, 105
Cumae   59
curia   33 f., 36, 128 f., 141
curse tablet   41

dance   27, 82, 191
dead   36, 38, 40, 47, 54, 56, 102, 112, 142
Dea Syria   173
de Certeau, Michel   48, 94, 101
demon   18, 47, 102, 148
densitiy   25–27, 36, 52, 60, 111, 173, 186
density   14, 25, 29, 35, 52, 56, 58, 97, 100, 158, 161, 165, 170, 188
deviance   4, 136, 151, 178
dies Alliensis   127–129
dies vitiosus   130
disaster   13, 114, 117–119, 126, 129, 143 f., 150
diversity   1, 4, 26, 57, 59, 73, 97 f., 165, 170, 173, 188

divination   62 f., 74, 152, 172, 188
divine agency   18, 70, 103
domination   14, 192
Durkheim, Emile   32, 34 f., 91

Egypt   40, 132, 157, 160
elite   8, 16, 26, 31, 39 f., 44, 56, 62–64, 91, 96, 112, 124 f., 136, 152, 155, 168, 175, 186, 192
– non-elite   3, 40, 96
emperor   39, 56, 84 f., 107, 109, 133–135, 139, 155–157, 174, 181 f.
enemy   160
entanglement   5, 11, 42, 51, 61, 67, 142, 150
Epicurean   67, 74
epiphany   99, 118, 154
ethnic   63, 82, 98, 100, 111, 170, 172 f., 178
ethnogenesis   14, 188
everyday   3, 33, 37, 44, 47 f., 91, 94, 102, 111, 148, 154, 156, 159, 161, 176
experience   1, 8, 12, 14, 17, 19, 33, 40, 42, 47–49, 78, 93, 98 f., 115, 117, 145, 149, 151, 155 f., 162, 183
extravagance   94

face-to-face   52, 77
family   14, 18, 22, 32–35, 102, 104–106, 145, 153
fasti   13, 71, 81 f., 85, 106, 109 f., 119–133, 135–140, 142–144
female   18, 82, 104, 162, 169, 173, 177, 185, 187
Feriale Duranum   133
festival   3, 35, 44, 59, 75, 104–106, 109, 111, 121, 127, 132–134, 136, 172, 174, 177
festive   21, 121, 140
Field of Mars   83, 141
Filocalus   142, 144
finance   26, 108, 111
fire   24, 32, 60, 80, 83, 106, 108, 119, 129, 131
– fire-fighting   60, 107 f.
flaneur   140
flood   13, 117–119, 131
flow   4, 6, 26, 28, 41, 71, 102–109, 140, 145, 152, 155, 174, 192

formation 8, 17, 24, 29, 49, 77, 106, 117, 157, 165f., 188, 193
forma urbis 82
Fornacalia 39
forum 57, 65f., 68, 72, 75, 83–85, 141
Foucault, Michel 3, 50, 96
freedmen 85, 177
fundamentalist 16, 45
funeral 113
funerary 8, 55f., 85, 87
Fustel de Coulanges, Numa Denis 10, 30–39, 45, 53, 176

gate 55, 83f., 181
Geography 95
ghetto 6
globalisation 1f., 4f., 37, 61
glocalisation 4
Göbekli Tepe 54
god, goddess 11f., 18, 23f., 33f., 36, 47, 59f., 64, 67–75, 77, 82, 102, 112, 118, 140, 151, 170–172, 182f., 186
governmentality 3
graffiti 41
group 24, 27–29, 39f., 49, 53–55, 77, 100, 103f., 138f., 144, 152–154, 157–159, 161, 167, 172–177, 187f.
grouping 10, 14, 29, 39, 49, 100, 106, 145, 161, 167, 173f., 193

habit 87
habitual 18, 36
hearth 32, 56, 102f., 106
henges 55
Hercules 34, 82f., 125
heritage 49, 57
Hermas 149, 161–164, 180–182
heterarchy 13, 43f., 57
heterogeneity 25, 38
holiday 22, 121, 132–134, 141
homogenisation 26, 98
hope 25, 28, 37, 99, 112, 143, 153

iconic religion 5f., 29, 98f.
iconography 88, 103, 109

identities 10, 14, 27, 29, 43, 50, 58, 95, 98, 120, 134, 143, 149f., 153–157, 163–167, 173–177, 188, 193
image 1–3, 6f., 20, 27f., 50, 54f., 66, 72, 81, 88, 100, 103f., 108, 114, 125, 141f., 153, 156f., 160, 162, 164, 169, 171, 173, 181, 183, 190
imaginary 99f., 108–110, 112, 114, 131, 142, 153, 155f., 172, 176f., 181
immigrant 2, 25, 28, 39, 99, 155, 174, 188
immigration 2, 6, 25, 37, 52, 99, 119, 145, 152, 176
individual 9f., 17, 22, 33–34, 43f., 71f., 93f., 114, 126, 145–162, 165, 175–178
individualisation 5, 14, 16, 145, 149f., 161, 164f., 193
industrialisation 2
information 41, 81, 123, 136, 141, 160
infrastructure 3, 44, 57, 86, 98, 115f., 138, 143f.
inhabitants 25f., 52, 59, 99, 114, 153, 170f., 190f.
inscription 40, 49, 86, 109–111, 117, 128, 133, 138, 141, 168f.
institution 6, 38, 76, 124, 149, 193
institutionalisation 13f., 46, 58, 108f., 149, 153, 161, 164f., 167, 172f., 175, 193
intellectualisation 9, 26, 58
intellectuals 9, 14, 20, 26, 28, 58, 74, 85, 119, 175, 188
interpretant 19
interpretation 19–21, 39f., 81, 100, 130, 151f., 175, 192
investment 26, 54, 59, 85f., 94, 107, 126, 188
Islam 10, 17
itineraria 82

Jenne-jeno 42
Jerusalem 6, 42, 59, 154, 158, 160, 162f., 172, 181, 187
Josephus, Flavius 163, 179
Judaism 14, 17, 154, 158, 166, 177–179, 183, 188, 193
Jupiter 33f., 59, 68, 74, 83, 118, 142, 158, 163

Kerma 42
kingship 42
kitchen 103

labour 1f., 26, 42f., 54f., 58, 92, 150, 186, 190, 192
landscape 21, 66, 95, 97, 140, 154
lar 13, 33, 38, 56, 69, 102–105, 107–109
Latour, Bruno 89
Lebenswelt 64, 66
legibility 41
lifestyle 3, 44, 182
lived ancient religion 5, 8, 16, 31, 44
lived religion 7–10, 16, 30, 44
Lyon 56, 143

magistrate 23, 36, 63f., 79, 107f., 110, 113, 121, 123f., 131, 138f.
male 18, 28, 104, 153, 162, 169, 175
map 49, 51, 82, 86, 95, 112, 141, 149, 181
market 105, 150, 152, 155, 165, 172, 176, 188, 191
materiality 9f., 12, 88–90, 92, 98f., 102, 112, 114, 132
material religion 6, 10, 49, 88f., 117, 120, 143
material value 94
Maya 40f.
meaning 16, 19f., 29, 32, 61, 95, 99, 101, 126, 140, 153, 155, 163, 166
media 6, 8f., 13, 19f., 24, 49, 89f., 94, 96, 108f., 117, 119, 135, 138, 144, 156, 160, 191, 193
Mediterranean basin 6–9, 14, 18, 27, 30, 78, 82, 87, 134, 145, 149, 177f., 194
megalopolis 1, 5
– metropolis 1, 5, 12, 39, 78, 88, 102, 104, 183
– metropolitan area 1
– polis 2, 31, 44, 169
– town 2, 25, 35, 37, 55, 83, 127, 152, 164, 168, 184–186
memory 48, 59, 86, 92, 115, 123, 126, 128, 140, 142
– commemoration 126f., 182
– commemorative date 133
message 20f., 88–90, 180, 182

migration 3f., 14, 28, 52, 150, 153, 155, 170, 188
miniaturisation 50, 94
mishnah 179, 182–184, 186, 188
Mithras 28, 154, 156, 159f.
modernisation 2, 7
monopolisation 45, 86
monument 113, 130
monumentalisation 6, 42, 54–56, 101
monumentality 13, 54, 82, 94, 100, 103, 108, 119, 134, 136f., 139
morality 12, 34, 77, 99, 150, 158, 161
Muslim 4, 56

narration 8, 127
negotiation 22, 48, 101, 103
neighbourhood 12, 39, 49, 60, 85–88, 104–106, 111, 114, 145, 174, 177, 187f., 193
– vici 12, 82, 104–111, 138f.
Neolithic 53, 77
network 9, 22, 27–29, 39, 43, 49, 52, 55, 58, 60, 97, 100, 137, 150f., 156f., 164, 174, 176, 188, 190
Nile 26, 78
– Tiber 81, 157, 168
– Yamuna 42
nobility 118
nundinae 105

object 18–22, 79, 85, 88–95, 99–101, 103f., 172
oikeiosis 146, 148
oracle 24, 131, 151f., 157, 181
Orbona 69
orphism 28, 150
Orsi, Robert 2, 7, 16
othering 169
Ovid, P. Naso 39, 59, 81, 105f., 121, 128f., 139–142

Palatine 69, 83
Palmyra 59
patiency 22
performance 22, 40, 48, 55, 59, 63, 74, 81, 84f., 92, 98, 113, 133, 139, 175, 177, 183, 191

Pergamon 59
philosophy 11, 17, 36, 62–64, 67, 69 f., 73–75, 145–148, 151 f., 176, 179
phratries 33, 36
place 3, 11 f., 20–23, 48–50, 56, 61, 79–84, 93, 96, 103 f., 119, 135 f., 138–144, 159–160, 192
place-making 49 f., 57
plausiblity 19 f
pluralisation 4, 166, 176, 193
pluralism 5
plurality 9, 14, 29, 72 f., 155, 166, 177, 188
polis religion 5 f., 8, 10, 30 f., 36, 39, 97
pomerium 84
Pompeii 102 f.
power 2–4, 7, 18, 22 f., 42, 44 f., 53 f., 92, 111, 191
Praeneste 133, 137
prayer 4, 21 f., 51, 90 f., 141, 163, 177, 191
prestige 22, 57, 86, 111, 155, 188
priest 24, 36, 73, 79, 82, 123, 173, 181, 185
private 8, 13, 23, 41, 64, 86, 107, 112, 114, 117, 139, 152, 171
procession 9, 21, 27, 57, 59, 113, 118, 125 f., 139, 151, 173, 183, 188, 191
prodigies 118, 129
producer 35, 43, 54, 92, 101, 161
profane 21, 123
profanus 21
professionals 173
property 23, 66, 86, 92, 112 f., 116, 173, 186
prophecy 29
public 8, 12 f., 22–24, 83 f., 108, 112 f.

qadosh 23
quarter 13 f., 42, 82, 104, 107–110, 133, 174, 188, 193
quietism 22

rabbis 179, 183 f., 186 f.
rationalisation 2, 58, 97, 132
readability 21
reading 6, 11 f., 16, 31, 77, 127, 132, 158, 161, 164, 173, 184 f.
regionalisation 5
regiones 82, 111

relevance 20, 38, 47, 54, 90, 99, 109, 112, 116, 136 f., 147 f., 156, 191 f.
religious action 3 f., 8, 11, 14, 27, 90, 92 f., 96, 140, 170, 191 f.
religious actors 2, 45, 103
religious agency 8 f., 18 f., 21 f., 29, 31, 45, 48, 90
religious change 8 f., 11, 14 f., 25 f., 30, 52, 61, 188, 191, 193
religious communication 10, 18, 20, 26 f., 29, 48–50, 53, 56 f., 61, 89–94, 98 f., 102 f., 151 f., 160, 175
religious diversity 73, 170
religious entrepreneur 152
religious ideas 6, 78
religious identity 166 f., 177
religious practices 14, 16 f., 38, 47, 108, 117
religious space 1, 27, 96 f., 175, 192
religious specialists 14, 60, 100, 141, 188
Religious Studies 2 f., 31, 78, 89, 116
resilience 10, 13, 42, 114–120, 124, 127, 129–133, 135, 137, 139, 143 f., 193
rhythm 48, 174
ritual 1 f., 6, 8 f., 11 f., 18–20, 22–24, 28, 30, 32, 35, 39–41, 50 f., 53, 55–60, 71, 78, 80–82, 84 f., 92 f., 98, 104–106, 109 f., 117–119, 123, 127, 129 f., 133, 135 f., 139–141, 160, 168 f., 172 f., 176, 178, 183 f., 188, 191
– *ritus Graecus* 168
river 66, 128, 168
– Ganges 42
– Indus 42, 78
– Mississippi 42
Roman empire 7, 9, 14, 17, 38, 154–156, 159, 162, 165, 173, 175, 186
Roman republic 11
Rouffignac 54
ruler 22, 40, 42, 44, 142, 157, 168, 190
rulership 43
rural 29, 51, 65 f., 96, 105 f., 142, 150, 184, 186, 190, 192

sacer 23, 92
sacerdotes 23
sacralisation 10, 18, 20–23, 29, 48, 50, 86, 91 f., 94, 98 f., 107, 109, 112

sacral kingship 50
sacredness 10f., 20–23, 33, 83, 88, 91f., 94f., 98f., 109f., 112, 120, 154
sacrifice 9, 32, 83, 111, 118, 130, 169, 175, 183, 191
sanctuary 21, 49, 60, 85, 91, 93, 99, 110, 125
Sarapis 172
Scheid, John 24, 31f., 37, 75, 110, 168
secular 3–6, 93
self 14, 48, 145–165
– inner self 148
– *persona* 28, 73, 148
semiosis 19
Semiotics 19, 88, 95
Seneca, the Younger 107, 147, 161, 177
settlement 10f., 25f., 29, 33, 47, 51–53, 55–60, 84, 115, 133, 152, 168, 190, 192
sibylline book 24, 131
Sigillaria 104
Simmel, Georg 27, 43, 140, 153, 161
situation 4, 14, 18, 20–22, 47f., 50, 54, 61, 77, 90–93, 154
slave 57, 68, 103f., 111f., 163, 170, 177f.
smell 40, 68, 92, 107, 141
Smith, Jonthan Zittel 5, 25f., 50, 59, 61, 93f., 99
solar 55, 71, 132
– solar year 119, 132
soul 33, 71, 73, 142, 146f., 150, 161–164
sound 40, 49, 74, 98, 141, 173
space 3, 9, 12, 25, 43, 47–50, 56f., 78, 82, 95–97, 100f., 137, 141, 191–194
– *espace* 43, 96
Sparta 72
spiritual welfare 2
standardisation 26, 41, 165
Stoic 66f., 69, 73f., 146f., 164
street 21, 40, 49, 80, 83, 102–105, 109, 111, 142, 173, 177, 185, 191
subaltern 3
subject 5, 9, 11, 16, 25f., 33, 40, 42, 55, 61, 78, 127, 129, 145, 148f., 157, 171, 178
subjectivity 10, 14, 86, 145, 193
suburban 63, 136–138, 142
Summanus 59
superhuman 47, 103, 191

tactics 94, 157
taste 40, 103, 169
telecommunication 50
temple 7, 9, 22, 30, 34f., 41f., 57, 59f., 65, 67–69, 72, 83, 85, 87, 93, 96, 113, 117, 125–127, 134–137, 140, 157, 162f., 171–174, 182, 186f., 192
Terminalia 105f.
text 24, 28, 51, 58, 62, 99, 144, 156, 190
theatre 9, 27, 65f., 72, 83f., 148, 183, 188
Thirdspace 96
time 27, 29, 48f., 54, 57, 70, 79–82, 91, 95, 124, 140, 142–144, 193
tomb 20, 32, 38f., 56, 85, 103
topography 21, 42, 57, 81, 95, 134, 137, 148
tourist 49
tradition 7, 10, 16f., 19f., 23–25, 29, 48, 50, 56, 60, 71, 73, 93–95, 98f., 107, 124, 128–130, 136, 138, 145–148, 150, 153, 160, 162, 165f., 177f., 187, 190
traditionality 93, 101, 112
transcendence 17, 48–50, 61, 86, 103, 148, 164, 192
translocality 4f., 50, 156, 174
Trier 59

universalisation 5, 11, 44, 154
urban environment 10, 18, 76, 89, 193
urbanisation 3f., 7–10, 12, 14, 27, 36f., 45, 47, 50–57, 61, 76–78, 99, 115, 145, 149f., 153, 155, 160, 167f., 178, 187f., 192f.
– planetary urbanisation 52, 115, 191
urbanity 5, 14, 24, 28f., 45–47, 52, 60–63, 73–76, 85, 100, 102, 115, 149f., 160, 162, 166, 182, 184, 188, 190–193
urban planning 1, 116
urban religion 1, 3–11, 14, 16f., 30f., 38, 44–47, 60, 64, 67, 75, 90, 99, 109, 115, 145, 166, 174f., 188f., 191
– urbanised religion 11–13, 31, 43, 45–47, 56, 58, 60, 62f., 75f., 120, 184, 188
– urbanising religion 13, 47, 76, 178, 188
urban space 2f., 6, 8–14, 21f., 25, 27–29, 41, 43–47, 52, 58, 67, 76, 80, 85f., 88f., 93, 95, 97f., 100f., 112, 114, 117,

120, 135, 137, 139, 142, 144 f., 169, 187 f., 190–193
– urban nucleus   81
urban studies   1, 3, 5, 25, 28, 31, 43, 184
Urciuoli, Emiliano Rubens   5, 25, 95, 100, 115, 187

Valerius Maximus   24
Varro, Marcus Terentius   12, 32, 59, 62 f., 70, 79–82, 92, 121, 135, 179, 192
Veii   59, 114
Vergil   114
Vertumnus   39
Vesta   32, 35, 39, 85, 119
vicomagistri   13, 89, 108, 110
village   25, 29, 51, 137, 184 f., 190

visibility   1 f., 12, 21, 29, 40, 43, 57 f., 137, 139, 143 f., 158, 170
visible religion   6, 88

wall   41, 55 f., 84, 94, 103–105, 117, 120, 125–127, 139, 142, 155, 164, 181, 186 f., 191
warfare   53, 84, 168
Weber, Max   1 f., 5 f., 31, 37, 58, 67, 95, 151
Whitehead, Alfred North   16 f.
wilderness   51
writing   6, 10, 26, 41, 46, 58, 62, 87, 124, 140 f., 144, 159 f., 171, 175, 182, 190
– literary   11, 40, 75, 96, 108, 116, 126, 129, 139 f., 144

RELIGION AND URBANITY ONLINE

Edited by Susanne Rau and Jörg Rüpke

- 200 entries – case studies and theoretical texts
- Open Access and ahead-of-print
- Will be available in 3 printed volumes upon completion

Religion and Urbanity Online will present important research contributions on religious change as well as the change of urban spaces and above all urban forms of life, practices and discourses on urbanness in Europe, the circum-Mediterranean region and South Asia. It will provide historians, anthro-pologists, and sociologists of cities and of religion with research articles as well as overviews. Case studies on cities or urban networks and on specific phenomena and processes will help to build a reservoir of knowledge on two overarching questions: What role do religious actors, practices and ideas play in the emergence and ongoing development of cities and "urbanity"? What role did urban actors, spaces and practices and the discourse on urbanity play in the emergence and ongoing development of religious groups and "religion"?

Open Access

For further information, please visit **degruyter.com/urbrel**

www.ingramcontent.com/pod-product-compliance
Lightning Source LLC
Chambersburg PA
CBHW051610230426
43668CB00013B/2052